Soft in the Middle

Soft in the Middle

The Contemporary Softcore Feature in Its Contexts

DAVID ANDREWS

The Ohio State University Press
Columbus

Copyright © 2006 by The Ohio State University.
All rights reserved.

Library of Congress Cataloging-in-Publication Data

Andrews, David, 1970–
Soft in the middle: the contemporary softcore feature in its contexts / David Andrews.
  p. cm.
Includes bibliographic references and index.
ISBN 0-8142-1022-8 (cloth: alk. paper)—ISBN 0-8142-9106 (cd-rom) 1. Erotic films—United States—History and criticism. I. Title.
PN1995.9.S45A53 2006
791.43'65380973—dc22
   2006011785

The third section of chapter 2 appeared in a modified form as an independent essay, "The Distinction 'In' Soft Focus," in *Hunger* 12 (Fall 2004): 71–77.
Chapter 5 appeared in a modified form as an independent article, "Class, Gender, and Genre in Zalman King's 'Real High Erotica': The Conflicting Mandates of Female Fantasy," in *Post Script* 25.1 (Fall 2005): 49–73.
Chapter 6 is reprinted in a modified form from "Sex Is Dangerous, So Satisfy Your Wife: The Softcore Thriller in Its Contexts," by David Andrews, in *Cinema Journal* 45.3 (Spring 2006), pp. 59–89. Copyright © 2006 by the University of Texas Press. All rights reserved.

Paper (ISBN: 978-0-8142-5154-6)
Cover design by Dan O'Dair.
Text design and typesetting by Jennifer Shoffey Forsythe.
Type set in Adobe Minion.

For Samuel, who did his sweet best to thwart this book

Contents

List of Illustrations		ix
Preface and Acknowledgments		xiii
Chapter 1	Introduction: Approaching the Softcore Feature	1
Chapter 2	Soft *v.* Hard	23
Chapter 3	The Disorderly Feminization of Classical Sexploitation: Tracing the Genealogy of Contemporary Softcore	45
Chapter 4	"Spicy, but Not Obscene": Industrial and Formal Retooling in 1980s Sexploitation	77
Chapter 5	Class, Gender, and Genre in Zalman King's "Real High Erotica": The Conflicting Mandates of Female Fantasy	110
Chapter 6	Sex Is Dangerous, So Satisfy Your Wife: The Softcore Thriller in Its Contexts	131
Chapter 7	Softcore as Serialized (and Feminized) Featurette: Postfeminist Propriety on Late-Night Cable	159
Chapter 8	The Softcore Public: A Cult of Bad Faith?	184
Chapter 9	Corporate Softcore and Its Discontents: Weightlessness and Weightiness at Playboy Enterprises	205

Chapter 10	"From Skin to Scream": Evolution and Elevation at a Cult Softcore Label	230
Conclusion	Whither Softcore?	251

Notes	259
Film- and Videography	288
Works Cited	305
Index	317

Illustrations

Figure 1	Soft, "deflective" stylization in the promotional art for high-end hardcore. © Studio A Entertainment and Andrew Blake, 2003.	20
Figure 2	Soft imagery and literary allusions in the promotional art for high-end hardcore. © Studio A Entertainment and Andrew Blake, 2002.	40
Figure 3	The paradigmatic image of soft-focus fantasy: Sylvia Kristel in a production still from Just Jaeckin's *Emmanuelle* (1974). © Trinacra, Columbia, and Just Jaeckin, 1974, and RCA/Columbia, 1984.	41
Figure 4	Rape as female fantasy in Russ Meyer's *Lorna* (1964). From the collection of Eric Schaefer.	55
Figure 5	An ad-mat for *Mantis in Lace* (1968), a fully softcore production that emerged from the roughie-kinky tradition. From the collection of Eric Schaefer.	59
Figure 6	Aspirational stylization in Joe Sarno's *Butterflies* (1974). Used courtesy ei Independent Cinema.	67
Figure 7	A scene from Joe Sarno's awakening-sexuality classic, *Inga* (1967). Used courtesy ei Independent Cinema.	70
Figure 8	The "empowered babe" in a production still from Al Adamson's *The Naughty Stewardesses* (1973). From the collection of Eric Schaefer.	72
Figure 9	Video-box art for *Young Lady Chatterley* (1977), a classical vehicle in the *Emmanuelle* mode. © Alan Roberts, 1977, and Monterey Home Video, 1996.	89
Figure 10	Sexploitation-style promotional art for the *Barbarian Queen* films. © Concorde—New Horizons and Roger Corman, 1985, 1989, 2003.	103

Figure 11	Equal-opportunity objectification in the promotional art for Andy Sidaris's *Hard Ticket to Hawaii* (1987). © Malibu Bay and Andy Sidaris, 1987, 2001.	105
Figure 12	Soft lighting of the low hero's chest in a frame enlargement from Zalman King's *Two Moon Junction* (1988). © Lorimar, 1988, and Columbia TriStar, 2000.	118
Figure 13	A frame enlargement from the autoerotic shower sequence of Zalman King's *Two Moon Junction* (1988): an immersion in female subjectivity. © Lorimar, 1988, and Columbia TriStar, 2000.	126
Figure 14	Glenn Close as Alex Forrest, the psychopathic *femme fatale* of Adrian Lyne's *Fatal Attraction* (1987). Theatrical erotic thrillers in the *Fatal Attraction* mold tend to front-load their sexual spectacle. © Paramount, 1987.	134
Figure 15	Sharon Stone as Catherine Tramell, the imperious *femme fatale* with pronounced exhibitionist tendencies in *Basic Instinct* (1992). This theatrical erotic thriller is markedly closer to softcore than earlier films like *Fatal Attraction*. © Carolco, 1992.	137
Figure 16	Though Jag Mundhra's *Night Eyes* (1990) represented a significant step in the development of the softcore thriller, the film's straightforward use of *noir* devices also posed obstacles to the same. © Prism Entertainment, 1990.	144
Figure 17	Video-box art for Alexander Gregory Hippolyte's *Carnal Crimes* (1991), a *noir*-romance hybrid that also qualifies as the first fully softcore erotic thriller. © Axis Films and Magnum Entertainment, 1991.	145
Figure 18	Promotional art on a "one sheet" for three ultra-low-cost MRG 16mm thrillers. Note the high degree of standardization in the titles. © Mainline Releasing, 2001. Used courtesy Robert Lombard.	154
Figure 19	Three more ultra-low-budget 16mm softcore thrillers from MRG. The promotional art accents a noirish quality that is carefully restricted in the films themselves. © Mainline Releasing, 2002. Used courtesy Robert Lombard.	156
Figure 20	A production still from *Emmanuelle* (1974), a crucial postfeminist influence on *Red Shoe Diaries* (1992–99) and many later softcore serials. © Trinacra, Columbia, and Just Jaeckin, 1974, and RCA/Columbia, 1984.	163
Figure 21	The second video anthology of Zalman King's pioneering serial, *Red Shoe Diaries* (1992–99). The use of "mystery lighting" in this promotional art emphasizes the upscale noirishness of King's psychosexual vision. © Showtime and Zalman King, 1992, and Republic Pictures and Zalman King, 1993.	166

Illustrations | xi

Figure 22 The "swinging Playboy male" as reimagined in the video-box art for a corporate softcore drama, *The Model Solution* (2001). © Indigo Entertainment and Playboy Entertainment, 2001. 213

Figure 23 The dark, self-reflexive promotional art for Tom Lazarus's first Playboy film, *Word of Mouth* (1999), suggests the director's departure from corporate softcore convention. © Mystique Films and Playboy Entertainment, 1999. 222

Figure 24 *House of Love* (2000) reinforced Lazarus's status as a corporate softcore "dissident." © Indigo Entertainment and Playboy Entertainment, 2000. 223

Figure 25 A frame enlargement showing the alien protagonist of Surrender Cinema's cult softcore hit *Femalien* (1996). *Femalien* is widely credited with introducing a new explicitness into contemporary softcore cinema. © Full Moon Pictures and Charles Band, 1996. 231

Figure 26 This DVD art for *Lord of the G-Strings* (2003) demonstrates Seduction Cinema's stress on exploitation-style art and its heavy promotion of the women it trumpets as "contract players." Used courtesy ei Independent Cinema. 238

Figure 27 A production still from *SpiderBabe* (2003), a higher-end spoof from Seduction Cinema. Used courtesy ei Independent Cinema. 242

Figure 28 A 2006 sales catalogue for Retro-Seduction Cinema. Used courtesy ei Independent Cinema. 245

Figure 29 A telling sign of the cultural penetration of the Janet Jackson affair: an ad for Siemens stoves. © Siemens and *The Chicago Tribune*, 2004. 252

Figure 30 Janet Jackson's notorious "wardrobe malfunction" may have contributed to contemporary softcore's current decline. © CBS and MTV, 2004. 252

Preface and Acknowledgments

My most formidable challenge in writing *Soft in the Middle* was the paucity of prior theorization on contemporary softcore itself. When I began this project in 2002, good work was at hand on the "classical" genres. Comparatively little research, however, was available on post-1990 softcore cinema—and if valuable, the work that was available was limited by narrow sampling and narrower agendae.[1] I filled this vacuum as I could by studying the generic matrices that have enmeshed softcore and its precursors. Thus I inspected the literature on classical exploitation and sexploitation; examined the research on other low-budget forms, including "cult" films and hardcore videos; and delved into the scholarship of theorists working in related media like noncinematic pornography (hard and soft), romance fiction, and soap opera.

The bulk of my research was, of course, devoted to softcore texts and the industry that produced them. Unlike colleagues working on older forms, I did not find it difficult to screen a representative sample of the genre. Nor was it onerous to view this material in appropriate formats. Though now in decline, softcore is nevertheless a current genre and an almost exclusively nontheatrical one. As a result, in my research, I watched more than 350 contemporary softcore features and nearly one hundred featurettes in all. (In addition, I examined scores of films from earlier strains of sexploitation.) Most of this material was purchased or rented on VHS or DVD, with a smaller segment taped onto VHS from premium cable channels like Showtime, Cinemax, and so on. The smallest body of material was recorded from

Playboy TV on a pay-per-view basis. Learning to recognize the genre before renting, purchasing, or taping it has had its comedy—yet as my remarks on genre cues indicate, such trial-and-error has also proved enriching.

This textual plenitude underscores one of the soundest rationales for a study like *Soft in the Middle*. Over the last fifteen years, softcore producers have disseminated a vast body of works. Insight into the genre fills in neglected sectors of film history and extends the reintegration projects of scholars working on other marginalized cinemas. My crude and no doubt conservative estimate places the total number of American softcore features produced after 1990 at no fewer than 1,500; this total would be doubled or trebled were featurettes added. These figures remain hazy because the self-conscious industry that spawned this "indecent" genre has maintained an evasive, under-the-radar stance that is reliant on a strategic refusal to refer to itself consistently. Unlike more mainstream fields (Hollywood) and less mainstream ones (hardcore), softcore has no trade magazines devoted to it and appears only elliptically in forums like *Variety* or *Adult Video News*. Outside the Internet forum Softcore Reviews, industry data is not readily accessible, and what is available is scattered, incoherent, and often unreliable.

My research has nonetheless yielded more detail than this space can possibly accommodate. Such profusion is partly the result of softcore's byzantine nomenclature. Because this deliberate multiplicity defies communication, the reader should bear in mind that pseudonyms are rife among softcore producers, players, and even critics. "Susan" is "Marie," and don't be surprised if she is "Jen" and "Michelle" as well.[2] While this type of diversity is motivated by an urge for career preservation, a different sort of diversity has been conditioned by an industrial urge for maximum profit. Softcore films are routinely edited into variants that conform to the market specifications of disparate distribution channels.[3] These films have also been retitled or recredited in transfer from one market to another and may appear under multiple titles in the same context at the same time.[4] Softcore films have, further, been recycled under new titles years after their release, and their "numbers" have been scavenged by producers intent on fleshing out "compilations" in which the identities of the performers are insignificant.[5] Straitened projects have even been known to replay their *own* numbers, as in Torchlight's *Beach Babes 2: Cave Girl Island* (1995). Sequeling adds another layer of multiplicity. Though difficult to convey, a sense of this diversity is indispensable to any account of the genre—and insofar as it suppresses the notion of the immutable aesthetic object, a mirage that still distorts areas of film studies, it may serve as a kind of critical corrective.

Which brings me to antiessentialism. One justification for studying softcore is that such a venture may be construed as a part of a wider cultural project of demystification and dehierarchization. Aesthetic ideology has in the main had a negative impact on softcore, contributing to the inferiority complexes that have shaped this middlebrow form of pornography. To observe these mechanisms with clarity, I have remained as neutral as possible regarding softcore "value," despite the myriad pressures to belittle or denounce. Hence, I seldom play to easy elitist prejudices by cataloguing softcore "incompetence." One reason to avoid this smug practice is that it tends to obscure what the genre is saying through its stylistic habits and thematic emphases, many of which are devalued by elite culture and thus too readily classified as "mistakes." Of course, a major obstacle to critical neutrality is the pejorative value that is more or less implicit to necessary terms like "softcore," "middlebrow," "pornography," and "bad faith." Where feasible, I have resisted an incipient highbrowism by engaging in frequent historical inquiries and by deploying disclaimers and a veritable legion of quotation marks. But in the end, one goes to press, so to speak, with the value-laden language one has.

My interpretive posture is somewhat more ambivalent. Antiessentialism implies the reception-studies view that meaning is an event, not an essence. As Mark Jancovich puts it, the "meaning of any text is not eternally inscribed within its form but changes, as it is positioned or repositioned in different categories, as [it is] consumed according to different competences and dispositions" ("Naked" 1). However, because my aim is to survey a "virgin" genre—one whose individual works have not, by and large, generated a critical response—I have sacrificed the rigor of a doctrinaire reception-studies approach so as to immerse the reader in texts and, to a lesser extent, to make my language flexible and thrifty. Consequently, I ask the reader's forbearance if I occasionally adopt phrasing that anthropomorphizes softcore as a univocal form whose meanings exist apart from its interpreters. (A useful critical shorthand, such a practice is in its extensions incompatible with my antiessentialist stance.) Besides yielding copious data, a willingness to engage the devalued text counters one of the more insidious expressions of elitist bias. Scholars in film studies, as in other popular fields, at times dispense with individualized interpretation and with such textual and industrial basics as the director's name under the rationale that these practices and details are tainted by essentialist ideas of artistic intention, the auteur, and the aesthetic object. Though sympathetic to such premises, I am wary of them because they may reinforce an elitist bias by implying that only "higher" genres "merit" interpretation. They may also support the myth that there is little "going on" in softcore (O'Toole 318). From a pragmatic perspective, then, the advantages of engaging the softcore text empirically as well as theoretically outstrip the disadvantages. Such a persuasion informs my consistent interpretive thrust.

❖

Other rationales come across, I trust, in the pages that follow. Rather than outline them here, it is incumbent that I now salute the individuals and organizations that have aided me. First, I thank my wife Chris, whose library privileges, editorial skills, and even keel made this curious project feasible. (Recent habits notwithstanding, I love you and our tyrannical Young People more than I love solitude.) I also thank my father, William Andrews, and my sister, Melinda Abraham, for reasons that I am sure they can guess. Major thanks go to Playboy's Tom Lazarus and ei Cinema's (now POPcinema's) Michael Raso, whose diligence and generosity yielded the interviews that enrich my final chapters. Eric Schaefer was munificent in sharing insights and providing images; I also thank Eric for the example of his scholarship. Robert Lombard was helpful and exceptionally patient in providing visual materials and crucial glimpses into restricted areas of the softcore industry. Jerome Klinkowitz, an old friend, provided comments on the manuscript that were as discerning as they were unexpected—and Linda Ruth Williams, a new friend, supplied words of encouragement and a variety of resources, including a wonderful book. Others who shared insight, material, and time include Brian Marshall, Alan Roberts, Tony Marsiglia, and Timothy McCarthy. Of the organizations that helped me, ei Cinema merits praise for showering rich materials on an economically challenged academic. Others that deserve mention include Creative Image, Softcore Reviews, Playboy Enterprises, Comcast, and the University of Chicago Library. (I also thank the fans who shared their ideas in the Softcore Reviews forum.) By publishing early forms of the pieces compiled here, several refereed journals molded this book. Thus my thanks go to Jon Lewis and *Cinema Journal*'s outside readers; Gary Hoppenstand and *The Journal of Popular Culture*'s readers; Gerald Duchovnay and *Post Script*'s readers; and Rebecca O'Connor and *Television and New Media*'s readers. *Bridge* and *Hunger* also deserve mention in this connection for publishing small chunks of this project. Last but far from least, the editors, readers, and staff members of The Ohio State University Press—including Malcolm Litchfield, Laurie Avery, Dan O'Dair, Lori Rider, Kathy Edwards, Jennifer Shoffey Forsythe, Heather Lee Miller, Constance Penley and especially Sandy Crooms and Maggie Diehl—merit gratitude and recognition for their creativity, expertise, labor, and unstinting patience. Thank you one and all.

Introduction

Approaching the Softcore Feature

I. DEFINITIONS, DISTINCTIONS, ANTECEDENTS

> *"It's not porn."*
> *"Pretty darn close, if you ask me."*
> —STAR STRUCK (2000)

Unlike its antecedents, the contemporary softcore feature is not the sort of film genre liable to recruit its audience through shock-and-awe sleaze.[1] Nor is it apt to depict the far reaches of sexual experience. That the genre has had a pervasive, if muted, R-rated presence at Blockbuster, the retail hegemon with the disingenuous family policy, testifies to the chameleonic tendencies that have over the past fifteen years been crucial to its success in distribution. Its most prolific forms blend in with the many genres that use sex as a selling point, so a trained eye is requisite to discern their cues in cable listings and on rental boxes. The titles of recent softcore erotic thrillers (or "softcore thrillers") are telling, with "sexy" phrasings like *Dangerous Pleasures* (or *Dangerous Desires*), *Wicked Temptations* (or *Wicked Sins*), and *Sex, Secrets, and Lies* (or *Sex, Secrets, and Betrayals*) offering reliable hints.[2] But even these locutions manage a seductive innocuousness that is difficult to differentiate from Hollywood formulations like *Fatal Attraction* and *Basic Instinct*. A further cue is a blunt descriptor, "strong sexual content," that accompanies the genre on rental boxes and before airing on premium cable networks like Cinemax. Cinemax's nickname, "Skinemax," suggests that cable is softcore's most distinctive habitat. There it exists modestly and without advertising in a specialized late-night niche created, it seems, with softcore alone in mind. Integral to the cultivated ambiguity of its pornographic character, softcore's blandness has been a critical factor in its sub-rosa prosperity. But the actual diversity, idiosyncrasy, and fragility of softcore are evident when it is subjected to the scrutiny it appears designed to avoid—and, in fact, the scrutiny the genre has heretofore almost entirely avoided.

Before surveying the genre, it is necessary to establish softcore's basic formal and historical outlines. Used generally, "softcore" refers to any feature-length narrative whose diegesis is punctuated by periodic moments (typically between eight and twelve, though more is not exceptional) of simulated, nonexplicit sexual spectacle. This dichotomous mix of narrative and "number" lends softcore its identifying format and rhythm, which resembles the hardcore structure that Linda Williams has so usefully compared to the Hollywood musical in *Hard Core: Power, Pleasure, and the "Frenzy of the Visible"* (1989). Though its narrative may derive from any genre, the genre's spectacle has proved less flexible—and rigidly heterosexist. It stresses extensive female nudity and heterosexual encounters with "bumping and grinding." The genre also leans on standardized forms of pornographic spectacle such as striptease numbers, tub or shower sequences, modeling scenes, voyeur numbers, girl-girl segments, threesomes, orgies, and the like.

A crucial distinction separates spectacle from number. "Spectacle" distinguishes segments that serve visual and affective purposes from those that serve diegetic purposes. But because spectacle and diegesis are relative terms whose referents cannot be fully isolated in narrative cinema, every feature contains spectacle in some form and to some degree—and almost every feature contains spectacle of a specifically erotic nature. But to observe that a film registers periodic "numbers" is to assert something stronger about its spectacle, its structure, and, presumably, its intentions, for this narrative-number structure is a traditional signpost of pornography. Similarly, in denoting this dichotomy, "softcore" is narrower than "sexploitation." The latter I construe as any narrative feature that, by foregrounding nudity, makes sexual titillation its most credible commercial appeal (see Schaefer, *Bold* 338). Only when such spectacle achieves a certain duration, regularity, density, and activity does sexploitation yield numbers, which manifest the illusion that two inimical structures divide the feature, creating a pluralist whole—and only then does it merit softcore designation. Softcore is, then, a subset of sexploitation just as number is a subset of spectacle; indeed, these distinctions work in tandem.

By flaunting its untraditional structure, softcore takes a crucial step away from mainstream "legitimacy" that nonsoftcore sexploitation has not always taken. This broad generic evolution has historically accompanied the maturation of alternative distribution networks specializing in sexploitation content. In America, these twin developments have occurred twice, once in the late 1960s and again in the early 1990s, culminating in two golden eras of softcore. For chronological specificity, I refer to the first coalescence of the genre as "classical softcore." Most prevalent during the four-year period prior to the release of *Deep Throat* (1972) and the advent of porno-chic, classical softcore was one of many overlapping genres that emerged after Russ Meyer produced *The Immoral Mr. Teas* (1959), the "nudie cutie" credited with inaugurating sexploitation. For precision, I refer to this sexploitation era as "classical sexploitation." The sexploitation texts of this period were exhibited on an alternate circuit of drive-ins, grindhouses, and arthouses that grew out of an earlier "exploitation" circuit that evolved, over the forty-year span prior to the release of *Mr. Teas,* outside the aegis of classical Hollywood.

Since the 1950s, "exploitation" has been an umbrella term subsuming low-budget genres viewed as alternative and déclassé. Employed thus, the term is tantamount to "B-movie," whose common usage also skirts history.[3] After film historian Eric Schaefer published *"Bold! Daring! Shocking! True!": A History of Exploitation Films, 1919–1959* (1999), it became possible to use this category more rigorously. Schaefer construes "classical exploitation" as a genre that "roughly paralleled the rise and fall of the classical Hollywood cinema" (*Bold* 8) as defined by David Bordwell, Janet Staiger, and Kristin Thompson in *The Classical Hollywood Cinema: Film Style and Mode of Production to 1960* (1985).[4] In this account, "exploitation" derives from the extreme, often fraudulent promotional techniques of the "exploiteers." Distinguishing the exploitation film from the Hollywood film was its form, which relied on "scandalous" spectacle and rudimentary narrative; its content, which capitalized on topics proscribed by the Production Code; its low cost, which necessitated a departure from Hollywood production values; and its exhibition and reception, which occurred on the circuit of alternative theaters beyond Hollywood distribution and amid the "carnivalesque ballyhoo" that was the goal of exploitation promotion (Schaefer, *Bold* 4–6). Exploitation's most distinctive subgenres, Schaefer explains, were classified "by the forbidden topic they exploited," with "sex hygiene, drug, nudist, vice, and burlesque films ... among the most frequently produced" (*Bold* 6).

Meyer's *Mr. Teas* and its imitators supplanted older exploitation forms, which could not match the sexual daring of the nudie cuties. In turn, this development sparked an explosive diversification, with subgenres like "roughies," "kinkies," and "ghoulies" succeeding the nudie cuties by the mid-1960s (Turan and Zito 10–25; Schaefer, *Bold* 337–39). Classical sexploitation's most sexualized subgenre, "classical softcore," emerged around 1968. Though films like Harry Novak's *The Secret Sex Lives of Romeo and Juliet* (1969) generated substantial profits in 35mm (Rotsler 55), classical softcore's vogue was brief, with the industry that produced it susceptible to internal and external pressures. As Schaefer avers in his article "Gauging a Revolution: 16mm Film and the Rise of the Pornographic Feature" (2002), 35mm sexploitation was by 1970 competing with low-end, youth-oriented 16mm features whose narrative-number structures blurred the still-nascent boundary between hardcore and softcore explicitness (12–22). These 16mm films represent a crucial interval in the development of the classical hardcore feature, which became sexploitation's most significant commercial rival.

The arrival of *Mona* (1970), the first hardcore feature, did not signal the immediate demise of classical softcore or of the larger sexploitation genre. Sometimes referred to as "softies" or "soft X," softcore films in 35mm and 16mm continued to be manufactured in the 1970s, with classical sexploitation hanging on in diverse forms until late in the decade. Softcore even experienced a brief new chic due to the popularity of *Emmanuelle* (1974), the French import directed by Just Jaeckin. Nonetheless, this was a decade of decline for sexploitation. That Columbia distributed *Emmanuelle*'s American release indicates a salient factor in this decline. Not only was classical sexploitation competing with hardcore, it was jockeying with post-Code (or "New") Hollywood, which sought to marginalize the sexploiteers by stressing simulated, inexplicit sexual spectacle in its own projects. The Supreme Court's ruling in *Miller v. California* (1973) contributed to this decline (Lewis 267–70), as did rising real-estate values spurred by urban renewal and suburban sprawl, which adversely affected the grindhouses and drive-ins, respectively (Schaefer, "Triumph" 23–24; Ray 132–33, 160; Stevenson 48).

The passing of the old exploitation circuit marked the end of sexploitation's reign as a theatrical force. But the emergence of new markets in home video and on pay cable meant that low-budget sexploitation would persist throughout the 1980s. Though softcore was during this period all but absent as an American film genre, new sexploitation cycles and subgenres appeared. No longer did sexploitation differentiate itself from Hollywood as classical genres once had. Instead, "contemporary sexploitation" (post-1980) has been marked by its tendency to imitate theatrical blockbusters like *Porky's* (1981) and *Fatal Attraction* (1987). By 1991, the maturation of sexploitation's nontheatrical markets—as measured by the new willingness of HBO and Showtime to finance upscale softcore—along with a moderation in the culture's antiporn attitudes led to softcore's renewal. Though the Axis softcore thriller *Carnal Crimes* (1991) spearheaded "contemporary softcore," the success of the genre's reconfigured paradigms triggered a diversification within the genre. For example, the triumph of director Zalman King's stylishly feminized *Red Shoe Diaries* program (1992–99) spurred the crystallization of a distinctive late-night cable subgenre: the softcore featurette aired in serial format.

Because its routinized production and broad, centralized distribution have been facilitated by corporate America, contemporary softcore has in its socioaesthetic temper proved more static and staid than its progenitors. The genre has nevertheless been subject to economic pressures that have occasioned steady modifications throughout this period. The most salient change has been economic: budgets have fallen drastically in both adjusted and actual dollars. As Linda Ruth Williams verifies, it was not uncommon for companies like Axis and Prism to put out 35mm softcore thrillers costing in excess of a million dollars (*Erotic* 8, 285, 292, 323). Since then, shifts in distribution stimulated by competition have eroded budgets, at once forcing labels out of business and remolding the genre. By 2005, contemporary softcore's major player, Mainline Releasing Group (MRG), could no longer afford to make the homogenized 16mm thriller that it had been churning out since 1998, most recently at a cost of about $130,000. Instead, MRG and companies like New City Releasing have shifted to shot-on-video vehicles that cost $80,000 or less; most of these features are intended for pay-perview. MRG and New City compete with even lower-cost, more youth-oriented "cult" producers like Seduction Cinema, which often shoots its softcore on video for less than $50,000. Aside from truncated shoots and reduced production values, the most significant concomitant of this deflation has been an accelerating flirtation with the hardcore industry. Though hardcore players have always enjoyed a place in softcore, only over the last six or seven years have they landed starring roles with regularity. This crossover talent is willing to work for relatively low pay and is reportedly comfortable with the increasing sexualization that has been mandated by producers (Lombard, "Casting" 2–3)—and that has been driven in part by a desensitization process that cable programmers have called the "satiation factor" (Jaehne 12). Though softcore remains a simulation genre, its spectacle is thus "harder-core" than in the early 1990s. Since 1996—when Surrender Cinema, a studio that openly emulated hardcore, released its cult hit *Femalien*—softcore has placed a greater stress on labial close-ups or "beaver shots," and the ratio of narrative to number has decreased across the genre. Additionally, within individual numbers, myriad hardcore mannerisms are apparent. These motifs have been imported from hardcore along with the players themselves.

In some respects, contemporary softcore's deflationary interaction with hardcore is reminiscent of the classical era. But it would be a mistake to press this analogy too hard. Classical softcore arose amid a distinct sexploitation industry that had itself arisen from a distinct exploitation industry; in turn, it provided a significant impetus in the formation of the nascent hardcore industry. By contrast, before 1990, it is difficult to refer to "sexploitation" as a discrete industry in the classical sense, for its post-1980 manifestations were tightly interwoven with low- and midbudget producers that supplied other segments of the nontheatrical market—and, of course, during this interval hardcore was itself an established industry. Contemporary sexploitation formed its own "middle" industry only after lower-budget producers using nonunion players undermined the production models of crossover studios like Axis Films, which had originally used Screen Actors Guild (SAG) talent. By 1994, the lines of demarcation between softcore and other segments of the film industry had clarified. The softcore industry at that point comprised a reliable group of comparatively low-cost labels (e.g., Playboy's Cameo Films) specializing in 35mm softcore and an equally reliable coterie of executive producers (e.g., CPV/MRG's Marc Greenberg), directors (Kelley Cauthen), composers (Herman Beeftink), talent managers (Creative Image's Robert Lombard), players (Monique Parent), and so on. Contemporary softcore is thus far more significant relative to contemporary sexploitation than classical softcore was to classical sexploitation. What is more, that softcore was deflationary from the start means it would be imprecise to classify its current downscale nature as a straightforward "degeneration." Though cost competition has indeed blurred the industry's identity—and is now fracturing its hold on mainstream markets, including premium cable—this dynamic, it should be recalled, was also responsible for softcore's initial isolation and *generation* as a distinct middle industry.

As a middle industry, softcore has produced a body of texts that habitually conform to "middlebrow" expectations. Though I discuss the middlebrow at length in chapter 2, it is worth noting here that the term designates a diverse and relative taste regime that is no less complex when used as a tool for understanding softcore than when applied to other cultural contexts. In any framework, the term "middlebrow" situates its referent in a classed hierarchy. The middlebrow person or object identifies with the values of elite categories but bears attributes associated with "lower" ones for which she, he, or it expresses a fascinated disgust. In a softcore context, this dynamic has yielded a conflicted textual character that without transgressive intent threatens to subvert cultural hierarchies, eliciting a distinctive and *distinguishing* criticism from highbrow quarters. But just as the middle class is not a monolithic grouping, neither is the middlebrow—and neither is softcore. Though my definition holds true for most areas of softcore, distinct segments of the industry, its texts, and its public have registered this middlebrow identity in different forms and to different degrees at different times.

Three rough categories are helpful in identifying and theorizing discrete aesthetic formations within contemporary softcore's middlebrow identity. The most important criterion linking softcore to the middlebrow is its pervasive feminization, which as I argue throughout this study acts as a kind of distribution "grease." It is thus notable that one of the principal variables differentiating these areas is the degree to which they target women by endorsing postfeminist ideas of the feminine. "Aspirational softcore" may be viewed as the genre's "upper middle" category. As a crossover form, aspirational softcore was most influential during the softcore industry's formation in the early 1990s and remains the genre's most expensive, stylized, and feminized category. Producers and texts in this category evince the greatest anxiety over pornographic classification and thus adopt tactics to blur the art-porn distinction. A common tactic is to mimic a feminized, nonadversarial art film model. Though upper-middlebrow directors at times romanticize transgression, their usual soft-focus idiom—first developed in a sexploitation context by classical "auteurs" like Radley Metzger, Joseph Sarno, and Jaeckin—betrays their basic traditionalism. Another blurring tactic is to avoid clear-cut, narrative-number formats. Crossover directors like King are known for fully softcore vehicles (the *Red Shoe Diaries* serial) as well as for sexploitation vehicles that fall short of softcore designation (the *Red Shoe Diaries* feature [1990]). The response to this category also provides identifying cues. Defenders of canonical standards reject this category as "pretentious," but as I note in chapter 7, contemporary feminists often laud its feminization. Nonacademic respondents divide more evenly. Some accept the aspirational producer's elitist strategy of situating his or her work as "erotica," while others disparage this effort as tantamount to elevating "arty pornography" above its "proper" station.

The contemporary era's most characteristic flavor is "corporate softcore," which is the dead center, so to speak, of softcore's middlebrow identity. Studios that specialize in this "middle middle" have generated the most prolific and routinized body of softcore texts, which have found their widest and most distinctive distribution in the late-night slots of premium cable channels such as Cinemax, Showtime, and the Movie Channel. Influenced by the erotic thriller and by King's reinvention of it, corporate softcore emerged around 1994, with its heyday lasting through 2001. Though this paradigm survives in diminished form today, several prolific labels (e.g., Playboy's Indigo and Full Moon's Surrender) halted production early in this decade while others (MRG, New City, etc.) curtailed their budgets. Corporate softcore is at once more conservative and more openly pornographic than the aspirational softcore that inspired it. Though corporate softcore does not disguise its narrative-number dichotomy, it does embrace an often contradictory fusion of pieties in a "semiadvertent" attempt to defuse its structuring impropriety. A Hollywood-based aesthetic, corporate softcore is distinctive for bland stylistics that favor smooth jazz, flat lighting, and posh milieus located somewhere-in-Los-Angeles. The middling values implicit to its corporate production and distribution register most overtly in its business *mise-en-scène*, which often focuses on heroines who confront sexual and professional obstacles in the workplace.

The third category, "cult softcore," may be framed as contemporary softcore's "lower middle." Cult softcore is the most masculinized, youth-oriented, populist, and openly pornographic softcore area. It is also the one area of contemporary sexploitation in which softcore is outstripped, as it were, by nonsoftcore sexploitation forms, for cult sexploitation labels like Roger Corman's Concorde–New Horizons outnumber cult softcore producers. But cult softcore *is* a growth area. Seduction Cinema is one of the few labels to accelerate production in the past five years, which points to the competitiveness of its 16mm and video formats. Cult softcore is the most inexpensive, heterogeneous, and promotion-oriented segment of softcore, in part because it is geared to home video rather than premium cable, which favors more upscale vehicles. The "cult" designation is apt in that cult softcore has, in contrast to corporate softcore, inclined toward story lines that adhere to the subgeneric distinctions (horror, sci-fi, spoof, stripper, strangulation, etc.) encouraged by the cult nexus as described by Jeffrey Sconce in his landmark 1995 *Screen* article on "paracinema." As chapter 10 argues, cult softcore studios like Seduction have profound links to the "world of 'lowbrow' fan culture (fanzines, film conventions, memorabilia collections, and so on)" surveyed by Sconce (373). Cult softcore has also expressed its masculinized, grassroots character via flirtations with transgression, excess, and sadism. In this respect, it represents a throwback to classical sexploitation, a nostalgic identity that Seduction has exploited with particular vigor.

These masculinized qualities are relative. Insofar as it represents a mainstream formation, cult softcore is still in the postfeminist "middle." It still evinces feminized qualities that moderate its insistence on excess and underscore its middlebrow character. Cult softcore labels like Seduction and Surrender (as well as Torchlight, Surrender's precursor at Full Moon) exemplify this duality. From its inception, Seduction's signature has been to balance low, masculinized forms of comedy against a "classier" girl-girl spectacle. In moving toward a more upscale, aspirational model, Seduction is perhaps repeating the maneuver that led to Surrender's demise earlier this decade. Various factors influenced Surrender's halt in production, including an inability to slash costs and a muddying of its paradigm.[5] After its success with *Femalien*, the label's films became less distinguishable from corporate softcore. This convergence demonstrates a fact worth stressing: these "middle" categories are useful but imperfect tools. Surrender is difficult to categorize because aspects of its Hollywood-based aesthetic have always suggested the tactics of corporate softcore. Similarly, early manifestations of the corporate softcore aesthetic like Cameo's *Play Time* (1994) and *I Like to Play Games* (1994) and Axis's *Friend of the Family* (1995) are difficult to distinguish from the aspirational vehicles of King and Alexander Gregory Hippolyte (a.k.a. hardcore director "Gregory Dark"), Axis's influential softcore pioneer. Still, the imprecision of these categories is a function of their utility, for they are defined by socioaesthetic liminality. At one end of the spectrum that they bracket, aspirational softcore blurs into the direct-to-video art film;[6] at the other, cult softcore blurs into "specialty erotica" and hardercore videos. It is apt then that both categories blur, "mid-middle," into corporate softcore.

Another strength of these categories is the framework they provide for theorizing softcore's registration of a complex Bakhtinian motif: the carnivalesque. Though the image of carnival is mostly absent from the staid world of corporate softcore, it is pervasive in both aspirational and cult softcore, just as it was in classical sexploitation and, before that, classic Hollywood noir (see Naremore 224–29). But these categories of contemporary softcore envision and *classify* carnival distinctly. In aspirational softcore, low carnival imagery is exploited and "exoticized" for the contrast it provides with the middlebrow spectator-protagonist, who is as a rule a white, heterosexual, middle-class female—an identity meant to evoke the upscale audience of this cable-friendly mode. In the work of King and Elisa Rothstein,[7] this manifestation of the exotic is often realized through scenarios in which the heroine is eroticized by her interactions with a sculpted, lower-class male who guides her through a masculinized "otherworld," which, like the hero himself, disgusts and attracts her in a classic middlebrow dynamic. What makes this dynamic a clear expression of the exotic is that it specifically locates the erotic mystique of the male sexual object in his class and gender differences *vis-à-vis* the heroine. This aspirational use of the exotic may be traced to Metzger and Jaeckin—but the processes that inform "exoticization" are analogous whether discussing the racism of exploitation's "Goona Goona" vehicles (Schaefer, *Bold* 267–82) or the now more acceptable "classism" long integral to King's vision. An aspirational stance seems to suppress feminist criticism of exoticization if (1) the middlebrow heroine's principal object is a lower-class white male, as in King films such as *Two Moon Junction* (1988), *Red Shoe Diaries,* and *Lake Consequence* (1992), and/or if (2) the vehicle in question is promoted as the creation of an all-female production team, as is true of Rothstein's serial *Women: Stories of Passion* (1997), which was in the late 1990s a darling of feminist critics.

A distinct expression of the carnivalesque is manifest in the masculinized, lower-brow softcore vehicles that pervade the cult nexus. In these self-consciously "naughty" features, carnival is not simply portrayed and othered but embodied and exuded. Like cult sexploitation in a larger sense—witness the films of Troma—cult softcore does not just depict carnival, it *is* carnival. In this world, men still "ogle" women, and both observer and observed figure as low cultural "others" unified by a ludic populism. This tendency toward populist excess is not, however, fully unrestrained by postfeminist propriety. Even Seduction, a company notorious for its ad-hoc scatology, betrays a postfeminist nature, which is most overt in aspirational projects like *The Seduction of Misty Mundae* (2005). Though it exploits gay and lesbian jokes, Seduction avoids ethnic slurs and positions its heroines as more refined and empowered than its heroes. As the next section clarifies, this accelerating feminization recapitulates the postfeminist, middlebrow transformation of softcore as it moved from the classical to the contemporary.

II. TWO THESES

"They said it was pretty bad, even for a nudie."
—STARLET! (1969)

The definitions, distinctions, and antecedents glossed above create a framework for interpreting contemporary softcore as a collection of neglected histories, a set of industrial practices, a system of audience orientations, and a body of self-conscious texts. In the pages that follow, I propose two broad theses, one of which is historical and straightforward, the other theoretical and deceptive. The first is that contemporary softcore is an exemplary postfeminist genre. This character evolved from consumerist tendencies manifest in classical sexploitation, whose frequent misogyny reflected its decentralized distribution and prefeminist identity. The second thesis is that softcore has long been a self-conscious, anxiety-ridden genre steeped in negation.

"Postfeminist" is so central to *Soft in the Middle,* and its academic usage so varied and contested, that a précis of my construction of the term is in order. (See also chapter 7.) Besides invoking the era that followed the emergence of feminism's second wave, "postfeminism" alludes to the sex-and-gender norms that have long informed and enmeshed softcore. Here Carol Clover supplies a crucial definition. Drawing on Tania Modleski, she defines postfeminism as "the appropriation of feminist thought for non-feminist purposes" (Clover 153; see Modleski, *Feminism* 3–22 and Projansky 20).[8] The softcore industry is "postfeminist" in this sense in that it has embraced depoliticized elements of second-wave ideology. Like other pop culture industries, softcore performs this ideological operation because it deems feminism as a movement outside the commercial mainstream. It also deems feminism sex-negative. Thus softcore redeploys feminist ideas in reliably mainstream forms that just as reliably foment heterosexual female display. This postfeminist "appropriation" is mostly limited to an advocacy of female agency, choice, and self-respect. Rather than developing such rhetoric into a coherent critique, softcore uses it as one of several tools to "feminize" the genre—to construct it, that is, as an apolitical, "female-friendly" space that conflates untraditional ideas of female empowerment with traditional feminine stereotypes and ostensibly feminine idioms. *Vis-à-vis* contemporary softcore, then, "feminization" refers to a mode of textual construction or stylization that co-opts feminism's broadest appeal while using conventional motifs to render said appeal unthreatening.

One impetus behind this gambit is that it allays a quintessentially "postfeminist anxiety" that is manifest at the producer level—and that is especially prevalent among men. Time and again, male softcore producers ward off figmentary attacks from antiporn feminists by pointing to their preference for strong heroines; to their "respect" for actresses; to their use of a soft, "refined" stylistic idiom; to their prioritization of romance over "pure fucking"; and to their commitment to narrative. Such assertions rarely embrace feminism even when they agree with feminist critiques. It is not entirely contradictory, then, that softcore texts register an opposite postfeminist anxiety through "backlash" scenarios that undermine feminist advances by depicting independent women as *unhappy* women. Because softcore is largely nonviolent and antimisogynistic, excessive instances of this type of antifeminist backlash are rare, appearing mainly in nonsoftcore erotic thrillers. But a more moderate backlash depiction—one equating female career success with gender insecurity, sexual frustration, and "bitchiness"—is a common softcore trope. Despite its backlash motifs, however, the genre remains most apt to critique male characters. A mild misandry is, in fact, a normalized component of softcore's presentation of itself as a female-friendly mode. In sexual matters, this misandristic disposition has led to a pointedly postfeminist bundle of double standards: whereas softcore adopts a permissive stance *vis-à-vis* female adultery, same-sex contact, masturbation, and rape fantasy, it places anticonsumerist restrictions on male adultery, same-sex contact, masturbation, and rape fantasy. The effectiveness of softcore's postfeminist feminization may be measured by the genre's consistent ability over the past fifteen years to secure a place in mainstream outlets. This effectiveness may also be measured by the absence of sustained feminist criticism of the genre—and by the congenial feminist response to softcore's most feminized subgenre, the softcore serial. The latter response is a small but salient phase of a "post-feminist milieu" in which, as Jacinda Read puts it, "the opposition between feminism and femininity is becoming decidedly less distinct" (61). What this vanishing distinction suggests, it seems, is that "post-feminist feminists" are growing increasingly amenable to the feminization strategies of softcore and other exemplary postfeminist forms.

Feminization is a fixture of both postfeminist culture and a broader consumer culture that advances its "consumerist" values through "commodity aesthetics" (Lury 42, 60). In *Consumer Culture* (1996), Celia Lury argues that a "*process of stylization is what best defines consumer culture*" (4; Lury's italics), wherein specialized commodities use aestheticization tactics to target discrete consumer desires and identity groups. As a case in point, Lury draws on Dick Hebdige's discussion of feminization in the British scooter industry (22–25). Of course, feminization also has a specifically American history, as Ann Douglas verifies in her book *The Feminization of American Culture* (1977). This history was transformed by feminism, which lent feminized styles new meanings. Transformations of this sort are at once postfeminist and consumerist in that they imply a liberalization of attitudes toward female consumer desire, including sexual desire. (It is no accident that culturalists often elide postfeminism and consumerism under a "commodity feminism" rubric [Goldman et al. 333–51; see Projansky 79–83].) In Lawrence Birken's account, consumerism (or *post-fordism*) erodes cultural hierarchies, sponsoring social fluidity and democratization through a subversive "complex of values" that, unlike older "productivist" values stressing "work, gender, and need," stresses "pleasure, genderlessness, and desire" (111; see also Lury 72–75, 94).

That Birken specifies that consumerism's antihierarchical impulse includes a slow drift toward genderlessness indicates that postfeminism and consumerism are not identical concepts, for postfeminism implies a "counterrevolutionary" insistence on gender. My term for the ideological overlap of these ideas is "postfeminist consumerism." As the default posture of the mainstream media, postfeminist consumerism signals modestly progressive values that maintain the gender system. This is, of course, the type of consumerism exuded by today's softcore. The heterosexism implicit in postfeminist consumerism is in a sense "the cost of admission" to the centralized distribution schemes like Cinemax and Blockbuster that have sanctioned softcore's growth and diffusion. A freer, more diverse, and potentially more radical consumerism was apparent in the shock tactics of classical sexploitation, whose producers were hardly averse to undermining fixed notions of sex and gender. Sexploitation was freer to explore such material due to its decentralized, nonmainstream distribution schemes. It is instructive that when "sexploiteers" crossed into mainstream theaters, they tended to revert to a neotraditional sex-and-gender regime—and to rely on early prototypes of softcore's current feminization strategies. Still, one should not sentimentalize the anarchic consumerism of classical sexploitation. If the genre was obsessed by sex-and-gender sabotage, it was even more fascinated by violence and misogyny. The mainstream aspirations that have determined contemporary softcore's postfeminist consumerism may thus be viewed as moderating forces that have filtered off the liberal *and* illiberal extremism of classical sexploitation.

In her closing remarks, Lury argues that consumer forces do not "flatten" value and inequity so much as "rework" and "redraw" them: "questions of difference, struggle and inequality will not disappear, but will surface in struggles between social groupings in different ways, including the politics of identity" (256). My reading of softcore history supports Lury's point. Classical sexploitation never made any broad move toward egalitarianism, and its successors have been less bold. This underlying traditionalism has culminated in a contemporary industry that seldom challenges heterosexual viewpoints—and that typically presents female same-sex contact as an accessory to such viewpoints. For this reason, a caveat is in order: *Soft in the Middle* only sporadically discusses texts identified with alternative sexualities. In making this choice, I trust that I am not repeating a move that Linda Williams has come to regret. In her "afterthoughts" on *Hard Core*, Williams has lamented that her pioneering study focused "on heterosexual hard-core pornography" and "the 'mainstream' as constructed by the then dominant discourse on pornography" ("Second" 171). Though sympathetic to this concern, I would note that softcore is more uniformly heterosexual and resolutely "mainstream" than the genres that Williams discusses. Moreover, *Soft in the Middle* is structured by industrial specifics in a way that *Hard Core* is not. Given how little is known about softcore—and given my space constraints—it would be capricious to vitiate this historical framework by devoting entire chapters to nonsoftcore "alternatives."

Lury's point about the persistence of inequity in consumer culture is most relevant to softcore's two main interlocking sexisms. If softcore narrative has developed a mildly misandristic nature as a function of its postfeminist transformation, softcore spectacle has only increased its commitment to female nudity. Producers have responded to antiporn arguments not by creating a more egalitarian genre but by balancing old categories of inequity against new. Postfeminist softcore has definitely *not*, then, adhered to a structuring demand of antiporn rhetoric: that pornography stop objectifying men and women unequally (Russell 49). While aspirational and corporate softcore *do* objectify the male body, softcore spectacle is geared to expose the female body. As Axis executive Walter Gernert puts it, "you need to keep the women in front of the camera. The guys are incidental, the guys are appendages" (Linda Ruth Williams, *Erotic* 65). But far from inflaming social criticism, this bias has quelled it. *Softcore's broad acceptance has been conditioned not by a curtailment of the exposure and objectification of the female body but by a rigorously feminized expansion of the same.* The implicit industrial assumption is that women will tolerate a sexist brand of spectacle if it is complemented by a diegesis that exudes an opposite inequity. This development likewise assumes that women are more offended by the integration of female nudity with motifs like sadomasochism, misogyny, violence, and transgression than by nudity *per se.*

It is no wonder, then, that so many different sexploitation strains have moved at an early stage to foreground female characters in the narrative. Most often accomplished by use of a female protagonist, this tactic maximizes female spectacle while enhancing a film's status (Linda Ruth Williams, *Erotic* 333, 352). Already apparent in burlesque, this development recurs at a number of significant sexploitation junctures, as when Russ Meyer transitioned in the mid-1960s from the male protagonist of the nudie cutie to the female protagonist of the "roughie" or when the midbudget softcore thrillers of the early 1990s began to shun the traditional *noir* hero in favor of the heroines common to later softcore. This maneuver is also discernible in insular corporate developments; consider Seduction Cinema's shift in 2002 from its early emphasis on buffoonish, nudie-cutie–like heroes toward more "refined" and even empowered heroines. An ironic consequence of the urge to objectify the female body more pervasively has, then, been to *subjectify* her character more pervasively as well. Look at a woman long enough, this sexist evolution almost says, and she can hardly avoid sprouting a personality.

Stock elements of softcore numbers reinforce this consistent expansion of female subjectivity. Just as softcore narrative has inescapable visual functions, so do the numbers have inescapable diegetic functions. Softcore's central visual signifier is surely the female breast. Though this icon often carries thematic resonance, other visual staples offer more reliable psychological dimensions. Most crucial is the female face, which, as a performative focus of the spectacle, is a legacy of classical sexploitation and other genres (burlesque, early art films, etc.) linked to the exploitation tradition. Psychological import may also be located in other motifs with similarly extensive histories. These include domestic images of a woman before her mirror or relaxing in her tub. Both motifs hint at what is, after the breast and face, softcore's most important image, not to mention one fraught with psychosexual resonance: the masturbating woman. Manipulated with craft, these and other stock elements, all of which imply degrees of agency, easily integrate with plots centered on female subjectivity and female desire.

Contemporary softcore has adopted a consumerist treatment of these motifs, allowing female desire free play both in the narrative and at its end. This postfeminist tolerance dovetails with the genre's depiction of women either empowered from the start or arcing toward such a state.[9] The genre's antecedents never matched this routinization. Prone to prefeminist and anticonsumerist inflections, classical sexploitation was more likely to resort to devices that restrict and punish free expressions of female agency and desire. That said, certain classical producers had by the late 1960s established middling paradigms that made such tolerance commonplace. The awakening-sexuality model adapted from European art films by aspirational sexploiteers like Metzger (e.g., *Therese and Isabelle* [1968]), Sarno (*Inga* [1967]), and Jaeckin (*Emmanuelle*) is conducive to female desire and the development of female agency. Other protocontemporary elements may be discerned in the suburban or "swingers" subgenre and the women-in-the-workplace cycles that portray nurses, stewardesses, teachers, and so on. When softcore reemerged in the 1990s, distributors followed King in selecting for the feminized devices that had helped earlier sexploiteers achieve "breakouts" from the sex circuit, signaling the mainstream viability of their forms. Apart from feminism, then, the central factor in the development of self-consciously female-friendly forms was the emergence in the 1980s of nontheatrical distribution networks ready to air middlebrow sexploitation. It is no accident that the programming of premium cable, the centralized scheme most identified with the revival of softcore in the 1990s, has traditionally reflected a tolerance of female desire (e.g., Jaehne 10–15). After all, cable's corporate ownerships have had little interest in offending a subscriber base that skews upscale and female.

It might be surmised, then, that female sexual desire is to postfeminist softcore what male sexual desire was to prefeminist sexploitation: a consumer impulse to encourage then indulge rather than to encourage then critique. To understand this hypothesis, it helps to have a rough concept of the ideological shifts implicit in the transitions from classical exploitation to classical sexploitation and from classical sexploitation to contemporary softcore. Drawing on Birken's terminology, Schaefer describes classical exploitation as deeply conflicted in that it regularly conveyed a "productivist" message that demonized the titillation that the genre was designed to foment (*Bold* 15, 41). In its lighter, more consumerist treatment of male desire, *Mr. Teas* signified a break with exploitation that was indicative of a broad, middle-class rejection of archaic anticonsumerist anxieties. If, as Schaefer claims, exploitation "embodied the tensions between the older economic system rooted in the ideology of productivity and the developing consumer-based economy," then sexploitation reflected the new climate of the early 1960s, in which "sexual desire, especially male sexual desire, was economically legitimate" (*Bold* 15, 339). Naturally, this deep tension did not dissipate overnight. Though sexploitation was geared to indulge a voyeuristic stereotype of male desire, it often did so by demonizing the liberation of female desire in the diegesis. But in contemporary softcore, this anticonsumerist bias has either been downplayed or reversed in a postfeminist, cable-friendly manner. As a result, if today's softcore positions any sexuality as a threat, it is usually male sexuality. Indeed, the classical era's intentional indulgence of male consumers through an expanding objectification of the female body led logically albeit ironically to more recent depictions that cater to women by glorifying female stereotypes while censuring male stereotypes. It might even be said that the male softcore viewer often backs into a masochistic identification scheme, buying "an erection," as Linda Ruth Williams puts it, "at the expense of having to listen to a diatribe against the average guy's sexual neglect of women" (*Erotic* 352).

Male masochism offers an apt segue into my second thesis, which is that softcore is a self-conscious genre steeped in abjection, pervasively defined by what it is *not*—and quietly enjoyed for what it *is*. Cultural, industrial, and structural realities reinforce this negative dynamic, which encompasses all aspects of the genre, here defined to include producers, consumers, and critics as well as texts. Culturally, the residue of the antisexual, anticonsumerist anxieties glossed above has combined with the hegemony of an elite, aesthetic ideology biased toward neo-Kantian ideas of disinterest to delegitimize forms viewed as narrowly or "secretly" sexual in their utility. Industrially, the dubiousness ascribed to implicitly masturbatory forms has been reinforced by softcore's deflationary economics, yielding a singularly contemptuous producer-product-consumer interrelation. It is instructive that I have *never* come across a person in softcore production who claims to have *aspired* to that industrial stratum. Instead, producers almost always view softcore as a transitional middle, as a path, that is, to something else. Aspirational producers aspire to "indie" art films, corporate producers aspire to major studio films, and cult producers aspire to nonsoftcore horror films. Still and all, softcore's specific textual realities have most fully conditioned its abject, negative position even among sexualized forms like the theatrical erotic thriller or, alternately, the hardcore video. That softcore has a dichotomous, narrative-number structure is decisive here—but as we shall see, the fact that softcore sex is simulated and nonexplicit is also significant.

Two ideas are helpful—indeed, *overhelpful*—in discussing these tendencies. One is Linda Williams's theory of "compensation" in hardcore representation, which she adapts from David James's ideas on striptease. According to Williams's construction of James, in striptease, "the art of dancing is played off against the non-art of the sexual act that the dance suggests. The artistry of performance comes to compensate for what is missing in discursive exchange between performer and audience" (Linda Williams, *Hard* 77). Williams expands on James's point by arguing "that each historically successive form of the representation of sexual acts using living, moving bodies must compensate its viewers for the formal limits of the medium." The stag film's total-visibility aesthetic and exaggerated amateurism assure the viewer that the sex is unsimulated and are ultimately offered as "compensation for the spectator's physical and temporal separation from the sexual performance he observes. . . . The hard-core sequences of the stag film are thus like a magnified and amateurized striptease in which the spectator sees more of the real sexual act as compensation for the loss of his own direct sexual relation to the performing body" (Linda Williams, *Hard* 78). The other noteworthy idea is Richard Dyer's nuanced albeit subtly essentialist construction of the term "structuring absence." According to Dyer, the "notion of a text's 'structuring absence' is a suggestive, even beguiling one, which is also much open to abuse. It does not mean things which are simply not in the text, or which the critic thinks ought to be in the text. . . . A structuring absence on the other hand refers to an issue, or even a set of facts or an argument, that a text cannot ignore, but which it deliberately skirts round or otherwise avoids, thus creating the biggest 'holes' in the text, fatally, revealingly misshaping the organic whole" (*Matter* 105). These two ideas are not exactly parallel. "Compensation" is an attempt to explain the interaction of producer, text, and viewer, while "structuring absence" has a more formalist bent. Nevertheless, Williams's idea resembles Dyer's in its negative workings. If we accept Williams's slant, such negations relate not just to texts, as Dyer argues, but to entire genres. And certainly, softcore and other "soft" sexploitation forms seem on first glance peculiarly apt candidates for this species of theorization.

Indeed, compensation seems to fit softcore sexploitation even better than stags and hardcore. As a simulated, peekaboo form emulating the mechanisms of striptease—which is also a standard softcore number—softcore posits a greater representational distance from actual sex than hardcore and thus seems to have more to compensate for. The idea is, then, applicable to the soft-focus tactics that "refine" the spectacle of aspirational films by decreasing their explicitness. In alluding to the stylization of Metzger's spectacle, Elena Gorfinkel has theorized that "the soft-core predicament" is a "prohibition of the explicit sexual act" that conditions an array of viewer compensations, including aestheticization but also encompassing production values often missing from hardcore (39). That a well-developed narrative may figure as one of these "absent" values suggests a common perception of how softcore narrative compares to the more slender narratives of hardcore or of how nonsoftcore sexploitation narrative compares to the more slender narratives of fully dichotomous softcore (e.g., Hardy 68–69). Take the standard reading of the roughie, which preceded both classical softcore and hardcore. As articulated in an early study like *Sinema* (1974), this reading describes the roughie's dramatic emphasis on action and violence as compensations for an absence of sex (Turan and Zito 19–25). The legal anxieties of the prehardcore era offer a rationale for reading sexploitation in this manner. As Schaefer puts it, "[b]ecause sexploitation movies could not bring up the curtain on the last act (they were busted often enough for nudity as it was), they were forced to sublimate sex into other activities" ("Triumph" 22). This legalistic explanation of why "the last act" (David Friedman's euphemism for active sex) is often absent is reasonable in classical contexts. Applied to contemporary texts, it is an anachronism—albeit a conventional one—that distorts discourse on sexploitation genres, which, like hardcore, remain largely unhindered by the law. The end result of this interpretive trend is that the manifest qualities of a sexualized text are perceived as "substitutes" for the greater explicitness of a more sexualized form, creating the illusion of a chain of abject genres each deferring its "real" or "desired" identity to other forms.

The utility of Dyer's notion of the "structuring absence" parallels that of Williams's notion of compensation. Because softcore so persistently yet so inexplicitly invokes sex, the genre's tactics for aestheticizing, obscuring, or cutting away from sex seem to indicate "a set of facts" that softcore texts shun, lacunae that indirectly "structure" the presences onscreen. These omitted "facts" are presumed to be hardcore sex and genital close-ups. Consider, for example, that one of softcore's most striking omissions is the erect penis, which American culture has traditionally construed as uniquely indecent if not obscene. Despite the fact that neither the law nor the MPAA places greater restrictions on depictions of unaroused male genitalia than on depictions of female genitalia—and despite the fact that avoiding the penis altogether disrupts the realistic illusion—the flaccid penis is also largely absent from softcore.[10] Such an absence is hardly surprising. The ingrained prohibition against phallic imagery is unlikely to be challenged by a middlebrow genre like softcore. But this straightforward acceptance of a broad taboo gains new significance when filtered through psychoanalytic reading styles that readily frame the unseen as determining the seen. After all, the idea that the penis—or, to be precise, the *phallus*, its more symbolic analogue—acts as a secret "overseer" is pervasive in discourses critical of "phallocentrism." It is little wonder, then, that this hermeneutical habit informs Linda Williams's reductive dismissal of softcore: "Hiding the penis merely yields 'soft core'; the phallus's power and dominance are still reproduced, only now in more indirect ways" (*Hard* 247).

What makes these intertwining concepts so tempting is that they seem to explain not only obvious internal trade-offs and glaring omissions but also more intricate biases and subtle silences, thus presenting the beguiling potential for an all-encompassing thesis. Though I have neither the space nor the inclination to detail this "ideal" thesis, its deterministic outlines may be touched on. Drawing on these concepts, the narrative-spectacle trade-off noted above might be extended to the sex-violence continuum that enmeshes most sexualized genres, such that violence is explained as a "structuring compensation" that varies in accord with the absence of hardcore sexuality. The emphasis on the female face would compensate for a similar absence. In turn, *all* the feminized details of softcore—from the fantasy emphasis to the literary devices, soft-focus effects, and current recourse to misandry—might be connected and dismissed as a postfeminist method of "bribing" female viewers into neglecting the sexism of the spectacle, which remains biased toward its *idée fixe* of male desire. Certainly, this theorization could be applied to the absence of children from softcore as well as to the genre's suppression of overtly racial and political themes. It could also be extended to corporate softcore's contradictory integrations of pornographic imagery and cultural piety. More impressive, this thesis might be delicately applied to the ironic internal absences and dubious external silences that attend the issue of autoerotic reception. Though male viewers have confirmed that they masturbate *to* softcore, the masturbating male is all but absent *in* softcore. Conversely, though softcore texts overflow with images of masturbating women, female consumers are peculiarly silent, thus obscuring their reception of the genre. Both omissions are fomented by the comparative invisibility of the softcore viewer in a nontheatrical era of private, domestic consumption. Notions of structuring absences and "compensatory presences" might be used to explain these interlocking gaps as the genre's complex manner of obscuring the "real" story of why it is produced, who consumes it, and how.

The supreme difficulty of discussing this shadow thesis, so to speak, is that each of its parts has some qualified utility and some qualified logic. Producer perspectives *are* marked by negation, and to some extent, such attitudes *do* condition the abjection of softcore texts from *Starlet!* (1969) to *Star Struck* (2000). Moreover, the compensation account of interlocking motifs

Figure 1. Soft, "deflective" stylization in the promotional art for high-end hardcore. © Studio A Entertainment and Andrew Blake, 2003.

like stylization, feminization, violence, and misandry is not only popular but in restricted respects persuasive. But ultimately, these negative accounts, no matter how pervasive or supple, do not provide a seamless understanding of softcore—and are convincing in neither their logical nor their historical extensions. Witness one permutation of the compensation account as registered in online responses to softcore: the idea that producers cram their films with spectacle *because* their plots are shoddy. This is a silly idea, but is it really less logical than the compensation account that suggests that softcore has a story *because* it lacks hardcore sex? If the latter is logical, why has hardcore ever had any narrative? And for that matter, why do hardcore auteurs like Candida Royalle and Andrew Blake frequently resort to soft-focus tactics? Wouldn't it be "better" if their works were more amateurish, as Linda Williams seems to imply? Here it is plain that realistic narratives and soft-focus styles confer the same distinctions in both hardcore and softcore. In focusing on softcore, it would be myopic to view "prestige" elements as sexual compensations in any inflexible sense.

These genres are too complex, and the responses they elicit too variable, to brook such brittle readings; no thesis as ahistorical and as overdetermined as the one outlined above can unify their diversity. For scholars, the danger of such a thesis is obvious: it encourages them to dismiss major textual elements. Such a method may even shade into one of softcore's most distinctive responses: *interpretive amputation*. As chapter 8 shows, it is common for consumers to treat the softcore dichotomy as if one part of its narrative-number unit either does not exist or does not contain the "essence" of the text, which is located in the other part. This pressure to amputate hails from myriad sources, including the assumption that all narrative genres yearn toward Hollywood paradigms or, contrarily, that all sexual genres yearn toward hardcore paradigms. More salient is the intercession of elite aesthetic ideologies that delegitimize genres perceived to have affective and utilitarian purposes. In softcore, this dynamic is exacerbated by the genre's masturbatory uses and misandristic meanings, which stimulate anticonsumerist anxieties among consumers. Especially among male viewers, such mechanisms have culminated in a distinctive tendency toward bad faith. Consumers often locate the essence of the text in its numbers, dismissing the narrative as in effect not "really" there, and then consistently belittle their own manifest preferences. Tellingly, these softcore "advocates" seldom use sacralizing terms, at most praising a film in practical terms that invoke craftsmanship but rarely artistry—as if to suggest that softcore is *intrinsically inartistic*. This middlebrow taste formation is singular, then, in that it renounces essentialist terminology but only as a qualified gesture of "good taste" in deference to the more proper claims on such terms made by consumers of elite genres. What could be a radical antiessentialist posture is no more, then, than the self-effacing cover for elitist mystifications.

By contrast, in their responses to aspirational softcore, consumers often focus on narrative to the exclusion of number. Despite these anxious reactions, softcore has thrived because producers and consumers prefer its base model *as it is* and not simply as a perverse compensation. What softcore "is" is a dichotomous form of sexploitation that relies on a synthesis of elements—all of which, from a scholarly perspective, are equally *there*. It is crucial to understand why producers and consumers often adopt opposite views, but neither these responses nor an "ideal" thesis grounded in theories of negation should encourage scholars to engage in similar reductions.

The chapters that follow explore the above ideas by tracing the history of softcore; by contextualizing it as an evolving "middle" in a postfeminist matrix; by examining its exemplary cycles, texts, and figures; and by analyzing its current reception. The second chapter considers the softcore-hardcore distinction from three perspectives: the history of the porn debates; the history of the middlebrow concept; and the history of soft-focus feminization. My third chapter looks at the classical genres from a current standpoint, focusing on industrial and generic trends relevant to softcore's contemporary identity. The fourth examines the 1980s as a transitional period in which technological, economic, and political shifts led to softcore's recession; when the form reemerged in 1991, it had a contemporary bearing, especially in its feminization and modes of exhibition. The fifth chapter looks at King, a crucial popularizer, focusing on the interplay of gender, genre, and class in his *noir*-romance hybrids. Chapter 6 focuses on the softcore thriller, an area in which the erotic thriller and contemporary softcore overlap. Chapter 7 looks at a fantasy-oriented subgenre, the softcore serial, analyzing the mostly affirmative responses that it has elicited from feminist critics. The eighth chapter analyzes segments of the softcore public so as to contextualize current softcore reception, which is distinguished by anxiety and bad faith, in terms of the scholarship on cult audiences. My ninth chapter proposes that the contradictory pieties of Playboy Enterprises' now-defunct corporate softcore model were a function of the company's corporate history. This chapter's second section focuses on director Tom Lazarus, whose "dissidence" illustrates the obstacles to auteurism emplaced by corporate softcore practice. Chapter 10 looks at cult softcore through a case study of Seduction Cinema, which mostly shoots on video. The transformations of this youth-oriented label recapitulate film history; exemplify salient distinctions between cult and corporate softcore; and provide contrasts with other softcore subsectors, many of which are trending downscale.

"We don't like nothin' soft; everything we touch is hard."
—*Faster, Pussycat! Kill! Kill! (1966)*

"I'm supposed to be soft, I'm a woman."
—*Hard Ticket to Hawaii (1987)*

Soft v. Hard

Over the past four decades, the word "softcore" and its relatives, "soft porn" and "soft focus," have become common pejoratives. One has only to peruse the title of Ann Douglas's essay "Soft-Porn Culture" (1980) to predict with confidence that it will belittle its subject, Harlequin romance.[1] Implicit to this put-down is that soft genres and techniques are devalued because they are pornographic. Yet this idea tells but half the story. Though some conjunction of "soft" qualities has allowed such media to flourish in the mainstream markets barred to more explicit media, references to the former are more uniformly derogatory than references to the latter. Soft forms are also, then, mocked for not being pornographic enough. Such a dismissal is evident in many reviews of recent American films that do not rise to the "hardcore" trend of European art films like *Intimacy* (2001) or *9 Songs* (2004), which feature unsimulated sex.[2] It is more evident yet in academic discourse, where expressions like "softcore" and "soft focus" are attended by "mere," as in Linda Williams's phrase, "[h]iding the penis merely yields 'soft core'" (*Hard* 247). Softcore really is, as the "other" Linda Williams puts it,[3] "the Cinderella of sexual theory," for it "always com[es] second." Though hardcore has its defenders, few outside a small "cult" of online fans are willing to defend softcore *as such*—and even they do so in a halting, embarrassed idiom that suggests bad faith.

The ultimate reason for this pattern of derogation is that soft forms are considered "hybrids" whose "impurity" represents a failure to conform to harder, purer, more masculinized ideals. This failure may be framed as a pretentious confusion, a *mistake*, or as a willful vulgarization of standards—but deemed intentional or not, it has usually been interpreted as tantamount to "crass" commercialism. There is something to such views. Producers have ensured the commercial maneuverability of soft forms through a distinction strategy that combines Porn's allure with Art's elevation. In this sense, then, the hybrid label and charge of commercialism are equally apt. What is irritating, though, is that such critiques obscure that *all* forms have a hybrid aspect and that even the most elite and ascetic forms have economic bases. At bottom, then, this pattern of derogation reveals the presence of patently ideological mechanisms that falsify history by masking the contingent impurity of *all* texts, codes, and values.[4]

This is not to say that soft forms should be lauded. Naïve modes of evaluation, pro or con, only reinforce dominant cultural hierarchies; they do so first by naturalizing the very idea of hierarchy, which depends on illusions of intrinsic value. For that reason, none of the defenses of "softness" that have gathered over the years has dented the larger bias against soft forms. These defenses have instead inclined toward status-quo ends because they accept our culture's most dubious premises, namely that certain aesthetic forms contain an ahistorical value; that certain ideas of gender linked to biological sex have an essential reality and value; and that there is something "in" sex that demands that it be treated in certain aesthetic fashions or risk becoming intrinsically degraded, degrading, or obscene. Without demystifying these foundational essences, which naturalize privilege and sexism, even academic approaches devoted to transgression seem as likely to bolster dominant hierarchies as to subvert them.

The following chapter exposes the essentialist assumptions that have informed the pejorative usage of "softcore," "soft porn," and "soft focus" in three different historical frameworks. (This approach has the advantage of introducing events and concepts to which I will refer throughout *Soft in the Middle*.) The first section compares the softcore-hardcore distinction as it crystallized during the advent of the sexual revolution to its altered condition following the rise of antiporn feminism and the wane of porno-chic. The next two segments traverse even broader ground. The second section focuses on the middlebrow taste concept, while the third surveys the history of that visual tactic once called "the soft style." In each context, elements deemed feminine and middlebrow have been so closely identified as to become virtual synonyms. Together, they have yielded an aspirational posture that has enlarged the distribution of softly sexualized texts while ultimately reinforcing "elite" perceptions of their inferiority.

I. PORNO-CHIC, ANTIPORN CRITIQUE

> *Erotica is soft core, soft focus; it is gentler and tenderer . . . than . . . pornography.*
> —ANN BARR SNITOW (256)

> *"Softness" is just people saying that women only like "soft" things, and that's ridiculous. That's ghettoising women.*
> —ALEXANDER GREGORY HIPPOLYTE[5]

The softcore-hardcore distinction was preceded by the erotica-porn distinction, which it closely resembles. In *The Secret Museum: Pornography in Modern Culture* (1987), Walter Kendrick observes that "erotica" and "pornography" gained their current inflections only during the middle of the twentieth century:

> Like "pornography," "erotica" is a modern coinage with a specious aura of antiquity. The OED dates its first English usage 1853 (just three years, that is, after the first published use of "pornographers"), as a category heading in a bookseller's catalogue. . . . "Erotica" seems to have entered the general vocabulary only in the 1950s and 60s, as "pornography" became increasingly tainted with low-class associations. A word was needed to designate the increasing number of books that, though they dealt with sex, somehow did so in a safe and classy way. (244)

As classifiers, "pornography" and "erotica" have not historically been rooted in concrete generic criteria. Instead, their usage has been dependent on patently subjective indices. *The Unabridged Random House Dictionary*, for example, defines "pornography" as "obscene writings, drawings, photographs, or the like, esp. those having little or no artistic merit," but construes "erotica" as "literature or art dealing with sexual love." Applying such terms, then, requires not just interpretation but evaluation as well—and it is notable that these terms suggest distinct approaches to authorial intention. Works deemed "erotica" are usually framed as having complex, heterogeneous intentions that combine the aesthetic (or literary) and the sexual (or pornographic). In this hierarchical economy, erotica is partly redeemed by its aesthetic aspirations but partly debased by its sexual intentions, which violate neo-Kantian principles of disinterest. By contrast, works devalued as "pornography" are viewed as having sexual intentions alone (Kendrick 206). As a result, cultural historians like Steven Marcus have often dismissed "erotica" and its cognates as "little more than euphemisms" (36n2). In making such a claim, Marcus is not casting doubt on the intention-based evaluation that informs this brand of classification. Nor does he reject the term "erotica" insofar as its middlebrow elitism aspires, however unsuccessfully, to a learned Canon that cloaks its contingent being in dubious ahistorical concepts. Marcus cannot, of course, attack the term on antiessentialist grounds because his scholarship is informed by highbrow principles.[6] Instead, he dispenses with "erotica" because he thinks it disguises the "secretly" unified intention basic to all pornography. In this reductive view, it is all Porn and, as such, "really" has one intention irrespective of the diversity that only "seems" to inform its disparate vehicles.[7]

"Hardcore" and "softcore" date to the 1950s and 1960s, respectively. More than "porn," "hardcore" initially invoked a purely negative referent. According to Kendrick, "hard core" came to prominence via the Supreme Court's 1957 *Roth* decision (196–98). "Hard-core" was linked adjectivally to "pornography" to construct a legal category of utterly worthless or "obscene" material, ostensibly giving the federal antiobscenity statute a stricter focus. Falling into this essentialist rubric were unsimulated sexual depictions whose only intention, the government's solicitor general smugly insisted, was to express the idea "that there is pleasure in sexual gratification," the "social value" of which was, "of course, nil" (qtd. in Kendrick 197). Fully explicit stag films were assigned to this category, as were unvarnished materials that emerged from an illicit underground in the 1960s and early 1970s. But it was not until the luminous success of *Deep Throat* (1972) had inaugurated the "porno-chic era" that "hardcore," like "porno," entered the linguistic mainstream.[8] The usage of "softcore" has been dated to 1965. This term also gained prominence by dint of porno-chic, which engendered a wider cultural awareness of how hardcore forms related to softer, less explicit genres—including "classical softcore," which had appeared on the sexploitation circuit prior to the arrival of hardcore in 1970. (That these relations were clear within the sexploitation industry as early as 1968 is indicated by commentators like William Rotsler and self-referential softcore films like *Starlet!* [1969].) The softcore-hardcore distinction achieved a new cultural clarity after the 1974 release of Just Jaeckin's soft-focus blockbuster *Emmanuelle,* which gained wide American distribution through a major Hollywood studio, Columbia, thus yielding a softcore analogue to *Deep Throat* (Willemen 13; Lewis 227–29).

Porno-chic suggested that the purely negative idea of hardcore—and, by extension, of sexual gratification—that was constructed under *Roth* did not reflect emergent attitudes. Given that *Playboy* founder Hugh Hefner had been preaching a "fun morality" since 1953 (Ehrenreich 45), there was little chance *Roth*'s anticonsumerist assumptions would go unchallenged in an era that made the *Playboy* model look staid. Starting in the 1960s, hardcore forms were perceived as a principal component of the culture's rapid embrace of a revolutionary sexuality. According to hardcore's proponents, explicit porn was a path to Reichian liberation (which neglected that Wilhelm Reich considered porn symptomatic of repression). This new viewpoint inverted *Roth*'s derogatory construction of hardcore "purity," lending "dirt for dirt's sake" an affirmative intonation. Conversely, as a function of its fully relative etymology, "softcore" gained a more ambivalent meaning. Whereas "hardcore" has connoted purity and unyielding commitment, "softcore" has connoted moderation and, more pejoratively, dilution and half-measures.

That divergences of this sort existed in the early 1970s is not surprising, for such contrasts had been implicit to the erotica-porn distinction for decades. From a current standpoint, though, it is surprising that these discourses did not substantiate the traditional understanding that women "[prefer] the 'erotic' over the 'pornographic,'" to use Linda Ruth Williams's words (*Erotic* 25). As it happens, the politics of gender identity governed the hard-soft distinction only after second-wave feminism had generated an outspoken critique of porn in the mid-1970s, as signaled by a concatenation of events, including the publication of Susan Brownmiller's *Against Our Will: Men, Women, and Rape* (1975), the formation of Women Against Pornography (1976), and the antisnuff campaign (1976; see Johnson and Schaefer 40–57). Before that juncture, hard and soft films competed for female consumers. Hardcore gained its first wide access to female audiences via three 1972 films—*Deep Throat, The Devil in Miss Jones,* and *Behind the Green Door*—and porno-chic's countercultural rhetoric was as likely to be evinced by women as by men.[9] This fact was particularly apparent in the sex film industry itself.[10]

Published in 1974, Kenneth Turan and Stephen Zito's *Sinema: American Pornographic Films and the People Who Make Them* is valuable for preserving the essentialist discourses that enmeshed the hardcore-softcore distinction at the height of porno-chic. Part porno-chic effusion, part scholarly tome, *Sinema* adopts a journalistic stance toward the sex film industry, disseminating the industry's ideas of itself to a wider audience. These evaluations often come from female sources; neither the authors nor the performers imply that they view one's sex as a significant ideological limit on the expression of sexual tastes. Instead of dividing the industry through gender concepts, then, *Sinema* partitions it along hard-soft lines, with women on both sides.

In an interview section entitled "The Hard and Soft of It," Turan and Zito sum up the industry's divided perceptions of itself by referring to softcore's ostensible "tastefulness" and to hardcore's uncompromising moralism:

> It may seem, as populist firebrand Tom Watson said of poor whites and blacks in the rural South, that hard- and soft-core pornographers are all in

the ditch together. Those involved, however, don't see it quite that way, and in most cases a clear demarcation line can be drawn between the soft- and hard-core folk. The former view themselves as perfectly respectable, if a little risqué, and see hard core as far too clinical and explicit to be tasteful. The latter, meanwhile, feeling an Old Testament moral rectitude about what they do, dismiss the people who mess with soft-core sex as hypocritical, if not worse. (94)

Turan and Zito's initial interviews—the first with Marsha Jordan, the "Queen of Soft Core," the second with Mary Rexroth, bohemian daughter of writer Kenneth Rexroth—embody this ideational divide. Jordan evinces a genteel perspective, rejecting hardcore on traditional grounds while embracing softcore as a "vital," romantic alternative (Turan and Zito 99–100). The more radical Rexroth counters Jordan by aligning the explicitness and straightforwardness of hardcore with health, nature, and truth (surely among Ideology's most basic keywords). By the same token, Rexroth critiques softcore for its structuring obliquity, which she frames as perverse and even pathological:

> "[I]t's the taunting and the lewdness and the striptease—I can't understand it." And as a corollary to this, Mary feels that for her "there is a kind of morality" about making a hard-core film as opposed to a soft-core film. "I won't do a soft-core film, and I won't do sort of standard beaver films because, as I said, I don't understand the tease trip. I think there's something lewd and dirty and sick and so on and so forth about soft-core films, I really do. You gotta know how to do that. I mean, I know how to fuck, I don't know how to do that." (qtd. in Turan and Zito 106)

Turan and Zito's subsequent interviews with Pat Rocco, a pioneer of gay sexploitation, and John Holmes, a sexploitation vet legendary for his hardcore performances, reinforce the nonsexist orientation of this essentialist debate. Like Jordan, Rocco views hardcore as antiromantic, preferring softcore for its greater capacity to portray "'the beauty of male love'" (qtd. in Turan and Zito 113). By contrast, Holmes idealizes hardcore by linking it to free speech principles and pure affective emotion (Turan and Zito 116, 118).

Through these prefeminist juxtapositions, Turan and Zito imply that the hardcore-softcore debate was in the early 1970s framed according to flexible consumer tastes. Given the emphatic feminization of contemporary softcore, this implication may seem counterintuitive. Alternatively, it may clarify what Linda Ruth Williams calls "obvious": that the contemporary softcore audience is defined not by gender but by consumer preference (*Erotic* 265).

(See chapter 8.) This reality has been masked by gender essentialisms that position "softness" as a nexus of "female" concepts and "hardness" as a nexus of "male" concepts. Antiporn feminism mostly reinforced such stereotypes. Hence, but a few years after *Sinema*'s publication, the hard-soft distinction had fractured along gender lines, a development attributable to the intervention of antiporn ideology. At that point, the consumer diversity that had once been implicit to the hardcore-softcore debate was overwhelmed by reductive ideas of sex and gender.

The antiporn era was inaugurated by a coalition of cultural conservatives, who would later be identified with Reaganism, and social progressives, including second-wave feminism's antiporn wing (Kendrick 228–39; Frug 254–63; Linda Williams, *Hard* 16–23; MacKinnon 137–38; Segal 59–70; O'Toole 26–60).[11] These groups had a mutual interest in reversing aspects of the sexual revolution, and both contributed to the Meese Commission Report of 1986. To conservatives, the entire liberationist turn in American life was a grievous moral error, while feminists embraced such liberation except where patriarchal forces within the revolution appeared to exploit female bodies for profit or pleasure. Lawrence Birken might argue that the counterrevolutionary logic of this coalition was that both groups relied on fixed ideas of gender to critique an emerging consumerist "system of values stressing pleasure, genderlessness, and desire" (111). In this account, antiporn feminism represents an anticonsumerist departure from that revolutionary, antiessentialist strand of second-wave thought that would eventually argue "that gender should be overthrown, eliminated, or rendered fatally ambiguous precisely because it is always a sign of subordination for women" (Butler xiii).

Within feminism's antiporn wing, prominent figures like Gloria Steinem, Susan Griffin, and Diana Russell lionized "erotica" as a safe, nonpornographic alternative to hardcore. Through this middle concept, feminists could sanction erotic forms, dodging an antisex label and attracting the support of women who had reservations about hardcore excess *and* the antiporn excess of Andrea Dworkin and Catharine MacKinnon. The erotica concept, whose gender intonation had been secondary, gained a gender-specific rationale: erotica was safe and "classy" *because* it was feminine. Antiporn endorsements of "erotica" thus tended toward the sexist and ahistorical, reflecting fantasies of reform rather than realities of form. That said, feminist definitions of "erotica" did include notable variations. Whereas Steinem and Griffin stressed love, Russell stressed dignity and equality, defining "erotica" as "*sexually suggestive or arousing material that is free of sexism, racism, and homophobia and is respectful of all human beings and animals portrayed*" (48; Russell's italics). Though in some respects ludicrous, Russell's formulation is also attractive in that it is based neither on inexplicitness nor on feminization. Under her egalitarian rubric, many hardcore videos would qualify as erotica but R-rated softcore films, which never expose male and female bodies equally, would not (see 69). This willingness to forego gender essentialism and the privileges sanctioned by it was at odds with traditional and untraditional orthodoxies alike. It is unsurprising, then, that feminism's default tendency was to valorize a counterrevolutionary "erotica" that was closer to Steinem's logic in that it equated the term with soft, feminized forms structured by gender inequity. Thus, in embracing "softcore erotica," pro-erotica feminists embraced concepts not far from traditional femininity. The hardcore-softcore schism soon emerged as a sexist division within feminism shunting women away from "bad" hardcore. This division was fortified with mostly groundless suppositions apropos the "natural" differences between male and female sexuality and, by extension, male and female porn (see Modleski, *Feminism* 151). Linda Williams sums up this trend by noting that "anti-pornography feminists have used this hard/soft distinction to label men's sexuality as pornographic and women's as erotic," with such "polar oppositions" linked to a "soft, tender, nonexplicit women's erotica and a hard, cruel, graphic phallic pornography" (*Hard* 6; see "Porn Studies" 6; see also Linda Ruth Williams, *Erotic* 39–40).

These counterrevolutionary ideas were co-opted by a neotraditional, postfeminist culture amenable to oppositions that maintained the gender system. By reinforcing gender stereotypes, such ideas helped reinstitute restrictions on female tastes typical of American culture before the sexual revolution (e.g., Henry Jenkins 2). Suddenly, revolutionaries like Mary Rexroth who did not favor soft prescriptions were informed that their tastes were not only "low" but a betrayal of their gender. In cinema, these biases contributed to the routinization of sexploitation as it morphed into contemporary softcore. In the late 1970s, shifts to private technology created a potential female audience for sexploitation that dwarfed porno-chic's "couples audience." Following Columbia's example, the conservative conglomerates who controlled cable distribution tailored their sexploitive offerings to the *Emmanuelle* model,[12] which favored a limited rhetoric of female agency as integrated with an upscale, sensual grammar—all to make soft, unthreatening products that adhered to what some antiporn feminists described softcore erotica as having *always* been. Of course, the emphatic feminization that regulates the softcore concept is not isolated to the softcore genre. The processes that have led postfeminist culture to persistently reduce complex sexual tastes to soft, feminized imagery are as evident in the "romantic," heterosexist stylistics of erectile dysfunction advertising—and even in *Bridgestone tire advertising*—as they are in softcore serials like *Red Shoe Diaries*.[13]

In going mainstream in the 1990s, softcore cinema became even more vulnerable to imprecise pejoratives. After the porn debates, a new stigma, "politically correct porn," became affixed to it. This was and *is* absurd. Softcore narrative is dominated by white, middle-class, heterosexual women, and its spectacle is molded by fixed sex-and-gender inequities. If "correct" connotes a commitment to sex-and-gender equality and to social diversity, then "correct" is precisely what softcore is not. Such pejoratives might have been more applicable had producers espoused Russell's notion of erotica, but that was not the case. Equally ironic is that feminists like Williams and Laura Kipnis, who yoke their interest in feminist transgression to hardcore explicitness,[14] have dismissed softcore as a function of their interest in hardcore cinema. Viewers who do not identify themselves as feminists have, then, disdained softcore as too feminist, too correct, to be erotic, while those who do identify themselves as feminist have disdained it as too timid, too mainstream, to be "authentically" feminist (see Linda Ruth Williams, *Erotic* 270). But a growing number of feminists have adopted opposite tacks. As a function of their postfeminist embrace of an antitransgressive, "domesticated" femininity, critics like Jane Juffer evince an affirmative view of softcore and other soft forms. But insofar as Juffer seems to have returned to the old antiporn tendency to draw counterrevolutionary links between "tender" genders and "tenderer" genres, her neotraditionalism is as likely to augment the perception of softcore's second-rate status as to subvert it.

II. THE STIGMAS OF THE MIDDLEBROW

Having stressed that feminization became central to the softcore concept during the antiporn period, I should now stress that said concept was implicitly gendered from the outset. A similar shift is apparent in the evolution of "erotica." Works classified as erotica have long connoted a secondary feminization via their middlebrow status. What changed after antiporn feminism was that erotica's feminization came to seem more essential than its middling rank, despite the fact that both qualities were accepted signs of erotica's relative "safety"—and of one another.

Given that softcore porn has, like erotica, come to be classified as middlebrow porn (Jancovich "Placing" 2–4, "Naked" 4–5), it makes sense that many traits of the contemporary softcore feature, including its feminization, are hallmarks of middlebrow taste formations. (Other traits include the genre's realism and narrative emphasis; its moderation; its pluralistic conflation of structures and styles; and its literariness.) Here the salient commonality is second-rate status. The term "middlebrow" specifically signifies such status and is therefore a tool of exclusion and condescension; hence my thesaurus even lists "boob" among its synonyms. Among highbrows, the middlebrow is more threatening, dubious, and dull than lowbrow "entertainment," a counterintuitive valuation that Jancovich ("Naked" 4) and Leon Hunt (160) have noted—and one that hardcore advocates have reflected. A historical critique of the middlebrow concept thus offers insights into softcore's derogation, which is part of the phenomenon that Modleski has called the "pervasive scorn for all things feminine" (*Loving* 13).

The great problem of the middlebrow concept is that it is almost impossible to invoke it without becoming a highbrow—without slipping, that is, into a graceless elitism naïve to its own contingency, essentialist in its ideas of purity, and smugly certain of the intentions behind mainstream production and consumption. Apropos softcore, highbrowism leads to reductions like the assumption that softcore forms represent "mistakes" and that softcore consumers "really" want something other than softcore. Subtly evident even in Pierre Bourdieu's antiessentialist writings on the middlebrow,[15] this elitism is a traditional way in which highbrows have identified themselves, valorizing their own tastes by deploying a reductive "expertise" to belittle alternative regimes. Because explicit "aesthetic choices are often constituted in opposition to the choices of the groups closest in social space" (Bourdieu, *Distinction* 60), highbrow distaste falls heavily on the middlebrow—or in my analysis, on the upper-middlebrow category of aspirational softcore—for such taste most resembles its own. Besides a Rortian fallibilism, the belief that guides my usage is that no intrinsic, noncontingent value resides in *any* taste regime, so middlebrow sensibilities and forms are never *automatically* mistaken. The "real" mistake of softcore consumers is to be seduced into bad-faith postures that signal acceptance of highbrow essentialisms that delegitimate their manifest preferences. They not need be embarrassed by their own tastes—though they would hardly recognize this from digesting the literature.

This pejorative slant, whereby a historicist survey subtly reinforces a historical devaluation, is perceptible in the terms in which Bourdieu and his interpreters construct the irony of the highbrow-middlebrow relationship. As they point out, the middlebrow has been misperceived as a threat by the defenders of the high despite the fact that the middlebrow is rarely adversarial (see Carroll 232). Drawing on Bourdieu's class-based analyses, Jancovich explains that, from an elite perspective, the "sin" of the middlebrow is not a premeditated effort to overthrow the values of high culture but its "premature" acceptance of those values as grounded in an incomplete understanding of the same:

> [T]he petite bourgeoisie become a threat precisely because of their reverence for legitimate culture, not their hostility to it. Aspiring to enter the bourgeoisie proper, they display an admiration for legitimate culture that is founded on their sense of exclusion from it. If they threaten to blur distinctions between high and low culture and so undermine the authority of the cultural bourgeoisie, it is because they are too eager to become a part of legitimate culture, a culture to which they are alien. ("Naked" 6)

That the middlebrow, according to Bourdieu, seeks to achieve a "legitimate" place "on credit" points to a characteristic often identified with middlebrow expression (*Distinction* 365): it uses terms and ideas without having absorbed them, running them together in a "confused" or "pretentious" way that threatens to dilute the "purity" of elite forms and values. Such confusion, often equated with a self-conscious name-dropping, reportedly exemplifies a middle-class phenomenon referred to by sociologist C. Wright Mills as "status panic," which Marianne Conroy has defined as "a deeply felt unease over the expression and recognition of prestige claims" (117). In this account, the middlebrow's nontransgressive posture is one registration of befuddlement. As a legacy of romanticism, the conflation of beauty and cultural distinction with transgression was institutionalized by modernism and has dominated the academy (Bourdieu, *Distinction* 47). The middlebrow's "panicked" desire for cultural respectability, the ultimate reason for shunning transgression, is an obstacle to that respectability—a fact the middlebrow, lacking insight into high culture by definition, cannot fathom.

Before a critique of the middlebrow could be formulated, the highbrow-lowbrow distinction had to crystallize. In *The Making of Middlebrow Culture* (1992), Joan Shelley Rubin explains that in English-speaking contexts the distinction's physiological character "derived from phrenology and carried overtones of racial differentiation. Transformed into a description of intellectual caliber, 'highbrow' was, in the 1880s, already synonymous with 'refined'; twenty years later, 'lowbrow' came to denote a lack of cultivation" (xii). Because these formations were first associated with reading tastes, the middlebrow was initially identified as an aspirational "female" space dominated by literary women bent on self-improvement. After Van Wyck Brooks called for a "genial middle ground" between highbrow literature and lowbrow entertainment, Margaret Widdemer in 1933 applied the term "middlebrow" to "the majority reader," whom she situated between the "tabloid addict class" and the "tiny group of intellectuals" (qtd. in Rubin xii–xiii; see also Levine). Thereafter, the term was invested with its lasting derogatory meaning by highbrow critics like Virginia Woolf, Dwight Macdonald, and

Clement Greenberg (see Carroll 16–49). Uniting these seminal critiques of the middlebrow was the idea that interchange between "high" and "low" represents a violation of the purity of both. Associated with folk art's "authenticity," the low supplants the middle in this hierarchy of cultural value because the middle is framed as a uniquely "inauthentic" fusion of high and low impulses driven by commercial purposes (see Wilinsky 84–86). As a result, in the alarmist rhetoric of these mid-twentieth-century diatribes, the middlebrow was depicted as a "slime" or "jelly," a soft, feminized "ooze" that threatens to blur or erase "natural" differences in class and taste (see Woolf 180–84; Macdonald, 54). In the postmodern era, these critiques have gained urgency as high-low distinctions have been dismantled, fomenting regular counterattacks by conservatives bent on retaining hard, masculinized standards that guarantee their institutional prestige. Distinguished by an elegiac tone, such jeremiads lament the loss, as James Twitchell notes, of the clear middle "border between Lower Aesthetica and Upper Vulgaria" (23).

At the same general moment that critiques of the middlebrow emerged in other fields, cinematic tastemakers, proponents of auteur theory in particular, began articulating the belief that a taste for the kind of mainstream storytelling that classical Hollywood was so good at was symptomatic of a middlebrow sensibility whose impurity was gendered feminine. Throughout the twentieth century, sacralization processes across the arts had favored a pure, modernist abstraction that (ostensibly) resisted commercial vulgarization, so it is logical that Hollywood's commercial and technical mastery of narrative realism would complicate postwar efforts to elevate cinema to the elite status accorded painting, music, and even photography. For this masculinized idea of cinematic purity to take hold, tastemakers also had to distinguish Cinema from classical exploitation films, which had replaced low nineteenth-century fictions and then early Hollywood films as the target of reformers—but only in their most aspirational incarnations did films in this low tradition represent a threat to highbrow taste formations. An auteur-based idea of film as elite Cinema did not gain wide acceptance until the 1960s. Ironically, film's fine art status was immediately rendered insecure by two other events of that tumultuous decade: the sexual revolution and the advent of postmodernist dehierarchization.

This complex of factors has informed the striking virulence with which highbrows have greeted producers like Jaeckin, Radley Metzger, Joe Sarno, and Zalman King, who have specialized in feminized, upper-middlebrow forms of sexploitation like aspirational softcore. Bent on protecting Cinema's hard-won, relatively recent, ever-insecure status, cinephiles have denounced these middlebrow auteurs as "interlopers" who threaten to dilute the medium's masculine purity. This distinctive invective is not applied to straightforwardly commercial films that "know their place" but has instead been reserved for vehicles whose synthesis of sexual spectacle and auteurism has yielded a provisional cachet. During the classical era, this cachet—and, by extension, this highbrow vitriol—often resulted from sexploitation's crossover distribution on the arthouse circuit, where sex films could gain the coveted and elastic "art film" designation.

Here Metzger's straddling of the high-low border between arthouse and grindhouse is instructive. According to Elena Gorfinkel, Metzger distinguished his work from that of his more lowbrow rivals, Russ Meyer most famously, by specializing in a feminized "art-porn hybrid" that "took advantage of the slippages, misrecognitions and overlaps between the grind-house and the art-house to maximise audience attendance" (28, 29). In the early 1960s, Metzger imported and distributed European art films (a term then even more synonymous with "sexy" foreign films than now) through his New York label, Audubon Films. Metzger edited these films to satisfy distinct audiences. Arthouses got the tamer spectacle, the unhappier endings, and the subtitles, while grindhouses got racier sex, "Hollywood endings," and dubbed dialogue. He also shot his increasingly female-oriented sexploitation films, which he referred to not as "exploitation" but as "'class specialty films,' or 'class sex'" (qtd. in Gorfinkel 30). He thus implied that his main appeal was to the "'sophisticated filmgoer, not to the skinflick audience'" (qtd. in Gorfinkel 30). In Gorfinkel's estimate, these overtures created the "alibi of a middlebrow spectator who wants, presumably, to be educated and edified more than entertained and aroused.... In an attempt to make arousal 'elegant,' Metzger's films can be seen as part . . . of a middle-class pornography, a niche market expanded to include less the maligned all male 'raincoat brigade'—envisioned as the true audience of sexploitation—but more the newly targeted 'date crowd'" (30–31). Gorfinkel concludes that "Metzger promoted an aspirational project . . . classing his films in terms of the already available and upper-middlebrow tenets of the art-house patron" (32). It is worth noting that even as Metzger's rhetoric of distinction worked to dissociate his films from the grindhouse audience, he still marketed his films to that group, drawing crossover audiences to arthouse and grindhouse alike. Though seemingly exclusivist, the director's elitist terminology was inseparable from his commercial object, which was to create films that could move freely through multiple venues.

Metzger's insight, then, was to discern the multivalent distribution possibilities of the art film. Since 1934, when the Czech film *Ecstasy* (1933) was released in the United States, Americans had equated this rubric with a titillating, "Eurosex" blend of nudity and sexual symbolism. As my next section indicates, this association could emerge only after Hollywood began enforcing its Production Code in 1934. Because pre-Code Hollywood was notoriously "sinful," until then no firm distinction could be drawn between salutary domestic "entertainment" and scabrous-yet-classy foreign films. By the late 1950s, the exploitation circuit had diversified to such an extent that certain theaters specialized in art films while others specialized in much less rarefied material. The prosperous vehicles, Metzger realized, appealed to more than one segment of the circuit. In this respect, Roger Vadim's Brigitte Bardot art film, . . . *And God Created Woman* (1956), offered Metzger a useful model, for its arty, heroine-driven sexualization enabled it to move "from art house to grindhouse with no alternation" (Schaefer, *Bold* 336).

It should not, though, be assumed that Metzger's aspirationalism—which yielded the soft, deflective surfaces of literary adaptations like *Carmen, Baby* (1966), *Therese and Isabelle,* and *Camille 2000* (1969)—was a "purely" mercenary pretense. In tandem with his industrial niche, the sexualization and feminization of Metzger's work made him vulnerable to this reduction, which is a variant of Marcus's rejection of erotica. Such critiques rest on three anticonsumerist myths. These writers imagine that there is something inherently dirty "in" commerce. They assume the existence of more-or-less "magical" Artists who secure distribution while evading market pressures. And they decide that art molded by commercial intentions cannot have been guided by other sincerities, specifically aesthetic ones. The last myth is *clearly* inapplicable to Metzger, who was subject to a middlebrow elitism that caused him to agonize quite unnecessarily over commercial compromises. In "Twice As Elegant," his interview with Turan and Zito, Metzger deploys an array of allusions that verify his taste and place him in the company of Ingmar Bergman and Stanley Kubrick; he also evinces sensitivity to a species of criticism that categorizes via reduction (69–70). The interview's subtext is his unhappiness at having been pigeonholed as "just another dirty filmmaker" supplying the raincoat brigade with masturbation material (Turan and Zito 68). It is no wonder that such dismissals bothered Metzger. They implied his violation of neo-Kantian principles of disinterestedness, which Bourdieu and others cite as the foundation of aesthetic ideology (*Distinction* 488–90), and his exclusion from elite culture as well (Turan and Zito 68–69).

Highbrow vitriol continues to greet revivals of Metzger's work. Bart Testa's 1999 *Spectator* article, "Soft-Shaft Opportunism: Radley Metzger's Erotic Kitsch," exemplifies such vitriol. This long essay is a peculiarly informative synthesis of insight and invective in which Testa subjects Metzger's films to elaborate analysis, all to situate the filmmaker as "the late-Sixties' preeminent charlatan of soft-shaft kitsch-eroticism" and as an arty "interloper" whose "critical recuperation should [not] be sought" (41, 52, 43).

Testa's caustic article is unusual in the detail that it devotes to Metzger's work, but it remains arbitrarily reductive in that it cannot admit that the director was perhaps motivated by sincere and *heterogeneous* intentions. Instead, Testa pretends to *know* that "Metzger was an erotic charlatan with no mission but securing his market niche" (45). Testa's elitist terminology specifically recalls the language of Greenberg's classic treatise "Avant-garde and Kitsch" (1939) and other influential highbrow critiques. (Indeed Testa even cites Greenberg to "prove" his devaluation of Metzger [46, 57n17].[16]) In these pieces, the middlebrow artist is always a feminizing "vulgarizer," who, as Macdonald puts it, "pretends to respect the standards of High Culture while in fact [he] waters them down and vulgarizes them" (37).

It is telling that Testa deploys the term "soft" to reinforce his snooty formulations and singles out Metzger's softest, most feminized devices to illustrate the filmmaker's pretentiousness and the particular worthlessness of his nonhardcore films (46–49, 54–55). Testa's derogatory uses of "soft" point to the high-middle dynamic that still informs the gendered connotations of "softcore." They also disclose the links that these mechanisms share with softcore's most distinctive and, from a highbrow vantage, diluted and diluting mode: soft focus. The history of this mode is my next subject.

III. THE DISTINCTION "IN" SOFT FOCUS

> Thus, when D.W. Griffith began to use his soft-focus lens to give added beauty or mystery to a shot and the idea was hailed as an advance in art, we had an era of fuzzy pictures which I am afraid did more to irritate the fans than to charm them. If a cameraman didn't have a real soft-focus lens, he merely threw his regular lens a bit out of focus and felt artistic for the rest of that day.
>
> —WILLIAM DEMILLE (qtd. in Bordwell et al. 96)

Soft-focus cinematography is softcore's most familiar distinction strategy.[17] This tradition derives from a long symbiosis. The soft effects still visible in the cheapest, shot-on-video softcore can be traced to the aspirational gestures of photographers and cinematographers in diverse genres and media. Leon Hunt reminds us that sexploitation's "cultural affiliations and modes of looking" diverge saliently from those of hardcore, a fact he attributes to sexploitation's genealogy, which represents "the convergence of two aesthetic/cultural traditions—the dubious 'respectability' of art photography and forms of lowbrow popular entertainment" (92). This history points all the way to impressionism, whose stylistics helped inspire photography's pictorialist movement. Photographers then disseminated the "soft style" to cinematography, where it manifested in the Hollywood films of the 1920s and 1930s. The soft style later became a middlebrow expedient liable to emerge in any cultural context. Its trademark glow has been closely linked to the 1960s and 1970s and is recalled as one of the sexual revolution's primary "looks," as implied by the phrase "the soft-focus seventies." During that period, aspirational sexploiteers like Metzger, Sarno, and Jaeckin widened their distribution by using soft focus to lend their imagery crossover appeal; similar tactics were used by softcore magazines like *Penthouse* and *Playboy*. When softcore films resurfaced during the postfeminist nineties, they did so under the middlebrow auspices of King, a soft-focus innovator.

Contemporary softcore still exploits the conceptual import of this genealogy. That is, the soft style still functions not as an autotelic aesthetic but as a fully conventional signifier of softcore's interest in romantic fantasy, female eroticism, and "sin"; it also suggests the genre's aspiration for a middlebrow seriousness and a spiritualized sexuality. Furthermore, soft focus has a practical benefit in that it limits explicitness. There has, however, been a penalty for "siphoning" impressionism's aura. Since the early twentieth century, soft-focus practitioners have been scorned for exploiting a middlebrow aesthetic that is shallow, derivative, pretentious, and far too feminine. Highbrows have, moreover, been singularly disdainful of soft focus *qua* sexploitation style, framing it as an endlessly recycled effort to "dress up" middlebrow porn as high art.

As a decisive influence on Hollywood's use of soft focus, pictorialist photography exemplifies an important early case of this dynamic. By the 1900s, impressionism had become an academic style with elite credentials and mass appeal. Hence it is logical that pictorialism—which is primarily identified with the first two decades of the twentieth century—attempted to establish its own aesthetic cachet through "an impressionistic soft focus and aestheticized poses" (Shiner 231). More notably, as the "most advanced and self-consciously artistic photography of the day" (Keith Davis 55), the pictorialist movement was the principal engine behind photography's timid move toward eventual acceptance as a fine art (see Bordwell et al. 292). Its manipulation of low-contrast developing, shallow focus, and idealized or spiritualized material contrived a moody, artificialized atmosphere that diverged sharply from the young medium's more typical naturalism. That photography's first broad fine art movement would capitalize on the medium's potential *qua* artifice made perfect sense, for it was photography's mechanized naturalism that had rendered it a suspect art in the eyes of influential critics like Lady Elizabeth Eastlake, Benedetto Croce, Charles Baudelaire, and George Santayana (Shiner 230).

Though respected artists like Edward Steichen, Gertrude Käsebier, and Clarence White contributed to the movement, pictorialism has in retrospect proved something of "an embarrassment" to photography critics intent on promulgating modernist and realist agendae (Keith Davis 55; see Sontag, *Photography* 119–20). As Keith Davis relates, "Even appreciative critics, who applaud the beauty of the images, tend to consider the movement as a whole intellectually shallow. At its least sympathetic, modernist criticism has judged pictorialism to be wrong-headed and retrograde, a willful violation of the medium's essential nature and shamelessly imitative of second-rate painting. For such critics, the pictorialist era represents a futile—if mercifully temporary—deviation from the historical path of 'real' photography" (55). The "real" is defined here as a hard-edged naturalism—thus the "straight photography" salon aesthetic is often viewed as a rejection of pictorialist aestheticization (Keith Davis 130)—and gendered as a masculine entity. It is unsurprising, then, that pictorialism, which was known for its inclusiveness of female artists, was rejected "as entirely too 'feminine'" by the modernists of the predominantly male Stieglitz circle (Keith Davis 124).

A similar interplay is visible in Hollywood's use of the soft style, but with new intonations of depravity. According to Kristin Thompson, cinematographers were, much like photographers, "eager to prove that cinema, too, was an art" (Bordwell et al. 292), so it makes sense that the soft style was one of film's early sacralization strategies. Hewing closely to pictorialism,[18] directors like D. W. Griffith duplicated the soft effects of still photography in their cinematography (Bordwell et al. 287). While a soft, shallow focus was considered useful for foregrounding a figure, the primary "justification for using the soft style was beauty—not simply feminine beauty, but beauty of the whole composition" (Bordwell et al. 288). But "feminine beauty" was not to be discounted. Throughout the 1920s and early 1930s, the soft style proved popular in "glamour" portraiture, which was favored by Hollywood actresses eager to enhance their pulchritude by obscuring their blemishes. Typically called "gauzy," these and other soft shots were often literally filmed through gauzes (Bordwell et al. 290–91).

Mark Vieira's *Sin in Soft Focus: Pre-Code Hollywood* (1999) demonstrates that this conjunction of soft focus and femininity was thoroughly sexualized during the silent and early talkie eras. This sexualization was a function of a more pervasive Hollywood eroticism that was either sublimated or banished after 1934.[19] Indeed, motifs that later became stock sexploitation elements—tub scenes, bondage motifs, orgies, even "lesbian" numbers—found their first expression in these Hollywood productions.[20] Because of the cinema's mass allure and specific appeal to the young, this sexualization was met with hostility by a familiar mix of conservatives and reformist progressives, which

Figure 2. Soft imagery and literary allusions in the promotional art for high-end hardcore. © Studio A Entertainment and Andrew Blake, 2002.

culminated in Hollywood's enforcement of the Code. But before that moment, the soft style had a very complex utility. The cinema's heightened eroticism led to an equation between soft focus and female immorality, an appeal that Hollywood openly exploited amid the difficult conditions of the Depression. Indeed, this equation was so central to the period that Vieira—who often refers to the soft style as "sinful soft focus" and to actresses like Clara Bow and Alice Faye as "sin in soft focus" (212, 75)—employs it as his titular paradigm. Intriguingly, the soft style was also used as an obscuring tactic that kept the censors at bay without diminishing a film's appeal, for it allowed studios to soften and disguise potentially objectionable female elements with the same "mysterious" élan that it deployed to soften and disguise female blemishes.

Of course, it was because of this overt commercialism that soft-focus sensuality was ultimately less successful at lending fine art cachet to film

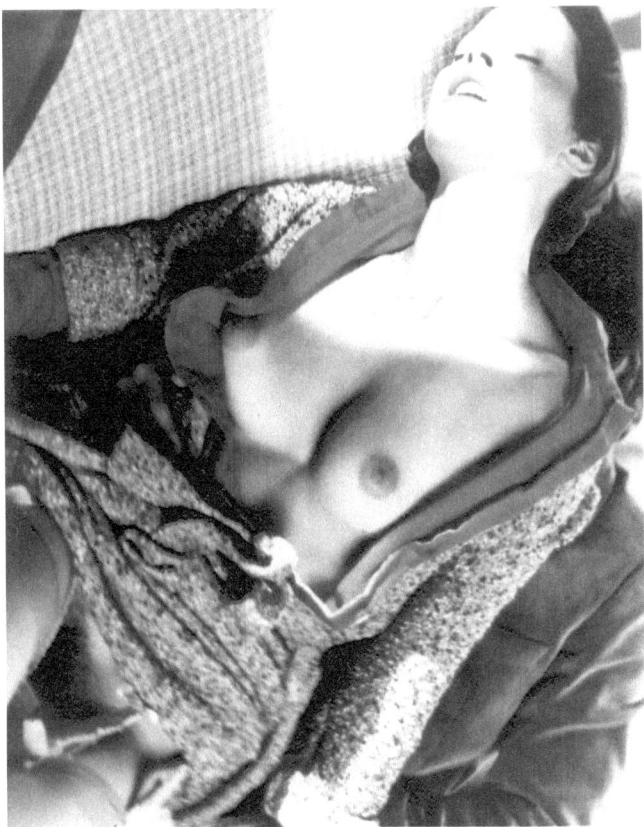

Figure 3. The paradigmatic image of soft-focus fantasy: Sylvia Kristel in a production still from Just Jaeckin's *Emmanuelle* (1974). ©Trinacra, Columbia, and Just Jaeckin, 1974, and RCA/Columbia, 1984.

than to photography, which was one of many reasons Cinema had to wait until after midcentury for the auteur movement to complete its "official" hierarchization. What is more, in its own time and/or in retrospect, the soft style in Hollywood productions of the 1920s and 1930s was criticized for its deviation from a strict, hard-edged realism—and from the use of related techniques like deep focus and the long shot—which influential theorists like André Bazin posited as Cinema's essential province. Just as pictorialism was critiqued by modernists as middlebrow, the Hollywood soft style was assailed for its feminizing pretensions, which, as critics pointed out, could lead to major problems in continuity (Bordwell et al. 292). William DeMille's flippant take on the soft style thus represents the common view that the style sacrificed much "in the name of superficial art." What this view does not admit, though, is that through this style the industry gained fan appeal through sex.

Through Hollywood usage, the soft style made a broad yet seamless transition from fine art strategy to distribution-savvy sexploitation technique. This segue influenced later, more openly pornographic forms, which were often content to use the established appeal of soft focus to position themselves as middlebrow and thus respectable enough to remain in the public eye. Postwar publications like *Playboy* and *Penthouse* differentiated themselves from déclassé porn[21] through a pluralistic juxtaposition of sexual materials and "serious" nonsexual materials, with *Playboy* in particular earning accolades for its fiction and reportage. By the late 1960s, these publications sought to enhance their legitimacy by featuring pictorials that aspired to be just as serious as their articles. Such aspiration was apparent in the pictorials' use of soft focus, which blended Hollywood's pre-Code penchant for soft eroticism with pictorialism's still-photo techniques. Indeed, Hefner was notably unwilling to concede that *Playboy* pictorials were any less elite than the rest of the magazine, insisting that its nudes had intrinsic artistic value—a stance that by turns incensed and delighted his more elitist critics (Jancovich, "Placing" 4). In recent decades, *Playboy* and *Penthouse* have reduced their reliance on soft lenses, but both continue to equate quality with stylization. *Playboy* is now known for idealizing its nudes through heavy airbrushing and a high-gloss finish, while *Penthouse* uses a broader range of techniques that includes grainy black-and-white photography.

After midcentury—and especially amid the "soft-focus seventies"—the influence of the soft style became too pervasive to plot individual legacies with precision. Indeed, by that point, this cultural cross-pollination was so pervasive and involute that Roger Ebert's notion that Jaeckin's porno-chic style imitated *Penthouse* imagery is entirely plausible.[22] As the examples of *Playboy* and *Penthouse* indicate, soft focus became a fully conventional cultural signifier of feminized sensuality that retained its upper-middlebrow hint of "serious" aesthetic interest. These significations were operative as well when soft focus made incursions into classical sexploitation by dint of the linked aspirations of Metzger and Jaeckin, and they would again be operative during the late 1980s when King redeployed soft focus as a postfeminist style that corporate softcore could subsequently adopt as a newly meaningful prototype. Since I have already looked at Metzger and devote my fifth chapter to King, it is appropriate that I focus briefly here on Jaeckin's porno-chic blockbuster, *Emmanuelle*—a film that, in addition to spawning dozens of official sequels and unofficial rip-offs, quite literally set the "template for 1,000 soft-focus softcore fantasy sequences on film and paper" (Cox 2).[23]

An X-rated French import, *Emmanuelle* functioned during porno-chic as a high-profile exemplar of the softcore concept. The film's solemn soft focus created an obvious contrast with the lowbrow comic realism of *Deep*

Throat, its hardcore *doppelgänger* (see Lewis 227). Like many other sexploitation directors, Jaeckin imported his soft style from fashion photography.[24] Known for "lavish set designs shot in soft-focus" (May 148–49), the Jaeckin style is so extreme that the shimmer that pervades *Emmanuelle* often threatens to swallow its heroine (Sylvia Kristel) whole; witness, for example, the girl-girl sequence that takes place on a squash court. A dreamlike soft focus is also apparent in the erotic still photos that motivate the heroine's initial descent into adventurism. This link to the protagonist's central motivation suggests that Jaeckin views soft focus as more than "frosting," more than a commercial glamour tactic. By linking his theme of metasexual discovery to aesthetics and soft-focus aestheticization, the director instead intimates that his trademark style is an ethereal effusion of feminine beauty[25] and a complement to the pious sexual education that Emmanuelle seeks, which resembles what Michel Foucault has called the *ars erotica* view of sex as experiential truth (57).

Jaeckin's earnest focus on his heroine's psychosexual transformation recalls the tactics of Mac Ahlberg in *I, a Woman* (1966) and harks back to heroine-driven art films of the 1950s and early 1960s. Sexploiteers like Ahlberg and Jaeckin might have been blamed for exploiting their actresses' physiques but could hardly be blamed for slighting their heroines' psychologies. Such "subjectifications" would prove crucial to softcore's efforts to insulate itself from censure and thus to expand into mainstream markets. What *Emmanuelle* does more plainly (and ponderously) than other antecedents is to underscore a postfeminist link between the soft style and female subjectivity. Such modestly progressive implications were absorbed into softcore's discursive vocabulary, establishing a soft-focus resource that directors like King, whose influence by Jaeckin is noted by Linda Ruth Williams ("Oldest" 25), could tap as a standard implication of this venerable legitimation technique.

This reasoning should not imply that *Emmanuelle* is free of regressive motifs. As critics have increasingly pointed out, the narrative, which is set in Thailand, has a paternalist and specifically colonialist logic (Willemen 13–14; Linda Ruth Williams, "Oldest" 26). The heroine's education is dominated by misogynists like the libertine philosopher Mario (former New Wave star Alain Cuny), who urges her to "step into a forbidden land of eroticism"—and then subjects her to a gang rape and makes her the "prize" in a brutal kickboxing match. The film's sexism is therefore closely linked to its "racist excursions into exotic domains" (Koch 152), where upper-class foreigners use lower-class natives as playthings. Jaeckin's earnest use of soft focus may, in short, be situated as a postfeminist feminization strategy that works not only to justify the film's pornographic effects but also to lend a metaphysical seriousness to its colonialist worldview.

Given that a subdued form of "the exotic" remains a stock motif of aspirational softcore, it is no accident that King and other producers have remained reliant on soft-focus feminization. But what I find most depressing about this is that critics still tend to dismiss "soft-shaft" directors like Metzger, Jaeckin, and King simply for using soft focus. These directors are, in other words, most often impugned for making an *a priori* "mistake," a middlebrow mistake—and not for using soft focus in a politically dubious fashion. (It should be remembered, though, that soft focus is one of many popular techniques criticized for being somehow essentially "nonparticipatory," so by that rather thin reasoning, it *has* been considered a political mistake.)

Indeed, that Jaeckin, like Metzger, continues to elicit highbrow invective confirms that soft-focus feminization is still (wrongly) perceived as a threat to aesthetic values and to the cultural distinctions that they seem to warrant. From a broad cultural perspective, then, Jaeckin's remarkable success has, sadly, only reinforced the vague sense of inferiority that has long interlaced a "debased" style (soft focus), an "impure" genre (softcore), a "diluted" class ethos (the middlebrow), and a "second-rate" gender (femininity).

This nexus of presumed abjection explains the negative slant of "softcore," "soft porn," and "soft focus." Their derogation is rooted in the essentialist illusion that soft, feminized, middlebrow forms are watered-down entities. Though such impurity marks their sexual nature as unthreatening and thus salable, they remain at best "easy pleasures" devoid of the redeeming purities, excesses, and transgressions of harder forms. What this dynamic also indicates is that, barring some unaccountably radical shift in cultural beliefs about sex, class, gender, and aesthetics, a genre like contemporary softcore is unlikely to ever have its cake (its niche in the commercial mainstream) and eat it, too (earn substantive cultural respect and, in a sense, self-respect). Though softcore has been distinguished from hardcore by its presence in the broadest outlets, its toleration there is predicated on its tacit acceptance of the elitist, antisexual, masculinized value system that constructs its principal textual qualities—including sexualization and feminization as well as "middlebrowness" and softness—as marks of inferiority. As we shall see, contemporary softcore almost invariably indicates that this formula not only institutionalizes cultural inferiority but also encourages self-consciousness, contradiction, and bad faith. It is unsurprising, then, that slighting references to "softcore," "soft porn," and "soft focus" have even pervaded the softcore genre itself.

The Disorderly Feminization of Classical Sexploitation

Tracing the Genealogy of Contemporary Softcore

Any comparison of the contemporary American softcore feature to its classical precursors is bound to reveal stark differences in repetition and standardization. Relative to its antecedents, softcore is today a fixed postfeminist genre with narrow room for ideological idiosyncrasy and improvisation; this is truest of the genre's most prolific strain, corporate softcore. Still, that sexploitation was in its classical phase less routinized than it has been over the past fifteen years (and over the past ten in particular) should not obscure the fact that elements of the genre's contemporary identity were already nascent in sexploitation at the time of classical softcore's inception in the late 1960s. This genealogy may, in fact, be traced back to the burlesque films of the 1950s. Such elements had an adaptive value that rendered them attractive under the altered political, economic, and technological circumstances of the late 1980s and early 1990s. When in those years American producers and distributors evinced renewed enthusiasm for softcore, they steadily favored postfeminist elements—and what had been a disparate, disorderly, often lowbrow form became a much more static and domesticated one.

Given classical sexploitation's bewildering immensity—director William Rotsler has, for example, estimated that two thousand sexploitation films were made between 1959 and 1973 (Turan and Zito 228)—my narrow focus on this particular lineage is a critical necessity as well as a useful way of charting a protocontemporary succession. The three principal elements of this succession are the use of a female protagonist, the emphasis on the female face, and the liberal treatment of female desire. The theme that organizes these devices is female subjectivity. By the time classical softcore emerged around 1967 or 1968, it was common, though not the rule, for sexploitation narrative to focus on the pyschosexual experience of a single heroine or, less commonly, a group of interlinked women, each of whom was the protagonist of a discrete arc. This convention had its complement in what remains one of the most iconic signifiers of softcore spectacle: the female face expressing or "performing" sexual ecstasy. The foregrounding of these twin elements contributed to the feminization and ideological moderation of the vehicles in which they appeared, yielding a trend toward tolerant, consumerist trajectories in which female subjectivity had increasing room to "play." Especially in the work of directors like Radley Metzger and Joe Sarno, the convergence of such motifs betrayed the intercession of a European art film tradition in which the "awakening" of female desire was a fixture as far back as the 1933 film *Ecstasy*. But this classical convergence was also an extension of a homegrown lineage rooted in burlesque films and nudie cuties.

One of classical sexploitation's most notable tendencies, its stress on misogyny, violence, and excess, complicates and contradicts this liberal progression. Indeed, some of the most significant categories of sexploitation, including roughies, kinkies, and softcore, rely on a crucial rape discourse. The prevalence of these shock tactics points to the genre's prefeminist character, which is linked to its nonmainstream exhibition. What I find most intriguing, however, is how subtly interwoven such tactics are with the feminization of classical sexploitation—and how often such tactics are thematically justified through the genre's larger focus on female desire. Nevertheless, the sexploitation paradigms that most clearly anticipate the contemporary either frame such tactics in a careful, feminized manner or avoid them altogether. These loose categories include the "awakening sexuality" paradigm, the "suburban" paradigm, and the "empowered babe"[1] paradigm. Coming to the fore in the late 1960s, the third category reflects the impact of second-wave feminism through its assertive, independent heroines who embody a "middle feminism." Typically depicted in the workplace, such heroines at times adopt action roles. By the mid-1970s, these paradigms had yielded a consistent body of sexploitation films that feature a progressive focus on a postfeminist form of female agency that neither rejects male companionship nor directly challenges the patriarchy—but that does resist male attempts to restrict female potential.

I. NUDIST FILMS, BURLESQUE FILMS, NUDIE CUTIES

As far back as early cinema, female nudity—or its soft, teasing promise—had a place on the screen. Whether through the exposure of a woman's foot, ankle, and calf as in the narrative featurette *The Gay Shoe Clerk* (1903; Linda Williams, *Hard* 65–67) or the draped spectacle of Fatima's "cooch dance" as recorded at the Columbian Exposition (1893; Lennig 36–37), this imagery excited a desire and a dread that contributed to the pervasive erection of obstacles (local statutes, censorship boards, the Production Code, etc.) blocking the commercial distribution of such material. During the 1910s and 1920s, hardcore stags[2] and various inexplicit products[3] were restricted to the private sphere, where illicit or semi-licit exhibition ensured their low profile. Though Hollywood was at that time notorious for its sexualization (Schaefer, *Bold* 295), the industry proscribed nudity through the introduction of its "Don'ts and Be Carefuls" in 1927 and its eventual enforcement of the Production Code in 1934. Inexplicit sexual content therefore became a prime attraction of classical exploitation, as screened in questionable theaters outside the aegis of the classical Hollywood distribution net. Contemporary softcore derives most directly from these publicly exhibited feature-length films.

Two exploitation subgenres are of special concern: nudist films and burlesque films. Other exploitation subgenres, including sex-hygiene films, vice films, and exotics, drew a portion of their appeal from fugitive glimpses of nudity (Schaefer, *Bold* 86–87, 267–71, 290–91).[4] But nudist films and burlesque films placed a more fundamental stress on such spectacle. Accordingly, these subgenres often display the rudiments of softcore's narrative-number organization; they also provide early instances of still-extant softcore devices. An intriguing aspect of their divergent sensibilities is their divergent treatment of the female body. Relative to burlesque, nudist films are less consumerist in their objectifications of female sexuality and posit a much less subversive idea of female desire.

For the most part, nudist films were documentaries recording the "outré" customs of the nudist movement (or "naturism") or narratives dramatizing the same. Exploiteers made these films available for American consumption mainly in the 1930s and 1950s. Two features that instantiate each "wave" are *This Nude World* (1932) and *The Naked Venus* (1958). Like most of the first wave (see Schaefer, *Bold* 296–98), *This Nude World* adopts an "ethnographic" documentary approach, depicting nudist camps in America, France, and Germany. Dominated by shots of nudists engaged in self-consciously healthy activities like tug-of-war and volleyball, the documentary reinforces nudism's idea of itself as a salutary, Thoreauvian lifestyle. *The Naked Venus,* by contrast, is a narrative interspersed with a static, posed brand of spectacle. Unlike the documentaries, it has a (very) loosely dichotomous structure that prefigures the nudie cutie.

The Naked Venus has a fairly simple plot. Bob (Don Roberts), an American painter of nudes, takes his French wife Yvonne (Patricia Conelle) to his native California, where his domineering mother discovers that she has been his model. In the ensuing struggle for Bob's affections, Yvonne flees with her child to a nudist camp. The plot culminates in a divorce trial in which nudity's aesthetic utility is used to validate nudity as such. According to the curator who certifies the value of Bob's work, "art essentially is beauty and as such pure—never morally objectionable . . . everything instrumental in bringing it about must be considered morally clean." In light of this "expert" testimony, the trial exculpates the French wife, who reconciles with Bob in France.

The Naked Venus's construction of a system of correspondences interlinking art, nudity, liberalism, and France had ample precedent. As the stir caused by art films like Malle's *Les Amants* (1958) verifies, American filmgoers of the day equated Europe, France in particular, with a classy but titillating blend of art and sex (see Lewis 129–33). But the film's association of artist model and nudist—and the inexplicable thread that has Yvonne turn to a nudist camp for sanctuary—is more peculiar. As Eric Schaefer notes (*Bold* 302), the nudist film's tendency to draw on "the discourse of fine art" was related to the nudist movement's use of ancient Greece to legitimate itself. Because this civilization's "refined" classical ideals are linked to its liberal attitudes toward the body, "the nudist films were made, although not always received, in a way that aligned them with art" (Schaefer, *Bold* 316). This tenuous link was useful in that it allowed nudism to replicate art's historical feat of insulating itself from the moral stigmas attached to its bodily content via neo-Kantian principles of disinterest. Witness the curator, whose role in the story is to extend this "purity" from art world to nudist camp. Nudist films in this mold, then, neutralize the threat of their passive nudity through two contrary didacticisms: the elitist discourse of fine art and the reactionary discourse of naturism.

Unlike the nudist, the artist model is one of few motifs common to the nudist film and contemporary softcore. As a justification of nudity, this motif has a long history. In the 1933 pre-Code film *Another Language,* director Edward Griffith used "a totally nude woman" in shooting an art class scene featuring Helen Hayes (Vieira 130; see 142). Now a straightforwardly sexualized device, the artist model is still common in aspirational films like Zalman King's *Delta of Venus* (1995) and Anne Goursaud's *Poison Ivy 2: Lily*

(1995). That this motif remains a staple is not peculiar, given its fitness for providing the aestheticized eroticism favored by softcore. More telling is the absence of the nudist. With the decline of the nudie cuties, the nudist, understood as an ideological figure and not a mere sunbather, disappeared from sexploitation, and contemporary softcore has not revived her. This absence is conspicuous in that sexploitation has relentlessly recycled any motif that facilitates integration of narrative and nudity; it is for this reason that strippers and nude models are formulaic figures. The nudists' antisexual rhetoric was, it appears, accurate. Despite the efforts of exploiteers to use the movement for titillation, naturism's claim "that sexual feelings were drained from situations where everyone was naked [was] a fact borne out by later studies" (Schaefer, *Bold* 297). Such anti-eroticism was reinforced by the movement's atavism, with its insistence on nature and childhood.[5] That today's softcore does not rely on nudism for titillation is no more surprising, then, than the fact that it does not rely on birth-of-a-baby footage, another exploitation staple once exploited as an "educational" source of female nudity.

Conversely, the burlesque film actively underscores its sexual potential. Its legacy to softcore includes a teasing yet consumerist attitude toward sexuality; a kinetic depiction of women, including hints of inner desire; and many individual motifs. A case could even be made for classifying burlesque as the first sexploitation form. Classical sexploitation has traditionally been dated to 1959, the year of Meyer's *The Immoral Mr. Teas;* this is the chronology handed down from producers to scholars (e.g., see Friedman 164). Yet in several respects, burlesque films like Meyer's *French Peep Show* (1952), Jerald Intrator's *Striporama* (1953), and Irving Klaw's *Varietease* (1954) and *Teaserama* (1955) form an even more compelling departure than the later nudie cuties.[6]

Schaefer supports his interpretation of *Mr. Teas* as a "decisive break from classical exploitation" by noting the film's consumerist insouciance (*Bold* 338). *Mr. Teas* ironizes exploitation's central "critique of modernity," parodying a reactionary theme formerly dramatized with utter gravity; this light, consumerist tone had become more acceptable during the post-*Playboy* era. That *Mr. Teas* and later nudie cuties scuttled the "square-up,"[7] an element crucial to exploitation's self-legitimation strategy, was in keeping with this ideological departure. According to Schaefer, the "lack of a square-up was perhaps the greatest point of divergence between classical exploitation and sexploitation and a clear indicator of the changed moral climate.... If the new sexploitation films did not wax philosophical about consumption in the same overt way that *Playboy* did, they were still a manifestation of the economic changes that had increasingly expanded the acceptable sphere of desire" (*Bold* 338–39). The problem with this useful insight is not its validity but its applicability to burlesque. Like later nudie cuties, burlesque films often jettisoned the square-up's didactic function. And the nudie cutie and burlesque were more open about sexual desire—heterosexual male desire, specifically—than the nudist film, which, like other exploitation forms, relied on classical exploitation's repressive social-reform trappings as cover for the voyeuristic desire to which its carnal spectacle intentionally appealed.

Witness *Striporama,* which does contain a square-up. Rather than cloaking itself in anticonsumerist rhetoric, the film's preface addresses a viewer whom it constructs as male so as to assert the pleasurable solidarity of spectatorship: "So Brother, if you are a connoisseur of the motion picture arts—and come in here to be critical of the production values . . . you better get the 'Hell' out to the Box Office right NOW and try to get your money back . . . On the other hand . . . if you came in here to see the GIRLS . . . and enjoy yourself . . . just sit back and relax. . . ." Here exploitation's moralistic self-consciousness and "productivist" ideology have been exchanged for a more consumerist anxiety anent class and taste. What differentiates this demotic entreaty from the middlebrow ideology of most contemporary softcore is its aggressive embarrassment. It freely admits its shortcomings and foregoes any pretense of "respectability" in favor of pure Entertainment. In Bourdieu's account, this belligerent defensiveness is the hallmark of the low, whose colonized sense of inferiority represents "a dominated 'aesthetic' which is constantly obliged to define itself in terms of the dominant aesthetics" (*Distinction* 41). But despite *Striporama*'s inability to provide the production values and other indices of taste and class that "dominate" its consumerist sensibility,[8] the fact that the film adopts this amoral posture at all marks it as, in a sense, more liberated and modern than many later sexploitation forms.

According to Schaefer, the most salient component of burlesque's modernity is its use of female performers who express themselves as desiring agents (*Bold* 310–24). If burlesque was addressed to men, its focus on female desire prefigured later sexploitation genres that attempted to attract mixed audiences. Performers like Tempest Storm and Betty Page upset demure traditions of femininity predicated on the positioning of women as inert objects. Instead, they cast themselves as active exhibitionists, who, complicit with the viewer-voyeur, expressed themselves in unmistakably erotic ways. Through an art "based on a complex relationship among dance, gesture, and costuming," these burlesque performers also call "attention to the performative aspect of gender" (*Bold* 315, 314; see Barthes 85–88). Ultimately, their art undermines ideas of fixed sex-and-gender identities, accenting the mutability of femininity *and* of masculinity. The linchpin of this critical *tour de force* is Schaefer's analysis of the drag passages in *Varietease* and *Teaserama* that feature Vicki Lynn, a female impersonator (*Bold* 317–19).

Nevertheless, as Schaefer notes, it is possible to overstate these arguments (*Bold* 323). Schaefer, it should be noted, offers a limited challenge to Robert Allen's thesis, which claims that burlesque curtailed the subversiveness of its performers as a result of its shift from its nineteenth-century middle-class milieu to its twentieth-century working-class environment where it acted "primarily as a vehicle for female nudity" (*Bold* 304). In building an opposite case, Schaefer seems to minimize the cinematic mechanisms that in the burlesque film contain female agency and eliminate fuller illusions of subjectivity. Allen argues that during burlesque's twentieth-century devolution, the female performer was all but silenced, and "without a voice it was all the more difficult for [her] body to reclaim its subjectivity" (240). Allen's reasoning is clearly pertinent to cinematic burlesque, wherein female performers generally do not speak to their audiences. Such voicelessness is in part a function of the genre's nonnarrative format.[9] The burlesque film has a loose dichotomous structure, which loosely divides between two distinct types of spectacle: mostly female dance routines and mostly male skit comedy. Deprived of diegesis, burlesque performers, unlike their counterparts in later sexploitation forms, do not develop the nonsexualized phases of their agency that might yield a realistic illusion of "personhood"—and thus they cannot fully transcend their mystified, exotic-other status.

The burlesque feature's more subtle legacies hint at forms of female subjectivity that would sprout in more narrative-oriented contexts. As noted, the female face has long been crucial to sexploitation performance. Though the burlesque feature never directly mimes the sex act, its use of the female physiognomy is its means of evoking sex with the presumably male viewer. Unlike contemporary stripper movies in which dancers interact with staged audiences, burlesque performers recall the early cinema by looking straight into the camera, unflinchingly welcoming the viewer's gaze. As Tom Gunning notes, early cinema was an openly "exhibitionist cinema" that established a dynamic "contact with the audience" (57). If the burlesque film sacrifices part of the affectivity of the female face by not enmeshing it in a narrative, it in a sense *regains* a different component of that affectivity by having the female face directly engage the viewer through an eye contact that energizes a whole range of sexual expressions. Witness *Teaserama*, a film in which the legendary Page, an otherwise hapless burlesque performer, shows a virtuosic mastery of pouty smirks, naughty smiles, and knowing glances.

The closest that burlesque comes to miming sex is its discreet, conventionalized simulation of female masturbation. In *Striporama*, *Varietease*, and *Teaserama*, the dancers often run their hands along their bodies during numbers, leaving a crucial gap between hand and body. According to Schaefer, autoerotic contact decipherable as such might have elicited penalties ("RE: Thanks," 20 Mar. 1). The image of the masturbating female was significant not only because it was relentlessly reused by producers who believed in its commercial appeal. It also had a polysemic resonance implying the agency "in" the female other and hinting more specifically that female pleasure always had a performative component. Another contemporary staple visible in ur-form in burlesque is the girl-girl number. In a domestic vignette situated near the start of *Teaserama*, Page helps Storm, recently arisen from bed, ready herself for the day, dressing her in a merry widow corset, combing her hair, and so on. This inverted striptease is accompanied by the same languorous gestures and eroticized smiles located in the strip sequences. Yet another "active" motif traceable to burlesque spectacle is the venerable tub scene, as exemplified by the "How to Take a Bath" segment of *Striporama*.[10]

But this focus on discrete motifs may overlook burlesque's most salient legacy. Amid an otherwise lowbrow, masculinized, prefeminist form is a stress on the intimate feminine details—what Linda Williams calls the "previously hidden, and often sexual, 'things' of women" (*Hard* 4)—that would become a crux of sexploitation's middlebrow, postfeminist feminization. Burlesque's glimpses of the woman before her mirror or in her bed, bath, or dressing room anticipate sexploitation's shift from a disorderly, classical genre into a much more domesticated, contemporary one. Given that the burlesque format heavily restricts the agency "in" striptease, it is notable that these glimpses are often a function of vignettes starring performers like Page, Storm, and Lili St. Cyr. If such mininarratives do not result in rounded illusions of personhood, they do at least suggest how difficult it is to dismiss a cinematic genre as "pure" spectacle.

At the conclusion of his section on burlesque, Schaefer notes that the nudie cutie's arrival meant that burlesque's challenging sexual spectacle had been "displaced by more conventional representations of passive female sexuality" (*Bold* 324). Indeed, far from extending burlesque's subversions, *The Immoral Mr. Teas* seems to have reversed them in several respects. This is not to downplay the impact of Meyer's nudie cutie. Valuable for deflating classical exploitation's anticonsumerist rhetoric, *Mr. Teas* would serve as a pivotal transition into more explicit, feminized sexploitation forms; it also proved to be a rich repository of sexploitation motifs. Such motifs begin with the burlesque performer and her tease, as encoded by the title. (Meyer even provides an early example of "product placement" by having his protagonist pass a marquee under which hangs a self-referential sign promoting *French Peep Show* and its star, Storm.) Other *Mr. Teas* devices that were later incorporated into sexploitation include the film's nude photography motif, its extensive bathing emphasis, its prostitution theme, its therapist figure, its assortment of mammary and phallic symbols,[11] and its voyeurism theme.

The last device was structurally decisive. It brought onscreen the voyeur implied by the eye contact of the burlesque performer. In nudist films, male observers are desexualized in accord with naturism's antisexual claims; thus the genre draws few links between internal and external observers. And while burlesque embraces its sexual content and suggests a male voyeur, it leaves the latter offscreen. *Mr. Teas* transforms the implied observer into its hero. It is no accident, then, that sexploitation's first stock protagonist is not female but male—and specifically, an oafish, middle-aged white man. Teas is the low "common man," to use Meyer's wry phrase, whom grindhouse exhibitors saw as making up the "raincoat brigade" that attended burlesque and, later on, sexploitation screenings. As I have noted elsewhere, the observer figure has traditionally been understood as an audience cipher (Andrews, "Convention" 23); *Mr. Teas* clarifies that this standard reading has a precedent in a crucial industrial transition.

But Meyer's bold move came at a cost, one that would ripple through later nudie cuties. Though he drew courage from decisions like *Excelsior Pictures Corp. v. Regents of the University of the State of New York* (1957), which ruled that nudity *per se* is not obscene, Meyer did not want to press the sexualization of his film beyond the implicit—beyond, that is, the lowbrow symbols and bawdy double entendres he played for laughs, perpetuating the "naughtiness" of the burlesque skit comedy from which *Mr. Teas* and the nudie cuties derived inspiration. By opting to build his plot around an eroticized voyeur, Meyer created an unprecedented erotic potential. In consequence, he exercised caution in his other tactics, including his judicious use of frame devices. Similar caution informs the film's imagery, explaining the nudie cutie's regressive reliance on largely passive female spectacle. Most importantly, Meyer constructed his protagonist's voyeurism as purely visual hence socially harmless, a model adopted by later producers.[12] Even in fantasy, Teas avoids contact with women, as when he jumps into a lagoon to escape a woman who sits beside him. He also avoids consensual contact with strippers; notice the segment in which he perversely enters a burlesque club from the side, peeping on the action rather than engaging in a consensual exhibitionist-voyeur relationship.

Teas's peeping does not culminate in masturbation or in signs of arousal. Besides Meyer's desire to avoid sex, antimasturbatory norms that construct autoerotic gestures as effeminate (and comic) inform this restraint. Later vehicles favoring a visibly aroused observer would opt for a female voyeur, letting her make vague, fluttery gestures or, in more explicit productions, having her palpate her breasts and genitals while miming climax with her face. As variations on the Teas figure, these eroticized observers show producers modifying the genre so as to augment female display. Such tinkering has reinforced the odd cinematic distortion that masturbation is a specifically female activity. Thus later, more atypical films that depict an autoerotic male observer on occasion do so in epicene terms.[13] A more significant corollary of this tinkering is that the new female observer, though objectified and sexualized, is positioned as a subject within the diegesis. Given the widespread assumption that the observer figure represented the audience, this autoerotic woman implied that sexploitation's audience was at least potentially female. As with other devices, the development of the observer involved a gradual process that, in tandem with the demand for greater female objectification, led to greater female subjectification—with women positioned as potential subjects inside and outside the diegesis (see Linda Ruth Williams, *Erotic* 341). Though at first tenuous, these implications grew so conventional that, by the 1990s, softcore vehicles routinely targeted female audiences.

II. ROUGHIE-KINKY MISOGYNY

Driven by liberal court judgments and an attendant increase in exhibitors willing to play sexploitation product, the 1960s witnessed a helter-skelter diversification of forms that persisted through the arrival of hardcore in 1970. Between the exhaustion of the nudie cutie around 1964 and the arrival of softcore around 1968, two overlapping forms, "roughies" and "kinkies," came to the fore (Turan and Zito 19–25). As Eithne Johnson and Eric Schaefer note, the "lines of distinction" dividing roughies and kinkies were not always clear (48). Generally, the roughie featured less nudity than the nudie cutie but had a fuller narrative. Thus it enhanced the stress on action, violence, and sexual interaction while limiting active sex. The kinky also had a fuller narrative but tended to accent underground sexual practices, particularly sadomasochism. It thus represented the most sexualized presoftcore form. In this phase, the heroine became a stock protagonist and female desire a stock theme. The combination of sexploitation's new emphasis on drama and its prehardcore, prefeminist emphasis on shock meant that female subjectivity was at this time simultaneously rendered in greater detail *and* subject to greater violence. Since sexploitation was so heterogeneous in its production and exhibition, the realization of these tendencies was patently multiform. A roughie like Meyer's *Lorna* (1964) is polished and feminized and takes aspirational pains to reconcile its attention to female nudity with an equal attention to female psychology as unified through the theme of

The Disorderly Feminization of Classical Sexploitation | 55

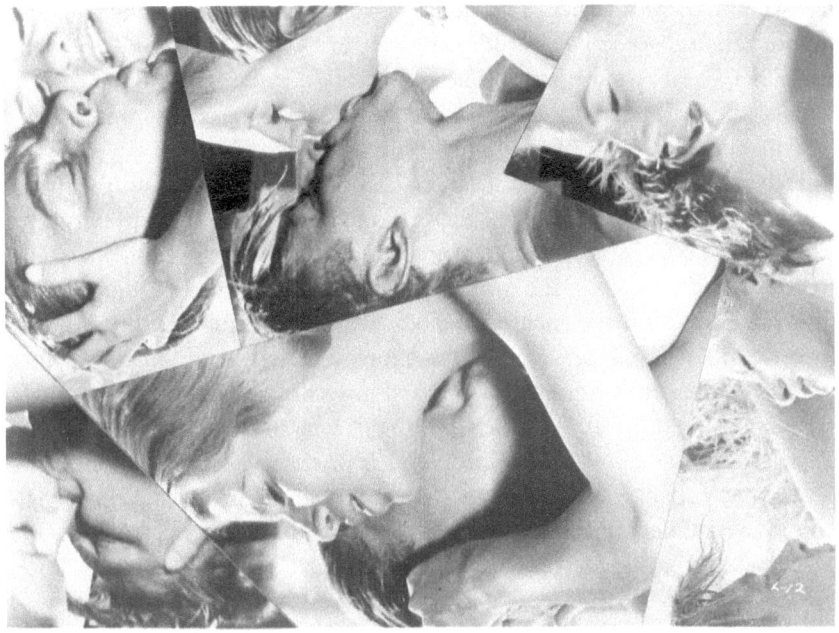

Figure 4. Rape as female fantasy in Russ Meyer's *Lorna* (1964). From the collection of Eric Schaefer.

female desire. At the "other" end of the spectrum, an ultra-low-budget opus like Michael and Roberta Findlay's *Flesh* trilogy maximizes the misogyny of the roughie-kinky model by deploying the female desire theme but still marginalizing female subjectivity, an outcome facilitated by a brutal reversion to a male protagonist.

Like *Mr. Teas, Lorna* embodies a complex set of impulses whose specific formal realization made an outsize impression on the films to follow. This complex ambivalence is already apparent in Meyer's inspiration: "'I said, now I must do something like the foreign films, only it will be Erskine Caldwell and it will be a morality play and we'll borrow heavily from the Bible and I'll find a girl with giant breasts'" (qtd. in Turan and Zito 22). Meyer's reference to foreign films is intriguing, given a neglected aspect of his work: its aspirationalism. Due to a taste for burlesque comedy and "giant breasts," Meyer has often been classed as Metzger's lowbrow double, which obscures his accomplishments as a cinematographer who developed a kinetic visual style—and whose work drew on the art film tactics of Ingmar Bergman and Roger Vadim.[14] In *Lorna*, this Metzger-esque feminization registers through soft, arty effects and a related stress on the details of the heroine's domestic existence, including her bathing habits.

The focus on the heroine's desire is the most vital component of this feminization. *Lorna*'s plot is rudimentary: Lorna (Lorna Maitland), a young rural heroine, longs for James (James Rucker), her young inept husband, to "make me feel the way he feels when he—" She experiences this rapture when raped by an escaped convict; the narrative ends when her husband kills her and her lover. Thus the film has something in common with the awakening-sexuality model that Metzger and Sarno adapted from European sources like Mac Ahlberg's *I, a Woman*. But like the softcore thrillers that reestablished softcore in the early 1990s, Meyer's aspirational roughie places a greater stress on violence than most awakening-sexuality films. On the other hand, *Lorna* differs from postfeminist vehicles in that it uses violence to free the heroine's orgasmic desire *and* to recontain it through the gothic action closing the film. Rendered as a rough schema, then, *Lorna*'s stress on consumerist pleasure is gendered feminine, classed as middlebrow, and located as urban. Its anticonsumerist counterstress on retribution is gendered masculine, classed as lowbrow, and located as rural. Such an antithesis serves as a patriarchal check against the social dangers of unbound female desire.[15] That this dénouement is to be read as a punishment of female "weakness" and of the scapegrace who abets it is articulated by the film's gothic preacher-narrator (James Griffith), a kind of walking square-up who warns, "Woe to the libertine who preys upon the virtue of the weak!"

Lorna's campy moral fabric insulates the film from censorship even as it parodies the antisexual reformism manipulated to the same end by classical exploitation. This complex relation to exploitation ideology implies that Meyer considered this overheated moralism more than "productivist" cover. It was, in fact, crucial to the film's consumer appeal. By pushing this exploitation tactic to violent, misogynistic excess, Meyer gears it to function as a supplement to the film's sexual spectacle, which offers less nudity than *Mr. Teas* and the nudie cuties. This supplementation effect is apparent in the film's two rapes. Neither depicts much sex, but both gain impressive immediacy through Meyer's violent theme and crisp, energetic style. A similar tendency toward integration—like many roughies, *Lorna* does not divide into a neat narrative-number structure—is visible in every segment involving Lorna, whose buxom physique provides spectacle whether in or out of clothes, whether washing dishes or acquiescing to a "semiconsensual" rape. Both *Lorna*'s violence and its female orientation may, then, be viewed as methods of offsetting the film's minimal depiction of nudity and interactive sex.

Meyer's parodic, excessive reversion to the exploitation ideology mocked by *Mr. Teas* clarifies that sexploiteers fashioned and refashioned their ideological visions in accord with a disorderly imperative toward consumer novelty. This bias toward the immoderate, which leads to as much violence as sex, is apparent among the grindhouse products categorized by the fetish-oriented "kinky" designation. Such films are no less likely than *Lorna* to focus on female desire—and, as the *Olga* series (1964–65) confirms, are more likely to manifest this focus through self-consciously unsettling ideas of gender. Produced by George Weiss and directed by Joseph Mawra, the black-and-white *Olga* franchise fuses the underground allure of Klaw's 8mm bondage loops starring Page with the feature-length traditions of the drug film and vice film (Landis and Clifford 12). The *Olga* films thus involve white slavery, prostitution, and drug rings. But the *Olga* films diverge from earlier exploitation paradigms in framing the crime boss as a woman whose monstrous "otherness" is a function of her transgressive gender identity.[16]

As the literal and symbolic boss of the series, Olga (Audrey Campbell) is an early exemplar of the dominatrix femininity that sexploitation marketed right through the porno-chic era, as confirmed by the 1974 production, *Ilsa, She Wolf of the S.S.* (Landis and Clifford 9–21, 218–22). Equally interested in sexual pleasure and criminal wealth, Olga is a sadist who, as the head of a syndicate, satisfies her desires by torturing female "employees" in a pervasively squalid milieu, upending the nurturing-womanhood concept that undergirded exploitation ideology. Olga's fetish for dominance is already set in *White Slaves of Chinatown* (1964), the first installment in the series, so the franchise does not delve into her psychology, as is common in films depicting a transformative "awakening." A low, prefeminist fantasy of evil, Olga's inscrutable self-possession ensures the stability of her otherness, which is crucial to the screechy moralism of the voice-overs that provide this inexpensive franchise with the majority of its dialogue.[17] But if this campy and decidedly masculinized formula treats its protagonist as pure spectacle, it leaves no doubt that she is an active subject, for she constantly treats women as objects, encouraging others to do the same. In the course of *Olga's House of Shame* (1964), seminude women are whipped, spanked, electrocuted, punctured, and literally treated like animals by other women. As this list indicates, Olga's brutal sexual consumerism favors other women, with most of the active sex scenes exuding a bisexuality that is a vital element of her transgressive dominance. Its most meaningful element, however, is her lack of containment. Unlike Lorna, Olga will not be reined in (i.e., victimized thus *feminized*) by patriarchal forces. This ongoing pattern is signaled at the close of *White Slaves* when Olga arranges her submissives by imperiously snapping her fingers in a photo session "that encapsulates the film's dominance/puppet-master theme" (Landis and Clifford 15). Like Olga's bisexuality, which has the benefit of maximizing female spectacle, this element is motivated by utilitarian purposes, particularly the decision of Weiss and his grindhouse distributor, Stan Borden of American Film Distributing, to serialize the Olga story.

Olga's lack of containment influenced Michael Findlay, who also worked with Borden, and contributed to the misogyny that dominates his first kinky, *Body of a Female* (1965), and his kinky opus, *The Touch of Her Flesh* (1967), *The Curse of Her Flesh* (1968), and *The Kiss of Her Flesh* (1968). Familiar with the *Olga* series, Findlay and his wife Roberta redesigned the sadistic camp of Weiss and Mawra to punish wayward women, an anticonsumerist posture suited to Findlay's "sex is bad, you are gonna be punished" sensibility as reported by friend and colleague John Amero (qtd. in Landis and Clifford 37). Amero verifies that Findlay "was absolutely influenced by the old Klaw style" (qtd. in Landis and Clifford 25), implying his reactionary nostalgia for the reliable containments of the older, less threatening tradition of burlesque films and bondage loops.[18]

Played by Findlay, Richard Jennings, the protagonist of the *Flesh* trilogy, is outraged by women, whom he refers to as whores, animals, and monsters. Consider the exemplary sequence of arch double entendres that *Curse* deploys to underline the protagonist's castration anxieties (e.g., "this little pussy is really a primordial carnivorous beast waiting to tear apart anything it can touch"). *Touch* explains this misogyny through a scenario in which Jennings discovers his wife, Claudia (Suzanne Marre), cheating on him with another man. Stunned, he flees to the streets of the Lower East Side, where he is struck by a car, losing an eye. He is thereafter unhinged and alcoholic, blaming all women for his wife's betrayal and his injury. Throughout this lo-fi trilogy, Jennings uses his knowledge as a weapons expert to gain revenge by killing society's most sexualized females, strippers and prostitutes, in addition to his wife. Women are threatened and murdered with baroque gadgets that include a poisoned flower, a blowgun, a crossbow, a circular saw, a cat's poisoned claw, a sabotaged dildo, a harpoon, a blowtorch, a poisoned ointment, and electrified earrings. The Findlays make no effort to generate sympathy for this murderous misogynist. But because the perspective is so often aligned with this excessive figure, the Findlays also do little to humanize the sketchy female "others" who are in effect relegated to minor roles by dint of Jennings's droning place in the foreground. This prefeminist element is, perhaps, the trilogy's most misogynistic attribute, for it indirectly supports Jennings's rhetoric by positioning women as the objects of its sexual and sadistic spectacle while denying them subject status in the diegesis.

Unlike earlier roughies and kinkies, the *Flesh* films approach a narrative-number dichotomy and contain fairly explicit spectacle. And by 1968, clearly softcore films like William Rotsler's *Mantis in Lace* and Doris Wishman's *Love Toy* had arrived. Though not always easy to differentiate from their antecedents,[19] these films are expansive in their sex, occasionally ranging like

Figure 5. An ad-mat for *Mantis in Lace* (1968), a fully softcore production that emerged from the roughie-kinky tradition. From the collection of Eric Schaefer.

Love Toy into a "wall to wall" category that minimizes diegesis. The idea that sexploitation needed to compensate its viewer for minimal sex no longer made sense. This point is significant, for shock tactics "justified" in part by a widespread compensation idea contributed to the negative female portrayals discussed above. Film genres, of course, are neither reasonable nor centralized, so it would have been unaccountable had producers suddenly sacrificed their reliance on misogyny, violence, and shock in 1968. Certainly, the Findlays did not do so, as low, porny productions like *Janie* (1970), *The Slaughter* (1970),[20] and *Altar of Lust* (1971) confirm. But by the end of the 1960s, a softcore had emerged that was less shock-oriented and less violent and thus distinct from new forms specializing in violence and gore as well as from those specializing in hardcore sex. Like their precursors, these softcore films registered conflicting impulses that complicated their moderation of the misogyny and violence typical of roughies and kinkies. This complexity is especially instructive when examined in terms of softcore's shifting rape discourse.

III. RAPE DISCOURSE IN CLASSICAL SOFTCORE

"You only get to know women via rape."
—ROMANCE (1999)

Though budgets remained below Hollywood standards across sexploitation in this era, individual producers employed diverse fiscal models. Some relied on microbudgets, with the Findlays making some films for under $7,000 (Landis and Clifford 25). The norm was higher. According to Schaefer, sexploitation films were "produced and exhibited in 35mm for $15,000 to $25,000, with 'a fair number' coming in at $40,000 ... a few of the more elaborate color productions made in 1969–70 cost more than $100,000" ("Gauging" 6). Entertainment Ventures Incorporated (EVI) and Boxoffice International Pictures, outfits headed by David Friedman and Harry Novak, were among the most prolific and lavish producers of classical softcore features. These studios represented the "softcore mainstream" inasmuch as such a thing could be said to exist during sexploitation's unruly heyday—which in 1969 yielded between 135 and 150 features (Schaefer, "Gauging" 6). As "the biggest [studio] in the sexploitation field" (Rotsler 51), Boxoffice released more than two dozen films between 1968 and 1973, most qualifying as softcore, while Friedman has reported that EVI softcore occasionally cost more than $70,000, with the costume-epic *The Erotic Adventures of Zorro* (1971) coming in at $72,000 (Rotsler 179).

One index of this mainstreamness was sexploitation's tendency to displace its abjection. "Displaced abjection" refers to the process through which nonelite genres seek a middle status by deflecting their felt inferiority onto lower forms (see Stallybrass and White 53). Schaefer draws on this idea to explain Hollywood's denigration of classical exploitation (*Bold* 14), a trend Jack Valenti and the MPAA perpetuated through implacable attacks on sexploitation after the lapse of the Code (Lewis 135–91; Schaefer, "Gauging" 19). The idea is also relevant to the antihardcore sentiments exhibited by softcore producers even prior to *Mona*'s arrival in 1970. Though shock-oriented grindhouse producers like the Findlays often narrow the distance between soft and hard forms—consider the "Squash Fever" segment of *The Curse of Her Flesh*, which culminates in a misguided attempt to restore a stag actress's virginity—they usually do so to exploit hardcore's *outré* status as Pure Trash. By contrast, producers like Friedman underscore hardcore's abjection so as to emphasize softcore's relative legitimacy and thus to reinforce the same. Though financial pressures eventually drove Friedman to hardcore, he was in the early 1970s an outspoken critic. Witness the 1973 interview with Rotsler, in which he declares, "I have no desire nor any intention of making a porno, because I have no respect for any of the people who make 'em" (175; 172–87). In the course of this diatribe, he compares hardcore to classical exploitation, the genre in which he got his start under Kroger Babb—but his point is to suggest hardcore's "carnival" debasement and to underscore his own rise in status. (Such sentiments also reveal his anxiety regarding the fragility of his new status amid a collapsing sexploitation market.) But softcore's embodiment of the displaced-abjection concept was apparent before the soft-hard dichotomy achieved its porno-chic clarity. In 1969, the Adult Film Association of America, an organization over which Friedman long presided, opposed lower-budget competition from 16mm simulation films, a protohardcore subsector produced by "'heat artists,' who went 'too far' and [gave] the exploitation industry a bad name" (Schaefer, "Gauging" 19). But like Friedman's antihardcore attitudinizing, this view obscured the fact that sexploitation gave itself a *good* name primarily through opposition to other devalued forms.

As *Starlet!* confirms, classical sexploitation also displaced its abjection through formal mechanisms. Inspired by "the great Hollywood epics" (Rotsler 184), *Starlet!* uses a self-conscious plot that concentrates on the softcore industry to promote its own studio, "the mighty EVI," which it presents as a sexploitation variant of the major studios with which it shared a Hollywood address. A realistic drama written and produced by Friedman, *Starlet!* deflects sexploitation's cultural inferiority onto another genre, the stag film—which, within a year of the film's release, emerged from underground reconfigured as a feature-length form. Though this perspective has the benefit of providing the film with inexplicit portrayals of both hard and soft production practices, in the end, the dual focus reinforces the anxiety that permeates this otherwise incoherent film: industrially and culturally, softcore was on the whole nearer to the underground world of stags and loops than to the mainstream world of Hollywood.

Though most acute in its rape sequence, incoherence pervades *Starlet!* The film's promotion, title, and opening segment imply a focus on the heroine's aspirations. But *Starlet!* wanders from this focus, complicating its attempt to distinguish itself from male-dominated stags. *Starlet!* gives its fullest attention to producer Kenyon Adler (Stuart Lancaster) and director Phil Latio (John Alderman), with their new starlet, Carol Yates (Deirdre Nelson), playing a subordinate role. Latio is a softcore producer who in his spare time directs "specialty" shorts for his boss, Adler. The pair contrive to repackage Yates, a stag actress, as a "softcore skinflick superstar" whom Adler renames "Starliss Knight" and casts as the lead in "A Youth in Babylon" (a title that Friedman later recycled for his autobiography). In their way is Maxine Henning (Kathi Cole), the fading starlet whom the rising Yates consigns to spaghetti westerns. Henning seduces Allison Jordan (Sharri Mann),

Yates's nymphomaniac roommate, who reveals Yates's "tarnished past." Henning's attempt to use this information backfires, speeding her to Italy.

By making Latio a director of "specialty films" and Adler his producer/consumer, the script undermines its effort to place a respectable distance between sexploitation and stags. This problem is exacerbated by the fact that *Starlet!* poisons the figure of the hardcore director. It first establishes this "poison" as a visual sleaziness. A sex film veteran, Alderman lends his role his usual disreputable air, as underscored in a scene in which Latio's moist, leering grin is framed in tight close-up as he directs a penetration sequence. That Latio soon pressures Yates to sleep with him reinforces this effect. Desperate to rise, Yates acquiesces—and has sex with Adler for similar reasons. Latio's sleaziness is lent more gravity when he rapes the virginal and drunken Linda Ford (Chris Mathis). This, the film says, is the kind of man who directs hardcore. The problem with such tidy moralism, of course, is that he is also the kind of man who directs softcore. Friedman has no desire to press this moralism into self-deprecation, so it is dropped.[21] There are no consequences for Latio, who is soon "normalized" as a comic figure in boyish league with Adler against Henning, the contained "lesbian" villainess. Though the corrupt hardcore director later became a stock type—and a standard mechanism through which posthardcore sexploitation films like *The Naughty Stewardesses* (1973) displaced their abjection—the device is too incoherent in *Starlet!* to impart indirect legitimacy.

Starlet!'s spectacle has similarly incoherent implications. Like the Friedman-produced *Zorro*, *Starlet!* features a girl-girl scene whose "tenderness" is reinforced by an aspirational stylization apparent mainly in that type of number; the Henning-Jordan lovemaking is thus differentiated by its "tasteful" soft focus. But the positive implication of this stylization is nullified by a patriarchal plot that critiques Henning and Jordan more steadily than it critiques a rapist. Unsurprisingly, then, the rape itself delivers the most befuddling attempt at artistry. As Latio forces himself on Ford, the cinematography alternates between over-the-shoulder shots that portray her on a bed and impressionistic point-of-view shots filmed from below, as if the victim were on a glass table. This effect ruptures the continuity and with it Friedman's Hollywood aspirationalism. But the moral equivocation implicit in this incoherence is what is most telling. Though possibly meant as hallucinatory, the rape's stylization comes off as an attempt at "sexy" sophistication; a more clinical treatment might have framed the horror more effectively. But given that the plot later dismisses the rape, it is likely the scene was not meant to be disturbing, at least not *very*. Indeed, the stylization seems designed both to convey horror *and* to corroborate Latio's remark, "Honey, you'll never have it so good."

This equivocation parallels that of the larger plot. It is not clear which character the camera identifies with, so it is not clear whose desire, or lack thereof, the audience is to sympathize with, that of the male rapist or that of the female victim. It is not, then, the likelihood that this nonconsensual scene is just another number that makes this scene peculiar. After all, this type of rape is "just another number" in *many* classical films. Witness Bob Cresse's *Love Camp 7* (1968), an Olympic release in which Friedman has a rape-oriented cameo—or EVI's *Zorro,* which opens its spectacle with a male-identified nonconsensual rape capped by a "shocking" gross-out.[22] In her chapter on rape-revenge films, Carol Clover argues that the decrease in nonconsensual rape scenes that conform to sadistic male stereotypes correlates with the 1975 publication of Susan Brownmiller's *Against Our Will* and the "feminist discussion of rape," after which rape is "seen not just as an individual act but as a social and political act as well" (144). "Although earlier cinematic rapes allow for a large measure of spectator identification with the rapist," Clover contends, "films from the mid-1970s go to increasing lengths, both cinematic and narrative, to dissociate us from that position" (152; see Projansky).[23] *Starlet!*'s oscillation between male and female identification and its normalization of its heterosexual rapist as a sleazy but not irredeemable "guy" merits consideration in this framework. The film's incoherence is not mere incompetence. It is also an antique of a prefeminist perspective that considered rape a distasteful extension of sexual harassment but not a crime akin to murder, a development that made the identification mechanisms of the rape-revenge film more possible (Clover 152). In turn, feminism's emphatic critique of rape and the cultural processes that support it made sadistic male fantasies of rape, incoherent or otherwise, less possible.

But the rape scene has not disappeared from sexploitation, where it manifests today in highly mediated, feminized forms. Classical softcore's use of semiconsensual rapes—which, as in *Lorna,* begins with the man forcing himself on the woman but ends with her epiphanic pleasure—may even be situated as a stage in sexploitation's move to the female-identified rape fantasies still common in aspirational softcore. This sort of scene was perhaps most famously realized in Sam Peckinpah's major-studio project *Straw Dogs* (1971), where it was juxtaposed with a nonconsensual rape (Projansky 35). But the semiconsensual rape has a long and very diverse cultural history. Steven Marcus (213) notes its presence in erotic literature like *The Lustful Turk* (1828), and Leon Hunt notes that it was a staple of British sexploitation (125). Though this category of rape scene has been criticized by feminists as patriarchal and "inauthentic," variations on it are central to the masochistic sexuality of romance fiction, which is mostly produced and consumed by women. Though such scenes do have, as *The Notorious Cleopa-*

tra (1970) proves, regressive implications, they represent a salient idea of female desire and a significant (if ironic) phase in sexploitation's feminization.

Boxoffice International stressed the semiconsensual scene as part of a larger rape discourse that was calibrated to its strategy of appealing to "discriminating" filmgoers who wanted "to see sex pictures but at their *better* theatres, not some sleazy house" (Rotsler 52; Rotsler's emphasis). More than EVI, Novak's studio tempered the violence and kinkiness of its imagery by stressing a burlesque-style comedy that referenced male and female desire and mediated shock. Two of the studio's most lavish productions, *The Secret Sex Lives of Romeo and Juliet* (1969) and *The Notorious Cleopatra*, embody this discourse.[24] Besides the semiconsensual scene, such discourse includes a ludic "dirty talk" linked to a tame sadomasochism; this unrealistic, comic banter muffles the impact of the rape discourse by implying consent. Boxoffice's rape discourse is not, then, essentially different from the more feminized and middlebrow discourse available in contemporary softcore, wherein rape's fantasy quality is carefully accented.

Directed by Peter Perry ("A. P. Stootsberry"), *Romeo and Juliet* and *Cleopatra* both qualify as softcore. Like *Zorro*, these costume spoofs feature articulated numbers with extensive bumping and grinding as organized by a thin narrative tissue that foregoes development so as to deliver populist skit comedy that relies on sexual double entendres, scatological remarks, homophobic jokes, sight gags involving body fat and necrophilia, and so on. As part of this low, masculinized formula, the heroines actively suggest that the language of force is a means of satisfying their desire. Juliet's spirited "Sock it to me"—a phrase whose link to NBC's *Laugh-In* (1968–73) confirms that this prefeminist idiom was also a mainstream idiom—is the refrain of *Romeo and Juliet*. And Cleopatra (Sonora) encourages Mark Antony's "threat" ("I will take you like I take my enemies, leaving you torn, weak, and ravished . . . leaving you feeling as if you've been raped 100-fold") by crying, "Oh rape me, rape me!" In *Romeo and Juliet*, such "rapes" are more ambiguous but still accompanied by the woman's expressions of ecstasy, as unmediated by pain or nonconsent. Thus, when a maid is flogged—with the cast chanting "whip her! whip her!" like a Euripidean chorus—she greets the lash with delight.

At its most violent, this discourse is realized through semiconsensual rapes that delay consent and complicate the fantasy. Uneven power divisions that cast females as submissives—a tendency that postfeminist softcore inverts—here seem most incoherent, ambiguous, and objectionable. Though *Cleopatra* focuses on a powerful black heroine who would be "queen of the world," it nevertheless contains two semiconsensual rapes, with the second implying that masochistic bliss acts as a "natural" check on female ambition. The film's fourth number begins as a virgin's ritual sacrifice—but rather than her life, the priest takes her virginity instead. Just as the promise that "she will shed much blood" comes true, the promise that "she will enjoy her sacrifice" is borne out when she succumbs to rape pleasure. This "joke" is reconfigured in the crowning ninth number, which serves as a dénouement. Here Enobarbus (Mason Bakman) rapes Cleopatra in the tub. Cleopatra fights but gradually asks for "more, more" in a parody of the film's earlier dirty talk. When Mark Antony finds them, he slaughters Enobarbus and brandishes his weapon. Cleopatra tries to save herself, claiming, "he raped me! I couldn't help it!" Unmoved, Mark Antony kills her but regrets his deed, killing himself. Thus the film delivers the ritual murder promised by the earlier number.[25]

That these films mix progressive and regressive sentiments lends classical softcore a consumerist heterogeneity that is today available mainly in cult softcore. In tandem with market shifts that impelled softcore into mainstream niches, the seepage of feminist ideas into pop culture suppressed sexploitation's most objectionable depictions, making the tolerant forms explored in my next section the future of softcore. Though this postfeminist trend has yielded a respectful bearing toward women, it has also restricted their depiction, mandating moderate femininities rooted in paternalistic "softness." By contrast, classical sexploitation's shock-oriented, prefeminist consumerism alternated between corroding and reinforcing fixed ideas of gender and sexuality. Thus sexploiteers depicted women not only as feminized submissives but also as masculinized dominatrices like Olga and Ilsa. Even in the "mainstream" films of EVI and Boxoffice, regressive meanings existed side by side with progressive ones. EVI's *Zorro*, for instance, features a gory nonconsensual rape geared to a sadistic male fantasy, but it also contains more liberal spectacle that deconstructs regressive identity fixities.

Zorro owes debts to previous incarnations of Johnston McCulley's story line, especially Douglas Fairbanks's screen original, *The Mark of Zorro* (1920). But *Zorro* is also indebted to burlesque. The punning swordplay, the homophobic yet subversive gay jokes, the imagery of "saucy senoritas": all play to a carnival machismo that mocks itself even as it revels in its own indecency. The film's most intriguing aspect—Douglas Frey's dual portrayal of Don Diego, encoded as a "queen," and of the hypermasculine Zorro—exemplifies this bivalence. Schaefer argues that burlesque may be read as leveling ideas of sex and gender (*Bold* 322). In this "spectacle of sameness," he notes, "the marks of gender difference—whether a veil and brassiere or an attitude of passive femininity or masculine power or bravado—were stripped away to reveal only desire." When "re-manned" by Helena (Penny

Boran), the effeminate Diego echoes this point: "Strip away all the linen and lace and the only difference between a queen and a whore is time and place." Given this figure's facility at performing the signs of the queen *and* those of the superhero, it is hard to see Zorro's masculinity as less discursive, as less of a masquerade, than Diego's effeminacy.[26] This epicene depiction might, then, be framed as a step toward Birken's idea of consumerist "genderlessness" (111) or as a return to the ancient "one sex" ideology discussed by Clover (13–17) and Thomas Laqueur. In any case, its fluidity contrasts with sexploitation's protocontemporary trend, which favored postfeminist or "neotraditional" sex-and-gender formations.

IV. THE ADOLESCENT, THE HOUSEWIFE, THE EMPOWERED BABE

As the 1960s gave way to the 1970s, sexploitation's embrace of the female protagonist increased, yielding not just spectacle but more bourgeois depictions of femininity as well. Eventually, the modest, Europeanized liberalism of the awakening-sexuality model found a more American expression in the empowered-babe movies that, in the wake of the success of *The Stewardesses* (1969), proliferated in the early 1970s, projecting a middle feminism. More than the image of the housewife of sexploitation's "suburban" cycle, this modestly progressive image of the working woman has served as a model for contemporary softcore. Admittedly, these trends existed amid a classical supergenre still replete with male protagonists and with violence, misogyny, and rape (e.g., see EVI's *The Adult Version of Jekyll & Hide* [1971], a softcore sleazefest replete with grisly rapes and castrations). But the structuring presence of postfeminist anxieties in even the lowest, most masculinized softcore of the 1970s (e.g., *Female Chauvinists* [1975]) predicted the genre's larger course, which was to sacrifice shock in favor of a more genteel consumerism rooted in gender traditionalism.

Bart Testa has noted the impact of Mac Ahlberg's *I, a Woman* (American release, 1968) on Metzger's *Therese and Isabelle*. According to Testa, in the "short interval before *I Am Curious (Yellow)* ... broke down legal barriers [in 1969], *I, a Woman* defined the erotic film by jettisoning exploitation plots and assuming an art-film model. The expedients seem simple: implant erotic experience in the subjectivity of its protagonist" (47–48). Testa's point is mostly valid. This feminized, aspirational film inspired verisimilitude, tolerance, and artfulness in sexploitation depictions of awakening female desire. But by concluding that "the most important code Ahlberg isolated from art-cinema was sex performed by a woman's face" (48), Testa overreaches,

Figure 6. Aspirational stylization in Joe Sarno's *Butterflies* (1974). Used courtesy ei Independent Cinema.

implying that this stand-in for explicit imagery came to the sex film via an overdetermined Bergman-Ahlberg-Metzger chain. Such a view neglects the significance that this sexploitation motif already had in the early 1960s (see Intrator's *Satan in High Heels* [1962]) and overlooks American influences on the same (from classic *noir*, burlesque, and so on).[27] Nor was Metzger alone in adopting this paradigm. By 1967, Sarno was in Sweden working on his black-and-white film *Inga*, whose historical place is comparable to that of Metzger's *Therese and Isabelle*. As one might expect, *Inga* is timid and not fully softcore. But *Butterflies* (1974), Sarno's much harder-core German film, confirms that the awakening-sexuality film could accommodate explicit display without sacrificing feminization. Indeed, as bookends to classical softcore's last successful theatrical period (and thus expressly evocative of hardcore's emergence during the same interval), *Inga* and *Butterflies* make more telling companions than *Inga* and its Sarno-directed sequel, *The Seduction of Inga* (1969/72).

A coproduction of Cannon and Inskafilm, *Inga* is the tale of Inga (Marie Liljedahl), a newly orphaned teenager. Reversing Dreiser's *Sister Carrie* (1900), the story begins with Inga traveling by rail from city to country. There, her financially and emotionally insecure aunt, Greta (Monica Strömmerstedt), attempts to capitalize on her sexuality. The plot effects an elaborate turnabout: the passive Inga learns to make her own decisions, fleeing the country with her aunt's lover, Karl (Casten Lassen), a budding writer. *Butterflies* picks up where *Inga* leaves off. The narrative of Denise (Marie Forsa), a farm girl initiated into sex by Fred (hardcore star Eric Edwards), *Butterflies* begins with its heroine's trek to the city. In Sarno's realistic cinema, sexual initiation is not a world-shattering event, which is why Inga ends wiser but not transformed—and why Denise does not grow up until *after* she leaves her bumpkin lover. Indeed, Sarno underlines that Denise is still "natural" when he has her first encounter not only lingerie but *underwear* while hitchhiking to the city, where she learns to adorn herself in femininity's signs. But Denise does end her tale more cynical than Inga, having met a man (Harry Reems) who has deepened her education through abuse and affection, demonstrating in ways that Fred did not sexuality's emotional range. At the end, Denise is hitching again—less innocent, perhaps, but still a subject in transition. This nonclosure creates the illusion of female potential beyond the frame that is crucial to Sarno's optimistic vision. (See *The Seduction of Inga*.) Such open-endedness dispenses with the violent containments common to *Lorna* and other patriarchal awakening-sexuality variants. It also dispenses with the addiction metaphors and pseudoscientific explanations that pathologize female desire in melodramas like *Alley Tramp* (1966), a Herschell Gordon Lewis project that extends and exaggerates Ahlberg's pessimistic references to nymphomania.[28]

Sarno's take on female subjectivity is more than just a tolerant open-endedness. Like Metzger, he establishes his aspirationalism through polished values and regular allusions to auteurs.[29] But his main way of establishing it is through an overt feminization adapted from films like Bergman's *Summer with Monika* (1953) and *Wild Strawberries* (1957). In this respect, Sarno's soft focus is most obvious; consider his use of this tactic in the tender montages that conflate wildflowers and romance in *Butterflies*. Also notable here are Sarno's self-consciously "sensitive" beach motifs in *Abigail Lesley Is Back in Town* (1975). Other feminized effects are less transparent and more meaningful. In their spectacle, *Inga* and *Butterflies* include segments that suggest the importance of apparel to the formation of sex-and-gender identity; that accent psychosexual stirrings as registered by the heroine's self-inspections in mirrors; that feature depictions of cunnilingus, implying male reciprocity in pleasure; and that contain moments of rapture as performed by the heroine's face, a device that in *Butterflies* has lost its obscuring function.

Inga's masturbation sequence is Sarno's most iconic use of the female face. This scene, in which the camera remains fixed on Inga's inverted face as she slips head first from bed to floor, uses its odd floor angle not to disguise the spectacle's fakeness but to obscure its authenticity. In his commentary for *Inga*'s Retro-Seduction rerelease (2001), Sarno claims that neither this scene nor the one in which Karl performs cunnilingus on Inga was simulated. The director reportedly wanted his close-ups of Inga's orgasmic face to be as realistic as possible to generate narrative depth. Because explicitness might have invited censorship, both passages were shot from "soft" angles; neither breasts, nor hands, nor genitals are evident in the masturbation scene. In other words, an aspirational desire for psychological realism led to hardcore tactics that culminated in an ironic timidity. *Butterflies* is interesting in this respect in that it shows how hardcore influenced specific sexploitation effects. As when filming *Inga*, Sarno encouraged his actors to "go all the way" (qtd. in Hallenbeck, "Sixties" 19), again hoping to enhance the psychology. But hardcore's arrival meant that he could finally capitalize on the graphic nature of his realism. Sarno's approach yielded a seamlessness seldom matched in porno-chic hybrids that supplemented softcore spectacle with hardcore inserts filmed separately (cf. Joe D'Amato's *Emmanuelle in America* [1976]). But if *Butterflies*'s almost-hardcore ethos does not disrupt the feminization of Sarno's awakening-sexuality model, it does modify the imagery through which this feminization is conveyed. Though the facial motif is still conspicuous in *Butterflies*, it is not as striking as in *Inga*. The later film also opts for medium shots where *Inga* opts for tight close-ups, and its cinematography is more straightforward, presumably because artifice and indirection were no longer necessities.

Sarno has recently said that he "concentrate[d] on faces" so as to construct "strong women" who were important "as people, not just as sex symbols" (qtd. in Hallenbeck, *Inga* 22). This empowerment rhetoric indicates a feminist sympathy that Sarno's *oeuvre* suggests but never fully develops. Inga is extremely passive. Denise is a more active subject and has a kinetic image in the spectacle—but there she is most often defined by men. These traits are in accord with the fact that the awakening-sexuality model has never been a radical form. In its contemporary resurgence, it has effected a modest progressivism at most. For producers, the advantage of this model is the low expectations it creates by dint of its use of an unformed, adolescent heroine. Even a minor reduction in this character's passivity may at the end of a film

Figure 7. A scene from Joe Sarno's awakening-sexuality classic, *Inga* (1967). Used courtesy ei Independent Cinema.

be read as signifying offscreen empowerment. Relative to films like *Inga*, *Butterflies* weaves a "round" example of this illusion in that it portrays a figure who weans herself from male dependence with the aid of other women, a diegetic transformation that is crowned by a masturbation number symbolic of self-sufficiency. Nevertheless, the fact remains that most of the narrative is devoted to Denise's phallic pursuits. The awakening-sexuality paradigm is, then, unlikely to yield films that deeply offend the left or the right. Along with its aspirationalism, the calculated inoffensiveness of this paradigm is one reason that it was recycled by contemporary sexploitation—and was particularly pivotal to softcore's rebirth in the early 1990s, a moment still politicized by antiporn sentiment.

The awakening-sexuality model looks downright seditious, though, when compared to the suburban model, which was another feminized strain pioneered by Sarno and others during classical sexploitation's presoftcore phase. A loose category, the suburban film may feature awakening-sexuality motifs, but its principal heroine is the housewife and its dominant subject adultery. This material is often realized through plots that center on "swingers" and "swapping," as in Rotsler's *Suburban Pagans* (1968). *The Agony of Love* (1966), another film made by Rotsler for Boxoffice, exemplifies a less frequent tendency to integrate these motifs with thriller arcs—and, in this case, with a temporary-prostitute device that anticipates a device later favored by softcore thrillers like *Secret Games* (1991). It is also notable that the adultery theme has been responsible for the sex-negative pessimism of the theatrical erotic thriller; that such pessimism was already apparent in the suburban films of a patently "liberated" era suggests this theme's negative potential.[30] When sexploiteers "crossed" suburban adultery with awakening sexuality, the former often trumped the latter, yielding dark, illiberal products[31]—which is why I consider Sarno's *Sin in the Suburbs* (1962) and Lewis's *Alley Tramp* suburban films though they contain dual mother-daughter heroines and notable awakening motifs.

But like awakening-sexuality films, suburban films have affected contemporary softcore by supplying a blueprint for placing an eroticized heroine in a domestic setting and by reinforcing the misandristic tendencies of postfeminist forms. Leon Hunt contends that the suburban cycle offered a "'feminine' space" such that the British variant constituted "a way of talking about female sexuality, or rather, specific types of female sexuality—thus the emphasis on the housewife" (105). This milieu maximized female display. Producers could also capitalize on its juxtapositions, with "the blandness and banality of the location offer[ing] a counterpoint to the activities going on there" (Leon Hunt 105). In American sexploitation, the most optimistic suburban films are those that view this "shocking" disjunction as a negative function of male desire, which may be overcome through the persistent benevolence of femininity (Turan and Zito 57). Unlike *Lorna*, such films do not frame the heroine's adultery as an expression of "bad" female desire but as a function of her temporary internalization of a "bad" male desire. A positive resolution depends on her rejection of this inappropriate desire *and* on her reformation of her mate "through an injection of femininity," as Moya Luckett puts it (151). Domestic female desire is thus constructed as essentially good *and* as antitransgressive.

Marsha, the Erotic Housewife (1970) exemplifies such a scenario. Marsha (Marsha Jordan) is a housewife whose bland exterior matches her habitat and contrasts with the "all-night session of drinking and sex" into which she descends once she discovers her husband's infidelity, which she self-destructively mimics. A happy ending is salvaged by her rejection of this gender-inappropriate contrast. It is no coincidence that it is a female friend, Phyllis, who helps her regain her virtuous blandness. Indeed, Phyllis is single not because she rejects "the love and tenderness" that Marsha prioritizes but because she believes that monogamous heterosexuality may only be maintained outside marriage. The most liberated attitude this softcore woman's film can muster is a cynical conservatism. Marsha conquers cynicism by publicly (and deceptively) humiliating her husband, which chastens him into returning to the domestic sphere. That this power play is necessary implies that her husband's middlebrow transformation signifies submission

Figure 8. The "empowered babe" in a production still from Al Adamson's *The Naughty Stewardesses* (1973). From the collection of Eric Schaefer.

and emasculation; he has, as Luckett might say, been forcibly "injected" with femininity. The double standards implicit to this resolution prefigure similarly misandristic attitudes that have proved more pervasive in contemporary softcore.

The suburban film's legacy persists in contemporary softcore thrillers as well as in major theatrical films like Ang Lee's *The Ice Storm* (1997) and the network television megahit *Desperate Housewives* (2004 on). Nevertheless, the suburban film's synthesis of domesticity and gender traditionalism has proved retrograde even by the standards of contemporary softcore. In a sense, the "empowered babe" of the contemporary working-woman film *begins* with the more progressive "middle feminism" that is the diegetic destination of awakening-sexuality films. As a result, the tolerant, optimistic inflection linked to this outcome is spread through the working-woman narrative. Though evident in aspirational softcore, such narratives have proved most prevalent in corporate softcore, which often follows the romantic and professional travails of career women.

The working-woman vehicle clearly manifests the intercession of second-wave ideology. Here I am *not* referring to the hypersubversive figure of "the angry woman" that Clover calls "[o]ne of the main donations" of the women's movement to horror and to popular culture (17; see 4). This militant type did make appearances in the classical genres. In a sense, she represented a variation on the subversive women of the roughies and kinkies, politicizing the sadism of Olga, Ilsa, and the top-heavy nightmares of Russ Meyer, who located power in breast size. But given that Clover's point is to confirm that feminist ideas and motifs were *broadly* appropriated by low-budget genres, it is perhaps predictable that this implacable woman was outnumbered by female types that registered more ambivalent feminisms. Indeed, the equivocal and ultimately yielding character who begins a narrative as an angry feminist but who comes to see "the error in her ways" provides one instance of such ambivalence. These figures have remained standard to sexploitation throughout the postfeminist era, unifying vehicles as widely disparate as *The Swinging Cheerleaders* (1974) and *House of Love* (2000).

The empowered babe supplies an even softer, more traditional expression of this feminist influence. That this heroine's independence constitutes no social threat is accented by her tendency to step outside the home only to step into a traditionally female career. Hence she serves as the focus of a slew of sexploitation cycles that fetishize historically female professions like stewardessing, nursing, teaching, modeling, and, in a figurative sense, cheerleading. Even in Crown International's *Superchick* (1973), which develops its liberationist rhetoric far more than most sexploitation films, the superwoman heroine is "disguised" as a stewardess, curtailing her transgressive potential. Affording a broad opportunity for passive nudity and active sexual spectacle while specifically disarming feminist critics, this quintessentially postfeminist figure ultimately served what became an overarching goal of sexploitation once its reliance on shock and transgression had ebbed: to maximize distribution in part by minimizing controversy. As a result, the empowered babe was not, like the angry woman discussed by Clover, a vindictive, alienated figure. If she offered modest critiques of sexploitive aspects of the patriarchy, she never rejected the patriarchy as a whole, typically maintaining a normalized situation in mainstream society. Popular as drive-in fare (Waller 135), this sexploitation strain was stimulated by the $25 million gross of *The Stewardesses* (1969), a figure so compelling that it was still inspiring the production of knock-offs like Independent-International's *The Naughty Stewardesses* in the mid-1970s (see Turan and Zito 64).

Roger Corman's New World Pictures routinized the empowered-babe paradigm, producing *The Student Nurses* (1970), *Private Duty Nurses* (1971), *Night Call Nurses* (1972), *The Young Nurses* (1973), *Candy Stripe Nurses* (1974), *The Student Teachers* (1973), and *Summer School Teachers* (1975). Corman's New World formula integrated nonsoftcore spectacle with a liberal story line: "Exploitation of male sexual fantasy, a comic subplot, action and violence, and a slightly left-of-center subplot . . . and then frontal nudity from the waist up, total nudity from behind, no pubic hair" (qtd. in

Morris 3; see Corman 181, 184). *The Student Nurses* was the first New World film to realize Corman's vision of "fetishized feminism." In this $150,000 melodrama, four young women confront a variety of male-oriented problems, including sexual harassment at work and romantic disappointment at home (see Pam Cook 126–27). *The Student Nurses* dramatizes one of second-wave feminism's founding precepts: the patriarchy operates in oppressive ways even within society's most liberal areas. Hence, Lynn (Brioni Farrell), the film's most socially conscious character—as demonstrated by her ultimate refusal to wear the nursing garb she considers politically co-opted—gets involved in Hispanic street protests only to find that sexism abounds even in this radical subsector. The film's most sexualized character, Priscilla (Barbara Leigh), is impregnated by a falsely "sensitive" biker, who, as an exploitation emblem of radical individualism, predictably abandons her. She attempts to get a legal abortion but is turned down by the unsympathetic all-male review board, prompting a companion to ask, "what do you expect from a bunch of men?" Later, a conservative male doctor performs her illegal abortion, illustrating that even men with regressive attitudes may embrace a middle feminism. Despite their use of female production talent—like many Corman films, *The Student Nurses* was directed by a woman (Stephanie Rothman)—New World films never endorse a separatist critique of the patriarchy. Instead, Corman's heroines work with their male opposites, adopting nurturing roles that effect a gentle, postfeminist enlightenment.

As a refinement of the haphazard *Stewardesses* (Turan and Zito 64), the Corman model was adopted by producers in films like *The Naughty Stewardesses,* which also critiques men of all persuasions. A significant variant on this empowered-babe formula is visible in comedy. Gregory Waller argues that sexploitation comedy was the period's "dominant and most interesting trend" (135). *Superchick* represents this trend at its peak postfeminist consciousness. American sexploitation comedy then grew less political and more youth-oriented, as indicated by titles like *Cherry Hill High* (1977) and *Cheerleaders' Beach Party* (1978). The major sexploitation vehicle of the early 1980s, the teen sex comedy, thus required only a slight toning down of the spectacle as supplied by a reversion to the voyeur hero—and the incentive supplied by mainstream blockbusters like *Animal House* (1978), *Porky's,* and *Fast Times at Ridgemont High* (1982). In *Superchick,* however, mild social protest still shares the foreground with mild spectacle.

This synthesis of what Corman considered equally exploitable cinematic elements is conspicuous in *Superchick*'s depiction of sexploitation icon Uschi Digart as Mayday, a militant "lesbian" feminist who seems to despise men *because* she works in misogynistic subgenres like the kinky. Upon finishing a nude scene in which she has been bloodied by a low-budget lashing,

Mayday enacts a humorous and sympathetic reversal by turning on her masked assailant to give him a tongue-lashing of her own. But Mayday's misandristic militance is pointedly differentiated from the gentle ethic of the "superchick" heroine, Tara B. True (celebrity astrologer Joyce Jillson). A stewardess trained in martial arts who in the climax foils a hijacking, True carries on affairs in several hubs, embodying her belief that "you can live as many different lives as you choose." Though her liberationism subverts marriage, it does not challenge heterosexual love—for True is "true" to each boyfriend. And though a (post)feminist, she advocates termination of the gender wars: "Why do men always have to win against women? Why compete? When we both give each other what we both want, we can't do anything but win."

True exemplifies one final trend worth noting. As a superheroine, she is an empowered babe in a masculinized action role. Other classical films exemplifying this trend include Andy Sidaris's $100,000 *Stacey* (1973), which represents the director's first attempt to place a heroine—in this case, "a very private detective" (Sidaris and Sidaris, *Bullets* 33; see 15)—in a crime-fighting vehicle. Produced with New World backing, *Stacey* is a precursor of the many 1980s vehicles, including Sidaris's own, wherein "soft" women adopt "hard" personae. It also prefigures 1990s softcore in which gender has little to do with the heroine's career, for by that point, women's advance into the workplace had lost much of its exploitable anxiety. In the early 1970s, however, this progress was so fraught with fear that women in nontraditional roles were demonized even in films sensitive to the sexual harassment of career women. This equivocal posture is evident in protoerotic thrillers like Centaur's *Invasion of the Bee Girls* (1973), a sci-fi vehicle in which Dr. Susan Harris (Anitra Ford) is a queen bee posing as a scientist. Though clearly harassed by male colleagues, she is ultimately too "hard" to be sympathetic. Like the drug-addled heroine of *Mantis in Lace,* Harris literalizes the threat that identifies the *femme fatale:* she kills her lovers by fucking them. A similar ambivalence is evident in the stock types of the women-in-prison film, a subgenre populated by strong, attractive women who often engage in repellent behaviors. Still, this subgenre is notable here for encouraging the development of a progressive, action-oriented, empowered-babe heroine as a function of sexploitation's larger tendency toward female objectification.[32]

Classical sexploitation was, in sum, a disorderly supergenre whose exhibition on an alternative yet very public circuit of theaters revealed the anxieties of a revolutionary culture in which sex-and-gender mores were under review. Its first cycles conformed to stereotypes of male heterosexual desire, but its diversification yielded new combinations that made gestures toward female desire as a function of a mandate for female display. Though this consumer expansion did yield misogynistic motifs and often demonized subversive expressions of female desire, its longterm trend favored empowered heroines, some of whom diverged radically from traditional femininity. The sexploitation market declined after 1973, with many producers switching to hardcore. Coupled with the emergence of second-wave feminism, whose impact on sexploitation was clear by 1970, this decline attenuated the diversity of the genre and favored a more genteel, evolutionary model that, relative to the transgressive excess of sexploitation's heyday, seemed rooted in gender traditionalism. This retreat into the homogeneity of postfeminist consumerism set the stage for sexploitation's distribution through more domestic and centralized media in the 1980s and resulted in softcore's reemergence as sexploitation's most reliable form. The cultural, technological, and formal adjustments that fomented this renaissance are the subject of my next chapter.

"Spicy, but Not Obscene"

Industrial and Formal Retooling in 1980s Sexploitation

For sexploitation, the 1980s marked a critical transition from public, theatrical modes of exhibition to private, nontheatrical ones. In this contemporary phase, "sexploitation" named a timorous genre and a diffuse, decarnivalized industry reliant on comparatively masculinized Hollywood paradigms; perhaps the best index of the genre's diminished fortunes was the recession of softcore, its most pornographic "outpost." In hindsight, what 1980s producers had to do to engender sexploitation's current softcore identity seems plain. They had to learn to harness the new modes of distribution and exhibition; they also had to differentiate their spectacle from the kind of sexual imagery available from other industrial sources. Ultimately, they achieved these ends by trending upscale; by favoring a feminized, middlebrow sexual spectacle that was relatively dichotomous but always inexplicit; and by securing the decisive support of the cable industry. At the end of the decade, two *noir*-inflected nontheatrical paradigms, the Zalman King romance and the softcore thriller, proved singularly capable in forwarding these purposes. Sexploitation gained wider distribution and acceptance, then, even as its sexual spectacle grew more extensive and specialized—as it emerged, in other words, as a specifically *softcore* industry. Yet these retoolings and redefinitions occurred gradually. As a result, the 1980s were littered with "cult" sexploitation cycles whose visual timidity and downscale impulses appear to mark them as "dead ends."

But this teleological idiom obscures the considerable continuity that interlaces these diverse forms. Such continuity is clearest in the gender formations typical of 1980s sexploitation. Though the postfeminist disposition of the *noir*-romance hybrids popularized at the end of the decade is obvious—which is one reason I devote chapters 5 and 6 to King and to the producers of softcore thrillers, respectively—it is less clear-cut in the decade's more chaotic, video-oriented strains, whose cult masculinization and visual timidity suggest a regression to the lowbrow, prefeminist mannerisms of burlesque, the nudie cutie, the roughie, and so on. If, however, these downscale forms broadly recall classical sexploitation, they diverge from the latter in that they rarely resort to overt misogyny as "compensation" for sexual coyness. Given that such coyness was specifically encouraged by antiporn feminism, it makes sense that the "remasculinization" of the decade's sexploitation was superficial at best, "diluted" as it was by broad postfeminist notions of female empowerment that often doubled as notions of male disempowerment. Indeed, in cycle after 1980s cycle, heroines are portrayed as voyeuristic, nonmasochistic agents whose synthesis of hard and soft qualities marks them as superior to their male opposites. Even when such heroines lack full protagonist status, they are often promoted to protagonist in sequels, most likely because producers realized that they offered something the heroes did not: the opportunity to maximize female display *and* to unify narrative and spectacle in postfeminist fashion.[1]

The chapter that follows develops this account of the decade's postfeminist continuity by looking at 1980s sexploitation from several angles. The first section, which surveys the collapse of sexploitation's theatrical market and the emergence of its nontheatrical markets on cable and video, concentrates on the industrial pressures that favored postfeminist forms and led sexploitation to routinize production of a feminized, aspirational form of softcore in the 1990s. Because this softcore paradigm first appeared in the classical era, the second section analyzes an unusual "Janus" text that bridges softcore's two golden eras. As one of few fully softcore films shot in the 1980s by an American, Alan Roberts's *Young Lady Chatterley II* (1985) is sequel to a 1970s softcore classic and forerunner to a pivotal strain of 1990s softcore. But this is also to say that the film's middlebrow feminization and overt pornographic thrust were in its own time anachronistic. For that reason, the chapter's final sections focus on the nonsoftcore cycles whose restricted masculinization and lower-brow tendencies were most representative of the decade—and were rooted, unlike Roberts's film, in Hollywood paradigms. The first of these examines the intersection of female (sexual) empowerment and male (sexual) disempowerment in the teen sex comedy. The chapter's final section critiques a number of sex-action vehicles made by Roger Corman and Andy Sidaris. Such films situate "empowered babes" in violent scenarios that include rape and bondage. But these films typically elect to defuse the misogynistic, roughie import of such imagery. This strategy is in accord with postfeminist anxieties that motivate the feminist rhetoric of the Corman films and the glossy visions of female mastery that pervade the Sidaris films. But it is crucial to note that a postfeminist logic also motivates the films' most traditional elements, including the rigid patriarchal thrust of Corman plotting and the soft paternalisms of the Sidaris style. Though paradoxical, the ambivalence of these approaches to female agency would prove common both in contemporary softcore and in the wider postfeminist culture of which it was a part.

I. INDUSTRIAL PRESSURE AND POSTFEMINIST REFORMATION

To understand sexploitation's metamorphosis into the feminized softcore of today, one must first look to the 1970s. As classical sexploitation's sexual outpost, classical softcore was peculiarly responsive to its new competitors, 16mm simulation films and hardcore features, and grew more explicit between 1969 and 1972. But this new frankness was revised by the Supreme Court's 1973 decision in *Miller v. California,* which gave states and communities power to proscribe material that they deemed obscene. Though *Miller* had its most direct impact on hardcore, it also worried exhibitors of R- and X-rated films, for it contained a clause hinting at the potential regulation of simulation films (Lewis 267). Once it became clear that the R-rating was safe, exhibitors became less receptive to X-rated films (Lewis 268), modifying a long-standing, panindustrial trend toward explicit cinema. The mobility of softcore, so evident in the breakout success of a Danish import like *Without a Stitch* (1968), was henceforth restricted, with the most sexualized movies limited to grindhouses in skid row areas where they faced direct competition with hardcore. Softcore collaborations by Perry Dell and Manuel Conde like *The Dicktator* (1974) and *Deep Jaws* (1976), X-rated comedies with the look and feel of the hardcore comedies of the day, attest to this pressure and to the equivocal identity it conditioned. Indeed, many sexploitation producers—including such luminaries as Radley Metzger, Roberta Findlay, Joe Sarno, and, despite his earlier protests, David Friedman—had to varying degrees embraced hardcore practices by the mid-1970s.

Sexploitation was being squeezed on all fronts. Hardcore's arrival hindered its ability to market itself as the most "sexcessive" cinema available, and Hollywood's post-Code emphasis on spectacle, including sex, hampered its ability to position itself as the "classiest" purveyor of sexual imagery. *Miller* compounded this difficulty by compelling a broad retreat from the soft X middle ground that might have afforded sexploitation a stable softcore purchase. Classical Hollywood had been defined by the narrative priorities of the Production Code, which, in proscribing a range of "indecent" spectacle, mandated the abandonment of sexual material to lower-budget film producers in America or abroad. But after 1968, the new MPAA system allowed Hollywood to reassert many aspects of its primeval sexuality. Hollywood co-opted, or reannexed, even more of sexploitation's traditional material when the MPAA hardened the R in 1970 (Sandler 206; Lewis 188).[2] Suddenly, even network television was encroaching on sexploitation territory.

On the other hand, Hollywood's new interest in sex held advantages for some sexploitation producers, especially those specializing in postfeminist and/or aspirational formulae. As Jon Lewis notes, the majors preferred the model that led to Columbia's success with the X-rated *Emmanuelle*. By "purchasing their soft core fully shot," Lewis contends, the studios stayed "out of the soft- and hard-core development and production business" (224–25). Ergo, sexploitation films with strong heroines, polished values, and developed narratives occasionally secured Hollywood distribution during the porno-chic era. This was the path of Cannon's *The Happy Hooker* (1975), a rather inexplicit, R-rated film starring Lynn Redgrave that was distributed by MGM. Such practices amounted to win-win propositions for the majors, which could always drop a sexploitation "pickup" if it proved too controversial or unprofitable. Such deals were far riskier for independent sexploiteers, who were even more vulnerable without them.

In the long run, sexploitation could not compete with Hollywood's prowess in effects, advertising, and distribution. Specifically, it could not compete with spectacle-based films like *The Exorcist* (1973), *Jaws* (1975), *Carrie* (1976), and *Star Wars* (1977). This new breed of Hollywood blockbuster further marginalized R-rated sexploitation. Even adroit studios like Roger Corman's New World, which survived by shifting among various low-budget genres, could not compete with the majors, which "dominated the exploitation genres with budgets ten times higher than ours" (Corman xi). As a result, by the late 1970s, New World was compelled to seek nontheatrical markets in home video and on "pay TV," where the competition with Hollywood was less acute (Corman xi). The major studios also eliminated sexploitation competitors by tightening their grip on theatrical distribution. As George Mair details, many theater owners had retained close ties with Hollywood studios throughout the postwar period despite the Paramount Decrees that after 1948 forced the majors to divest their chains (102–3). When Reagan-era deregulation allowed the studios to repurchase theaters, revisiting the "vertical integration" of Hollywood's classical heyday, the disadvantage that sexploitation producers had faced all along was newly exacerbated.[3]

The most severe distribution crisis facing sexploitation was, however, the collapse of its own circuit of arthouses, grindhouses, and drive-ins. Though there is anecdotal evidence that "a considerable portion of the country, especially the South ... provided a stable [theatrical] market for softcore materials well into the 1980s" (Bowen, DVD), it is nevertheless clear that a pattern of distribution problems had begun eroding sexploitation production long before that. Starting in the early 1970s, urban renewal projects, suburban sprawl, and rising land values all contributed to a steady contraction of the sexploitation circuit. For example, by 1980, the drive-in circuit had declined to roughly three thousand venues; by 1990, that number had dwindled to one thousand (Schaefer, "Triumph" 24; Stevenson 48). This process did not have to play itself out to disrupt fragile sexploitation networks and eliminate susceptible producers. Even a small but reliable outfit like Sam Sherman's Independent-International, producer of *The Naughty Stewardesses*, folded in the face of seemingly minor disruptions:

> [In] the late 1970s and early 1980s there developed a shortage of drive-ins to play the product. Due to rising real estate values, outdoor theaters began to fall to land developers and pictures like *Game Show Models*, *The Chorus Girls*, and *Teammates*, which dealt with equal rights for women (even on the high school football field), found it increasingly difficult to find play dates. As the drive-ins tumbled, the independent subdistributors began to tumble with them. Late and nonpayments from the ailing subs started putting a financial crunch on independent distributors like I-I [Independent-International]. It became more difficult and expensive to produce new movies, where large sums of money needed to be recouped in order to break even, and older pictures with newfangled titles were pushed back into the marketplace to scrounge up what little revenue was left. Those remaining subs were now turning down pictures that did not fit their own market criteria and I-I chose not to sink their own money into new pictures. With a company whose prime market was the drive-in, Sherman realized that the future of I-I was dwindling into secondary markets he had little interest in. ... I-I moved away from the theatrical end of things and into the export end of distribution, television, cable, and even their own home video label, Super Video. (Ray 132–33)

Sherman's ability to transition "away from the theatrical end of things" has led Fred Olen Ray to describe him as a "survivor in the graveyard of [his] contemporaries" (133).[4] Other producers like former Corman protégé Larry Woolner of Dimension Pictures proved much less adaptive (Ray 161). As gentrification took its toll on grindhouses, most of which vanished long before those of Times Square (Landis and Clifford 5–6), the last of America's softcore producers went hardcore or left the business. At the same time, older sexploiteers with experience in classical exploitation were retiring or dying.

Such changes were part of a pervasive shift in film consumption, which was being privatized—or *decarnivalized*—in ways that television experts had long predicted. A prime determinant of the general falloff in moviegoing was the growth of Home Box Office (HBO), which experienced its "golden era" from 1978 to 1983 (Mair 37, 42). This lucrative phase was followed by a decline in HBO's growth linked to the expansion of home video. For sexploitation, then, the irony was that it fell apart for lack of distribution at the same time that nontheatrical technologies opened broad new markets desperate for product—and suited to *its* products. Consider cable, whose programming needs multiplied after HBO adopted a twenty-four-hour format in 1979 and spawned a twenty-four-hour affiliate, Cinemax, in 1980. Showtime then shifted to a twenty-four-hour format in 1981 and merged with the Movie Channel in 1983. With so many channels and so many time slots—and with Hollywood producing a limited slate—it was natural that programmers would resort to "cableporn," allowing viewers to "see tits and ass on cable" (Mair 88, 83). As Ginia Bellafante puts it, "the ability to show bare female nipples—and to get endless mileage out of low-budget R-rated movies—has been one of the prime attractions of pay cable ever since its birth in the 1970s" (76). Cable historians Thomas Baldwin and D. Stevens McVoy concur, observing that it "has always been accepted that uncut, R-rated movies are a major appeal of the big pay networks" (135).

It is hardly shocking, then, that recycled sexploitation turned up on cable during the late 1970s. Indeed, low-budget "drive-in movies"—which scholar Gregory Waller has dubbed "softcore sexploitation"—had by the early 1980s settled into their new habitus "as late-night filler on Cable TV movie channels" (135). Though HBO and Showtime generally shunned X-rated films, the 1970s had generated a plenitude of timid, R-rated sex films like *Superchick* useful to their purposes. Some early services like Quality Cable Network and Warner Amex's Qube pay-per-view system offered "toned-down softcore X films" (Baldwin and McVoy 135–36; see Mair 84), with the latter providing descriptions in 1980 that would not appear unusual on the premium channels of today:

> PASSIONS OF PLEASURE. When a man dreams about a beautiful blonde, it leads to the ultimate fantasy—a man, his wife and his mistress. $3.50.
>
> MUSTANG, HOUSE OF PLEASURE. A unique look at the infamous Mustang Ranch, Nevada's legal brothel. $3.50. (qtd. in Baldwin and McVoy 135)

At this time, few of the giant services risked airing hardcore (Mair 84; Ford 2). Even the Playboy Channel, founded in 1982 as a joint venture with the Cablevision unit Escapade, almost never showed hardcore and avoided X-rated simulations.

Given cable's interest in sexploitation, why did HBO's golden era coincide with the contraction of sexploitation and the disappearance of softcore? The answer hinges on economics first and class, taste, and gender second. While many services could buy the rights to old sexploitation films, only the most capitalized concerns could afford the risky practice of "prebuying" (what from a producer perspective Corman calls "preselling" [xi]) films from Hollywood or from independents. This practice was critical to production in that it gave sexploiteers something to show a bank, allowing them to finance the rest of a picture—and circumventing Hollywood investment, which put them at a disadvantage. In one common arrangement, cable or video entities fronted 50 percent of a film's production cost in return for negotiable distribution rights, with the balance financed by a bank.[5] Also common were arrangements in which cable services prebought the rights to a block of films (Baldwin and McVoy 133; Corman 207). With its huge backer (Time), HBO has since its inception had the resources to subsidize production, which it began doing in the mid-1970s (Mair 13, 78). By 1987, HBO had become one of Hollywood's largest customers *and* the largest producer of movies in the world (Mair xviii). But HBO has long favored Hollywood fare. In financing independents, it has tended to promote middlebrow values, reflecting the concerns of its early operators, who worried that HBO might alienate subscribers with "junky or offensive movies" (Mair 6). Golden-era HBO was therefore more likely to spend tiny sums to air old sexploitation films than risk larger expenditures on unknown quantities. With a rich parent of its own (Viacom), Showtime mimicked HBO. Playboy also had ample resources. Under its twenty-nine-year-old president, Christie Hefner, the service dove into production agreements in 1982. Unlike HBO, it evinced an immediate readiness to finance sex comedy and occasional softcore by the likes of Chuck Vincent and Alan Roberts. Playboy funding was, in fact, the main reason American softcore was produced at all in the 1980s. But this sponsorship came too late to sustain an entire form. By 1982, the age of video was upon the industry, but even this large and democratic—albeit unstable and decentralized—source of revenue arrived too late. HBO's early dependence on recycled sexploitation was decisive.

Ironically, HBO soon signaled that a feminized softcore paradigm, one that classical sexploitation had pioneered fifteen years earlier, matched its emerging adult strategy. Consider the arthouse sensibility that HBO imposed on Cinemax. Due to adverse conditions—competition from video, pressure from other cable operators, a shortage of Hollywood films with buzz, a decline in construction—HBO revamped Cinemax in 1984 through a renewed stress on adult fare (Mair 108). According to HBO programmer Bridget Potter, Cinemax would be "spicy, but not obscene" (qtd. in Mair 109). By indicating that films like *Young Lady Chatterley* (1977), *The Happy Hooker Goes Hollywood* (1980), and *Intimate Moments* (1981) exemplified this "new" approach, Cinemax implied that it would favor a traditional arthouse stress on female protagonists, inexplicit facial imagery, and light, consumerist narratives. Given that these films were all produced at an earlier time, HBO was clearly not yet spotlighting its own jointly produced sexploitation. But it *was* demonstrating that neither it nor its affiliates were afraid of sex. *Young Lady Chatterley* is a highly sexualized film directed by Roberts, who also directed *The Happy Hooker Goes Hollywood* for Cannon and *Young Lady Chatterley II* for Playboy. (The latter film would run on Cinemax as well.)

By adhering to the spicy-not-obscene ethos, HBO was also certifying that it would *not* subsidize the lowbrow excess associated with the grindhouses and, to a lesser extent, the drive-ins. Too much bad publicity was at stake. Old-school producers like Friedman embraced the view that *all* publicity was good. By the 1970s, this willingness to risk public censure had stimulated a reaction from antiporn groups affiliated with feminists and the Christian right. Such groups claimed that porn bred violence, especially against women. Eithne Johnson and Eric Schaefer have identified the antisnuff campaigns of 1975–76—which focused their wrath on *Snuff* (1976), a risible sexploitation hoax—as crucial in galvanizing these coalitions and in replacing the liberalism of porno-chic with the conservatism of porno-fear (40). In the wake of these campaigns, groups like Women Against Pornography (WAP) and Morality in Media targeted cable sexploitation (Mair 86–88; Jaehne 10). The latter even sponsored mailings from Roger Staubach that warned of "smut peddlers," who, aided by the "great medium of cable TV," could "now explode into your living room" with images of "[h]omosexual acts, women being brutally molested and raped" and with "explicit movies of women tied and beaten, raped with guns and other deviant sexual acts, all of which claim to be entertainment" (qtd. in Mair 88). Staubach's paternalistic, homophobic rhetoric was not mere hype, for violent, misogynistic films like *Snuff* did exist in profusion. But unlike the distributor of *Snuff*, who profited smartly from theatrical receipts inspired by the affair (Johnson and Schaefer 43–46), the new breed of nontheatrical distributor rarely cultivated controversy. This aversion to negative publicity—which factored in the emergence of the softcore thriller—marked a major divide between classical and contemporary sexploitation. Most often, this aversion was driven by the needs of the larger pay services, which had the most centralized networks and the most corporate alliances to consider. But by 1984, cable operators working with a multitude of pay services had a history of seeking a "balanced" sexual approach so as to mute outcry from advocacy groups. According to Baldwin and McVoy, in the early 1980s, operators in rural areas often coupled a premium channel "with a Christian channel to counterbalance the effect of the R movies" (136). Similarly, corporate giants like Cablevision and Comcast designed "the original pairing of lowbrow Escapade with highbrow Bravo, the cultural program service . . . partly as a response to questions of taste likely to be raised by franchising authorities" (Baldwin and McVoy 136). HBO and Showtime achieved similar balance—and did their operators a significant favor—through the feminized, aspirational disposition of their sexploitation content.

How might this look in actual practice? In her 1983 *Film Quarterly* article "Confessions of a Feminist Porn Programmer," Karen Jaehne details her early 1980s experience selecting pornographic films, including recycled sexploitation, for play on the late-night service of a pay cable station in Washington, D.C. Given her location, Jaehne was perhaps more sensitive to FCC restrictions than most programmers (11–12). There is, though, no reason to think her sensitivity to and distaste for "special interest groups like Morality in Media and WAP" was unusual (Jaehne 10). More telling is that she saw her audience as 60 percent female and gives evidence suggesting that she perceived cable as a whole as having "a dominantly female home audience" (Jaehne 15). Thus Jaehne and her peers, all of whom were women and some of whom were feminists ("albeit *sans* radical rhetoric" [10]), took "women's sensibilities into account":

> The actual increase in fantasy and decrease in brutality in adult movies has been found to be in a direct relationship to the increase in female viewers. . . . One immediate observation was that women preferred less fragmented shots of sexual acts (fewer shots of isolated genitalia), slow rhythms in the editing of such sequences, and legitimate motivation for erotic relationships (obviously rape was eliminated as a "legitimate" motivation). To the programmers, it also meant incorporating more plot-oriented, complex films with an emphasis on the male/female erotic relationship as a cause for sexual contact. (15)

Jaehne saw her nonviolent programming choices as gendered feminine. Moreover, she perceived them as situated in a distinctly middlebrow position within a hierarchy of erotic films. Though her director "was eager to have what she called 'classy classics,'" Jaehne had to be careful not to pick anything *too* complex, for "no matter how carefully done, no matter how psychologically sound the motivation, the classification 'high-brow' eliminated [certain sex films] as potential programming" (11; 12).

Cable's emerging taste for the tamest drive-in fare and for Europhilic art-house content suggested, then, a postfeminist, middlebrow strategy that negotiated controversy and evaded boycott by situating a spicy, feminized eroticism as a decorous alternative to a "living-room explosion." What differentiated premium cable from a service like the one for which Jaehne worked was that the former used its very similar programming biases to subsidize production. By 1991, this strategy had led HBO and Showtime to forge licensing agreements with discreet, cable-oriented studios like Cinema Products Video (CPV), and by 1994, this market trend had stimulated the emergence of a specialized softcore industry "between" the hardcore market and other mid- to low-budget sectors of the nontheatrical film market. For an idea of the production potentials driving the formation of this industry, consider that between 1991 and 1995, CPV—a studio that is notable here only because it was the forerunner of Marc Greenberg's Mainline Releasing Group (MRG), which has remained a top softcore purveyor—supplied premium cable with thirty staid softcore films like *Novel Desires* (1991) and about seventy feminized featurettes for softcore serials like *Love Street* (1994–95).[6]

Contemporary sexploitation's cable-sanctioned feminization is not, as Jaehne's article demonstrates, a self-defensive sham that has only pretended to appeal to women. As Jaehne notes, her programming choices were driven by a postfeminist consciousness grounded in customer surveys (15). And premium cable has since its inception targeted women more consistently and far-reachingly than channels like Jaehne's, with its sexual content growing feminized as it has become more familiar with its own demographics. On cable, even small subscriber bases are valuable because they indicate disposable income—and women are among the broadest of cable's bases (Baldwin and McVoy 282). The advent of "narrowcasting," that is, the process of targeting specific market segments, meant that women would become the target of many channels. For instance, by the 1990s, Lifetime was openly marketing the "female" attitudes that it had flaunted since its introduction in 1984. Fostered by Reagan-era deregulation,[7] such strategies have led to the "multiplexed" networks of today, through which distinct HBO and Showtime entities target specific consumer types. The subgroup that cable covets most is the "upscale working women" category, which Nielsen has charted since 1976. Such women "attract advertisers not only because they remain the primary household consumers, in the tradition of women historically targeted by radio and TV, but also because they have considerable money to spend on their own pleasures" (Juffer, *Home* 200; see Gomery 1).

Given that "[m]ost of the profits in contemporary cinema [have been] generated in video stores" (Naremore 163), it is worth questioning why the softcore industry has reflected cable biases more than video biases. The answer is that home-video distributors have tended to be more diverse, democratic, and class-blind than cable (Naremore 163). They have seldom, in other words, embodied coherent bundles of tastes. It has been even rarer for them to combine such "bundles" with centralized distribution schemes and large revenue streams. Consequently, though home video has since the 1980s underwritten many areas of sexploitation, it has not encouraged the same level of routinization as cable. Of course, Blockbuster, which still shapes softcore production practice,[8] represents the enormous exception to this rule. But it is clear that the softcore industry did not form in response to family-oriented Blockbuster so much as learn to accommodate it after the industry had adopted a default corporate softcore sensibility in the mid-1990s (see Juffer, "No Place" 55–56). Also implicit to home video's unpredictable sexual palate is that it is a private format but not a broadcast medium. For that reason, the rape metaphors that antiporn paternalists like Staubach have aimed at televisual sexuality have not lent themselves to video, which requires people to perform an act of consent by transporting a consumer choice into the home. By contrast, cable is a "'high penetration' (as it is truly called) medium" that is easy translated into assaultive and paternalistic terms (Jaehne 10). Cable transmission has therefore remained more likely to generate controversy than home-video exhibition despite the fact that there is greater sexploitation diversity on a Blockbuster shelf than a Cinemax schedule.[9] Given the *far* greater sexploitation diversity that has been available through mom-and-pop outlets—and that has recently proliferated through online means—it is clear that home video has supported a generic range loosely approximating the whole of the classical sexploitation circuit, while cable has subsidized tame variants on arthouse and drive-in fare, eschewing the more visceral, masculinized forms of the grindhouse. Throughout the 1980s, such diversity was implicit to the cult sexploitation category, whose producers relied mainly on video distribution,[10] and it would continue to be evident there once this category spawned cult softcore labels like Torchlight, Surrender, and Seduction during the 1990s.[11]

In its lowest, most "cultish" vehicles, video sexploitation has, then, been more masculinized than cable sexploitation, daring feminists and cultural conservatives to take umbrage to its "classical" synthesis of objectification and violence. But this impulse was curtailed by opposite postfeminist anxieties—with the result that 1980s sexploitation never matched the diversity or disorder of classical sexploitation. Films of the 1980s in the cult sexploitation rubric align their heroines with implacable strength and appropriate a feminist idiom more reliably than 1970s vehicles. Witness Academy Entertainment's *Blue Movies* (1988), which foregrounds characters displaying feminist sympathies, including one doing research on "mass media's influence on sexual identification." And these films often temper their objectionable traits through a lower-middlebrow comedy that muffles their violence—and through ironies that place a crucial distance between them and the grindhouse products that they knowingly parody. This parodic historical continuity indicates a familiar strategy of 1980s sexploitation, which has qualified as a "cult" area not only insofar as coterie audiences have favored it but also insofar as its producers have commodified their own parsimony, turning lo-fi necessities into nostalgic distinctions. Even the name of Fred Olen Ray's 1986 start-up, American Independent Productions, is a camp homage to Samuel Arkoff's teen exploitation outfit, American International Pictures (also AIP), where Corman cut his teeth.

Before moving on, I should make three points about these video-oriented sectors, which comprised the majority of sexploitation produced in the 1980s. First, in this period, sexploitation relied on ultra-low budgets and thus had ultra-low values. In an exemplary arrangement, Ray presold *Hollywood Chainsaw Hookers* (1987) to Camp Video, allowing him to raise half of the film's budget of $50,000 in return for American video rights (188). This left him the option of licensing the film elsewhere, so he negotiated a richer pickup with the more established distributor Vidmark (Ray 195). (Along with Vestron, Vidmark was a major financier of low-cost direct-to-video genres in the 1980s.) But such financing restricted his budgets to the ultralow $60,000–$125,000 range, which yielded campy, lo-fi values. Second, though producers like Corman and Ray clearly made sexploitation films—besides *Hollywood Chainsaw Hookers,* Ray was responsible for *Beverly Hills Vamp* (1988) and *Bad Girls from Mars* (1989)—they seldom specialized in sexploitation alone. This survival-oriented flexibility ensured that sexploitation would remain diffuse in this era, indistinct from other low-budget sectors of the nontheatrical market. Finally, like their classical forebears, the new sexploiteers depended on lurid plots, titles, and promotions. Over-the-top video box art was a requisite for inexpensive cult films whose monsters, chainsaws, and breasts had to compete on retail shelves with much slicker contemporary Hollywood fare selling the same spectacle.[12] This youthful promotion, whose excessiveness is ironic and hence unthreatening, marks another constitutional divide between a video-oriented cult sexploitation aesthetic and sexploitation's emerging cable aesthetic, which favored more restrained signals and required less promotion. Such restraint would be most completely realized by corporate softcore, whose bland video box art offers one proof that home video was not its primary market.

Figure 9. Video-box art for *Young Lady Chatterley* (1977), a classical vehicle in the *Emmanuelle* mode. © Alan Roberts, 1977, and Monterey Home Video, 1996.

II. *YOUNG LADY CHATTERLEY II*, A JANUS TEXT

As one of a handful of fully softcore American films shot in the 1980s, Alan Roberts's *Young Lady Chatterley II* (hereafter *YLCII*) is automatically intriguing, and its interest deepens on examination. In its complex Janus function, *YLCII* is meaningful to any survey of 1980s sexploitation. On one hand, the film is emblematic of the spicy-not-obscene aspirationalism to which premium cable was yoking its identity as early as 1984. On the other hand, *YLCII* is emblematic of sexploitation's theatrical past, for it was sequel to a classical film in the *Emmanuelle* mode. Such multivalence implies that *YLCII* was an anomaly among the masculinized, downscale, timid films that dominated 1980s sexploitation. But even here there is complexity, for the film's Playboy-style comedy links it to the era's most prevalent and masculinized form, the teen sex comedy. These impulses, at once alluding to sexploitation's past, present, and future, coincide neatly in the film's careful, conflicted, highly discursive depiction of rape.

YLCII is not faithful to D. H. Lawrence's novel. Though Roberts envisioned his first *Chatterley* film in the same reverential terms as later adapters, including Jaeckin and Ken Russell, he could not interest investors in such a concept. But because "*Emmanuelle* was the rage and *Lady Chatterley's Lover* had the same classic quality" (3), Roberts did manage to adorn each installment with literary trappings. To that end, he secured ritzy, Euro-style locations (including the Bernard Cornfeld estate in Beverly Hills) and deployed fractured allusions to Lawrence (both plots revolve around a wealthy married landowner [Harlee McBride] who pursues her gardeners). As a result, *YLCII* resembles the softcore imports of the 1980s, many of which were dubious adaptations driven by erotic names like Lady Chatterley, Emmanuelle, Fanny Hill, and O. The 1980s alone spawned four Chatterley vehicles, with dozens of Emmanuelle (or "Emanuelle") films appearing in the same interval. But unlike Roberts's films, imports like Lorenzo Onorati's *The Story of Lady Chatterley* (1989) were dramas. By transforming his first *YLC* film into a latter-day comedy, Roberts took advantage of a mid-1970s vogue for heroine-driven sex comedy. He retained this scheme in *YLCII*, though sex-com fashion had by 1985 shifted toward the frustrated teenage male, a trend Roberts acknowledges through a secondary figure. The sequel was made after Playboy approached Roberts during the early 1980s to shoot a 16mm serial using the same actress and location; eventually, the concept was redesigned as a 35mm feature with a final cost of $310,000 (Roberts 1). After playing on the Playboy Channel, *YLCII* aired on Cinemax and Showtime. The film was also licensed to Vestron and even appeared in a narrow, R-rated theatrical release under the alternate title *Private Property*.

YLCII's peculiar sensuality derives from its *Emmanuelle*-style liberationism and its Playboy-style materialism. Though forced to translate *Emmanuelle*'s metaphysical aesthetic into comic terms, Roberts mimicked the film's ostentatious sensuality, including its gauzy soft-focus, hedonistic *mise-en-scène*, and slick values, in his *YLC* films. Indeed, American audiences might have recognized the *Emmanuelle* stamp before viewing the first *YLC*, whose promotion featured a "Beautiful X" tag line that alluded to Columbia's famous "X was never like this" line (see Lewis 228). In *YLCII*, this sensuality shades into a Playboy aesthetic, a blurring that is evident in the sequel's tendency to fabricate sensuous imagery from luxury goods. A drift toward materialism is also apparent in *YLCII*'s sexual consumerism. Like Emmanuelle, Roberts's Lady Cynthia Chatterley is a liberated, sex-positive quester. But because *YLCII* is a comedy, it lacks the gravity of *Emmanuelle*. Roberts's light hedonism—which prefigures the "weightlessness" of corporate softcore, especially that of the Playboy variety—is striking in its handling of adultery. Antisexual, anticonsumerist anxieties have often manifested in classical and contemporary sexploitation genres through the figure of the bored wife, whose wayward desire portends destruction; this formula has a notable place in the erotic thriller. But in *YLCII*, Cynthia's adultery is not just guilt-free, *à la Emmanuelle*; it is *not* an issue. Even amid porno-chic, *YLCII*'s liberationism would have seemed self-indulgent. In the antiporn 1980s, it was, like the film's softcore structure, an anachronism.

YLCII introduces an anticonsumerist theme as a source of comic tension that must be dispersed for the narrative to regain its consumerist equilibrium. A common pornographic trajectory, this arc is not in itself remarkable. What is notable is that this tension is associated with Judith Grimmer (Sybil Danning), who evokes both sides of the antiporn coalition that contributed to the wane of porno-chic, a development that coincided with the release of the first *YLC* film. In a sense, then, Judith functions as an *anti*-antiporn device. Styled as a devout Catholic, Judith is also a false feminist whose misandristic repressions imply a complex misogyny that is revealed as such through the intercession of Cynthia, whose postfeminist liberationism is situated as a "truer" feminism. In reacting to a bad marriage—as she puts it, the "lust and feral desires of my husband seduced him away to other women"—Judith has become a repressive-purity stereotype whose self-loathing manifests in her notion that "the evil beast lurks" in female sex organs. She thus coerces her male relatives to join the priesthood and views Cynthia (whose estate she, her brother Robert [Steven Kean Matthews], and son Virgil [John St. Angelo] visit in the course of the diegesis) as an enemy. Cynthia neutralizes the narrative tension implicit to Judith's antisexual stance via an array of numbers culminating in Judith's semiconsensual rape. Cynthia begins by co-opting Judith's relatives. Her seduction of Robert is the least exceptional element of this pattern, though it does require her to nullify his "productivist" belief that sex "is meant to be enjoyable, but for a purpose." Cynthia's more consumerist idea of sexual pleasure as an autotelic good is integral to her nurturing femininity, which the film defines as maternal during her seduction of the teenaged Virgil.

Virgil is an intriguing figure. His age- and gender-specific frustration links him to the low-budget sex-coms that proliferated after *Porky's* and *Fast Times at Ridgemont High*. But since *YLCII* is softcore, his frustration has little chance of enduring. This point is clarified by the film's opening pattern of *coitus interruptus,* which places Cynthia in a comic role traditional to men. Just as her frustration "lapses" into pornographic surfeit, Virgil's frustration yields to satiety, first with Cynthia and then with interchangeable servants. Such abundance is rare in all but the most sexualized teen sex-coms—but when it does appear, it is accompanied by clear feminization tactics. A case in point is *My Tutor* (1983), a Crown project sponsored by Playboy and featuring the cinematography of Mac Ahlberg and the acting of a young, credibly frustrated Crispin Glover. A film that still runs on cable, *My Tutor* is a traditional teen sex-com except for its postfeminist stylization, which softens the disempowered hero (Matt Lattanzi) as a condition of satisfying his lust. The hero's older female tutor (Caren Kaye) educates him in French, sex, and manners. Like Cynthia, this figure is a nurturer whose tutelage has a feminist dimension: it is an altruistic expression of solidarity with the hero's girlfriends. In *YLCII*, Cynthia's role is more intricate in that she must first disabuse her charge of a hurtful ideology by using maternal tones to coax him into obeying "male" desire ("your mother's not here, Virgil, and there are no evil beasts, just soft and moist and warm"). Only then can she guide him in satisfying "female" desire ("go slower, slower, no hurry"). Like the entire scenario, this advice has been standardized by contemporary softcore, which depicts liaisons between teen males and older females in the warm, fuzzy terms of student-teacher metaphors. Such metaphors are most evident in softcore's most feminized subgenre, the softcore serial. By linking the liberationist comedy of the classical era to the "frustrationist" comedy of its own era, *YLCII* anticipates the contemporary.

Cynthia seduces Judith by way of Thomas (Brett Clark), the gardener who is her consistent sexual object. Her interactions with Thomas represent another way in which *YLCII* looks back and forth in time. The gaze that Cynthia levels at Thomas's buff, semiclad body inverts the traditional gendering of porn's subject-object relation. As the object of Cynthia's gaze, Thomas is configured as an other whose fetishized difference *vis-à-vis* the female subject is further "exoticized" by class difference. (Adam West's bare chest is also the object of Cynthia's ogle, but the exotic-other accent is absent because West plays a campy professor—and because he is Batman.) Later in the decade, this distinctively gendered and classed dynamic would become the crux of Zalman King's appeal. Thomas also anticipates the King hero through his antifeminist conviction that sex is the key to revealing a woman's essential femininity, which may be obscured by careers, pieties, and other acculturated "illusions." Thomas thus resolves to "help" Judith through coerced sex that he expects will "become" consensual, for he believes she has "more fire beneath her skirt than ice." Though his "backlash" attitude is incorrect—which Cynthia confirms in labeling him "a chauvinist"—this aspect of his postfeminist construction is not discordant given his low social background and his comic narrative function. What is discordant is that the middlebrow heroine agrees to his "remedy." An anomaly even then—or, in a post-Brownmiller, post-Dworkin decade, *especially* then—Cynthia's rape complicity is an ironic extension of her female solidarity.

Of course, *YLCII* has no intention of depicting a nonconsensual rape, and in this respect, it is of its time. Though Judith's violation offers an opportunity to adapt Lawrence through an allegorical display of brute "phallic reality," the film is too proper to seize this opportunity, offering instead the softest of semiconsensual motifs. After Thomas tricks Judith into meeting him in his hut, Judith, Bible in hand, spurns his coarse advance. But he does not respond with roughie violence. Instead, he shifts to a discursive approach, asserting that she is "primarily a woman. You hide her very well, but I know she's in there." After a pause in which no coercion is suggested, Judith yields, melting into his embrace. This "rape," then, pivots on two quick exchanges: Thomas cedes power to Judith, who cedes it back to him. Thomas does not take "no" for an answer, but neither does he force Judith's pleasure. Thus the sequence blends romance-novel surrender with a scrupulous maintenance of consent. Here *YLCII* is far softer and more postfeminist than *Emmanuelle*, which subjects its heroine to a nonconsensual rape. In today's softcore serials, the convention is to underscore a rape's unreality or to stipulate the mechanisms through which the female "victim" ritually controls her "rape." But because Cynthia does not know that Thomas will desist at Judith's behest, her role in this rape conspiracy is out of sync with the more cautious aspects of its presentation.

In the end, Judith's narrative arc conforms with convention by supporting Thomas's antifeminist misogyny. It does so, however, not through hardcore frenzies but through softcore scanties: beneath Judith's prim attire, she has all along been wearing the fiery signifiers of "true" womanliness. Her antisex trappings banished, she is exposed as a vivacious cliché with wild hair and revealing clothing. That *YLCII* at this point signifies Judith's "essence" through fashion rather than action is consistent with its softcore vision, which always stresses eroticism's mediated nature. Indeed, that Thomas captivates Judith with language, not force, reflects one of *YLCII*'s steadiest patterns. For example, the film also underscores language's power to captivate during Cynthia's seductions of Robert and Virgil. This allure is further accentuated by the instructive sequence in which Cynthia describes her fantasy man during a slow, languorous massage. In the aforementioned segment, Cynthia's masseuse (Barbara Stewart) works her clitoris as the camera lingers on her face and breasts—and all the while, Cynthia narrates a fantasy about a "sensitive and yet manly" stranger, whom the film later realizes as, naturally, a Frenchman. The excitement registered by Cynthia's theatrical face, the film's central image, is as much a response to the act of public fantasy as to the masseuse's manipulations.

YLCII's contemporaneity is most evident when the film's literary frills combine with dense oral textures to suggest that "authentic" female desire is tantamount to verbal fantasy. Like the surrender theme, this idea is common in romance and other "female" genres, including the woman's film. It has also retained its place in the art film; Jean-Jacques Annaud's just-shy-of-softcore *The Lover* (1992) offers a fairly recent case. It makes sense, then, that King also embraced this sort of literariness, most influentially through the epistolary framework of his *Red Shoe Diaries* serial.

III. MALE DISEMPOWERMENT IN THE TEEN SEX COMEDY

In the 1980s, few sexploiteers followed Roberts in lending their projects dichotomous structures. At that juncture, softcore procedures were rare even at Playboy, which, like other mid- to low-budget studios, financed more hero-driven teen sex-coms than heroine-driven sex-coms. It was more common for teen sex-coms to imitate *YLCII*'s feminization than its pornographication. It is no accident, then, that even sexploitation's downscale, masculinized sex-coms emphasize female empowerment, often countering antiporn ideology in the process. If such comedies at times revert to the tame, adolescent voyeurism and low double entendres of the nudie cutie, they also blend such attributes with "safe" postfeminist proprieties. Typically, this middling ethos was as crucial to their licensing for cable distribution as the fact that they mimicked theatrical paradigms in the first place.[13] Here it bears reiterating that unlike the old sexploitation market, whose formation was contingent on the nudie cutie's stark contrast with Code-era Hollywood spectacle, the new nontheatrical markets relied on voyeuristic, post-Code sex-coms that often *were* Hollywood spectacle. HBO and Showtime, it seems, needed the confidence of experience before pioneering their own distinctive softcore. But because these films were for half a decade the raciest new releases on cable, they deserve mention as a pivotal phase in the development of more specialized forms of sexploitation.

The social sensitivity of films like *My Tutor* was influenced by blockbusters like Bob Clark's *Porky's* and Amy Heckerling's *Fast Times*. Though pointedly low in its comedy and imagery, *Porky's* includes a strong racial tolerance theme, while the more middlebrow *Fast Times* contains joint male-female protagonists, a format that allows it to explore the gender-specific effects of teen sex, including abortion. In a typical gambit, later vehicles like Universal's *Private School* (1983) adapted the joint-protagonist schema popularized by *Fast Times* as a device for yielding greater female display—reminding us that, after the lapse of the Code, Hollywood was not above trends previously ascribed to low-budget sexploiteers alone. Hence the subjectification-via-objectification dynamic that in the classical era culminated in feminized biases may be observed in teen forms. Recent big-budget projects like *American Pie* (1999) and particularly *The Girl Next Door* (2004) perpetuate this trend, yielding strong women who socialize men by imparting sensitivity lessons—much as they do in softcore cable serials.

The teen sex-com openly panders to ideas of female superiority. This bias is an organic though oblique expression of the core theme of much contemporary sex comedy, which is the absurdity of male heterosexuality and its inflated claims to power and status (Dyer, *Matter* 114–17). Even the nudie cutie—whose women are typically flattened objects—tends to situate women as higher beings. Still, the analogy with the nudie cutie should not be overdrawn. The deflations and frustrations of the two forms are distinct. If the hero emblematic of the nudie cutie is Meyer's Mr. Teas, the maladjusted voyeur who flees active contact with women, the hero emblematic of the teen sex-com is Clark's Pee Wee (Dan Monahan), whose tireless pursuit of such contact provides *Porky's* with comic tension. Thus the teen sex-com's peephole voyeurism, iconically realized in the *Porky's* shower spectacle, figures as a frustrating deferment, not a liberating end-in-itself, as in *Mr. Teas*. Further, the postfeminist women of the sex-com are rounder, more humanized figures than the passive, prefeminist objects of the nudie cutie.

To verify how basic postfeminist female agency was to 1980s sex comedy, it helps to focus on Chuck Vincent, whose low-budget sex-coms pursue the teen-frustration paradigm without the niceties of more mainstream films. As a gay man who began by making straight sexploitation films like *Voices of Desire* (1970), Vincent was an early convert to hardcore, starting his own production label, Platinum Pictures, in 1981 (Gerli 198). He edited his narrative-heavy films to suit foreign and cable markets, with his soft-X cuts of hardcore films offering one of the era's steadiest varieties of softcore.[14] Known for arthouse hardcore like *Roommates* (1981) and *In Love* (1983), he was among the first directors to negotiate multipicture deals with the Playboy Channel (Ford 2), which produced *Preppies* (1982). Besides *Preppies*, Vincent's filmography features many teen sex-coms, including *Hollywood Hot Tubs* (1984), *Sex Appeal* (1986), *Wimps* (1986), and *Student Affairs* (1987). Though they focus on young men, these comedies supply forceful supporting women who dominate and manipulate the male characters. Typically, this "male disempowerment" theme is sexualized, as indicated by the films' lowbrow, self-conscious references to female orgasm, male masturbation, and porn.

That this master theme and its supporting motifs pertain to Vincent's hardcore background is clear. But they may also be linked to Vincent's sexual identity. Drawing on Richard Dyer, Jake Gerli has examined Vincent's hardcore output through the lens of his homosexuality. Gerli argues that Vincent's interest in bad sex and lack of interest in sexual representation as a whole "constitute queer strategies of representing heterosexual sex," the function of which is to displace and destabilize "the fantasy of utopian heterosexual intercourse as encountered in pornography" (199; 198–215). Gerli does not discuss the director's heterosexual sexploitation, but his approach implies that Vincent may have kept returning to sexploitation comedy because he felt it suited his talent and vision more straightforwardly than heterosexual hardcore. For whereas the qualities that Gerli situates as queer work *against* the emerging conventions of hardcore, the same qualities work *with* the emerging conventions of the teen sex-com, which mandates a timid, self-reflexive spectacle and an often dystopian perspective on straight sex and masculinity.

Female orgasm is a dystopian staple of Vincent's work and the teen sex-com broadly because it is a reliable device for underlining male futility. Linda Williams has argued that pornographic genres identify female "frenzy" with female orgasm (*Hard* 50). But the teen sex-com is self-conscious enough to acknowledge that this "evidence"—which in soft genres is often limited to facial conventions and noisy "M&G's"[15]—may be fraudulent. In mocking men, the sex-com underscores the intentional, performative nature of female orgasm. Men can neither predict nor direct female pleasure; nor can they be sure of the motives informing its dramatization. A converse impotence is indicated by films that suggest that female frenzy is credible enough but that men are ancillary to it—*or* that men cannot squelch it once they start it. The first device registers a basic male anxiety. The second is an unintended consequence of male fantasy. By exploring both male shortcomings, most memorably via Kim Cattrall's turn as "Lassie," *Porky's* helped cement these ecstatic motifs as standbys of the teen sex-com.

Vincent's richest comedy utilizes these standbys. In *Preppies,* three college freshmen are manipulated by two sets of women divided by class but united by mercenary intent. Both the preppy women and the working-class women hope to secure the freshmen's bank accounts. Gold-digging is the sex-com's main motive for "faking it." (In contemporary softcore, which explores this motif from the vantage of female subjectivity, love is the culprit.) This truism is borne out in Katt Shea's droll performance as Margot, the domineering girlfriend of the trust-fund designee, Chip (Dennis Drake).

Margot advises her dim friend Trini (Linda Wiesmeier) to regard virginity as a "time deposit." Margot retains Chip's interest while preserving her "capital" by letting him palpate her naked flesh through a glass door. She treats orgasm as a similar exchange. Shea's finest thespian moment may be the scene in which Margot, dressed in bra, panties, and frou-frou knee socks, models for her friend the performative flattery of a preppy wife,[16] teaching Trini to "swirl the head from side-to-side and wave the arms in gentle motion." Margot climaxes this recital with M&G's that she refers to as "slow purring, guttural moans." By contrast, in *Sex Appeal*, Monica (hardcore icon Veronica Hart), one of the working-class hero's more upscale lovers, comes to orgasm so rapidly, uncontrollably, and *authentically* that the hero's input is diminished—and with it, his self-esteem. This ludic outcome represents a double twist. Prior to sex, Monica indicates the impossibility of satisfying her. Initially, her volcanic responsiveness disrupts this expectation in accord with male fantasy—but in the end, such hyper-sensitivity reinforces this expectation in accord with male futility. In the context of the teen sex-com, female orgasm, authentic or otherwise, is a teasing signifier of failed masculinity; it is also a motif that Vincent seamlessly integrates with class anxieties.

A related and even more distinctive element of the teen sex-com's construction of male sexuality is its acknowledgment that men as well as women masturbate. Such an admission would be refreshing were it not for the sex-com's fortification of traditional sex-and-gender biases. From its inception, classical sexploitation tended to valorize female masturbation. Such a bias became more static and predictable after feminism's politicization of female masturbation during the early 1970s (see Laqueur 74–80, 400–413). By the mid-1970s, sexploiteers were intentionally endorsing this liberation of clitoral sexuality in films that include Joe Sarno's *Butterflies*—which, by concluding with a masturbation number, symbolizes the heroine's new freedom from phallic domination. Ever intrigued by the feminine "mystery" of autoeroticism, sexploiteers have since then lent female masturbation a middle-brow seriousness as expressed through postfeminist motifs that connote self-sufficiency and choice. This affirmative valence has remained fixed even as the politicization of female masturbation has receded in post-1996 softcore, occasionally returning to full view in aspirational vehicles such as Elisa Rothstein's Nancy Friday–inspired serial *Women: Stories of Passion*.

But as Thomas Laqueur notes in *Solitary Sex* (2003), masturbation was never rehabilitated for heterosexual men. Especially in pop culture, male masturbation remains unredeemed and irredeemable, marked by "fear, embarrassment and abjection" (Laqueur 417–18). In making this argument, Laqueur alludes to late 1990s blockbusters like the teen-sex variant *There's*

Something About Mary (1998) as well as *American Pie* (82, 418). The teen sex-com formed this negative stance toward male masturbation during its first vogue in the early 1980s. Female masturbation was at that point still politicized by liberationist sentiment, so the teen sex-com focused its negativism on male masturbation, generating a structuring contrast with later softcore convention, which has lavished pro-sex positivism on female masturbation while ignoring male masturbation. Only insofar as it, too, ignores male masturbation does the teen sex-com treat its hero kindly. The teen sex-com is sexploitation's closest "male" equivalent to the awakening-sexuality model, and it is notable that it is most positive in its valuation of "budding" male sexuality when its hero is most feminized, as in *My Tutor*. But what male sexuality can never do is bud in homosexual or autoerotic directions—a point as true of the films of a gay director like Vincent as of those of heterosexual directors. Though explorations of "lesbianism" and onanism have been standard in awakening-sexuality films since the 1960s, teen sex-coms of a similar style avoid motifs that still bear traces of Freudian stigma, as if this evasion were a condition of their affirmation of male sexuality.

Teen sex-com depictions of male masturbation are low, ludic, and nonerotic, suiting them to Vincent's tastes. They are, in fact, yoked to the subgenre's taste for gross-outs. (Here *American Pie* and *There's Something About Mary* are to the point.) Such depictions are also expressive of male disempowerment. Driven by bodily necessities he cannot control, the adolescent hero is compelled by sexual scarcity and social ineptitude to seek solitary relief, the ritual exposure and interruption of which underlines his phallic futility. *Fast Times* contains an influential instance of such a scene—but a similar scene from Vincent's *Sex Appeal* is no less exemplary. Cowering in a bathroom with a "Playhouse" magazine that conflates *Playboy* and *Penthouse,* the hero (Louie Bonanno) of *Sex Appeal* is thwarted by a mother's intrusions. The details bespeak awkwardness, impotence, and low, Freudian shame. Witness the clumsy mechanics of penis, porn, and pants; the proximity of the toilet; the overbearing voice of the Mother.

In alluding to print and film porn, *Preppies* and *Sex Appeal* manifest a related signature of the Vincent *oeuvre:* self-referential devices and plots.[17] Here again, Vincent might be viewed through his sexual identity. Dyer has discussed the tradition of self-reflexivity in gay porn videos ("Idol" 105–9), and Gerli has examined self-conscious aspects of Vincent's hardcore (204–12). But in the context of a broad discussion of sex comedy, the self-reflexiveness of Vincent's sexploitation is again most usefully read as a means of reinforcing heterosexual male disempowerment. Consider that *Preppies* and *Sex Appeal* both refer to Vincent's hardcore, including collaborations with Ron Jeremy and Candida Royalle like *Fascination* (1980) and

Sizzle (1980). These references are subtly linked to the abjection implicit to the male masturbation motif. As *Sex Appeal*'s toilet scene shows, the teen sex-com construes porn as a sign of male weakness. This view buttresses Alan Soble's *anti*-antiporn contention that "pornography is not an expression of the reality of male power, but an expression of men's *lack* of power" and "an admission that men must accept the social advances of women" (*Marxism* 7; Soble's italics). One pillar of antiporn orthodoxy is that men use porn as a tool of seduction and, by extension, of rape (Russell 80–82). Vincent counters this orthodoxy in a self-reflexive fashion. In *Sex Appeal*, his would-be Casanova uses *Fascination* as a comically *inutile* tool of female seduction. The director also counters this thesis by having one of *Preppies*'s lower-class females (Jo-Ann Marshall) pose as a preppy writing a sociology paper titled "The Male Response to Popular Erotic Cinema." She subjects the male preppies to hardcore films like *Sizzle,* making them instantly pliable. In the teen sex-com, then, porn is a self-reflexive signifier of male heterosexual disempowerment; it may also function as a self-reflexive signifier of female heterosexual empowerment.

In addition to covert images of female dominance, Vincent's sex-coms supply overt images as well. *Sex Appeal* contains a pair of dominatrices and a mystery woman (Tally Chanel) whom the hero cannot control even in his fantasies. These films also contain more positive images of female empowerment, including the hero's sympathetic sister (Marcia Karr) in *Sex Appeal* and the protagonist's smart, assertive girlfriend (Donna McDaniel) in *Hollywood Hot Tubs.* What is more, in this context of male frustration and deferment, misogyny is comprehensively ironized. Besides the fact that the "illuminating" nuggets that the hero of *Sex Appeal* gleans from his self-help book are plainly camp (e.g., "women love to talk; be a patient listener—that big mouth of hers has several other uses"), their suave chauvinism is so discredited as to render them absurd. In Vincent's work, women may embody all the qualities, positive and negative, that men embody, save one: they are not made ludicrous and low by their sexual desires. Almost without exception, they are creatures of choice, not necessity.

Vincent also produced sex-coms outside the teen area, including *Young Nurses in Love* (1987), which parodies the earnest career-woman films that Corman pioneered in the early 1970s, and *Slammer Girls* (1987). As a women-in-prison parody, *Slammer Girls* exemplifies a trend of 1980s sexploitation comedy, which often borrows motifs from adjacent genres with a similar interest in female strength. Hence, "slasher-coms" like David DeCoteau's *Sorority Babes in the Slimeball Bowl-O-Rama* (1988) and Ray's *Bad Girls from Mars* or *Hollywood Chainsaw Hookers* were not uncommon. These hybrids reconfirm what I have been arguing by way of Vincent: even when it is ultra-low-budget, ultra-lowbrow, and masculinized, direct-to-video sexploitation is no less "postfeminist" in its advocacy of female agency and choice than the midbudget, middlebrow, feminized softcore that premium cable would help finance from 1991 to 1996.

I should close by briefly returning to *Blue Movies,* a buddy film that exemplifies the characteristic postfeminist anxiety of 1980s sexploitation. The porn-actress heroine (Lucinda Crosby) of this self-conscious film-about-film is ferociously independent and dignified, which leads her to verbally assault the malign and impotent male caricatures around her. She thus demands respect from one set of male producers ("[h]aving sex on film for money is my choice, but I want to be treated like a goddamn human being while I'm doing it!") and joins with a feminist academic in demanding that another set of male producers demonstrate their solidarity by working naked. If *Blue Movies* is a measure, sexploitation comedy had in tandem with sexploitation generally responded to feminism through a broad ideological shift, becoming more deferential to the powerful women whom it continued to objectify—and more self-abasing, indeed more masochistic, *vis-à-vis* the ideas of male desire that it increasingly stooped to satisfy.

IV. SEX OBJECTS *QUA* ACTION FIGURES

The proliferation of action dramas in the 1980s is one indication of sexploitation's intensified dependence on Hollywood formulae. The female-empowerment imperative that is central to 1980s sexploitation is most masculinized in this area. The heroines of such films routinely master the same codes of machismo that prove sex-com heroes deficient. In that sense, these empowered babes are sexploitation's response to Rambo, Conan, and Bond. Here the most exemplary sex-action forms are *not* the most prominent ones. In this period, the women-in-prison film underwent a notable resurgence—and the teen slasher and the erotic thriller were among the most influential low-budget forms of this or any period. But though these film categories depend on nudity and violence, none is as straightforwardly reliant on action spectacle as, say, a Rambo film. As a result, their heroines have action and aggression thrust on them. This is clearest apropos the "victim heroes" of nudity-driven slashers like *The Slumber Party Massacre* (1982). Such women must confront a killer or die (Clover 21–64). By contrast, the sex-action films on which I focus here offer postfeminist heroines in the *Superchick* manner. These heroines actively embrace lives predicated on violence.

Within this sex-action subset, the two most intriguing paradigms are Corman's sword-and-sorcery model and Sidaris's babes-with-guns model. As exemplified by the *Barbarian Queen* films (1985, 1989), the sword-and-sorcery model is notable for its relatively hard, politicized heroines and its odd fetishization of rape. The *Barbarian Queen* vehicles may, in fact, be viewed as a delicate postfeminist balance of three discordant elements: a timid rape-and-bondage spectacle, an incoherent feminism, and a *very* patriarchal plot structure. Though in most respects different from the Corman films, Sidaris films like *Malibu Express* (1984), *Hard Ticket to Hawaii* (1987), *Picasso Trigger* (1988), and *Savage Beach* (1989) are governed by a postfeminist logic that precipitates similar balancing acts. These films are visual democracies that value the objects of their glossy, materialist spectacle as largely equivalent "eye candy." At its most liberal, this spectacle has the potential to provide gender-bending pleasures—but ultimately, any impulse toward genderlessness is checked by postfeminist anxieties that compel Sidaris to adhere to safe, paternalistic sex-and-gender representations.

The *Barbarian Queen* films represent a Hollywood-derived alternative to the much harder category of rape-revenge vehicle exemplified by Meir Zarchi's 1977 film *I Spit on Your Grave* (Clover 114–65). These Corman films specifically capitalized on a vogue for rape-inflected comic book fantasy first popularized by Universal's blockbuster *Conan the Barbarian* (1982). Corman writer Howard Cohen adapted the *Conan* model in *Deathstalker* (1983), but in Dino DeLaurentiis's *Red Sonja* (1985), he discerned a more fitting Hollywood vehicle for the Corman sensibility, which favored politicized material. In the *Barbarian Queen* films, a feminist narrative arc ostensibly motivates rape imagery. But given how often the films present such spectacle—or more precisely, how often they *refer* to it, since they do not depict penetrative acts—rape is plainly their central resource, the one that they mean to "exploit." It is more logical, then, to assume that this imagery motivated Cohen to find a feminist "solution," one that made rape spectacle acceptable at a time when rape was uniquely politicized, than to assume the converse.

The first *Barbarian Queen* announces its interest in rape-and-bondage spectacle before the credits roll. The film's preamble depicts the abduction of an adolescent girl by horsemen in the pay of an oppressive regime. (The girl is plucking pink flowers by a river, no less.) Ravishment is left implicit. The girl's tunic is rent, the deed itself posited by a medium close-up of a soldier unbuckling his belt. In sequence after sequence, this pattern is repeated: soldiers rip the clothing from their female victims, with the camera lingering long enough to show nipples and horrified reactions but never long enough to simulate penetration. *Barbarian Queen* supplements this rape-tease, so to speak, with roughie-kinky degradations in which women are histrionically soiled, bloodied, and bound to racks. *Barbarian Queen II* follows a similar pattern, though its rape references are even more fleeting, its torture devices even more baroque.

This is patently postfeminist sexploitation in that rape is somehow at the center of a spectacle that cannot simulate rape. The stand-in for rape simulation is a variant on the bodice-ripping device of romance fiction—and, more lately, of Super Bowl halftime shows. By combining the violent exposure of breasts with female reaction shots, the Corman rape-tease reconfigures the indirection with which nonsoftcore sexploitation has traditionally referred to sex: not through bumping and grinding but through furtive close-ups of female breasts and faces. (Ironically, prefeminist films in the roughie-kinky nexus also relied on rape violence as "compensation" for elliptical nudity.) In several passages, the *Barbarian Queen* films imply that exposure of the breast is *itself* an ultimate violation—a crime, that is, on a par with penetrative rape, which had in turn been placed on a par with murder by dint of feminist activism (Clover 152; see Projansky). If this overvaluation is a product of a particular cultural moment, it is also a product of R-rated constraints. The interplay of all these factors may be discerned in the sequence in *Barbarian Queen II* in which the villain Hofrax (Roger Cudney) exposes the heroine's breasts only to recoil, declaring them "an awesomely disgusting sight." In harder-core films or in verbal media, the misogyny of Hofrax's outburst would likely be applied to female genitals. But like rape simulations, labial and vaginal references are off-limits to the R-rated *Barbarian Queen* films, by default shifting the misogynistic onus to the breasts.

The Corman vehicles are exceptional not in their rape imagery, which is no more than a timid pattern of allusions, but in the diegetic contortions that the use of this material sets in motion. Corman is famous for plots with left leanings, so it is predictable that the adoption of uniquely sensitive material exacerbates this tendency. The resulting agitprop obscures the classic rape-revenge mechanisms outlined by Clover. Throughout *Barbarian Queen*, women fight alongside men, handling weapons skillfully. Though victim-heroes are in evidence, most of these women are not compelled to fight.[18] Alloyed to this spectacle is a thin anti-authoritarian rhetoric that in combination with rape-revenge arcs yields feminist import. *Barbarian Queen II* best articulates this political content. Unlike the heroine of *Barbarian Queen*, who accepts her transformation into a bride, the sequel's heroine violently opposes a similar metamorphosis into a "lady."[19] This opening vision of resistance is supplemented by the heroine's later encounters with female vigilantes and matriarchal rebel bands. Through violence (mud wrestling), the heroine proves that she is not "too much of a lady to be of any use" to the rebels. Her feminist arete is matched by her strident principles,

"Spicy, but Not Obscene" | 103

Figure 10. Sexploitation-style promotional art for the *Barbarian Queen* films. © Concorde—New Horizons and Roger Corman, 1985, 1989, 2003.

which are evident early on when she asserts that "men don't understand power—they think all it's good for is getting more."

Despite this independent streak, Corman's *Barbarian Queen* films work toward patriarchal resolutions. The feminism of these films—which, as noted, is a function of the particular spectacle that they exploit—put the Corman teams at pains to differentiate their vision from "actual" feminist militancy, which they presumed would alienate audiences that enjoyed the roughie-kinky imagery. As a result, these films follow the postfeminist contours of Corman's first New World film, *The Student Nurses,* in which empowered babes experience problems inspired by patriarchal institutions but mostly work within the patriarchy for progress. The only difference is that, in the 1980s films, the patriarchal content seems exaggerated to offset the exaggerated feminism.

The plot of *Barbarian Queen II* is exemplary. The film develops a vision of female solidarity yet still foregrounds the symbology of potency, paternity, and kingship, with the plot hinging on the heroine's patriarchal loyalty. On hearing of her father's death, this female Telemachus earns the enmity of Hofrax by refusing to divulge the secret of her father's magic scepter, the guarantor of kingship. Her rationale is that she has not viewed her father's corpse. Should she use the scepter while her father is alive, he would die. Her loyalty is tested through crises from which she could rescue herself by handling the scepter. Each time, she abstains for love of her father—who it turns out really *is* dead, in a sense rendering the entire plot *de trop*. That the scepter is an eroticized, incestuous sign of the patriarchy and of women's vital but subordinate place within it is acknowledged when she informs her enemies that "having the scepter in your hands does not give you the secret of its power," which cannot be accessed without "the blessing of womankind." This motif is central, then, to forging the "middle feminism" identifiable with Corman since 1970. The wisdom of collaboration is reinforced by two points. First, it is revealed that the "autonomous" female rebels have similar loyalties and want to supplant a specific patriarchy, not *all* patriarchy. Cooperation between the sexes is further justified by the film's portrayal of its supporting villain (Cecilia Tijerina). This young sadist inverts the heroine's feminist virtue by confirming that "girls are stronger than you think" in their equal capacity for evil. A matriarchy ruled by this villainess, it is indicated, would be no less oppressive than a patriarchy ruled by misogynists.

Relative to the Corman heroines, the Sidaris heroines are softer and less political. In this, they hew closer to the postfeminist heroines of contemporary softcore, which is logical given the filmmaker's popularity with late-night programmers from the late 1980s on. The Sidaris vision is also closer to softcore in its pervasive sexualization, which is remarkably free of antisex attitudes. The *Barbarian Queen* films barely qualify as sexploitation, indicating the throwback dishonesty of their exploitation-style video box art, which is far more sexualized than the films. Sidaris's films, by contrast, are all but softcore. *Malibu Express* contains thirteen regularly paced nude sequences, five of which involve active sex. The only element disqualifying these films from softcore designation is that their spectacle more than complies with R limits. (Shots of bumping and grinding are, for instance, rarely held for more than a few seconds.) These independent films also prefigure the contemporary in that they treat men as sculpted sex objects but do not expose male bodies as fully or as often as female. Moreover, the glossy weightlessness of the Sidaris vision anticipates the mood of corporate softcore.

Still, it would be a mistake to lump Sidaris films with more routinized forms. Though these protosoftcore forms exhibit still-extant motifs and register postfeminist anxieties, they are idiosyncratic in imagery and transitional in humor, with a bawdiness rooted in Russ Meyer and burlesque. Indeed, these films throw a unique window onto sexploitation history. Sidaris is the only sexploitation filmmaker that I know of to have directed films in four different decades, all without lapsing into hardcore or Hollywood.[20] Whereas his first films feature classical icons like John Alderman, recent works feature contemporary icons like Julie Strain. Drawing on his classical experience, Sidaris and his independent label, Malibu Bay, made four movies in the 1980s, which led to eight more sex-action films in the 1990s. Sidaris began

Figure 11. Equal-opportunity objectification in the promotional art for Andy Sidaris's *Hard Ticket to Hawaii* (1987). © Malibu Bay and Andy Sidaris, 1987, 2001.

with a female detective in *Stacey* but reverted to a more traditional action hero in *Seven* (1979). After *Malibu Express*, however, he opted for joint protagonists, with female leads gradually overshadowing male.

If the Sidaris hero is thereafter diminished, he is not, as in so many sexploitation progressions, marginalized, for the Sidaris formula relies on the eroticization of men as well as women. Paramount in this formula is not the sex or gender of the object but its conformity with a slick, prepackaged look. Sidaris films thus offer a consumer-oriented democracy of sex-and-gender types. The glossy carnival exhibitionism that drives Sidaris to supply viewers with fancy vehicles, expensive houses, lush locales, campy guns, odd weaponized gizmos, towering explosions, and bloody dismemberments also drives him to provide Playmates, *femmes fatales*, martial arts experts, macho men, *Playgirl* centerfolds, James Bond playboys, bodybuilders, and transvestites. Sidaris, in short, produces eye candy at its most flexibly "pure," achieving on midlevel budgets a diversity and a luster rare in 1980s sexploitation.[21] In *Hard Ticket*'s DVD commentary (2001), Sidaris's wife and producer Arlene Sidaris claims that "the essence" of their popularity is "beautiful people." But what unifies Sidaris spectacle is not traditional beauty so much as visual artifice. This "spectacle for spectacle's sake" leads, as in burlesque, to gender-bending motifs that underscore the constructedness of human appearance.

This thesis is verified by Sidaris's twin sex-and-gender typologies. Sidaris's female imagery ranges from Playmate spectacle, wherein soft, passive women are marginalized as "bimbos," to less conventional spectacle, in which harder, *larger* women conflate sex and death. In the former area are pornographic figures like Faye (Kimberly McArthur) and May (Barbara Edwards), who giggle their way into the hero's boat and shower in *Malibu Express*. In the latter is *Hard Ticket*'s sinister musclewoman (Lory Green), who performs a martial arts routine in body oil and diapers dyed black. The middle is a hybrid space in which traditional beauties play law agents and assassin *femmes fatales*, combining curvaceous femininity with athletic professionalism. These types share a common exterior, so Sidaris differentiates them psychologically. In *Picasso Trigger,* he aligns heroine Donna (Dona Speir) with an interior softness that is naïve, yielding, and loyal, but he aligns *femme fatale* Pantera (Roberta Vasquez) with an interior hardness that is cynical, unyielding, and treacherous. Donna's postfeminist arc is to learn to accept that she can carry a phallic pistol *and* remain true to her internal "woman." In *Hard Ticket,* her coheroine helps her get past any sense of disjunction by counseling anti-intellectual acceptance. When Donna reminds Taryn (Hope Marie Carlton) that "drug-enforcement agents can't afford to get soft," Taryn drops her top for an impromptu shower, blithely asserting, "I'm supposed to be soft, I'm a woman."

The subversive potential of Sidaris's largely amoral approach to sex-and-gender spectacle is, then, counteracted by his postfeminist narrative tendencies, which reconcile the contradictions of said spectacle with mainstream values; this feat is accomplished through the demonization of "excessive" gender constructions and the valorization of neotraditional "tough girls" like Donna and Taryn. But if Sidaris disparages outright gender sabotage, he idealizes a moderate gender reconfiguration. (As Sherrie Inness argues in *Tough Girls: Women Warriors and Wonder Women in Popular Culture* [1999], such neotraditional "play" is common to strong heroines throughout postfeminist culture.) These dynamics are also visible in Sidaris's male typology. The Sidaris men range from ultratraditional to antitraditional, with extremes rendered negative. The musclemen of *Malibu Express*—played by actors hired for biceps and bodybuilding titles, much as the actresses were hired for breasts and *Playboy* credits—are villains. These marginal yet eroticized figures correspond to the "bimbos" in that their acceptance of an established heterosexual identity is exaggerated. Among the male figures occupying the other pole are the transvestites played by Michael Andrews in several Sidaris films. In *Hard Ticket,* his villainous "Michele" persona corresponds with the evil musclewoman in that both adopt an ultratraditional exterior associated with the opposite sex. In the middle reside the sculpted macho men, sinewy martial arts experts, and suave playboys who portray Sidaris's heroes and *hommes fatals*. Sidaris's neotraditional heroes are in-between figures. In men and women, then, Sidaris rewards a moderate gender retooling, which he aligns with virtue, happy endings, and attractiveness. But he also aligns in-betweenness with anxiety. The heroes' covert feminization—rendered as a failure of masculinity, just as Donna is troubled by her sense of feminine inadequacy—is signaled by the inability of the heroes of *Malibu Express, Hard Ticket,* and *Picasso Trigger* to shoot their *excessively* large guns straight. Hence the heroines must often rescue these handsome "ladies' men," a situational vulnerability that reinforces their feminization.[22]

The viewer hardly needs these signals to discern the heroes as feminized. That they are positioned as slick, artificialized objects conveys the *to-be-looked-at-ness* that Laura Mulvey has described as traditional to femininity, especially as constructed by classical Hollywood (19; see also Berger 45–64). Feminization is, then, most obvious among the most artificial males. Sidaris's transvestites confirm this point—but it also holds true for the hypermasculine men, whose feminization is reinforced by a stereotypic vanity and fussiness and by sexual ambivalence. Sidaris's principal male types are all, in fact, epicene—and they all displace their feminization onto others, yielding a motif that slips smoothly from one type to the next. Witness *Malibu Express*, in which Cody (Darby Hinton), the macho hero, differentiates himself from Stuart (Andrews), the closeted transvestite, by labeling the latter "light in his loafers." Cody's sexuality is then questioned by other men, including a highly artificial muscleman (John Brown) who mocks Cody as a "pretty boy" only to problematize his own masculinity by asserting that he may "wanna fuck [Cody]." The broader question raised by these characterizations is whether any male treated as an exemplar of a prefabricated look can ever "be" masculine, given that masculinity is aligned with nature. Cody's macho "prettiness" exemplifies this dilemma. Though based on a 1980s type popularized by Tom Selleck (Magnum, P.I., is Cody's direct model), Cody's look has a long history in gay iconography. Macho is the "conscious deployment of *signs* of masculinity" and thus an "exaggerated masculinity" whose "exaggeratedness marks it off from the conventional masculine look on which it is based" (Dyer, *Matter* 42, 40; Dyer's italics). Such visual excess undercuts macho's naturalness, transforming its working-class symbols into "pure signs of eroticism" (Dyer, *Matter* 40). This combination of excess and eroticism is what attracts Sidaris to macho. Ultimately, his preference for the "spectacular" male means that unproblematic depictions of masculinity elude him. The diegetic signals outlined above may be Sidaris's wry acknowledgment of the inevitable gender inadequacy encoded in his visual practices.

It is notable that the pleasure that the director and his producer wife take from their movies transcends traditional and neotraditional categories. Sidaris has an impolitic habit of dissecting female parts in his DVD commentaries—in his *Hard Ticket* remarks, he points out "some beautiful, large, American breasts," all but neglecting the "cute little thing" attached to them—so it is interesting that Arlene also admires the chests, arms, and abdomens of their heroes, duplicating the low "male" way in which women ogle men in Sidaris films.[23] Most telling is that the Sidarises are liable to gush in unison in response to characters of either sex. In the *Picasso Trigger* commentary (2001), Arlene directs Sidaris to "look at [Steve Bond's] arms!" "He looks great," Sidaris agrees. "He sure does!" she responds. And both express open-mouthed titillation when reviewing the *Hard Ticket* sequence in which Andrews recalls Vicki Lynn's classic transvestite-striptease performances. The surface aim of Sidaris's glossy burlesque is to satisfy heterosexual tastes—but its deeper, more consumerist thrust may be to assert that identity distinctions need not differentiate or otherwise obstruct spectator pleasure.

So many aspects of Sidaris's *oeuvre* support Judith Butler's analysis that genders are "sustained social performances" (180) that it is worth asking why Sidaris ultimately favors essentialism. Why, that is, does he favor Carlton's character, whose anti-intellectual acceptance of her feminine "softness" contradicts the complexities of her social violence? For one thing, Sidaris is an anti-intellectual himself, so it is not clear that he has explored the implications of his spectacle. But a more satisfying answer discerns the postfeminist logic of Sidaris's neotraditionalism. Given his irrepressible eagerness to please and equally irrepressible sexism, it is predictable that he has proved susceptible to the postfeminist anxieties that in the 1980s compelled producers across sexploitation to embrace female agency. Sidaris thinks that his sexist humor, which the more middlebrow Arlene notably disavows, is funny, *pleasing*, but he is aware that it may give offense. Thus his commentaries alternate between impropriety and defensiveness. It is clear that the same equivocation has led him to develop the paternalistic themes and styles that restrict his development of untraditional pleasures. When justifying his films—often as if in response to a generalized antiporn feminist—Sidaris *always* points to their ostensibly profemale traits. His heroines, he argues in his *Hard Ticket* commentary, "do what they want to do when they want to do it." He extends this to the actresses themselves by noting their authority on his sets, going out of his way to describe how Carlton ghost-directed certain *Hard Ticket* numbers. But he slides into a paternalism that implies female *disempowerment* when he stresses his obligation to avoid putting "our women in compromising situations where blood and guts are graphically shown" (Sidaris and Sidaris, *Bullets* 27).²⁴ Sidaris's postfeminist anxiety has paradoxically encouraged him to "protect" women to accent their self-empowerment. He has also implied that postfeminist anxiety has conditioned his use of traditional styles, including *Hard Ticket*'s soft-focus numbers: "And we do it rather sensuous—and sometimes [they] said, 'oh, you're doing those pictures'—our pictures are so, so sensitive and soft, there's never any mean violence and sexual innuendos."

Sidaris's use of a feminized aesthetic is, then, linked to his gender traditionalism, his paternalism in particular, and is motivated by a postfeminist anxiety. Such anxiety limits his most consumerist visual mechanisms, which tend toward genderless pleasures. This quintessentially postfeminist incitement to gender traditionalism could not have been foreseen by antiporn forces. But if contemporary sexploitation is any index, it has been among their most significant legacies to postfeminist culture.

The decisive factor in the shift from the classical to the contemporary was the gradual move from public to private modes of exhibition, which contributed to upheavals in low-budget genres, including a temporary reduction in sexploitation's explicitness that all but eliminated softcore. An ironic function of this shift was that the classical era's emergent feminization was interrupted as masculinized Hollywood models like the teen sex-com dominated the shrunken sexploitation marketplace. Softcore's return was ensured once premium cable had by the mid-1980s established its middlebrow palate; this eminently safe taste formation would later justify enhancing sexploitation's explicitness. But softcore's exceptionally feminized sensibility was also anticipated by the fact that even masculinized sexploitation forms like teen sex-coms and sex-action dramas bore a postfeminist imprint in the era of Reagan and Rambo. By decade's end, cable programmers favored the softest of these forms, including Sidaris's babes-with-guns cycle. The type of sexploitation that cable liked the most—that is, the *noir*-romance hybrids purveyed by Zalman King and numerous other producers who had incrementally remolded the theatrical erotic thriller into the nontheatrical softcore thriller—were also the upscale forms that led most directly to contemporary softcore.

Locked inside all women was the same secret place where fantasies are born.
—*Delta of Venus* (1995)

Class, Gender, and Genre in Zalman King's "Real High Erotica"

The Conflicting Mandates of Female Fantasy

For two decades, Zalman King has been synonymous with an aspirational form of sexploitation addressed to women. The first decade was King's influential period. Between the 1986 release of Adrian Lyne's lucrative *9½ Weeks*, which King produced and cowrote,[1] and the 1995 release of the Anaïs Nin adaptation *Delta of Venus*, which he directed, the filmmaker made a string of films with elegant production values often financed in part by Hollywood labels. Some of his efforts, like *Two Moon Junction* (1988) and *Wild Orchid* (1990), enjoyed limited theatrical release, while others, like *Red Shoe Diaries* (1990) and *Lake Consequence* (1992), first appeared on cable, with all doing well on video.[2] But King exerted his greatest influence through the softcore serial. In 1992, the *Red Shoe Diaries* (*RSD*) feature spawned the eponymous Showtime series (1992–99), which yielded sixty-seven half-hour featurettes, most of which have a softcore format. More than any other entity, *RSD* proved that a softcore program could deliver consistently high ratings (Bellafante 76; Backstein 308–10).

It is also true that more than any other *individual,* King facilitated the emergence of contemporary softcore, a pornographic genre that has proliferated in nontheatrical niches since 1991. King's upscale models helped reverse sexploitation's decade-long association with teen sex-coms and other timid, lowbrow cycles, opening a respectable path to greater explicitness—

and to the use of a distinctly softcore, narrative-number format. Such was not a distinction that he ever wanted or invoked. Indeed, he has rejected as "a bit humiliating" accounts of himself as a softcore director or "an arty pornographer" (Epstein 3; Sibert 2). Thus his directorial efforts have all along tended to stop shy of a regular softcore format—which even holds true for most of the *RSD* episodes he directed. But his imitators, including his fellow *RSD* directors, have shown no such compunction. If it is not, then, precise to refer to him as a softcore director, it is entirely correct to view him as a decisive figure in softcore's contemporary development.[3]

Given this influence, King's work merits in-depth scrutiny, especially in regard to its feminized, aspirational disposition. It is important to recall here one of the cardinal points of my preceding chapters: King did not invent this paradigm. Rather, he updated strategies that had proved effective for classical filmmakers like Radley Metzger and Joe Sarno.[4] These upscale filmmakers diversified their appeal by crafting aspirational sex films capable of playing all segments of the classical circuit—and, with luck, of crossing into adventurous mainstream houses. The most successful American films in this category, including Sarno's *Inga* and Metzger's *Therese and Isabelle*, stopped short of a narrative-number format—for aspirational sexploiteers were initially leery of adopting an openly pornographic structure. But the success of such films paved the way for more explicit works. The most successful simulation film of all, Just Jaeckin's *Emmanuelle*, was a fully softcore import that secured broad Hollywood distribution by dint of its feminized, soft-focus posture. The *Emmanuelle* phenomenon proved that in a tolerant cultural climate, a softcore vehicle with the "right" ideological contours might achieve a towering success. That this phenomenon was no anomaly was confirmed when the *RSD* serial debuted in 1992. But as in the classical era, contemporary sexploitation moved through increasingly explicit stages before arriving at this breakthrough. What makes King singular is that he made *two* distinct contributions to softcore's renaissance. Not only did he produce the contemporary period's one nonpareil softcore vehicle, he had earlier crafted a number of influential just-shy-of-softcore sexploitation vehicles that heralded softcore's revival. More specifically, his *noir*-romance hybrids hastened the arrival of the period's first softcore subgenre, the softcore thriller—which itself usually figured as a *noir*-romance hybrid with feminized, aspirational contours. In his interview with Linda Ruth Williams, Alexander Gregory Hippolyte (hardcore's "Gregory Dark") indicates that King and *9½ Weeks* had appealed to him, stimulating him to "explore some things" in softcore (*Erotic* 277). King's influence on *Carnal Crimes* (1991), the first contemporary American softcore film and the first fully softcore thriller, is clear, as is true of many softcore thrillers produced by Axis. The popularity of these nontheatrical films prompted Showtime to commission *RSD*. (See chapter 7.)

The key to King's success was his early realization that premium cable was predisposed to his feminized brand of arthouse eroticism. Recognizing that "if you don't have distribution, you're really in trouble" (Armstrong 2), King has throughout his career striven to create sexploitation vehicles that, by fomenting the least distribution resistance, flow through as many channels as possible. It made sense, then, that he prioritized the taste formations favored by cable programmers, for what sells on cable sells on video. (The converse has not held true nearly as often.) King has thus been most outspoken in targeting the female audiences most prized by cable programmers—but as he freely admits (Armstrong 4; Epstein 3), and as Linda Ruth Williams points out (*Erotic* 129), his synthesis of light suspense, romance, and nudity appeals to "mixed-gender consumers." His *noir*-romance hybrids were, then, engineered to prosper in a variety of nontheatrical niches. In this, King resembles Metzger more than anyone else. As a producer-distributor, Metzger claimed to target "'sophisticated married couples,'" but he also outfitted his "art-porn hybrid" to circulate among distinctly classed sites, including drive-ins, grindhouses, arthouses, and even mainstream theaters (Gorfinkel 30, 28).

King's followers learned from King what Metzger's followers had learned from Metzger: that feminized, aspirational paradigms make it possible to disseminate softcore pornography in the broadest array of outlets, including some fairly mainstream ones. For that reason, it is by no means startling that contemporary softcore has grown increasingly dismissive of men in narratives aimed primarily at women—despite the fact that even the most female-oriented vehicles remain dependent on heterosexual male audiences, as indicated by the genre's patently unequal reliance on female nudity. Such narratives often bolster postfeminist oppositions between a low, voyeuristic male heterosexuality that is at best undiscriminating and at worst barbaric and a more complex, mysterious, middlebrow female heterosexuality. Though King is hardly dismissive of male sexuality, by routinely subordinating it to a "higher" female eroticism, he fostered the masochistic mold in which later softcore films would appeal to heterosexual male viewers.

King's fascination with female sexual fantasy is responsible for his main formal legacies to softcore, which include an expressionistic stylization that is most evident in his sexual spectacle. These legacies also include a narrative formula in which romance motifs slowly overshadow *noir*-inflected motifs. King's staple characters, a white middlebrow female protagonist and a low white hero, undergo inverse transformations during his narrative. As a result of an "awakening" triggered by the hero, the heroine becomes more assertive in her sexual desires. Conversely, the hero, who first resembles a noirish *homme fatal*, becomes less assertive, revealing a sentimental streak. Hence, the anxiety induced in the heroine by the hero's "exotic" otherness diminishes as the narrative proceeds. In the end, the low hero's middlebrow reformation establishes him as the crux of King's postfeminist effort to satisfy dual audience yearnings: one for a "consumerist" exploration of sexual desire through spectacle-based narrative development and the other for a more traditionalist assertion of heterosexual romantic values through narrative closure. Put most simply, the low male is intricately feminized in conformity with ideologically polarized perceptions of female fantasy.

After briefly surveying King's aesthetic, I explore these diegetic patterns in detail. Unlike the *RSD* serial, which has been treated by a number of scholars, King's crucial early features have not been adequately critiqued. Hence they serve as the main objects of my analysis, with *Two Moon* serving as my default text.

I. THE INTERPLAY OF STYLE, SPECTACLE, AND NARRATIVE

King's signature style has, it seems, occasioned a signature scorn. Consider that noted softcore director Tom Lazarus has defined the phrase "to Zalman King it up" as the production of "manipulated, over-produced, dissolve-riddled, non-linear-because-they're-afraid-to-deal-with-sex-head-on, soft-focus-fluff" (Andrews, "Personal" 28–29; 27). Such mockery of "the Zalmanesque" is itself telling, for it verifies King's cultural penetration while revealing a traditional elitist distaste for the feminized middlebrow. Thus, as noted in chapter 2, a similar invective once greeted the similarly stylized films of Metzger and Jaeckin.[5] Lazarus's swipe is also instructive in that it isolates King's expressionistic, antirealistic thrust, which departs from the mainstream cinematic values derived from classical Hollywood realism. King's sensuous aestheticization is a direct complement of his thematic obsession with female fantasy. In features like *Two Moon* and *Delta* (and in many *RSD* featurettes), this erotic theme introduces fissures of ambiguity that the dreamy, Zalmanesque style only widens. But the most notable aspect of this stylization is indirect: King's signature aesthetic performs subtle antipornographic functions crucial to his just-shy-of-softcore distribution strategy.

King's most obvious artifice is visual. Besides using soft lighting, lenses, and filters, he softens his surfaces through saturated coloration, plush draperies and fashions, slow motion, and *very* languid pacing. King heightens these effects in his editing, which relies on dissolves, fades, wipes, graphic matches, and other heavily worked surfaces. He also makes liberal use of montage as a shorthand for romance or nostalgia. His locations are opulent, including the business backdrops determined by his cable-friendly interest in career women[6]—though King's dips into exotic spectacle, especially in moments of lush, carnival kink, have occasioned a very different opulence. But if this is a cinema of sensual excess, it is also postfeminist cinema that aspires to middlebrow esteem, not to lowbrow shock. Through continuity devices, King muffles shock, enhancing the dreamy sexuality of an *oeuvre* that might be identified as "David Lynch lite."[7]

King's use of smooth jazz is another component of his oneiric style—not to mention an influential motif in its own right. Used as a nondiegetic accompaniment to sexual spectacle, smooth jazz is so automatic in today's softcore that it is possible to forget that the device is an arbitrary product of history derived from postwar stereotypes associating sex and sax. Smooth jazz became a sexploitation staple in the nontheatrical erotic thrillers of the late 1980s—and by the mid-1990s, King's recycling of George Clinton's scores had cemented smooth jazz into a *de rigueur* softcore convention. Clinton worked with King on the production of *Wild Orchid II* (1992) and indelibly marked softcore through his compositions for the *RSD* serial. This partnership guaranteed the livelihoods of later softcore impresarios like Herman Beeftink and Nicholas Rivera, who remained rooted in the industry that crossover innovators like King and Clinton fostered. Of course, King's scores do make use of other types of music. King often opts for classical, which is apt given his aspirational thrust. No less typically, he selects a youthful pop. But because his main address has been to middlebrow taste formations, smooth jazz has long been his most reliably "tasteful" erotic sound.[8]

King's most idiosyncratic aural devices for creating an oneiric mood are verbal and literary. Here it should be specified that these soft, sensuous effects are elaborately gendered and classed. In her article on the *RSD* serial, Nina Martin points out that King's work "contains many characteristics of 'women's' genres," notably "romance novels and 'feminine' fiction" (47). King's reliance on the literary is an extension of the middlebrow stress that these "female" genres place on literariness itself.[9] It is also an extension of the aspirational tactics of Metzger, Sarno, Jaeckin, and even Alan Roberts—though King has deployed these flourishes more fully than his precursors. The most striking (and to my taste *grating*) trait of the *RSD* serial is its repetition of discursive phrases, a tic present in King features that rely on voice-overs motivated by a literary frame device. Thus, in both the *RSD* serial and feature, voice-overs articulate the diary entries; similarly, in *Delta*, they voice the heroine's forays into literary erotica. The ambiguities of these tropes, which alternate between fantasy and experience, serve as the self-reflexive theme of the voice-overs themselves. Witness the *RSD* featurette "Auto Erotica" (1992), wherein the heroine often asks, "Was he real, or did I make him up?" King works this question into an incantation so as to heighten the episode's air of indeterminacy.

If King's moody style feminizes his work in a class-oriented fashion, it does so in part by restricting sexualization. In sexploitation, the dual utility of soft stylization has long been to convey sexual content *and* to render it inexplicit. In King's filmy scheme, sexual atmosphere displaces sexual detail such that viewer pleasure is contingent on empathy as well as voyeurism. In "Auto Erotica," for instance, discursive repetition is one of many devices expressive of the hero's disorientation of the heroine, whose fractured perceptions are further fragmented through recollection; the goal of this technique is to elicit viewer identification with the heroine's erotic predicament. King has confirmed that his narrative model is rooted in romance, not porn (Armstrong 4), so it is notable that romance fiction uses style and metaphor to similar ends. As Jan Cohn has argued, romance writers "reach for high-flown, often tortured attempts at erotic metaphor," culminating in a hazy "discourse thick with sensuality" (25, 26). The writer's expressionistic goal is to recapitulate within the presumably female reader the heroine's roiled psychology during her conflicted encounters with the hero, whose words "more than his actions carry the force of his sexual potency" (26).

The director's stylistic signatures are, then, of considerable psychological import. This dimension is also crucial in that it allows King to classify his own work as "real high erotica," which he defines as sexualized forms based "heavily in the characters . . . you identify with the character and you take the journey with the character" (Kleinman 6, 5). Conversely, he links "low" or "bad" erotica to the abandonment of psychology—and, by extension, of viewer identification with the heroine's psychosexual "journey"—in favor of a harder, blanker explicitness. It might be surmised, then, that in King's *oeuvre* aspirational style fortifies narrative development and suppresses "bad" pornographic elements. King's stylization also foments narrative-spectacle integration, allowing him to suppress the pornographic in another fundamental way: by thwarting the emergence of a regular narrative-number softcore structure.

Here again the filmmaker's reliance on romance motifs is integral to his just-shy-of-softcore stance. King's most obvious debt to romance is not his style but his use of the "virtuous heroine," a figure who has also discouraged the emergence of pornographic dichotomies in fiction. Though romance publishers have satisfied increasing consumer demand for sex (Cohn 25n14), they have refused to muddle the genre's identity by hewing too closely to literary erotica, a more flexible category that often does imply a pornographic structure. As a result, "hot" imprints like Silhouette's Desire label do not achieve a narrative-number structure.[10] In romance, the central limit on the development of regular "numbers" is the use of a center of consciousness (i.e., the heroine) who remains faithful to unwilled erotic feelings instilled in her by the hero.

Similar restrictions limit the spectacle in King's early films, wherein heroines usually obsess over one male.[11] In those features that most resemble romance, especially *Two Moon* and *Wild Orchid*, the narratives work to establish a sustainable relationship between the principals and end happily. These principals engage in sex prior to closure; in *Two Moon*, April (Sherilyn Fenn) has sex with Perry (Richard Tyson) three times before their resolving tryst. But such scenes are tame. Even in films with ambivalent (*9½ Weeks, Lake Consequence, Delta*) or unhappy endings (the *RSD* feature), the heroines remain fixed on one male character, with punitive conclusions threatening only those heroines who betray domestic relationships (*RSD, Lake Consequence*). Particularly in *9½ Weeks, Wild Orchid II*, and *Delta*—which in addition to the abundant sex contain sex-underworld subplots, a staple of porn—the potential to organize erotic spectacle into sexual numbers is there. But by stressing psychological development diegetically and stylistically, King remained only "halfway across the river" throughout this career phase (Armstrong 2). Even in the *RSD* featurettes he directed—which were more pervasively eroticized than his earlier projects and far shorter, containing less room for plot—King avoided obvious descents into "bad" softcore. He managed this feat through irregular pacing, interspersing his story lines with uneven doses of spectacle. But he also managed it by amplifying his already thick stylization (*viz.*, "Auto Erotica"), a strategy whose triple antipornographic function was to claim aesthetic distinction, to limit explicitness, and to enhance identification with the heroine all at once.

II. THE MANIFOLD TRANSFORMATIONS OF A LOW HERO

Although romance motifs play a decisive role in King's early features, it is easy to oversimplify them by overlooking that they engage in a dynamic interplay with motifs from the woman's film,[12] classic *noir*, and the erotic thriller. Though secondary to the heroine, King's low male hero is complex and has elaborately gendered narrative functions. In *Men, Women, and Chain Saws* (1992), Carol Clover proposes that "the sex of a character proceeds from the gender of the [narrative] function he or she represents" (16). But as she also notes, character types embody many functions, which may conflict in their gender coding. The main function of King's low male is to serve as his heroine's heterosexual object, with his literal sex following from this role. But his secondary function is to register the heroine's new assertiveness, which proceeds from the hero's erotic effect. On her sexual "awakening," she grows more masculinized as he grows more feminized; in a sense, he causes his own emasculation. These shifts in the hero's secondary function are reinforced by shifts in the meaning of his class position. At the start, the hero's abjection signifies his raw machismo, which simultaneously agitates the heroine and controls her. At the end, his low status accentuates an emotional vulnerability with a socioeconomic subtext. This play with gender and class reflects a similar play with genre. Thus, by the conclusion, the domesticated hero resembles a traditional romance heroine, implying the heroine's ambivalent elevation to hero status.

As the Mickey Rourke characters of 9½ Weeks and Wild Orchid show, King's low hero is not always low in economic capital—though he does always have a humble backstory that explains his frank sexuality and low mannerisms.[13] That said, the working-class heroes of Two Moon, Lake Consequence, and the RSD feature embody this hero in his "purest" state, for King's impecunious heroes are most clearly identified with animal sexuality and nature. Such depictions are a commonplace of pornographic genres. As Simon Hardy puts it, "to be a working-class man or a black man in a porno narrative is really to say that one has a big cock.... [S]exual potency and lack of social refinement are so closely connected by the text that they become signs for each other" (89–90). What makes King's work distinctive is that in his *oeuvre* these significations are contingent on the intercession of a middlebrow heroine, whose perspective is aligned with the camera, with the viewer, and with social normality. King's bare-chested hero becomes an exotic, "alien" other through the heroine's fetishization of the class and gender gulfs that divide them. In America (as opposed to Britain), this mystification of a working-class white man by a middle-class white woman represents an acceptable use of the exotic. Indeed, this King motif has even drawn praise from American feminists who laud its placement of a woman in the subject position (e.g., Martin 49–50). But the mechanisms that inform this use of the exotic do not essentially distinguish it from King's "exploitation" of blacks and gays as "exotic accents,"[14] a tactic that has outraged reviewers (e.g., Elias 64). Nor is it fundamentally different from historical uses of the exotic to mystify the sexuality of women, nonwhites, and "other" classes, whose exploitation in classical genres has been documented by scholars like Eric Schaefer (*Bold* 277–82).

This classist, sexist dynamic is launched through a paradigmatic scene in which the principals engage in a mutual "first look." In *Two Moon*, April initially observes Perry in a posture that accents his bare chest and mean status as a carnival worker. Similar scenes introduce Tom (Billy Wirth), who plays a construction worker/shoe salesman in *RSD*; Billy (Billy Zane), an itinerant landscaper in *Lake Consequence*; and dozens of heroes in the *RSD* serial, which favors similar class and gender configurations. The low hero's early power over the heroine is all visual: he is a beefcake exhibitionist and a leering voyeur. He attracts the heroine's gaze to his body and then confronts it with his steady return gaze, causing her to flinch; *Lake Consequence* contains a strikingly stylized example of this visual exchange. A central index of the heroine's new masculinization is her eventual mastery of the hero's exhibitionism and voyeurism, which she later confirms by attracting someone else's gaze and then feminizing it into a flinching "glance" through her newly imperious return gaze. These patterns are clearest when, as in *Two Moon*, the heroine subdues the hero himself in this manner (about which more anon).

If King's hero grows more feminized as one index of the heroine's increasing assertiveness, he is also intricately feminized from the start. Though the purely verbal hero of romance fiction also masters the heroine through exhibitionism and a rigid stare, this literary combination does not necessarily entail the hero's feminization. But because King's low male is a specifically visual construct who flaunts his anatomy in a cinematic medium, such behavior automatically complicates his masculinity, for it accentuates his position as object of the heroine's "glance" and of the external viewer's gaze. As a result of this double objectification, King's low male exudes the same Mulveyan *to-be-looked-at-ness* noted of Andy Sidaris's in-between heroes—an epicene trait that King reinforces through other cues like Perry's "Fabio" hair in *Two Moon*. In tandem with this peculiar *to-be-looked-at-ness*, the hero's dark, smoldering sexuality almost inevitably cul-

Figure 12. Soft lighting of the low hero's chest in a frame enlargement from Zalman King's *Two Moon Junction* (1988). © Lorimar, 1988, and Columbia TriStar, 2000.

minates in his configuration as an *homme fatal*. Such characterization represents a further layer of feminization, for as a staple figure of classic *noir* and of the erotic thriller, the *homme fatal* represents an obvious variation on the *femme fatale*.

As a function of his feminization, the hero is often more distinctively eroticized in King's spectacle than the heroine. Unlike full female frontal nudity, which is a stock King motif, full male frontal nudity is only an occasional feature of the director's work. But otherwise, King enthusiastically idealizes the male physique. Witness the sequence in which Perry first seduces April in *Two Moon*. This segment begins with a gender reversal that self-consciously inverts the thousands of female shower scenes that pervade the film's sexploitation precursors: April finds Perry in her shower, where he muses girlishly about the impact of her shampoos and conditioners on his hair. In the seduction scene that follows, King devotes his most lyric visuals to Perry's face and chest. With April in shadow, the camera pans the hero's legs and buttocks, using natural light to accent his curves in a dramatic, expressionistic manner that recalls the *femme fatale* spectacle that opens *Body Heat* (1981). The prevalence of male spectacle throughout King's oeuvre offers a clear indication that his target audience skews female. That the internal viewer of this spectacle is frequently the heroine herself supports such an inference—and, as if any doubt remained, King often refers to his target audience in a literal fashion, as when he has Molly (Margaret Whitton) of *9½ Weeks* yell at her television, clamoring for a soap opera star to doff his shirt. As sexual consumers, King implies, women appreciate "eye candy" as much as men. Only when this fantasy material appears in the flesh (as it does for the heroine) is it cause for anything but benign visual delight.

Which is to imply that when the low hero does materialize, he inspires equivocal emotions that comprise not just sexual desire but anxiety and even disgust. The heroine's genre literacy apparently contributes to her anxiety. Though excited by the hero, she worries that he is only playing with her or, worse, that he is playing her—that is, that his psychosexual gamesmanship signals the stratagems of an *homme fatal*, a type that she plainly recognizes. But the King hero only masquerades as an *homme fatal*; his real deception is to hide the sentimental heart of a middlebrow heroine within the genre trappings of a cynical operator. One reason that the heroine has difficulty discerning his inner sentimentality is that he exposes her to low settings dominated by exotic menace. Often imagined literally through fairs and festivals, this carnivalesque category encompasses any milieu in which classes mingle, upending social convention. Thus in *9½ Weeks* this category includes an open market, a street festival, and a red-light district. A standard *noir* motif (see Naremore 229), such backdrops disorient, disarm, and disrobe the heroine. Because the hero has insight into these "other" worlds, they are at first an extension of his mysterious mastery. But because they are specifically abject, carnival settings finally dramatize the hero's power to nauseate the heroine.

King uses low heroes in low settings because the low, as a masculinized category, has a tremendous symbolism for the higher, more feminized classes whom his middlebrow heroine represents (and to whom she presumably appeals). "The primary site of contradiction," Peter Stallybrass and Allon White assert, "the site of conflicting desires and mutually incompatible representation, is undoubtedly the 'low.' Again and again we find a striking ambivalence to the representation of the lower strata (of the body, of literature, of society, of place) in which they are both reviled and desired" (4). This bourgeois "ambivalence" verifies that the low is inescapable, for "the top *includes* that low symbolically, as a primary eroticized constituent of its own fantasy life. The result is a mobile, conflictual fusion of power, fear, and desire in the construction of subjectivity: a psychological dependence upon precisely those Others which are being rigorously opposed and excluded at the social level" (5; Stallybrass and White's italics). Stallybrass and White's ideas have obvious application here. King's low heroes are emblematic of the heroine's fantasy life, which fetishizes social elements excluded from her mainstream existence. King manipulates this symbolic relation during the openings of films like *9½ Weeks, Two Moon, RSD,* and *Lake Consequence,* wherein the heroes appear to emerge directly from the heroines' fantasies. Consider the shower sequence early in *Two Moon* in which April imagines a succession of carnival workers, including Perry, *before* actually meeting them. The effect of such tactics is to indicate that these heroes, who appeal to the heroine's "lower body stratum," are an intractable part of her being. But one hazard of experiencing an object previously relegated to fantasy is that it will lose its mystique, becoming an object of simple disgust. This possibility is dramatized via the heroine's repeated descents into carnival, whose drab reality in the end leaves her revolted or just cold. Because carnival is "too disgusting for bourgeois life to endure," as Stallybrass and White put it, "its specular identification [can] only be momentary, fleeting and partial" (183). Hence, even when King's heroine is dominated by her desire for the low, it is clear that her acculturated disgust is only provisionally suspended.[15] Though the standard opening of a King narrative enacts the middlebrow heroine's "return" to the low as an "object of nostalgia, longing and fascination" (Stallybrass and White 191), prolonged exposure to the hero precipitates her rejection of the class formations that he represents. Such a conclusion is facilitated by her new aggressiveness, which only makes her more likely to assert the superiority that structures her social position. For this formula to attain anything like a happy ending, the low hero must shed his distasteful properties, assimilating himself to the heroine's bourgeois attainments.

It is not surprising, then, that in King's early films, the move toward closure precipitates the "subjectification" and demystification of the low male, with each feature except *RSD* revealing that the hero's internal values are closer to the heroine's than his gamesmanship has implied. That *RSD* avoids this pattern—avoids, that is, turning its low male into a Hallmark card—is a function of a screenplay that divides its attention between two males who embody distinct preconceptions of female fantasy. The low male, Tom, is a hypersexualized adventurist. His stunted emotional life is dramatized by his inability to express sincere regret over the heroine's suicide. Indeed, his most telling response to the heroine's death evokes a pornographic sense of the interchangeability of women: "All I know is that they all love shoes, and they go on buying them till they die." The more middlebrow Jake (David Duchovny), by contrast, satisfies a stereotypically female longing for a family man whose undying commitment certifies his adoration of his lover as an individual. As a result, he is rendered as a bland, almost neuter sentimentalist whose haunting, vaguely self-righteous sense of loss is perpetuated in his ongoing role as the host of the *RSD* serial.[16] This distillation of two separate fantasies into two separate fantasy men is a departure from King's typical scheme, which fulfills a low, consumerist fantasy of sex in its beginning and middle and a more domestic, traditional fantasy of love in its conclusion—all through the same low figure.[17]

King anticipates this emergent understanding of his low hero through stock signals. Like artists in other popular genres, King links dog ownership to a sentimental paternalism. This predictor of the *homme fatal*'s nonfatality is present in *Two Moon* and *RSD*,[18] with a parallel symbolism generated via the hero's relationship with a mysterious waif in *Wild Orchid*. In a related cue, the hero demystifies his otherness by situating it as the legacy of a fractured childhood. Thus he suppresses one feminized quality (his erotic otherness) in favor of new ones (his emotional vulnerability, his repressed desire for love and commitment, etc.).[19] At the end of *9½ Weeks* and *Wild Orchid*, the Rourke character discloses childhood details in a last-ditch effort to win the heroine. Though it fails in *9½ Weeks*, this ploy works in *Wild Orchid*, mainly because the hero has yet to consummate his affair with the heroine (Carré Otis). *Two Moon*'s Perry refers obliquely to his own troubled boyhood through his mockery of April as a sheltered suburban "princess." In *Lake Consequence*, Billy persuades Irene (Joan Severance) to return to her boy, sparing him the pain that Billy endured in his own childhood. By depicting one of its principals as an adulterous parent, the erotic thriller almost always foreshadows an anticonsumerist dénouement steeped in guilt and punishment; this was the formula exploited by *Fatal Attraction* and its myriad imitators, including Lyne's own *Unfaithful* (2002). In *Lake Consequence,* Irene's boy represents the potential for such guilt.

The most significant aspect of the low hero's transformation is financial. King's low males either need money or have been driven by boyhood deprivations to spend their lives amassing it. Nevertheless, these men ignore financial incentives when dealing with heroines, certifying the purity of their feelings. In *Wild Orchid,* the hero purchases a key property in a maneuver that threatens to ruin the heroine's first professional assignment, which appears to substantiate her view of him as an *homme fatal.* Later, he quietly signs the property over to her, but only after their relationship appears dead—as if to prove that in pursuing the property he was neither buying her affection nor looking for financial gain. The impecunious heroes of *Two Moon* and *Lake Consequence* evince the same disinterest. In *Two Moon,* Perry returns a wallet to April after cavalierly picking her pocket, throws a wad of cash at a freakish carnival operator (Herve Villaichez), and at his most dire moment refuses April's five-thousand-dollar bribe to leave her alone. Such scruples prove pivotal in courtship. April's grandmother (Louise Fletcher) has promised her a great inheritance if she marries a bland fiancé (future softcore icon Martin Hewitt) who belongs to her social set. April almost does—but in the climax, her grandmother, hoping to coax her to the altar, fabricates a story that depicts Perry as an extortionist. Recognizing the canard, April musters the courage to abandon her class.

Here the resemblance to romance is striking. Though the wealthy, controlling Rourke type matches the Silhouette guidelines for a romance hero (see Cohn 42), King's impoverished male has an intriguing link to a different romance figure: the heroine. Cohn argues that romance fiction concerns the heroine's fragile economic position in a society in which marriage remains a woman's surest path to security (3).[20] Because economics lie at the heart of romance, they also inform its ideas of virtue. For this reason, "[r]omance vigilantly protects the heroine's economic innocence; it is more precious than her chastity" (Cohn 46). The heroines of postfeminist romance may dabble in premarital sex but may never marry for financial ends—may never, that is, embody the identifying trait of that most reviled romantic type, the gold digger. Indeed, Cohn views the heroine's irresistible eroticization in the presence of the hero as an elaborate proof that his appeal to her is unwilled and thus financially disinterested (29–30).

Given his distress, the disinterest of the impoverished King hero represents a diegetic gambit that defends his "economic innocence" as steadfastly as romance defends that of its heroine. It also feminizes him by placing him at the mercy of others, for as Clover puts it, "those who save themselves are male, and those who are saved by others are female" (59). Occasionally, this pecuniary weakness is literalized through physical altercations in which "male victims are shown in feminine postures" (Clover 12). In *Two Moon*, Perry's most noble and ostentatious act of disinterest, flinging cash at the carnival operator who pinches pennies on safety, precipitates a confrontation in which he is beaten and his dog knifed. April and a low female, Patti Jean (Kristy McNichol), manage to extricate him from his savage beating, but this rescue does not staunch his economic bleeding. He is dismissed from the carnival, where he enjoyed limited sway, sinking ever lower in status. It is almost too obvious to point out that Perry's concluding "conquest" of April—who, even if she forfeits her grandmother's property, has a lawyer's future—may be read as her rescue of him, a character of few resources and fewer prospects. Variations on this scenario inform not just *Two Moon* but the many King projects using low heroes.[21] That this feminized economic innocence is even written into the low hero of *Return to Two Moon Junction* (1993), a sequel that credits King only for his characters, suggests how basic this motif is to the filmmaker's narrative formula.[22]

It is possible, then, to read the low hero's narrative subjectification, through which he loses the "mystery" crucial to his initial *homme fatal* mystique, as a narrative-spectacle trade-off. A figure like Perry sacrifices the feminization of his "otherness," while gaining the feminization implicit to his growing passivity and vulnerability, his new function as the character who is acted upon, who is rescued. Hence he comes to resemble the traditional romance heroine, whose subjectivity is qualified by the thrall in which the hero's brute sensuality holds her. Such heroines are "enslaved" through their inert gaze at an active exhibitionist. On the other hand, King's heroines learn to wield an aspect of the *homme fatal*'s (and *femme fatale*'s) mystique and ultimately offer a contrast with the traditional romance heroine. In a sense, she becomes more like the romance hero. As the narrative waxes, figures like April or Elena (Audie England) of *Delta* harness their own exhibitionism, gaining active power over men, with this enhanced agency also duplicated in nonsexual aspects of their lives.

It is instructive that the middlebrow heroine does not necessarily welcome the hero's reformation. Indeed, in several King projects, she greets his symbolic shift from Sex to Love with disgust. If the romance novel heroine instinctively uses romance to achieve financial security, the King heroine, who often already has security, is intent on romance itself, which she equates with an erotic mystery desirable in its own right. These heroines want to become mysterious-objects-of-desire and want their lovers to remain mysterious-objects-of-desire. In the *RSD* feature, Alex (Brigitte Bako) is motivated to pursue her affair with Tom by her recognition that she and her fiancé Jake have become so familiar, so dully transparent to one another, as to represent a single subjective entity. "I want my mystery back," she exclaims in her diary, a confession that signals both self-disgust and disgust with Jake.[23] By contrast, throughout their emphatically sexual affair, she and Tom remain opaque to one another, sustaining their mutually pleasurable otherness through an uneasy, erotic two-step of verbal one-upmanship and rough sex. But if prolonged contact leads to the demystification of the low hero, the King heroine's middlebrow distaste for his low status returns to the fore, thus proving Stallybrass and White's point that "disgust always bears the imprint of desire" (191). In short, the disgust that initially intrigued the heroine *qua* desire is redirected at the male, with her new animus intensified by previously fetishized class differences.

Hence the King feature reveals a basic contradiction in the Western ideology of romance, which constructs otherness *and* identification as "romantic." In the timeless manner of Hollywood melodrama, films like *Two Moon* and *Lake Consequence* smooth over this kink to achieve happy endings. The abrupt transformation of the heroine—who embraces a stereotypically female idea of love and security, unaccountably renouncing the pleasures of adventurism—and the gradual transformation of the hero are crucial to such endings. In this respect, the *RSD* feature is more consistent in its sad ending, which necessitates no improbable character shifts. The suicide of its heroine may be read as an admission that romance, no matter how untraditional, wends back to the same tedium.[24] Like desire itself, such realizations are not easily gotten over.

III. CONFLICTING IDEAS OF FEMALE FANTASY IN *TWO MOON*

A concise look at *Two Moon*'s dénouement adds detail to the above. In *Two Moon*, the heroine articulates an increasingly disgusted disillusionment with the hero in a mildly sadistic pattern that dovetails with her growing domination of their relationship. April first expresses distaste at Perry's deportment (in this case, his binge drinking) just after their first tryst and just prior to his confrontation with the carnival operator, a trajectory that strips several layers from his already diminished mystique. Rather than rebutting April's condescension, Perry lamely (albeit accurately, in a sense) insinuates that she has somehow appropriated his "mojo": "The lady's gotta secret, dontcha? I ain't got no secret. I ain't got nothin' except a bike and a truck—and a post-office box in Clearwater, Florida." Soon after their second tryst, April again chastises Perry, this time for making a pass at the motel "help." She vents her scorn in violent, masculinized curses that culminate in her emphatic assertion that Perry is "beyond social redemption." This pattern of disgust and abuse is crowned when she lambastes him one last time prior to their final tryst. Her commentary concisely reflects the oscillation between disgust and desire standard to King's middlebrow heroines:

"You know, you're a real son of a bitch. At first you excited me. Now you repulse me. You've got no mystery. Everything you are—"
"—is between my legs."

That Perry completes April's sentence without disputing her point—his only substantive response is a pointedly masochistic declaration of love—suggests the feminized passivity with which he greets her classifying critiques. Two earlier sequences had depicted him as supine during April's attacks; his declaration of love reconfigures such helplessness in verbal terms. This final sequence also contains the imagery of defenselessness, for Perry underlines his transformation into a committed, obeisant lover by showing April his new puppy.[25] In its aggression, his old dog matched his former cockiness; by contrast, his new dog matches his newfound vulnerability. On several symbolic levels, then, Perry acts like a traditional romance heroine proving her fitness for marriage.

April accepts his implicit proposal. She ditches Chad, her fiancé, at the altar, invading Perry's shower in a reversal of his former invasion of her own. In terms of her explicit desire for mystery-based romance, this exchange of potential spouses makes little sense. A pallid but loving member of her class (whom April loves, much as Alex loves Jake in *RSD*), Chad never had mystery for her. But it is also true that by the time she selects her low lover over Chad, the former has long since exhausted his own mystique. On its face, her choice forfeits one tedium-inducing love match for another, sacrificing an inheritance in the bargain. Of course, the force of this monogamous romance, which focuses from the start on April and Perry, is to smooth over this seeming contradiction. Nevertheless, the only way to intellectualize April's choice as a psychosexual decision is by recourse to sadomasochistic logic. Given April's growing taste for sexual agency, it is consistent to think she has chosen Perry because of her power over him, which includes an unchallenged right to humiliate him. April, it seems, prefers being the hero, the top, to being the heroine. Perry, not Chad—who likes to arrange her future a bit neatly—offers her this possibility, justifying the financial risks of her choice.[26]

This admittedly fanciful reading has a twofold appeal: it makes sense in terms of April's development as a "postfeminist consumerist" and in terms of King's parallel development. Consider that April's movement toward a masculinized form of sexual consumerism is implicit from the start. The shower sequence in which she first imagines Perry establishes this trajectory by depicting her as a voyeur intent on self-gratification. Said sequence

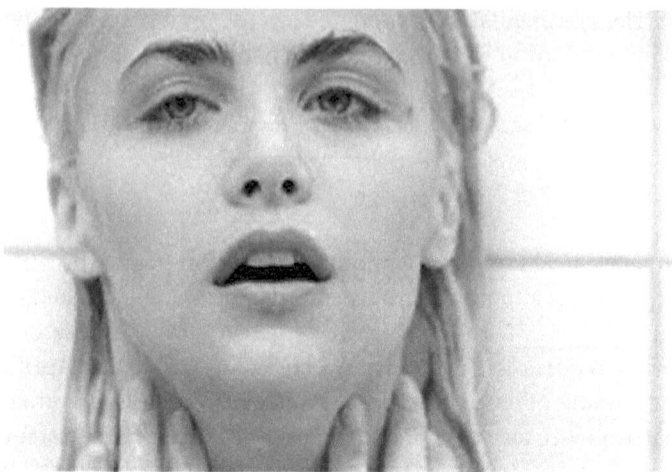

Figure 13. A frame enlargement from the autoerotic shower sequence of Zalman King's *Two Moon Junction* (1988): an immersion in female subjectivity. © Lorimar, 1988, and Columbia TriStar, 2000.

begins in a traditional sexploitation manner: April turns toward the camera, which frames her breasts as the object of the spectacle. This passive vision is modified, though, when she removes a tile from the shower wall, enabling her to peek into a men's locker room—and moving her nipples offscreen. The peephole that frames her gaze aligns her vision of disarticulated penises and buttocks with that of the film's consumer.[27] Unlike the director of a teen sex comedy, King does not play this locker-room voyeurism for laughs. As clarified by subsequent shots of April slipping to the floor and earnestly masturbating, he instead uses it to perpetuate a postfeminist understanding of female autoeroticism as a serious, aesthetic affair bespeaking self-gratification and agency. Indeed, though this shift away from the peephole threatens to "re-reverse" the objectification—that is, to return the spectacle to a more traditional female focus—April's breasts remain marginal to King's composition. In a series of stylish jump cuts that switch from one stern, literally steamy shot of April's face to the next (there are seven in all), King instead sinks the viewer into his heroine's autoerotic fantasy, reminding the viewer of the subjectifying effect originally enjoyed by this facial motif in postwar art films and their classical sexploitation imitators. Among these shots of April's face, King intercuts three shots of straining male bodies. Having noticed the portentous arrival of a carnival in an earlier scene, the heroine now imagines the carnival workers themselves, using her locker-room visions to flesh them out, so to speak. As she reaches orgasm, her fantasy fixes on Perry, whose face and chest emerge in her consciousness. King then fabricates a graphic match comprising several male chests. He manipulates this continuity device as a bridge to his next sequence—wherein April visits the carnival and meets Perry, who is now situated ambiguously as a fantasy-sprung-to-life.

At the start, then, April is positioned as an active voyeur, an active subject; by the end, she has become an active exhibitionist, an active object. The film's succession of shower scenes chronicles the integration of these distinct forms of agency, with the final one—in which April invades Perry's shower, seducing him in a reversal of his inaugural seduction of her—serving as a resolving flourish. During the earlier seduction, Perry had observed that her self-paralyzing stare at his body had authorized his forwardness. "You invited me," he whispers huskily. "It's all right there in your eyes." Though feminists have often insisted that the gaze *is* agency, King's romance sensibility reminds us that an opposite tradition aligns the gaze with the loss of agency. (Similarly, Perry loses control over the course of the diegesis even though he is increasingly subjectified through scenes that align the camera with his perspective. The subject position guarantees sympathy, not power.) It is no accident, then, that as a prelude to their climactic tryst, April strips and dons a blindfold, forfeiting her voyeurism so as to isolate and perfect her exhibitionism. She then parades in front of the enthralled Perry before tearing at his clothes. King thus underlines that April's control is at this stage more active and complete when she is not subject to the gaze. Only at the end, in the shower sequence that concludes the film, is she able to direct an encounter with Perry by exposing herself to him *and* looking him in the eye. Through this incremental development, King also stresses that April has transformed into a sexual consumerist who returns to that which tastes good rather than to that which is mandated by the conventions of class and gender. Consider that April's "ravaging" of Perry during their final tryst at Two Moon Junction completes an earlier scene in which she tears at his clothes in a restaurant, stopping shy of public sex.[28]

Two Moon thus signifies an early step in King's invention of an idiosyncratic, postfeminist sensibility stressing female agency as expressed through heterosexual self-gratification. That this consumerist ethic is present throughout King's *oeuvre* supports the sadomasochistic reading of *Two Moon*'s dénouement outlined above. It is notable that King, like his characters, has only gradually adopted this ethic. It is much less apparent, for instance, in *9½ Weeks* than in *Two Moon*. In the earlier film, the heroine (Kim Basinger) experiences an erotic awakening closer to an occupation than to a liberation in that it is controlled by a man and embedded within a sadomasochistic dynamic to which she never fully consents. Her most independent action is walking away—and even this self-liberation is qualified insofar as it is her insistence on a traditional romance leading to a traditional family. *Delta* also ends with the heroine leaving the hero, but in its case, the film as a whole supports King's postfeminist construction of it:

> *Delta* is probably the most significant piece because the way we chose to do the story was about a woman who gives up the idea of romance for her own sexual liberation. . . . It really is a feminist movie in a way because she becomes more and more in touch with her own weakness, thinking that a man will supply this romantic idea that she has. As the film progresses she becomes more and more in touch with her own sexuality and sensuality. She takes control of it and by the end of the film she is on her own and forsakes her lover because she is having too much fun being liberated. (Epstein 2)

Delta contains several details—a semiconsensual rape, blacks and gays used as exotic accents, and so on—from which many liberal viewers would no doubt distance themselves. But King is right to label the film "feminist" (though "postfeminist" would more precisely situate the film's apolitical ethos[29]) in that his tendency is to depict heroines as active, independent consumers who satisfy idiosyncratic desires, often without recourse to the restrictions of monogamy. After 1995, new King vehicles like his *ChromiumBlue.com* project (2002) stressed, as he puts it, "recreational sex full on" (Epstein 4). "That's where I'm headed. The women that I know and dig treat sex the way men treat sex. They get the guys they want; they fuck them and go on with their lives."[30]

But because *Two Moon* is less consumerist and pornographic than *Delta*, the sadomasochistic reading of its dénouement is not fully compelling. Though this reading reconciles *Two Moon*'s contradictions by pointing to consumerist tendencies within the text and within King's larger *oeuvre*, it fails to admit that *Two Moon* contains equally real elements that conform to more traditionalist ideas of sex, gender, and love. After all, if the film's dénouement is inconsistent with April's adventurist arc, it *is* consistent with the low hero's transformation into a doggishly loyal mate and with the film's myriad borrowings from romance fiction. Like Perry, then, April is in the end an incoherent figure whose shifting characterization represents King's attempt to satisfy disparate female fantasies. April's abrupt reversion to sentimentality only truly makes sense if it is viewed as a traditional form of narrative closure engineered to satisfy a stereotypical female fantasy that has been deferred as the heroine has explored more consumerist, spectacle-based sexual fantasies. Though King consistently cultivated a sophisticated female demographic, he seldom abandoned the broader audiences favoring traditional outcomes. It is not, then, that he did not personally prefer consumerist endings but that his stress on distribution kept him from unifying his earliest features according to this thematic inflection. Ironically, until

Delta, King's desire to access the broadest markets—a practical expression of his consumerist ethos—restricted his ability to express his "feminist" consumerism in direct, consistent film language.

The *RSD* serial encouraged King to move toward the greater consumerist unity available in a midcareer film like *Delta*. With the pressures of a status-quo, feature-length format removed, the filmmaker opted for a more sexualized structure that relied on even greater flourishes of style to replace the identification mechanisms previously supplied by a traditional narrative line—and to deflect attention from an increasing flirtation with the pornographic. Not surprisingly, in their conclusions, *RSD* featurettes are more likely than King's early features to embrace the psychosexual liberation discernible in the "open" closure of *Delta*. The astonishing success of the *RSD* serial implied an audience for this ideological slant, persuading King to pursue it in subsequent projects. It should be noted, however, that even if the *RSD* serial's consumerist, hypersexual format foregrounded the untraditional,[31] it did not entirely discourage the traditional. The guarantor of *RSD*'s "productivist" undercurrent was Jake, the host that functions as a static female fantasy of heterosexual romance *qua* commitment and identification. As such, Jake often acts as a reminder of the costs of a mystery-based adventurism. Even *RSD*'s most liberated, pornographic featurettes return at the end to the grief-obsessed sentimentalist of the *RSD* feature. This structural alternation at times effects the same narrative and ideological "whiplash" induced by *Two Moon*'s contradictory conclusion.

Jake's function has not been fully understood. In "*Red Shoe Diaries:* Sexual Fantasy and the Construction of the (Hetero)sexual Woman" (1994), Nina Martin observes that using Jake as a commentator on female-authored letters precipitates a "conflict in the subjective control of the narrative. . . . [A]ny freedom of female sexual expression exhibited in the [letters] is impinged upon by Jake's own subjective desires and imperatives" (45). Because Jake's perspective is informed by the grief produced by Alex's adventurism, he punishes the letter writers "every time they put on the red shoes in what he deems is an inappropriate heterosexual relationship" (Martin 55).[32] Unfortunately, Martin fails to subject Jake to rigorous analysis, construing him instead as an unproblematic exemplar of the patriarchy. Jake *is* a patriarchal figure, but he is also a feminized construct calibrated to an idea of female desire. In concluding with the assertion that what "is important is not necessarily *where* one stands but that no limitations are put on others in some prescriptive definition of feminism and female desire" (56; Martin's italics), Martin thus indicates two blind spots. First, she neglects that some women prefer a "prescriptive definition," and, crucially, that this taste "explains" Jake more than any other determinant. Second, by tacitly downgrading a mainstream female fantasy, Martin places her own narrowly feminist limitation on women's "freedom to construct *any* fantasy" (55; Martin's italics). That King has at once catered to regressive female fantasies and to more progressive, consumerist tastes only proves that we all live within the supple paradox of consumer capitalism, a phase in which consumer forces have had little trouble exploiting anticonsumerist ideologies as different as marriage and modernism.

Zalman King's most significant formal legacies include an oneiric, aspirational stylization and a hybrid narrative model in which motifs derived from romance trump those from *noir*-inflected erotic thrillers. The director's romance motifs are by-products of his cable-friendly interest in female subjectivity—an interest so central that his primary male types are all geared to satisfy divergent preconceptions of female fantasy. These King paradigms had a formative impact on contemporary sexploitation. During a ten-year window that saw the return of the softcore feature, King was crucial to the upscaling of sexploitation, which was in turn crucial to premium cable's willingness to finance and air increasingly sexualized forms. This category eventually included King's *RSD* serial, the longtime Showtime flagship that spawned a very prolific subgenre of softcore serials. Though King has not elicited uniformly positive appraisals from politically minded commentators, the success of his feminized paradigm did inspire cable programmers to commission serials like *Women: Stories of Passion* (1997), which briefly attained darling status among feminists. (See chapter 7.)

The irony of King's success is that it engendered so many imitators, so much lower-cost competition, that his aspirational sexploitation soon lost its hold on the niches that it helped establish. In the late 1990s, King attempted to work within these downward economics, as indicated by his role in features like *A Place Called Truth* (1998), which relied on softcore actresses like Jacqueline Lovell and Kira Reed and softcore distribution through Playboy. In *ChromiumBlue.com*, King revisited his upscale vision of "real high erotica." But by declining to support this lush serial beyond its first thirteen episodes, Showtime confirmed that King's "reign" as the contemporary era's chief "auteur of erotic fantasy" was over (Epstein 3). Nevertheless, given sexploitation's longer history, it seems likely that if King adheres to his feminized, aspirational paradigm long enough—and if he returns to the ideological contradictions that proved so uniquely marketable during the advent of the current softcore cycle—his "phase" will come again.

Sex Is Dangerous, So Satisfy Your Wife
The Softcore Thriller in Its Contexts

When discussing the erotic thriller, critics persistently allude to expensive Hollywood films like *Fatal Attraction* or *Basic Instinct* (1992), as if to imply that such films represent the "essence" of this contemporary genre. This reduction has its rationale. Theatrical erotic thrillers have exerted an undeniable cultural sway—and their economic significance is not to be discounted. Unfortunately, this limited focus has made the genre's lower-budget, nontheatrical forms that much more "invisible."[1] Any honest appraisal of the genre's multiplicity must pay heed to these superabundant thrillers, which have long proliferated on the edges of the mainstream marketplace. The difficulty is that these low-cost vehicles are so manifold in type that no single survey can theorize them in detail, much less situate them in their contexts. Thus the following chapter centers on one subgenre, the softcore erotic thriller or "softcore thriller," and refers to cognate forms mainly to clarify this generic strand. My assumption is that by analyzing one of the erotic thriller's least understood segments we may reorient our understanding of the broader category. Because the softcore thriller was also the first fully softcore category of contemporary sexploitation, this approach has the further benefit of clarifying critical developments in the history of contemporary softcore.

Two other premises are central here. The first is that this heterogeneous field is organized by a uniquely profitable abstraction: *sex is dangerous.* The anxiety of the erotic thriller is a relentless repackaging of this simplification, whose economic potential lies in its combination of sexual mystification and conservatism. As the components of "erotic thriller" indicate, the genre promises a dual spectacle: sexual action and violent suspense. The theatrical erotic thriller often integrates these forms of spectacle, as in the rough-sex idiom popularized by Michael Douglas in *Fatal Attraction, Basic Instinct,* and *Disclosure* (1994). Accordingly, this subgenre tends toward violence throughout its spectacle, precipitating the common view that the "erotic thriller means two minutes of nudity and 60 minutes of violence" (qtd. in Loftus 220). But this perception is myopic. Softcore thrillers, for instance, mostly detach sex from violence. Today, the lowest-budget projects often invert the ratios of theatrical projects, such that well over 50 percent of a softcore thriller's running time is devoted to sex—and such that specialized devices mute the danger and the gore. These polarized affinities lead to my other major premise. The erotic thriller may be framed as a sex-violence continuum in which the two principal formal variables tend in inverse directions depending on industrial factors like budget level, film gauge, and distribution mode. The cheapest softcore thrillers, then, are also apt to be the most sexualized, least violent of mainstream erotic thrillers.[2]

Numerous ideological variables shift in tandem with these formal and industrial determinants. The most salient are sexual attitudes and gender biases. Like the slasher (Clover 21–64), the erotic thriller frames gender as an adjunct of sexuality and thus as a danger in itself. Along with violence, then, certain regressive ideas of gender have contributed to the fearmongering that has limited the sexualization of the theatrical erotic thriller. This inhibition is plainest in noirish vehicles whose misogyny is a function of a persistent linkage of aggressive women and sexual danger. Other segments of the genre, however, rely on an opposite set of gender biases to liberate sexual imagery. As the erotic thriller grows more pornographic, its mood brightens, becoming more postfeminist and consumerist. In accord with other softcore subgenres and in discord with most theatrical erotic thrillers, the softcore thriller is a feminized area tolerant of female sexuality and sanguine anent femininity. But since sexual darkness is a generic necessity—without it, an erotic thriller could scarcely be recognized as such—sex must be poisoned somehow. The onus usually falls on men. Thus the softcore thriller has maintained a jaundiced view of male sexuality as a subordinate yet critical element of its feminized pornographic scheme. The softcore thriller's consumerist thrust is, in short, moderated by its gender specificity, which has liberal and illiberal corollaries. These interlocking biases have been most conspicuous in the subgenre's postfeminist treatment of adultery.

Implicit to the above is that the softcore thriller is neither static nor monolithic. Thus my discussion looks at the subgenre's two most distinctive periods, focusing on the producers representative of each. As it happens, the softcore thriller has never been more distant from its theatrical counterparts than it is today. This stark deviation derives from a more subtle set of divergences that accompanied the introduction of a softcore format into a midbudget cycle that dominated the market for nontheatrical erotic thrillers from 1990 to 1996. (Because this cycle was the first wave of contemporary softcore films, it also dominated the softcore market in said interval.) Though these midbudget softcore thrillers evoke the theatrical erotic thriller's *sex is dangerous* stance, they modify it as well, injecting consumerist nuances like *it is dangerous not to satisfy your spouse* and *it is dangerous not to satisfy yourself.* The cycle's most iconic figure is the housewife who strays from a derelict husband. Though her "awakening" proves disastrous in the short term, it usually effects a bright postfeminist resolution in the end. This character arc in turn motivates a narrative-number format whose sex is not "front-loaded," as in ultraconservative, anticonsumerist films like *Fatal Attraction,* but spread throughout the diegesis. Such patterns have been reinforced by the cheaper, harder-core thrillers that proliferated after 1996, many of which were shot on 16mm and which today may be shot on video. The pornographic temper of these softcore thrillers is made evident by their frank consumerism, which methodically dismisses any character or idea that threatens erotic gratification—or, in more industrial terms, that obstructs the free flow of spectacle. Because contemporary softcore studios have no interest in violating cultural pieties, recent softcore thrillers have tended to opt for unmarried heroines—yet those that *do* opt for married heroines offer an index of the subgenre's heightened consumerism. By the opposite token, even the cheapest, most current softcore thrillers remain reliant on feminization strategies that, in a quintessentially postfeminist dynamic, uphold the gender system and ultimately blunt the subgenre's consumerist thrust.

The sections that follow explore these themes in loosely chronological fashion. The first considers the cultural conditions informing the erotic thriller's initial theatrical popularity; it also briefly analyzes *Fatal Attraction* and *Basic Instinct.* My next section delineates the gradual emergence of the softcore thriller—and, in turn, of contemporary softcore—from a background of less pornographic sexploitation thrillers. The chapter's final segments scrutinize the midbudget softcore thrillers shot on 35mm by Axis and the cheaper, more recent softcore thrillers shot on 16mm by MRG.

I. TWO THEATRICAL EROTIC THRILLERS

The softcore thriller is more directly derived from theatrical erotic thrillers than from the low-budget cycles and subgenres (e.g., the teen sex-com) that dominated sexploitation during the 1980s.[3] The reason for this is readily understood. Unlike classical sexploitation, which in 1960 offered filmgoers a

Figure 14. Glenn Close as Alex Forrest, the psychopathic *femme fatale* of Adrian Lyne's *Fatal Attraction* (1987). Theatrical erotic thrillers in the *Fatal Attraction* mold tend to front-load their sexual spectacle. © Paramount, 1987.

very stark alternative to Code-era Hollywood, contemporary sexploitation tended during the 1980s to emulate big-budget paradigms so as to compete more effectively in home video outlets, which merchandised theatrical and nontheatrical projects side by side. Consequently, it is more informative to ask why Hollywood initially embraced the erotic thriller—as popularized by directors like Brian De Palma (*Dressed to Kill* [1980], *Body Double* [1984], *Femme Fatale* [2002]), Lawrence Kasdan (*Body Heat* [1981]), Adrian Lyne (*Fatal Attraction, Unfaithful* [2002]), Paul Verhoeven (*Basic Instinct*), Uli Edel (*Body of Evidence* [1992]), Phillip Noyce (*Sliver* [1993]), William Friedkin (*Jade* [1995]), and Damian Harris (*Bad Company* [1995])—than to ask why the sexploitation industry did the same.

Noir theorist James Naremore has argued that Hollywood's traditional taste for slick but inexpensive pictures combining sex and violence contributed to the gradual transformation of classic *noir*, whose cynical sexual style was restricted and defined by the Code, into the more explicit erotic thrillers of the New Hollywood (165). The noirish sexuality of this theatrical form has generated the greatest popularity amid moments of cultural anxiety during which the permissiveness precipitated by the sexual revolution has been temporarily repressed. According to Brian McNair, these periods of "porno-fear" include the 1980s and our current decade (*Striptease* 63; see McNair, "Porno-Fear" 17–19). That the genre has capitalized on anticonsumerist (or "productivist") anxiety is understandable. The theatrical erotic thriller in particular gains its regressive mystique from its stylized equation of sex and death; unlike more liberationist forms, its "sexiness" is contingent on the taboos it promises to subvert. To exist at all, the Hollywood erotic thriller requires a degree of permissiveness—hence its post-Code tenure—yet its appeal is most pronounced when such freedom has occasioned unease.

Many factors conditioned the transformation of the porno-chic of the 1970s into the porno-fear of the 1980s. The Reagan revolution was indicative of a broad revulsion against the liberationist "excess" of the 1960s and 1970s. A growing awareness of the AIDS crisis, in tandem with antiporn feminism's equation of pornography with degradation, rape, and murder, redoubled the sense of counterrevolution. That the new mood favored cinema with a *sex is dangerous* slant was indicated by the popularity of films like Paul Schrader's *Hardcore* (1979) and Bob Fosse's *Star 80* (1983). As a depressing "tale of a god-fearing American family torn apart by the wicked ways of the L.A. porn industry" (McNair, "Porno-Fear" 17), Schrader's film was particularly adept at exploiting the new anxieties about cultural pornographication. Soon distributors with sexploitive leanings were commissioning their own antiporn exposés. To cite one case, Vestron Video had Alexander Gregory Hippolyte—who later made influential softcore thrillers for Axis Films International and was as "Gregory Dark" a hardcore director himself—shoot the pseudodocumentary *Fallen Angels* (1985).

The theatrical erotic thriller must be placed in this context. Though a handful of films explore the same seamy territory as Schrader's, few express porno-fear so literally. Instead, they preserve their eroticism by exploiting a generalized "sex-fear" lent gravity by AIDS and feminism. That Lyne's *Fatal Attraction* and Verhoeven's *Basic Instinct*, which Naremore calls the "most commercially successful films noirs ever made" (263),[4] exemplify these dynamics has been suggested by their critics. Thus *Fatal Attraction* has been cited as evidence of a postfeminist "backlash" against feminism as well as a "stern moral lesson for men on the dangers of sexual promiscuity in the time of AIDS" (McNair, *Striptease* 152; see Linda Ruth Williams, *Erotic* 50, 54–55; see also Faludi and Willis). Such readings likewise indicate the exceptional power of these films' *femmes fatales*, Alex Forrest (Glenn Close) and Catherine Tramell (Sharon Stone). According to Naremore, these women are "among the most frightening femmes fatales in the history of movies—chiefly because they are viewed without the constraints of old-fashioned censorship and without the mollifying romanticism of Hollywood in the 1940s" (263).

Because *Fatal Attraction* and *Basic Instinct* have wielded a greater influence on sexploitation thrillers than any other pair of Hollywood films,[5] they merit extensive scrutiny. It is with some regret, then, that I limit myself to basic socioaesthetic insights.[6] Whereas *Fatal Attraction* has a moralistic front-loaded sexual structure, *Basic Instinct* uses a more regular sexual structure that almost qualifies as softcore and that hinges on consumerist detachment. This formal divergence dovetails with the emergence during the five-year period bracketed by these films of the fully softcore thriller from its background of less pornographic, less consumerist sexploitation thrillers.

Like the later *Unfaithful*, *Fatal Attraction* depends on its sex-violence scheme to drive its anticonsumerist arc. (Try to imagine a moralistic, sex-negative film that places its violence first and its sex second.) Lyne's front-loaded spectacle, which includes two inexplicit scenes of boy-girl intercourse and one fellatio number *sans* nudity, is frenetic and brief. It serves as a prelude to a more extensive pattern of rage escalating to violence, which ends when the *femme fatale* is destroyed, restoring The Family. This front-loaded structure clarifies Lyne's point: sex and violence are interrelated frenzies, so sex is nothing to trifle with. Thus the film offers its hero an empathy devoid of sympathy. In this Old Testament vision, Dan Gallagher (Douglas) has cavalierly opted for infidelity and deceit and must reap the whirlwind. Or, as a police character puts it, "it's his bed, I'm afraid he's going to have to lie in it"—with "his bed" figuring as the entire narrative framework. Alex's depiction has more depth. Her psychotic ramblings draw energy from an off-kilter resemblance to feminist rhetoric. Consider her central refusal to be treated "like some slut you can just bang a couple of times and throw in the garbage." Several other elements contribute to the film's rigid didacticism. In the erotic thriller, the presence of a child—the ever-proscriptive Young Person[7]—is a more reliable predictor of a guilt-ridden trajectory than the presence of a spouse alone. But without its front-loaded sexual structure, *Fatal Attraction* would lack both sense and gravity.

The film also contains motifs that the softcore thriller would later remold into the *it's dangerous not to satisfy your spouse* scenario. One of Lyne's subtlest effects is to establish Dan's frustration in a passage nestled between his first encounter with Alex and the segment depicting their affair.[8] In this scene, Dan prepares to go to bed with his wife (Anne Archer) when the latter reminds him to take out the dog. On returning, he finds his young daughter (Ellen Latzen) in bed with his wife, who explains, "It's only for

Figure 15. Sharon Stone as Catherine Tramell, the imperious *femme fatale* with pronounced exhibitionist tendencies in *Basic Instinct* (1992). This theatrical erotic thriller is markedly closer to softcore than earlier films like *Fatal Attraction*. © Carolco, 1992.

tonight, honey." Her implicit promise is qualified by the fact that she is to leave the next morning with their child for a trip to the country—an absence that accommodates his adultery. In a softcore thriller, the director would invert the genders and then shunt the blame onto the spouse, implying he invited his destruction by neglecting his wife's "needs." But because erotic thrillers treat male infidelity as a self-indulgence with lasting effects but no final justification, these motifs remain only nascent in *Fatal Attraction*.

As "the steamiest adult thriller" made for a major studio (O'Toole 152), *Basic Instinct* has a more consumerist appeal. Douglas plays another flawed figure, "castrated cop" Nick Curran (Linda Ruth Williams, *Erotic* 187), whose least sympathetic traits include homophobia and a fetish for rough sex verging on rape. His dalliance with the all-too-menacing *femme fatale* hastens the murder of his cop partner (George Dzundza) and leads him to mistakenly shoot Beth (Jeanne Tripplehorne), a psychologist and former girlfriend whom the film treats more roughly than *noir*'s standard "good girl." But unlike *Fatal Attraction*, *Basic Instinct* does not follow a productivist arc. The victims of Nick's adventurism are "partners," not relatives bound by blood or marriage, so the destruction triggered by his indiscretions seems minimal by comparison.

Informing this contrast is a divergent portrayal of erotic pleasure. Whereas *Fatal Attraction* links such pleasure to Dan's loss of domestic control, *Basic Instinct* links it to Catherine's seamless assertion of a sadistic narrative control. Though ultimately revealed as a calculating murderess, Catherine remains a charismatic artist figure whom filmgoers have admired (McNair, *Striptease* 122). Her most impressive attribute is not her propensity for murder, which is common among *femmes fatales*, but rather her cold assertion of a diverse sexual palate. Asked if she is sorry that a lover has been killed, she replies, "Yeah, I liked fucking him." She offers neither explanation nor apology for her bisexuality and never indicates that she values one sex or gender over another. Catherine also deviates from *noir* models in refusing to assert her power through deceptive conflations of love and lust. Only a lazy egotism convinces Nick that their affair is more than a sadomasochistic partnership. But as with many *noir* heroes, Nick's cynicism is exposed as a flimsy mix of scar tissue and pretense. Though he feigns Catherine's lack of sentiment by calling her "the fuck of the century," he alternates such glibness with softer professions of love and their tacit yearnings for reciprocity.

Catherine's chilly consumerism is intertwined with the film's approximation of a narrative-number format.[9] *Basic Instinct* has five boy-girl, straight-sex sequences, and the director's cut features extensive bumping and grinding in four of five. The film also contains scenes such as the infamous "crotch shot" in which Catherine asserts her power by revealing her body; this blunt exhibitionism complements porn motifs like bondage and girl-girl imagery. Such spectacle is interspersed with the diegesis, with three parallel passages—each dominated by the menacing image of Catherine astride her man—lending the film unity by their placement in the beginning, middle, and end. Unlike *Body of Evidence*, *Basic Instinct* does not use its just-shy-of-softcore format as a basis for *Fatal Attraction*–style moralism. This format is instead inseparable from the film's fascination with Catherine. Because the Hitchcockian plot leaves the killer's identity ambiguous until the closing shot, the film supplies nothing like a "moral center" to support the viewer in adopting something other than aloof detachment. So while *Basic Instinct* never endorses the *femme fatale*, it never develops a critique of her, either, allowing the sex and nudity to flow to the end. In the absence of a more compelling choice, Catherine's consumerist ethos dominates the film, becoming largely identical to it.

Basic Instinct's synthesis of mystery and detachment is a clever integration of story and spectacle. But despite its effectiveness, the film's narrative-number scheme has not become a softcore-thriller cliché because it is difficult to reduce to formula—and too discomfiting for porn. Drawing on Patricia Mellencamp, Stephen Neale argues in his 1980 treatise *Genre* that spectacle offers a break from narrative, "contributing towards an economy which in many ways is the antithesis of that of the genres of suspense" (30). Though applicable to the softcore thriller, these ideas are less applicable to a theatrical film like *Basic Instinct*, whose interlocking numbers are, according to Verhoeven, suspense scenes "disguised" as sex (McQueen; see also Linda Ruth Williams, *Erotic* 243–44). The director has insisted that the film's sex would have been subject to cuts had it *not* been violent, showing one counterintuitive way in which Hollywood has evaded porn's sex-positive ethos.[10] Ergo, tension only escalates in the course of *Basic Instinct*'s spectacle. The viewer fears that Catherine will kill Nick while fucking him, literalizing the *femme fatale*'s most anxious symbolism. In contemporary softcore, where distributors have discouraged producers from crafting ultraviolent numbers, such combinations are rare. Instead, softcore has promoted a consumerist ethic with an optimistic postfeminist inflection, meaning that it is both less violent and less subversive in its ideas of sex and gender.

In retrospect, *Basic Instinct* suggested that porno-fear, which had once helped sell a moralistic eroticism, had receded.[11] After all, by the time that Verhoeven's "licit sex movie" was released in 1992 (O'Toole 152), softcore's rebirth was clear, with sexploitation niches dominated not just by erotic thrillers but by *softcore* thrillers. Naremore claims that *Basic Instinct*'s approximation of a softcore format acknowledged the economic might of a nontheatrical market that would balloon by the mid-1990s into a seventeen-billion-dollar-per-year economy (161–62)—and that the success of this high-profile sex film disseminated the low-budget influence[12] to later major-studio films such as *Sliver*, *Showgirls* (1995), and *Striptease* (1996). The year 1992 also saw a Democrat's election to the White House, signaling the onset of a more tolerant period in which the American government ceased pressing obscenity cases. Not long after, the Internet exploded with porn and the cinema experienced a vogue for *anti*–porno-fear films like *The People vs. Larry Flynt* (1996) and *Boogie Nights* (1997).

II. SEXPLOITATION *NOIR* INTO SOFTCORE *NOIR*

During the transitional interval after *Fatal Attraction*'s release, the market for nontheatrical erotic thrillers lacked the clear lines of demarcation that it would exhibit by 1992. But even before the American release of the first softcore thriller, *Carnal Crimes,* in 1991, nontheatrical erotic thrillers mimicked either *film noir* or the slasher or both. Of these trends, the *noir* impulse was dominant and remains discernible even in today's ultra-low-budget softcore thrillers. Nontheatrical producers privileged *noir* not only because their immediate theatrical models did the same but also because *noir* imagery offered an established stylistic resource long favored by Hollywood and the larger style culture. Such imagery was more familiar than slasher iconography and far more upscale in its appeal.[13] Moreover, even during the Code era, *noir*'s appeal was distinctly sexualized. *Noir* stylization, in short, legitimated sexploitation spectacle even as it augmented the same. However, as early as 1991, softcore thrillers tended to restrict their *noir* iconography in ways that distinguished them from sexploitation thrillers that stopped just shy of a softcore dichotomy. These subtle divergences from *noir* prototypes indicate that *noir* devices presented sexploitation producers with certain problems that became more prohibitive as their narratives became more sexualized. *Noir* effects thought to confer legitimacy on nonsoftcore sexploitation thrillers were viewed by distributors as potentially delegitimizing softcore thrillers. Softcore producers like Hippolyte were thus compelled to improvise a *noir*-romance hybrid that was more independent of theatrical models than earlier contemporary sexploitation subgenres.

Noir posed two practical problems. As we shall see, *noir*-inflected Hollywood erotic thrillers rarely lent themselves to softcore adaptation. For another thing, *noir*'s edginess spooked distributors wary of controversy that might jeopardize fragile corporate alliances. These difficulties were extensions of *noir* fundamentals. Though *noir* is hard to pin down (Rausch 114–19), erotic thrillers seem faithful to it in integrating psychosexual darkness with stylized suspense that embroils cynical, down-on-their-luck antiheroes and treacherous-yet-irresistible *femmes fatales.* From a softcore standpoint, there are two problems with this desolate vision: its use of a male protagonist fails to maximize female spectacle, and its use of the *femme fatale* tends to demonize female sexuality. The latter trait may result in anticonsumerist arcs that further curtail the flow of spectacle, as in *Fatal Attraction.* Even worse, it may be labeled misogynistic. In a postfeminist world, sexploitation producers intent on broad distribution cannot openly exploit female sexuality and openly demean it. Indeed, since *noir* stylization has been favored because its prestige facilitates distribution, such combinations make little sense.

Noir misogyny, it should be noted, is rarely unequivocal. Though positioned as villainous "others," *femmes fatales* like Alex Forrest and Catherine Tramell have an ambiguous righteousness that situates them as sex-and-gender dissidents whose deepest function is to challenge inequity. Indeed, for most of film history, *femmes fatales* have been identified with the transformative depredations of the "modern world," which is forever in danger of slipping from patriarchal control (Pust 77–79; Zizek 8–12; Crowther 115–17). As far back as the silent era, "vamps" like Theda Bara discerned the meaning of their eroticism. "The vampire that I play," Bara remarked, "is vengeance of my sex upon its exploiters. You see, I have the face of a vampire, perhaps, but the heart of a feministe" (qtd. in Pust 79). The masculinity-in-crisis paradigm of "Michael Douglas *noir*" is, then, one phase of an unfolding process. In *noir*-inflected films of all periods and all industrial categories, men condense their frustration into a misogynistic ethos, the crude articulation of which generates indirect sympathy for the *femme fatale*.[14]

That said, feminism and AIDS did contribute to the creation of *femmes fatales* with specific historical resonance. If anything, this currency has been more overt in nonsoftcore sexploitation thrillers than in theatrical erotic thrillers. Directed by Kristine Peterson and produced by Roger Corman's Concorde–New Horizons,[15] *Body Chemistry* (1990) exemplifies such topicality by lifting slogans from second-wave feminism. Hence *femme fatale* Claire Archer (Lisa Pescia) is a sex researcher who proposes "to establish a physiological proof of a well-known social theory that most crimes of violence linked with sex are not about sex at all, they're about power." Though inspired by *Fatal Attraction*, *Body Chemistry* anticipates *Disclosure* in that it has Claire assert professional power by harassing its hero, Tom Redding (Marc Singer). Like the Douglas character in *Fatal Attraction*, Tom imagines that he can have a night of turbulence while his wife is away for a country weekend. Instead, by pressuring Tom to engage in increasingly violent antics, Claire confirms that her thesis—namely, that "the sex drive of the average Joe is driven by some dark desire for domination"—also applies to the average Jo. She destroys Tom's marriage and nearly incinerates his family in a postfeminist dénouement that pointedly revises *Fatal Attraction*. On one hand, the good girl/wife (Anne Archer look-alike Mary Crosby) does *not* stand by her man. On another, the *femme fatale* murders the hero, emerging "victorious" to star in increasingly pornographic sequels.

Body Chemistry generates little *gravitas*. For one thing, Pescia's performance effects the complex vulnerability so crucial to Close's performance only in a discordant closing passage. But the main reason *Body Chemistry* fails to recapture *Fatal Attraction*'s moral heft is that it is itself closer to softcore than its antecedent. *Body Chemistry* deploys twice as many sex sequences as *Fatal Attraction* and features porn motifs that Lyne has resorted to only under the auspices of Zalman King. Hence the flow of erotic spectacle persists much longer than in *Fatal Attraction*. This sexploitation structure undercuts the director's attempt to mimic Lyne's moralistic arc, with Peterson's "front-loading" not front-loaded enough. *Body Chemistry* is in the end too dependent on consumerist titillation to embody *Fatal Attraction*'s antisexual, anticonsumerist logic.

Though *Body Chemistry* contains enough social critique to problematize any tag of misogyny, it risks such designation by using a sadistic, sexualized *femme fatale*. If just-shy-of-softcore sexploitation thrillers like *Body Chemistry* often take this risk, fully softcore thrillers do not, presumably because their pornographic architecture makes *noir*'s misogynistic potential less ambiguous. Predictably, *Basic Instinct*'s imitators are among the minority of softcore thrillers that clearly occupy a "softcore *noir*" niche (rather than *Body Chemistry*'s "sexploitation *noir*" niche). The most successful vehicle in this category may be *I Like to Play Games* (1994), which was made by Cameo Films, a Playboy label.[16] One of few softcore thrillers to have achieved obvious "cult" status, *I Like to Play Games* is energized by the pouty, naughty-girl performance of Lisa Boyle. Boyle plays Suzanne, an ad executive who darkens the outlook of its happy-go-lucky hero, Michael (Ken Steadman). Like Verhoeven's *femme fatale*, Suzanne is a charismatic consumerist who flatly asserts her desire: ceaseless sexual gamesmanship. She disdains Michael's efforts to impose on her a feminized notion of love, insisting instead on her right to find a lover who matches her outlook—and to discard any man who does not. Thus, in a classic *femme fatale* gambit, she enumerates the double standards of the men she spurns. Despite these subversive elements, it is doubtful that many feminists would laud the film given its finale. Until Michael "wins" in the climax by all but drowning her, Suzanne is a bewitching dominatrix who uses the word "love" only as cynical pretense. But after her dunking, she whispers a sincere "I love you" as Michael stalks away. All it takes to win this "witch"—that is, to pacify her, remolding her into the traditional female masochist to whom Michael has no attraction—is a savage, atavistic punishment.

Though dark, this ending still strikes me as a failure of nerve. Relative to other fully softcore films, *I Like to Play Games* is distinguished by its adherence to *noir* prescriptions. Its antihero undergoes a cynical decline; its *femme fatale* is controlling and masculinized; and its stylized diegesis even includes suspenseful sex. But relative to theatrical erotic thrillers, *I Like to Play Games*'s violence is tame. And while the film's ending is antiromantic, no one dies, unless one reads the *femme fatale*'s emasculation as symbolic of her death. (Consider that *Basic Instinct* pointedly avoids any analogous "castration" of its *femme fatale*.) *I Like to Play Games*, in short, confirms that transferring the *noir* impulse to a softcore context tends to deplete its energy.

More routine instances of softcore *noir* corroborate this point more clearly. Witness the early Hippolyte softcore thriller *Night Rhythms* (1992), whose cost Linda Ruth Williams puts at $1,250,000 (*Erotic* 291). This film is most *noir* in its cinematography, which is so reliant on chiaroscuro "mystery lighting" that it portrays a radio station as operating in almost total darkness (Naremore 173). The film also features a *noir* hero, Nick West (Martin Hewitt), and a gender-war subtext. But the deviation from *noir* is what is pertinent. Though *Night Rhythms* depicts violence, it is isolated from the sex and is neither extensive nor graphic. And the hero is from the start an elaborately feminized construct whom one character deems a female "fantasy come to life." Nick is thus a polarizing figure. Men are threatened by his on-air credo of female pleasure, but women adore him—driving a sexual structure of eight numbers plus scattered stripper spectacle (see Linda Ruth Williams, *Erotic* 350–51). Nevertheless, two women do frown on his unfettered lust. One is Bridget (Delia Sheppard), a coworker and militant lesbian *femme fatale*. This backlash figure is another incarnation of sexploitation's entirely conventional postfeminist propensity for antifeminist characterization. Hence, after being foiled in her attempt to frame Nick for murder, Bridget critiques him as "so goddamn macho. . . . We're all just sex machines to you, aren't we?" The hero's lone romantic interest is Cinnamon (Deborah Driggs), a good girl (which in softcore means an *ex*-stripper) who also critiques him. But unlike Bridget, Cinnamon brings Nick into conformity with middlebrow pieties by wooing him with devotion, affection, and aptly spicy sex. In the end, Nick is a changed man whose feminized ethos espouses female pleasure and traditional love. This happy ending frames *Night Rhythms* as an optimistic melodrama that is at odds with its *noir* motifs somewhat in the manner of *film gris*.

Such "dilutions" explain Hippolyte's discontent with the softcore market that he and Walter Gernert (the other half of hardcore's "Dark Brothers") pioneered at Axis from 1990 to 1996. "[A] lot of that erotic thriller shit is just like network TV," Hippolyte has lamented. "[I]t's the worst, most unimaginative stuff you could come up with" (Petkovich 84). An intense man criticized for pressing his hardcore to dark, misogynistic excess, Hippolyte gravitated to the erotic thriller on going mainstream. But the distributors that helped finance his softcore—Magnum, A-Pix, Academy, Imperial, and so on—reportedly resisted his efforts to amplify the *noir* surrealism that attracted him. This conservative pressure led him to soften negative female types in *Mirror Images* (1991) and to employ a dual, male-female perspective in *Animal Instincts: The Seductress* (1995), which he had hoped to confine to a noirish male viewpoint (Petkovich 78, 81).

Similar dilemmas inform the softcore thriller's origin. My view is that the first softcore thriller—and the inaugural contemporary softcore film of *any*

Figure 16. Though Jag Mundhra's *Night Eyes* (1990) represented a significant step in the development of the softcore thriller, the film's straightforward use of *noir* devices also posed obstacles to the same. © Prism Entertainment, 1990.

subgenre—was Hippolyte's first Axis film, *Carnal Crimes*, which he was working on as early as 1989 but which was not released in America until 1991 (Petkovich 78).[17] Yet an alternative account could present Jag Mundhra's million-dollar *Night Eyes*, which made up to $30 million after Prism released it on video in 1990, as the first softcore thriller (Linda Ruth Williams, *Erotic* 1, 2, 56n2, 63). The Internet response to Mundhra's film confirms that its unrated version has often been received as softcore. But while the undeniably influential *Night Eyes* is more sexualized than previous

Figure 17. Video-box art for Alexander Gregory Hippolyte's *Carnal Crimes* (1991), a *noir*-romance hybrid that also qualifies as the first fully softcore erotic thriller. © Axis Films and Magnum Entertainment, 1991.

sexploitation thrillers, it does not qualify as softcore by my definition due to the irregular pacing of its spectacle and its reluctance to depict bumping and grinding. Granted, this is a fine distinction, so it is unwise to prioritize either film—or to pinpoint softcore's reemergence too rigidly. A better strategy is to situate these two nontheatrical thrillers as having a relational significance that is clear when they are viewed in tandem.

Night Eyes and *Carnal Crimes* are rooted in industrial contexts whose subtle divergences correlate with the relative noirishness and porniness of each film. Though both vehicles were financed by companies specializing in the same midbudget, nontheatrical sexploitation formulae, the producers of *Night Eyes* had broader links to theatrical markets, including a distribution deal with Paramount, while the producers of *Carnal Crimes* had more direct affiliations with the hardcore industry. It is predictable, then, that whereas *Night Eyes* has a comparatively evasive sexploitation structure, *Carnal Crimes* flaunts a pornographic dichotomy. On the other hand, Mundhra's film has the contours of classic *noir*, while Hippolyte's film is equivocal in its *noir* effects. The dark, masculinized *Night Eyes* divides its attention between a working-class *noir* hero (Andrew Stevens) and a rich, eroticized heroine who gradually emerges as a treacherous *femme fatale* (Tanya Roberts). The more romanticized *Carnal Crimes* focuses on a neglected wife (Linda Carol) whose middlebrow pursuit of Self-Knowledge and True Love elicits viewer sympathy, defusing criticism of her sexualization. *Carnal Crimes* sacrifices the *noir* hero to gain the abundant female imagery afforded by a female protagonist—which precipitates a feminization strategy that further softens its *noir* motifs.[18] This approach should sound familiar. Stylistically and ideologically, Hippolyte's *noir*-romance hybrid hews to the aspirational model that King relied on in his just-shy-of-softcore narratives from the mid-1980s onward. Hippolyte has indicated a conflicted relation to King and has at times denied his influence altogether (e.g., Petkovich 78). Most recently, however, he has indicated that King's contribution to *9½ Weeks* spurred his own work in softcore (Linda Ruth Williams, *Erotic* 277–78). Such ambivalence is unnecessary. What is most important about *Carnal Crimes* and Hippolyte's later thrillers is that they have straightforwardly pornographic formats. Hippolyte borrowed this innovation neither from King nor from other erotic-thriller producers. It came instead from his hardcore experience.[19]

The competitiveness of Axis's *noir*-romance hybrid convinced its rivals to adopt softer narratives and harder numbers. After the release of *Carnal Crimes,* Prism released unambiguous softcore films and Mundhra directed softcore vehicles, including feminized Axis projects like *The Other Woman* (1992) and *Sexual Malice* (1993). Though nontheatrical thrillers had been trending toward softcore for years, Axis's importation of hardcore candor and practice was pivotal in precipitating the nontheatrical erotic thriller's final swing toward softcore—and away from "undiluted" *noir.*

III. THE MIDBUDGET SOFTCORE THRILLER

Between 1990 and 1996, softcore thrillers were on average much more expensive than today, not infrequently budgeted over one million dollars—which was enough to purchase a 35mm film with slick values on a par with made-for-television movies (which, as cable-financed projects, these movies quite often were).[20] In this interval, Shannon Tweed, Shannon Whirry, and Monique Parent became icons in a softcore star system that arose absent Hollywood-style promotion (Naremore 163), as it had during the classical era. During the early 1990s, the erotic thriller was so popular—and the understanding of its subgeneric distinctions so rare—that players who specialized primarily in *softcore* thrillers had little problem crossing into more mainstream vehicles, including soaps and other television melodramas. On the other hand, though hardcore directors such as Hippolyte and Paul Thomas (whose softcore pseudonym is "Toby Phillips") had a crucial impact on softcore's contemporary renaissance, it was much less common then than today for players with hardcore "celebrity" to land leading softcore roles. These middling attributes were all crucial to establishing softcore as an unthreatening industry that could survive without salient theatrical distribution if it could establish itself as a dependable home video genre *and* as an inoffensive late-night cable genre.

As the preeminent producer of midbudget softcore thrillers, Axis Films not only pioneered the cycle but also routinized its production, making no fewer than two dozen films in this category by 1996. Many of the company's films focus on upscale married women whose lack of fulfillment leads to adultery—a character arc often recycled by Axis's imitators. Like theatrical erotic thrillers, these vehicles underscore the risks of infidelity. But they also stress that a lack of fulfilling sex is equally risky and rarely "punish" heroines for adultery, which distinguishes them from big-budget erotic thrillers like Lyne's *Unfaithful*. These softcore thrillers even make the counterintuitive suggestion that infidelity can empower women to realize traditional ideals. Adultery frequently leads softcore heroines to the self-awareness and self-esteem requisite to leave irredeemable marriages, allowing them to form more stable love matches. Established by *Carnal Crimes*, this postfeminist trajectory was recycled by Axis's rivals in films like Thomas's *Killer Looks* (1994) and Andrew Stevens's *Illicit Dreams* (1995). But the notion that female infidelity can fortify a faltering family was even more routine, as confirmed by Hippolyte's *Secret Games* (1991) and *Animal Instincts* (1992) and by Mundhra's *The Other Woman*. Conversely, softcore thrillers frown on male infidelity—and the subgenre's feminized slant, as evident in gynocentric narratives and soft-focus stylistics, has sanctioned other misandristic double standards. Though the theatrical erotic thriller often fixates on the perfidy of the *femme fatale*, the subgenre is actually less sexist in this respect than the softcore thriller. Films like *Fatal Attraction* and *Basic Instinct* are driven by the "bad" behavior of both their male and female principals. But midbudget softcore thrillers overwhelmingly assign guilt to male characters alone, such that the softcore heroine's infidelity *and* any danger that results from it are commonly blamed on neglectful husbands and on psychopathic *hommes fatals*.[21]

Directed by Hippolyte, *Animal Instincts* and *Secret Games* initiated a significant subpattern within the softcore thriller's housewife paradigm: suburban heroines remedy their ennui and dysfunction by becoming "temporary" prostitutes in the *Belle de Jour* (1967) mode. In *Animal Instincts,* the responsibility for the heroine's adultery is displaced onto her husband, David Cole (Maxwell Caulfield). David's undetected voyeurism interferes with his ability to satisfy the strenuous "needs" of wife Joanna (Whirry), driving her to cheat. When he discovers her fucking the cable man, he also discovers that he likes "to watch." Realizing that he—or his sexual preference—is to blame for Joanna's infidelity, David does not reprimand her. In fact, he is so enthralled by her spectacle that they enjoy terrific sex. The couple decides that having David secretly watch Joanna prostitute herself with rich men allows them to satisfy both their needs at once. Though this porno scenario inevitably arcs toward thriller violence, Joanna in the end gets what she "always wanted . . . Love." As in classical "suburban films" like William Rotsler's *The Agony of Love,* a housewife's prostitution is linked to nymphomania. But whereas prefeminist vehicles often focused on the destructive effects of unfettered female sexuality (see also *Alley Tramp*), *Animal Instincts* positions its heroine's hypersexuality as a taste formation, not as a pathology subject to sexology's moralistic "cures." As if to stress that there is no necessary conflict between a radical sexual consumerism and family values, the Coles' libertine arrangement acts within a traditional rubric, reinforcing family ties.

Secret Games is more striking in its profemale disposition. Its heroine, Julianne (Michele Brin), adores Mark (Billy Drago), her architect husband, but is dissatisfied by her cloistered existence in a swanky abode. Though Mark is ultimately sympathetic, his benevolence initially comes across as paternalism. He thoughtlessly belittles Julianne and defines his love for her as an ability to imagine "all of [her] possibilities." He also neglects her individual desires during sex. When Mark reneges on his promise to spend a day with her, Julianne allows a friend (Catya Sassoon) to take her to an upscale bordello inhabited by other wives and run by an affectless yet caring madam (Delia Sheppard). Though shy, Julianne is "awakened" by two clients. Unfortunately, her second client, Eric (Martin Hewitt), has evaded the brothel's screening and soon manifests a controlling nature. In time, he threatens not only Julianne but Mark as well. In the climax, Julianne is compelled to shoot

Eric so as to save Mark. *Secret Games* then ends with "dénouement sex"—a crowning number offered as proof that a couple has resolved its differences—that is gratifying for both participants alike. Like David Cole, Mark comes to realize that he is culpable and that Julianne has been telling the truth in claiming "all I ever needed was you." This resolution upholds the socially acceptable misandry routinely evinced by Julianne's peers. "Men don't understand how to please a woman," one of the prostitutes, reclining topless by the brothel pool, counsels her one day. "You have to train them, like pets . . . Women touch more. Women are more considerate."

Secret Games's most significant contribution to film history is its adaptation of the aspirational stylization of classical sexploitation films in the "awakening sexuality" category. Whereas classical directors like Joe Sarno and Radley Metzger applied the soft-focus, sex-positive aesthetic of this category to "budding" adolescents, Hippolyte applies it to married women. This deviation from American softcore practice was rooted in Hippolyte's French sources (Petkovich 78), especially *Emmanuelle*. Though even a cursory comparison of *Secret Games* to *Belle de Jour* reveals Hippolyte's systematic dependence on Buñuel's plotting, ultimately the film privileges the sex-positive valence of *Emmanuelle* over the more negative (and potentially more misogynistic) outlook of *Belle de Jour*. Like the Just Jaeckin film, *Secret Games* uses its soft aesthetic to reinforce a liberationist story line that forgives and even affirms female infidelity. This gendered aesthetic is quite manipulative. For example, the soft style is most overt during Julianne's "flowering" in the bordello. A notably "sensitive" female client (Parent in her softcore debut) is the first to overcome the heroine's timidity in a sequence whose hazy glow signals the "rightness" of Julianne's experimentation. Because this glow also suffuses her first numbers with Eric, the viewer is led to believe that he is no less sympathetic than her bisexual client. But as the diegesis darkens, this effect recedes from the couple's encounters, leading the viewer to recognize him as an *homme fatal*, that is to say, a negatively feminized man. In the *noir*-inflected climax, Hippolyte's cinematography abandons soft lenses altogether, imparting the film's final idea of sexual sadism as a specifically masculine trait.

Despite its female orientation, the housewife paradigm had obvious regressive tendencies, so the brevity of its prominence is understandable. If anything, the depiction of women as prostitutes was, in this context, less problematic than the striking passivity of heroines like Julianne of *Secret Games* and Diana (Rochelle Swanson) of *Secret Games 3* (1994). In Hippolyte's work, such passivity is a function of the director's preference for a cold, fashion-oriented consumerism—which informs everything from his static pictorialism and reliance on absurdist decor and dress to his Francophile description of *Secret Games* as "a cross between *Belle de Jour, Emmanuelle,* and a Chanel commercial" (Petkovich 78). But most softcore directors have favored less idiosyncratic paths to "legitimacy." Softcore thrillers have thus tended since the mid-1990s to focus on a more independent, respectable "working girl": the career woman.[22]

Insofar as its heroine is a career woman *and* a repressed wife who peeps on a prostitute, *The Other Woman* offered an early prediction of the softcore thriller's shift from its housewife phase to its more progressive empowered babe phase. Directed by Mundhra, *The Other Woman* was made with input from Hippolyte and Axis producers Gernert and Andrew Garroni. Its heroine, Jessica Mathews (Lee Anne Beaman), is a successful journalist but an "unsuccessful" wife. Though married to Greg (Adrian Zmed), a caring, attractive writer who likes to expose his chest, Jessica has little interest in sex. Worse, her uptight personality elicits gender-war friction at work, where she snipes with sexist males and with an intern whom she deems an irresponsible slut.

In framing Greg as the neglected spouse, *The Other Woman* upends Hippolyte's housewife paradigm. Jessica's suspicion that her husband has been unfaithful drives the action, sending her in pursuit of "the other woman." Her inquiry focuses on Traci (Jenna Persaud), a porn model and prostitute whose sexualized profession, dark skin, and low status invert her own identity as a buttoned-up, white, middlebrow journalist. Jessica's glimpses into Traci's life rekindle memories of her mother in a bisexual tryst. These girl-girl flashbacks—whose surreal mystery is accented via soft lenses—position the youthful Jessica as the observer of a primal scene, a pop-Freudian scenario that explains her later frigidity. Until she replays this scene in her own tryst with Traci, she cannot manifest her essential self, which is vivacious and yielding. After gratuitous violence plays out at the end—like many softcore thrillers, *The Other Woman* is a softcore woman's film whose violence is strained—Jessica realizes that Traci, as a cipher of her repressed femininity, was "the other woman," but not in the negative sense she had presumed. "I'd found the other woman," Jessica declares in closing. "And she was me."

In voice-overs, Jessica describes herself as "brilliant, totally in control, about as feminine as a printing press." Thus she frets that careerism has warped her Female Self. But *The Other Woman* suggests that a career offers no impediment to a "true" femininity (which is aligned, as always, with a pro-sex heterosexuality).[23] Jessica's careerism facilitates the adventurism through which she overcomes her repression, allowing her to open up to her husband. This combination of postfeminist anxiety and pop psychology also implies that the self-neglecting career woman has the same ironic obligation as the neglected wife: to improve her marriage, she *must* pursue extramarital lusts. Which is to say that the contrast between Jessica's stern reaction to her husband's presumed adultery and her forgiving attitude toward her own indiscretion is not addressed. This typically postfeminist double standard—which applies a tolerant, consumerist paradigm to female infidelity and an intolerant, anticonsumerist paradigm to male infidelity—was repeated throughout softcore's midbudget cycle, surfacing in early cases like *Carnal Crimes* as well as relatively late ones like *Illicit Dreams*. Ultimately, such bias must be framed as the result of the nontheatrical erotic thriller's introduction of a softcore format, which further encouraged producers to build plots around sympathetic female protagonists, to foreground feminized styles, and to deemphasize *noir* motifs.

Though the cheaper vehicles that circulated after 1996 tend to use younger heroines, they still exude gender biases that emerged in generic interplay with adultery motifs derived from theatrical vehicles. Such biases still have the "liberating" effect they had in 1991, lending distributors cover to purvey pornographic products in centralized channels. That said, it is now obvious that the softcore thriller's distinctly postfeminist reliance on largely traditional ideas of gender has limited the form's consumerist diversity and squelched any drift toward "genderlessness." Recent examples indicate that the form has grown more explicit and specialized, yet such change has occurred within a rigid scheme that brooks no threat to its heterosexist assumptions of sex-and-gender fixity. Thus the softcore thriller has never revisited the liberationist, gender-bending excess of classical sexploitation, whose decentralization fostered greater variety than has proved possible within the more corporate, routinized networks of today.

IV. THE LOW- AND ULTRA-LOW-BUDGET SOFTCORE THRILLER

By 1994, softcore had coalesced as a distinct middle industry within the nontheatrical market. This process was sparked by deflationary pressures that did more than just lower budgets. They also isolated nonunionized, softcore talent from unionized (SAG), B-list talent and compelled producers to resort to increasingly inexpensive means, including the use of truncated shoots as well as 16mm and (later) video cinematography. Such pressures also precipitated a diversification of forms, such that the softcore thriller became one softcore subgenre among many. (The latter development was spurred in part by a consumer backlash against "stupid and senseless" violence and the erotic thriller's early dominance of contemporary softcore [Anonymous 1].[24]) Within the softcore thriller, competition redoubled trends established early in the decade. The audience "satiation factor" that has been accepted as an item of faith by cable programmers since the early 1980s in effect encouraged a harder-core ethic among producers (Jaehne 12)—which, in turn, exacerbated the softcore thriller's postfeminist consumerism.

Competition also fostered and in turn eliminated dozens of labels, including Axis and Prism.[25] (Here I am *not* referring to "one-off labels" that are transient by definition.) From 1997 to 2005, when the low-budget model and its sub-$400,000 cost structure dominated softcore, MRG was the most consistent purveyor of softcore thrillers. The successor to CPV, one of softcore's first contemporary labels, MRG is a cable-oriented corporate softcore studio formed in 1997 by Marc Greenberg, who may be the most prolific executive producer in softcore history (MRG, "Company Profile"). MRG's endurance over this span was predicated on the flexibility of its corporate umbrella, Mainline Releasing. Mainline has specialized in *ultra*-low-budget (below $150,000) to midbudget nontheatrical categories, including children's films, and maintains two labels that market distinct types of softcore thriller. While the MRG label has churned out low- and ultra-low-cost softcore thrillers, its Magic Hour affiliate has produced a costlier, less prolific type. Launched under CPV, the Magic Hour brand has been mostly reserved for "prestige" thrillers like *Sexual Predator* (2001) and Kelley Cauthen's similarly slick *Bare Witness* (2002), which cost around one million dollars. These 35mm softcore thrillers recall their midbudget antecedents in more than just budget. They also rely on B-list SAG talent like Angie Everhart, Richard Grieco, and Daniel Baldwin and on distribution by major video labels like Columbia TriStar. Relative to MRG's specialized 16mm softcore thriller, the Magic Hour softcore thriller is more noirish and less explicit, broadening its distribution by enabling it to pass for a "mainstream" type of erotic thriller.[26]

Mainline's flexibility is also verified by the complexity encapsulated within its MRG label. Though MRG has produced some 35mm thrillers, prior to 2005 the label relied mostly on 16mm thrillers. This type of vehicle was shot in a week or less with eighty-page scripts. In 2004, it cost around $130,000, including postproduction expenses (Lombard, "Re: One Other," 30 June [1]). This ultralow cost allowed MRG to produce 16mm thrillers in abundance, peaking at about fifteen per year at the start of the millennium. Though production later declined, falling to ten per year by 2003 and zero by 2005 (Lombard, "Re: One Other," 10 Feb. [1]), MRG's use of a routinized model undermined its rivals, including 35mm softcore labels at Playboy and Full Moon, both of which had expired by 2003.[27] At the same time, MRG began shifting to an even cheaper video format. By 2005, film was obsolete at MRG, which began shooting thrillers solely on video, having scheduled seven such projects by March of that year. This change has reportedly lowered costs to around $80,000 per feature.[28]

It is safe to assume that the softcore thriller would not have established its cable niche had porny, downscale thrillers like those recently made by MRG spearheaded the market. Besides shooting on 16mm and moving into video, MRG has slashed costs by casting prominent hardcore actors (e.g., Randy Spears) and actresses (Syren, Ava Vincent, etc.) in lead roles. Longtime MRG casting director and Creative Image talent manager Robert Lombard has led this innovation, which he describes as a "lonely fight" opposed by insiders who view the trend as encouraging a decline in production values; as hastening the exit of an older, more established cadre of softcore-only actresses;[29] and as reinforcing a stigmatized link to porn ("Journey" 1–2; see "Casting" 2–3). Values *have* suffered in these 16mm thrillers, but the plainest signs of decline—poor mixing, resolution, and lighting—cannot be blamed on the players. Still, other adjustments can be linked to this influx, including relatively inept acting, the use of longer, more explicit numbers, and the introduction of hardcore mannerisms.[30]

Clearly, softcore thrillers of this ilk are more specialized than their antecedents. Though these 16mm films compete on the same video store shelves with theatrical erotic thrillers, the poles of the erotic thriller have never been farther apart. Though MRG's thrillers are still steeped in murder, violence is treated as "the ob/scene" in Linda Williams's sense: it is coyly pushed offstage. One MRG tactic for muffling the violence includes blacking the screen at violent moments. This common device, so striking in the climaxes of cheapies like *Dangerous Pleasures* (2001) and *Wicked Sins* (2001), has the virtue of affordability. By contrast, this effect is rare in Magic Hour's more brutal and expensive films, to my knowledge appearing only in one late Tweed vehicle, *Forbidden Sins* (1998). A new tendency to "disguise" the *femme fatale* is even more intriguing. On occasion, this device surfaces in midbudget vehicles. The Magic Hour release *Sexual Predator* contains a vivid instance—and the device recalls the significant midbudget thriller *Night Eyes*.[31] But as deployed by the ultra-low-cost 16mm film *Bare Deception* (1999), this device has a clear anti-*noir* function. The protagonist of *Bare Deception* is a lovely, seemingly gentle heroine (Tane McClure) who in the end is jarringly revealed as a brutal, remorseless killer. Until then, she lacks *any* hint of the erotic menace of the *femme fatale*. Like the blackened screen, the hidden *femme fatale* nudges violence offstage, saving money, diminishing shock, and preserving a mystery the viewer has no chance to unravel or suspect. In ultra-low-budget softcore, the purpose of this tactic is to allow producers to make use of a *noir* motif with misogynistic connota-

Figure 18. Promotional art on a "one sheet" for three ultra-low-cost MRG 16mm thrillers. Note the high degree of standardization in the titles. © Mainline Releasing, 2001. Used courtesy Robert Lombard.

tions while largely maintaining a properly postfeminist posture *vis-à-vis* the "pornographied" heroine. Which is also to say that MRG has reinforced the larger trend toward female protagonists. In the early 1990s, CPV often opted for heroes in softcore *noir* like *Strike a Pose* (1993). But of more than two dozen MRG thrillers analyzed for this chapter, only one opts for a hero.[32] Though MRG still refers to *noir,* its use of *noir* tropes has been moderated by parsimony and propriety. The hidden *femme fatale* offers a peculiar demonstration of how these factors may combine, transforming venerable motifs.

This low-budget specialization has led to a more consistent sexual consumerism than in the midbudget films. Some 16mm MRG films convey this inflection indirectly. To wit, a supporting character may criticize the heroine's sexual openness, with the narrative working to marginalize his or her antisexual stance. But in other films, this consumerism is blunt, such that some heroines challenge the erotic thriller's foundational illusion by explicitly demystifying the erotic. In still others, the heroine exudes a breezy bohemianism, which perseveres through death and deceit to become the final word on sex—and which relaxes the generic bias against male infidelity.

Sinful Deeds (2001) exemplifies the first trend in that it marginalizes the antisexual ethos of a supporting figure. Here the heroine is Julie (Syren), a middle-class Asian American who strips because she loves to dance but has not been given occasion to put her "classical training" to work. Her boyfriend David (Frank Harper) is so unable to accept her profession that his normality is questioned. His prejudices further the suspense by situating him (falsely) as a murder suspect. The crux of this arc is an inadvertently comic passage in which he happens upon Julie in a tub-induced autoerotic frenzy. Rather than watch and enjoy—which in softcore is a harmless, bourgeois convention—David interrupts her rapture, muttering in rage, "I'm not good enough for you, you have to pleasure yourself?" In a postfeminist, exhibitionist subgenre that exalts female masturbation, anticonsumerist attitudes of this sort amount to fringe extremism. No wonder that the heroine soon rushes from his house in fear.

Whereas *Sinful Deeds* opts for indirection, *Young and Seductive* (2003) is so bluntly consumerist that it verges on the didactic. In this cheapie, Nina (Julian Wells) is a researcher writing a treatise on Internet dating. According to one interviewee, the Web is a consumer's dream, for "there are sites devoted to every taste imaginable," forming an "all you can eat" buffet. But several of Nina's subjects die as a result of their taste for "erotic asphyxiation." Popularized by Nagisa Oshima's art film *In the Realm of the Senses* (1976), asphyxiation has been a nontheatrical cliché since appearing in noirish classics like *Body Chemistry* and *Naked Obsession* (1990). Often mystified as an antibourgeois practice and then demonized in the same terms as sex slides into death, asphyxiation is suited to regressive erotic-thriller prescriptions. But Nina does not accept such logic. Though exposed to peril, she maintains that "erotic asphyxiation is not about violence, it's about sensual stimulation; depriving the brain of oxygen is meant to awaken the senses, not to deaden them." Nina's rationalism—which is never challenged, since the killer's use of this specific murder method seems almost random—is integral to her effort "to demystify sex, to make it less taboo, [for] the more open people are talking about sex, the less power it has as a weapon." By closing with a long number, the film bolsters her contention that consumerist sex is not *a priori* dangerous.

Figure 19. Three more ultra-low-budget 16mm softcore thrillers from MRG. The promotional art accents a noirish quality that is carefully restricted in the films themselves. © Mainline Releasing, 2002. Used courtesy Robert Lombard.

Young and Seductive's rationalist sensibility demystifies the sex-death linkage, subverting the erotic thriller's cardinal illusion and qualifying as an anti–erotic thriller outlook. But Madison Monroe's *Love Games* (2001) shows that a blasé, anti-intellectual bluntness yields parallel meanings. *Love Games* is a rarity among later softcore thrillers in that it focuses on a married couple. Its upscale housewife, Monica Harris (Venus, star of hardcore videos like *White Wife, Black Cock 2* [2003]), is a bohemian ex-model who encourages her husband Paul (Paul Johnson) to participate in role-playing diversions that lead to adultery. Their swinging embroils them in a murder plot from which they barely escape. In the end, Paul states the obvious: "Playing all these games can get you in trouble." "I suppose," Monica blithely replies, "but it was fun." This cavalier coda crowns a pattern of contradictions that subverts the narrative's efforts to establish adventurism as a portentous activity. Indeed, the film ends with the couple revisiting its initial game, generating a feckless continuity that nullifies any potential for antisexual moralism. Far from random, these paradoxes foment corporate softcore's distinctive "weightlessness" and represent a consistent industrial strategy. (See chapter 9.)

Love Games's most interesting element may be its guiltless approach to male infidelity, which at first indicates that in this crucial detail MRG's 16mm softcore thriller managed to press its consumerist vision beyond the gendered limits of its midbudget precursor.[33] But closer inspection confirms that *Love Games* conforms to postfeminist propriety in that it is the heroine who encourages and directs the infidelity of the properly reluctant hero. The film's postfeminist consumerism is, then, still more rigidly socialized than that of a prefeminist swinger's film like Metzger's *Score* (1972). Because *Love Games* does not transcend the gendered codes instituted by its midbudget precursors, it cannot recreate the genderless, bisexual consumerism that surfaces in many classical vehicles—and that in *Score* culminates in boy-boy spectacle. One may conclude, then, that the consumerism of a cultural form like the softcore thriller is "postfeminist" insofar as it clings to largely traditional sex-and-gender hierarchies, thus refusing the subversive potentials implicit to a "purer" sexual consumerism.

Such variations exemplify tactics common to MRG's ultra-low-cost thrillers. If they seem to press the erotic thriller's capacity for sexual tolerance to its gendered limit, implying a form more precisely referred to as "anti–erotic thriller," such is not the case. Nonmainstream outlets sell hundreds if not thousands of even cheaper hardcore thrillers like David Stanley's *House of Lies* (2003) and Veronica Hart's *Love and Bullets* (2004), wherein the sex is more graphic and the violence less so—as produced by corporate hardcore purveyors like Vivid, VCA, Wicked Pictures, and Adam & Eve.

In the erotic thriller, form and logistics have maintained a dynamic dialectic with ideology. This thesis holds true for microcosmic motifs like sexual position and for macrocosmic structures like format. The overlapping fields that comprise this sprawling genre may be framed as a sex-violence continuum in which the focal variables trend in inverse directions as influenced by an array of formal and ideological factors with complex historical and industrial underpinnings. At the level of subgenre, the most crucial variable has been sex. The mainstream nontheatrical erotic thriller's introduction of a narrative-number structure into a midbudget cycle in the early 1990s was pivotal to the formation of its more recent lower-budget cycles. The postfeminist consumerism of these patently pornographic, feminized softcore thrillers has today diverged sharply from the violent, pessimistic, often misogynistic sensibility of theatrical erotic thrillers, which still adhere to the sex-negative logic implicit to their *noir* motifs.

As contemporary sexploitation's first softcore subgenre, the softcore thriller has a privileged place in this study. It was also the middle increment of a crucial sexploitation progression bookended by two distinctive Zalman King vehicles: the just-shy-of-softcore *noir*-romance hybrid and the softcore serial. Because the latter "bookend" developed into a prolific subgenre in its own right, it is the focus of my next chapter.

Softcore as Serialized (and Feminized) Featurette

Postfeminist Propriety on Late-Night Cable

In the first softcore serial, the recurring "host" is Jacqueline Stone (Ava Fabian), a romance novelist regularly depicted topless as she reads letters from her mainly female fans, who divulge their most intimate adventures. Jacqueline's enigmatic expression suggests mild titillation, a supposition reinforced by her deshabille and the obvious decadence of her life on a sumptuous estate. In the second serial, Jacqueline's counterpart is also a female writer, but one who is depicted as an anonymous, Nancy Friday–like researcher surveying the diversity of female erotic fantasy. The main thing that the viewer knows about "the Interviewer" (Elisa Rothstein) is that she is harried by the logistics of meeting her subjects. Unlike Jacqueline, the Interviewer wears frumpy clothing and reacts to her subjects not with autoeroticism but with an earnestness that evokes equal parts female empathy and scholarly motive.

Plainly, these recurring hosts generate distinct connotations for the programs that they frame. In the first, *Erotic Confessions* (1994–99; hereafter *EC*), the unbuttoned host provides "eye candy," a function seemingly calibrated to a voyeuristic idea of male desire. In the second serial, *Women: Stories of Passion* (1997; hereafter *WSP*), the Interviewer's frustration, prim attire, and empathy apparently signal a restriction on female nudity. The surprise is how similar the featurettes framed by each device actually are, with one after another limning the narrative contours of female fantasy—and exposing the visual contours of female anatomy. But from a historical standpoint, this continuity is predictable. Both shows were inspired by Zalman King's *Red Shoe Diaries* (*RSD*), the aspirational serial that in 1992 spawned the softcore subgenre to which each show belongs, and each character is a variation on Jake (ergo *Jacqu*eline), the *RSD* host played by David Duchovny. Moreover, both shows belong to the same ideological and industrial contexts: namely, the overlapping histories of postfeminist cultural production, American sexploitation cinema, and premium cable programming.

Given the affinities uniting these and other softcore serials, it is instructive that feminist critics have singled *WSP* out, praising it above other serials, including *RSD*. This darling status implies the show's uniquely effective deployment of standard feminization strategies—most of which have been present in sexploitation since the 1960s, and many of which have had a pointedly postfeminist character since the early 1970s. *WSP* may, in fact, be situated as the most effectively feminized vehicle in a field of softcore serials that in turn qualifies as the most feminized sexploitation subgenre ever. But neither *WSP* nor the softcore serial represents a basic departure. To understand this feminist receptiveness to softcore feminization strategies, one must consider that it signals something basic not in contemporary sexploitation but in contemporary feminism. It reflects, that is, not how feminist sexploitation has become—for sexploitation has long recoiled from feminism *per se,* which it construes as repressive, anti-erotic, and unmarketable—but how amenable to sex-and-gender stereotypes critics have become amid a postfeminist climate in which, to revisit Jacinda Read's locution, "the opposition between feminism and femininity is becoming decidedly less distinct" (61).

The softcore serial is, it should be noted, a prodigious, meaningful area of cultural work in its own right. Since 1992, hundreds upon hundreds of softcore featurettes have been produced, mostly to no fanfare. Conversely, King's fairly pricey *RSD* serial has had a wide sway. It was a factor in Showtime's new competitiveness with HBO in the mid-1990s. It was, further, the first softcore program to be touted by a premium cable network and the first to deliver consistently high ratings, which it did until ending its run in 1999 (Backstein 308–10; Bellafante 76). In the wake of this popularity, dozens of lower-rent serials—including not only *EC* and *WSP* but *Love Street* (1994–95), *Hot Line* (1994–96), *Beverly Hills Bordello* (1996–98), *Intimate Sessions* (1998), *The Pleasure Zone* (1999), *Nightcap* (1999–2000), *Passion Cove* (1999–2001), *Hotel Erotica* (2002–3), *The Best Sex Ever* (2002–3), and the like—have premiered on Showtime, the Movie Channel, HBO, and Cinemax, with these byzantine networks rerunning the shows years after production. When the subgenre's influential role in cable's development is added to its place in sexploitation history, it becomes apparent that a thorough survey of this form is overdue. Conducting this survey through the lens of postfeminism is, I think, conducive to discerning the subgenre's mechanisms most clearly. Moreover, this approach has the benefit of suggesting that any method with an investment in traditional ideas of femininity may be ill-equipped to achieve such clarity.[1]

As noted, a number of feminists have evinced a stake in this subgenre. They have expressed disappointment when shows like *RSD* do not meet their standards and have lauded an ostensibly all-female production like *WSP* that "corrects" *RSD*. To grasp what these critics are inclined to applaud, it helps to outline the softcore serial's sex-and-gender biases. Apart from serialization, its identifying trait is its obsession with female fantasy. This theme dictates the subgenre's confessionalism and aspirationalism, which are among its main feminization strategies. Such strategies operate at three levels: the narrative, which focuses on white, middle-class, heterosexual women; the spectacle, which is so committed to female nudity that it alternates with no contradiction between heterosexual bumping and grinding and same-sex "girl-girl" encounters; and the arty style, which is dominated by soft visuals and smooth scores. But because the subgenre's most unstinting imperative is toward female nudity, the sincerity of its appeal to women is equivocal. Indeed, the female-friendly diegesis and feminized style collaborate with the female-focused spectacle, often in exceptionally ironic ways. Even the subgenre's timid devices—like *WSP*'s buttoned-up host—and its frequent misandry ultimately seem geared to relieve women of their clothing. By no means, then, would it be a stretch to read the subgenre's feminization as a manner of facilitating and satisfying a stereotype of heterosexual male desire. Given the subgenre's antimale elements, producers have clearly construed this "male" desire as masochistic, myopic, or both.

Besides its structuring inequities, the subgenre's most crucial element is its nonadversarial stance, which creates an unchallenging forum that rarely melds analysis with fantasy and spectacle. That the softcore serial privileges strong women and female empowerment themes might imply that it is geared to accommodate feminist critiques—but like soap opera and romance fiction, it distances itself from feminist correctness, which it treats as a felt burden. If these shows evince any hostility, it is apolitical, directed against heterosexual men construed as instances of a universal masculinity, not as instances of power structures that oppress men and women alike by imposing spurious gender essentialisms. These serials view "bad" male behavior as an organic effusion of the male biological sex. Such behavior can be ameliorated through the intercession of females who tutor their men, feminizing (*civilizing*) their baser aspects. As a set of traits constructed as "natural," femininity is an unexamined virtue here, so double standards abound and even interlock. Women who perpetrate the behaviors branded "bad" when performed by men are treated more favorably than their male counterparts, especially when such behavior leads these women to doff their clothing.

The assimilationist diversity and middlebrow artsiness of the softcore serial must be framed in this context. Though this subgenre is more apt to highlight social diversity than any other softcore sector, it does not press such diversity into the service of race- or class-based critiques. Instead, it subordinates such concerns to conflicts that focus on sex, gender, and romance, which it usually frames as universals. This nonanalytical approach submerges the specifics of race and class, precipitating a return to "incorrect" stereotypes that only token examination reveals as such. As a result, even *WSP* exploits the "exotic" as an erotic resource rooted in racist, classist, and sexist stereotypes. Regressive images also inform the subgenre's recourse to art-world scenarios. Such plots mostly position the female heroine as a passive, sexualized muse, dispensing with the female empowerment theme that is the subgenre's most consistent feminist piety.

These comments should not be interpreted as highbrow diatribes. Many areas of postfeminist popular culture rely on dubious ideas and images as shortcuts to convey vast amounts of information (Dyer, *Matter* 12–13). Moreover, elite cultural areas are not exempt from market-driven, stereotype-based processes and do not necessarily transcend illiberal or essentialist attitudes through complexity, experimentation, and critique. My reason for identifying these formal and ideological elements at the outset is that they are so central to the subgenre that no analyst can neglect them—a point that is doubly true for analysts interested in representations of femininity. While the softcore serial does far more than pay lip service to notions of female agency, it has nevertheless done so first and foremost to "grease" the distribution of female spectacle.

I. POSTFEMINISM, SEXPLOITATION, PREMIUM CABLE

As noted in chapter 1, my use of "postfeminist" refers to the era that followed feminism's second wave. It also refers to distinctive discourses in recent American culture. On one hand, a postfeminist text appropriates "feminist thought for non-feminist purposes" (Clover 153). If the accent on "authenticity" informing this usage is naïve, such a definition is undeniably applicable to the softcore serial, which, like sexploitation historically, has embraced feminist ideas of agency but distanced itself from "actual" feminists. My use of "postfeminist" also points to a possibility broached by Read, Joanne Hol-

Figure 20. A production still from *Emmanuelle* (1974), a crucial postfeminist influence on *Red Shoe Diaries* (1992–99) and many later softcore serials. © Trinacra, Columbia, and Just Jaeckin, 1974, and RCA/Columbia, 1984.

lows, Sarah Projansky, and other feminists: that today's feminism treats femininity less critically because mainstream depictions of femininity have absorbed and reflect marketable components of its former agenda. Postfeminist processes present in concentrated forms in sexploitation have thus been manifest throughout popular culture. In this account, the second wave modified the culture, and feminism changed with it. Feminism lost its identifying purpose and fractured into postfeminist "tastes," which were amenable to the apolitical confection of feminine stereotyping, female sexualization, and feminist rhetoric consistently dished up by postfeminist culture.

In *Watching Rape: Film and Television in Postfeminist Culture* (2001), Projansky offers a précis of the semantic diversity implicit in the current usage of "postfeminist" (66–89; see also Hollows, *Feminism* 190–97; Kim 321; Phoca and Wright). Though Projansky's categories of postfeminism are all relevant, "pro-sex postfeminism" is most pertinent, for it suggests why feminists have been hesitant to critique the softcore serial's inequities: feminists have been demonized by "backlash" depictions in popular culture even as said depictions have co-opted feminist rhetoric to justify female display. "Pro-sex postfeminist" discourse thus defines older incarnations of feminism as sex-negative, reducing the movement to its antiporn fringes; it also "construct[s] sexual interaction with men as a core desire for women" (Projansky 79). According to Projansky, pro-sex postfeminism has four strands: "commodity feminism postfeminism," "to-be-looked-at postfeminism," "do-me postfeminism," and "masquerade postfeminism." Commodity feminism postfeminism is a component of popular entertainment that is even more evident in advertising. This distinctive discourse connects a feminist rhetoric of agency and choice to a postfeminist consumerism "that call[s] for and support[s] constant body maintenance" (Projansky 80)—and that is therefore closely allied to traditional femininity. The other pro-sex discourses use the same ideas to justify the gendered pleasures of female sexual display. To-be-looked-at postfeminism prioritizes voyeuristic male pleasure while do-me postfeminism and masquerade postfeminism stress the exhibitionist pleasures that an active heterosexuality, including its "excessive" display, may provide women (Projansky 82–83).

As chapters 1–4 argue, sexploitation has evinced these pro-sex discourses since at least 1964. They were in place, then, *before* there was a general recognition of what second-wave feminism would become in the wake of Betty Friedan's 1963 book *The Feminine Mystique*—which helps explain why sexploitation was so quick to translate feminist ideas into a distinctly postfeminist idiom in the late 1960s and early 1970s. Here a review helps. If sexploitation began as a déclassé, masculinized form featuring a comic male hero and marginal women who contributed little but nudity, it soon became something else. Russ Meyer's 1964 film *Lorna* is recalled for injecting a "roughie" impulse into sexploitation. But it is also memorable for its foregrounding of a hyperbolically endowed heroine; its commitment to narrative; and its use of feminized, art film tactics. Ultimately, the latter traits insulated sexploitation from censorship and helped expand its distribution. They also contributed to an emergent postfeminism. In *Mudhoney* (1965), *Faster, Pussycat!*, and *Vixen!* (1968), Meyer built on *Lorna* by creating a hypersexual "girl power" equating large breasts with strength. (Doris Wishman took this tactic to its carnival extreme in her films with Chesty Morgan, *Deadly Weapons* [1973] and *Double Agent 73* [1974].) Formally, this excessive female display, along with its implicit marginalization of men, allowed sexploiteers to maximize female spectacle even in narrative segments with little nudity—a factor not to be discounted in discussions of sexploitation's historical reliance on female protagonists.

As sexploitation moved toward softcore, upscale sexploiteers like Radley Metzger and Joe Sarno confirmed that a feminized, aspirational paradigm devoid of shock tactics provided an optimal synthesis of female spectacle and respectability. Many of their films portray young heroines in the throes of erotic awakenings. Such characters are sex-positive questers who learn to voice individual desires—but by avoiding the "castrating" spectacle favored by Meyer's women, these heroines hew closer to traditional femininity. Once feminism's impact was clear, sexploiteers encoded political specifics into various cycles. Despite its undercurrent of gender traditionalism, the feminized, aspirational paradigm proved hospitable to feminist ideas, especially those linked to awakening-sexuality motifs. Feminism's revaluation of female masturbation and of clitoral sexuality in general proved attractive to aspirational producers, who in the mid-1970s organized postfeminist scenarios like *Butterflies* and *Emmanuelle* around such themes. As a vocal supporter of feminism and a producer who promoted women, Roger Corman is notable for having adapted nonaspirational vehicles to postfeminist purposes. But neither the "fetishized feminists" of his women-in-prison vehicles nor the empowered career women of films like *The Student Nurses* embrace feminism as such (Pam Cook 127). Fearful that such scenarios might alienate audiences, sexploiteers embraced an ad-hoc, pro-sex "middle feminism" that rejects gender-based separatism. As a result, gender-war plots in which women reject the patriarchy led to backlash depictions that equate feminism with chaos and evil. Witness the protoerotic thriller *Invasion of the Bee Girls*, which is a clearer antifeminist allegory than the more celebrated backlash film *Fatal Attraction*.

After the decline of theatrical sexploitation in the mid- to late 1970s, sexploiteers were compelled to seek nontheatrical markets. In hindsight, it seems natural that premium cable would then become sexploitation's favored mode. Showtime, HBO, and their affiliates offered broad, stable, centralized distribution and specialized, late-night exhibition. But if cable was willing to program sexploitation in the 1980s, it was at first unwilling to finance its production—as if it were waiting for producers like Zalman King to establish a record of satisfying its postfeminist arthouse tastes, which were a function of audiences that skewed upscale and female (Jaehne 15). By 1991, cable had fostered the return of softcore. But since premium cable was a mainstream medium with no interest in shocking audiences, it channeled this renewal through narrowly feminized, aspirational forms. King's *noir*-romance hybrids, including the *Red Shoe Diaries* feature, formed a vital increment in this evolution. They combined the intrigue of the theatrical erotic thriller—which, as the "hottest new ticket on the cable dial" (qtd. in

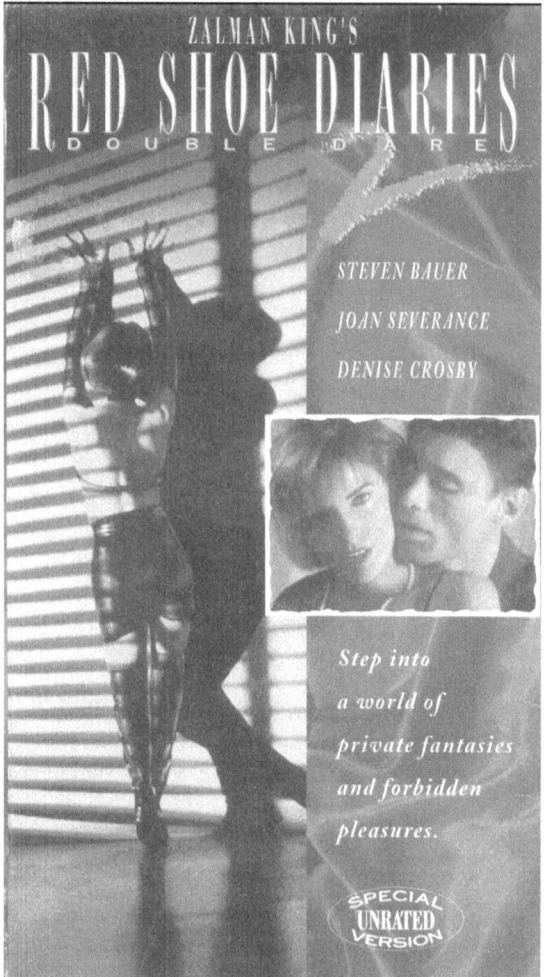

Figure 21. The second video anthology of Zalman King's pioneering serial, *Red Shoe Diaries* (1992–99). The use of "mystery lighting" in this promotional art emphasizes the upscale noirishness of King's psychosexual vision. © Showtime and Zalman King, 1992, and Republic Pictures and Zalman King, 1993.

Naremore 164), played well on the premium channels of the late 1980s—with awakening-sexuality motifs. Indeed, the softcore thriller, contemporary sexploitation's first softcore subgenre, was a *noir*-romance hybrid that integrated lush surfaces and visions of upscale consumerism with postfeminist scenarios that depict a heroine's growing psychosexual assertiveness—and that, in a typical pro-sex gambit, depict female adultery as necessary to such growth. In 1992, Showtime capitalized on softcore's nontheatrical popularity by having King use his *Red Shoe Diaries* film as the "pilot" of a fantasy series. Often focusing on the sexual adventurism of "frustrated" career women and relying on traits associated with "women's genres," this breakthrough program triggered waves of imitators. In the process, *RSD* pioneered a new softcore subgenre: the softcore serial.

Industrially, then, the aim of sexploitation's feminization strategy was from the start to expand distribution by claiming a respectability equated with female approval. Early on, this strategy had a postfeminist flavor, combining antifeminist depictions with feminist ideas of empowerment and pro-sex attitudes with feminist roots. Also crucial was a rhetoric of "femaleness." Producers signaled this "intrinsic" authenticity through their manipulation of the term "erotica" and attempted to verify it by pointing to textual details like soft-focus stylization and narrative complexity; they also attempted to verify it by gathering testimonials from "real" female producers and viewers for use in ad campaigns. The emergence of the softcore serial thus indicates fresh refinements to this component of sexploitation's feminization strategy. Because it was a televisual, serialized subgenre without theatrical aspirations, this subgenre could present itself as a private, domestic, and in that sense "authentically" female softcore form.

To situate this subgenre precisely, one must read *against* such rhetoric. One way to do this is to stress the links that unite the softcore serial to the softcore feature and to cinematic sexploitation generally.[2] It is worth stipulating that this form *is* a variant of the softcore feature. Though I mostly refer to this subgenre as comprising *serials*, it is not wrong to refer to it as comprising discrete *featurettes*. Granted, the featurette—which often spans just under thirty minutes, as in *RSD* and *WSP*, and as little as sixteen, as in *EC*—departs from the feature in its running time. But since the narrative-number pacing of these simulation formats is largely analogous, the feature and featurette are both recognizably "softcore." Another reason for grouping these variants is their emphasis on narrative closure. That softcore serials are often referred to as "anthologies" reflects the importance of the subgenre's closed, featurette nature. Though televisual serialization implies "flow," in this subgenre such continuity is limited to a host seen at the start and, less often, at the end—and serials like *Love Street* eliminate this figure altogether.

By bearing in mind the subgenre's reliance on "bad," "phallocentric" closure, the analyst may avoid the essentialist valorization evident in much of the scholarship on a televisual woman's genre like soap opera, which is much less reliant on closure.[3] Here it is instructive that the softcore featurette often conveys its gender biases through twists, symmetries, and epiphanies. Indeed, a mild misandry is such a normalized component of this subgenre that it often serves as the precondition for the kind of reversal or twist so prevalent at the end of featurettes[4]—which is an ironic reminder of the inadequacy of any method that would identify closure, cinematic or televisual, with "maleness." On the other hand, such closure does not imply that the featurette is rigidly plot-oriented. It is actually less reliant on suspense than the softcore feature, which is more rooted in thriller convention. Like a short story, the featurette enjoys a degree of autonomy from the plot-oriented suspense that confines longer narrative media. Featurettes often adopt free-form, stream-of-consciousness tactics common in the literary sketch (or "vignette"). Stylization of this sort lends *RSD* and *WSP* a surreal, music video sensibility.[5] Given the subgenre's aspirationalism and interest in fantasy, such artifice is justifiable. Yet these departures from traditional realism do not imply that the subgenre has cultivated a "postfeminist" or "postmodernist" openness. Indeed, featurettes often substitute literary sources of closure for more traditional ones, supplanting a more Aristotelian climax with an epiphany that pretends to present the essence of a specific narrative context, indirectly imparting a "sense of an ending." Likewise, the featurette often resorts to binding devices that yield closure by creating symmetries between beginnings and ends.

Another reason for stressing closure is industrial. Cable programmers have prized the closed, abbreviated nature of the featurette for its utility. Individual featurettes may be lumped with others, creating a feature-length unit consisting of two, three, four, or even five featurettes, or they may be detached into self-sufficient parts. Featurettes may thus be used as late-night "filler," moving viewers from one feature presentation to another.[6] The shorter the unit, the more flexible it becomes, which is one reason many serials are shorter than *RSD*. This factor may seem inconsequential, but industrially it is no small thing, for each of the premium channels is today an elaborately multiplexed network with dozens of late-night slots that did not exist just ten years ago.[7]

Of course, the initial industrial purpose of the softcore serial was not to serve as filler but to increase viewership. Here the popularization of the softcore serial may be viewed as the by-product of two types of jockeying. On one hand, King gave Showtime a fresh advantage in its competition with HBO, which had until the early 1990s treated Showtime as a "perennial also ran" (qtd. in Backstein 303; Mair 111–15). Between 1995 and 1999, Showtime's subscriber base nearly doubled to 22,300,000 homes (Backstein 305). By many accounts, *RSD* was a salient factor in Showtime's surge. Though rarely advertised today, the softcore serial relied on heavy promotion during its initial proliferation. Showtime made *RSD* its "flagship and best-known program" through such promotion, targeting women in some spots and men in others (Backstein 304, 308, 309; Bellafante 76). Showtime further accented the idiosyncratic feminization of its erotic sensibility in campaigns for later shows like *WSP* (Juffer, *Home* 223–24), whose rhetoric of female authenticity provided marketers with a reliable angle. As a result, *WSP* briefly became Showtime's "highest-rated late night program" (Eby 1).

On the other hand, that HBO and its affiliates jumped on the *RSD* bandwagon indicates that King's confessional format offered premium cable an advantage in its larger competition with network television, home video, and theatrical Hollywood. Even more than the softcore feature, the softcore serial supplied cable with a signature erotic vision. King's postfeminist aspirationalism also allowed cable programmers to amplify the sexual explicitness of their shows without violating "good taste," further indicating the medium's commercial uniqueness. Though premium cable avoids the NC-17 rating, its programmers have not, like Hollywood, avoided NC-17 content—for that is what cable's TVMA-rated softcore mostly is.[8] In a sense, then, the strategies of premium cable have resembled those of classical sexploitation. Much as theatrical sexploitation once marketed itself as an alternative to network television (as restricted by the FCC) and classical Hollywood (as restricted by the Production Code), cable has marketed itself as a risqué alternative to network television (as still restricted by the FCC) and contemporary Hollywood (as restricted in effect if not principle by the MPAA).

The softcore serial is no longer central to premium cable. Soon after *WSP*'s debut, the vogue for "trumpet[ing] the soft-core project" waned (Backstein 316). Competition drove down the cost-per-featurette of many serials while increasing their sexual density.[9] The form's deteriorating values meant that *RSD* would strike television critics as both the pioneer of the genre and its qualitative peak (Backstein 309). One factor in this decline was a shift in Showtime's rivalry with HBO. In the late 1990s, HBO developed *The Sopranos* (1998 on) and *Sex and the City* (1999–2004). Showtime countered with stylish evening soaps like *Queer as Folk* (2000–2005) and *The L Word* (2004 on), which focus on gays and lesbians. Having once defined itself through alternative takes on heterosexuality, Showtime now defines itself through alternatives *to* heterosexuality, positing credible views of groups it once depicted as "exotic" others. This shift from the (seemingly) firm realm of heterosexuality to the (apparently) fluid realm of alternative sexualities is offset by a stylistic shift from soft, flexible fantasy to a harder, more stable realism. But it would be wrong to downplay the links between the two types of serials. As Karen Backstein puts it, the "soft-core series gave hints of what cable could evolve into and how it could compete by offering adult-oriented fare that the commercial networks could not" (304).[10]

In two different eras, feminism gave sexploitation the tools to survive, develop, and prosper. But even in sexploitation's most feminized subgenre, this postfeminist inflection has entailed neither any identification with feminism nor any deep realization of its ideals. It is intriguing then that over the past twelve years increasingly postfeminist feminists have shown a gathering unwillingness to critique the subgenre's inequities, often because they fixate on female agency as reliably as the subgenre itself does—and thus they marginalize issues of equality and diversity with similar alacrity.

II. PROPRIETY VS. CORRECTNESS IN SOFTCORE SERIALS

> *"I like the idea of cataloguing what women want, what women think, not what's politically correct to want."*
> —"MIND'S EYE" (WSP, 1997)

The conspicuous feminization of the softcore serial indicates overlapping impulses. It *is* an attempt to satisfy certain estimates of taste and propriety; it *also* implies an attempt to conform to ideas of political correctness. "Propriety" and "correctness" are, of course, relative. "Propriety" refers to a broad, mainstream form of correctness, while "correctness" connotes minority interests. Most pejoratively, the term implies prejudicial pandering. Its positive connotation is left implicit, for the term is rarely used affirmatively. This subtext suggests the ideals—empowerment, equality, diversity—that liberalism exalts and putatively fosters. The companies that have financed the subgenre are by all accounts conservative, so it is safe to say that the softcore serial has aimed for a broad postfeminist propriety, not a narrow feminist correctness. The serial is so conservative, in fact, that its depictions provide a useful graph for sorting out which ideas once narrowly identified with feminism have achieved mainstream status.

Martin pioneered discussion of this subgenre in "*Red Shoe Diaries:* Sexual Fantasy and the Construction of the (Hetero)sexual Woman" (1994). In this important essay, Martin notes *RSD*'s central feminization, using this link to "'women's' genres" as a basis for a feminist appraisal of the serial (47). In questioning whether *RSD* "posits any resistances to masculinist discourses," Martin systematically tests King's serial against various standards of feminist correctness (45). Because Martin's essay appeared at about the same time that softcore coalesced as a distinct industry, its priorities are helpful not only in discerning *RSD*'s tenuous relation to feminism but also in discerning the postfeminist propriety of the larger markets energized by King.

Martin is revealing in her mix of praise, blame, and silence. Reflecting her feminist advocacy, she commends *RSD* for its empowerment of female characters and tolerance of their sexual fantasies, biases she deems emblematic of the show's larger empowerment of its female spectators. For Martin, the show is laudable for positing a female narrative subject and for positioning men as sex objects (49–50). Martin also praises *RSD*'s "construction of [female] fantasies based on real desires," an authenticity that she deems responsible for the show's rejection of the idea that women have trouble separating fantasy and reality (50). Her main objections also result from her valorization of female subjectivity, so her most incisive criticism involves King's choice of host. Because Jake's point of view encloses and evaluates each featurette, any freedom of female expression "is impinged upon by Jake's own subjective desires and imperatives" (Martin 45). Less consistent is her criticism of the show's unequal objectification. As Martin notes, "the object of the gaze fluctuates within the narrative—more often than not, women are the objects, even though they are narrative subjects" (49).

Martin's other criticisms are secondary. She considers the show's heterosexuality patriarchal. Even when *RSD* strays from a traditional framework by exploring female same-sex desire, it reduces such desire to "just another spicy alternative in the realm of heterosexual experience" (Martin 52). In her end comments, Martin regrets that *RSD* is "addressed specifically to white, heterosexual women," making no effort "to confront the interconnected oppressions of race and gender that exist in contemporary culture" (56). This criticism seems disingenuous given that Martin herself evinces little interest in such issues. After all, though *RSD* may not *critique* these "oppressions," it does *register* them through its "exoticization" of lower-class white males and minorities. Said dynamic in turn raises interesting questions of class, race, and gender about which she is likewise reticent. The closest that Martin comes to acknowledging one of King's most consistent "signatures"—he singles out lower-class male objects for middle-class female subjects—is to applaud the *RSD* feature for "pointedly" depicting its middlebrow heroine as she lustily watches its proletarian hero "at work on a construction site, taking off his shirt and so on" (50). She thus expresses no concern about the implicit sexism and classism of the feminized framework that she endorses throughout her article.

In this economy, female narrative agency trumps all other feminist/liberal values, including equality. Martin deprioritizes equality even when major structural inequalities affect female characters in seemingly problematic ways. Jake's role is central to Martin's critique, for it threatens to subvert the heroine's narrative control. The larger inequity of the spectacle, which exposes women more than men, does not elicit comparable concern from Martin, for it does not directly undercut female subjectivity. "Although there may not be much uncovered to look at," Martin observes, "the diegetic women are shown as looking [at men] and as deriving pleasure from looking" (49). Martin is saying, then, that the energy that King devotes to his narrative construction of women is *enough*. The fact that he has privileged his heroines in the diegesis is adequate "compensation" for their unequal treatment in the spectacle. This reasoning in effect limits Martin's interrogation of *RSD*'s visual inequity, which in a narrowly feminist sense she deems incorrect. Indeed, Martin specifically excuses this incorrectness through a disclaimer that acknowledges the "need for *propriety* in a soft-core cable series" (49; my italics).

Martin's uncritical acceptance of this visual inequity assents to the softcore serial's cardinal strategy. The subgenre systematically defends its central impropriety and selling point, female nudity, by conforming with mainstream propriety in most other respects. The result is a patently unequal treatment of male and female bodies and, if we accept Martin's logic—which assumes a direct link between empowered female characters and empowered female viewers—of male and female viewers as well. Note that these visual inequities do *not* follow from legal inequities. Even the male genitalia are not *a priori* obscene and can be depicted flaccid in both R-rated and TVMA vehicles, just as female breasts, buttocks, and genitals can be depicted there. Of course, as Martin has indicated, male nudity is widely considered more improper or "indecent" than female nudity. That the penis is absent from the softcore serial indicates that corporate softcore studios in particular recognize this differential impropriety and have no interest in adding "nonessential" male nudity that might complicate the distribution of the more "essential" commodity, female nudity. The persistence of this structuring inequity is a complex aesthetic and sociological phenomenon, yet the most obvious reason that this imbalance persists is that it is rarely challenged. Such silence reinforces the idea that the penis is improper and unwanted and, in sum, unprofitable. Even Martin, who presents herself as an arbiter of feminist correctness, is not agitated by its absence.

There is, though, evidence of a female heterosexual desire for a more equitable form of softcore. In the Softcore Reviews forum, female consumers have repeatedly expressed displeasure over the lack of male exposure. In June 2005, one female viewer even asked MRG casting director Robert Lombard why softcore is so "cautious about [male] frontal exposure. . . . The scenes often strategically avoid their cocks."[11] Similarly, Linda Ruth Williams has quoted a "female porn user" who, after criticizing "'mainstream porn,'" claims that there is "'a real need for porn for single women. We want erections, attractive men, things that don't look fake'" (*Erotic* 275n29). But I have encountered no feminist critics demanding penises.[12] This omission is crucial in that sexploitation has been uniquely responsive, if not precisely or uniformly so, to feminist criticism. History suggests that the softcore industry would be more willing to risk breaching mainstream ideas of propriety regarding the exposure of penises if doing otherwise risked breaching feminist ideas of correctness—and generating negative publicity.

As executive producer of *WSP*, Elisa Rothstein has an interesting take on this issue. She qualifies as an "antifeminist feminist" typical of postfeminism's pro-sex areas. Though she evades a feminist label—like most softcore producers, she collapses feminism into sex-negative images (Eby 4–5)—she has feminist sympathies as conveyed by her unhappiness that "there was and is a double standard" in her Playboy-financed serial. "[O]ne of the few things I have not been successful in fighting with them is about male nudity," she notes (qtd. in Eby 4). "They have no problem with complete female nudity." But Rothstein lets Playboy off the hook anecdotally: "I ran an art gallery in New York for many years, and we had a show with a lot of beautiful portraits of female nudes, and there was one of a woman sitting on a bed, wearing a skirt but no top, and she had very large breasts, and lying next to her was a completely naked man. We had hate mail coming in to the gallery, and people were just incensed that we were showing a penis; it didn't matter there were fourteen pairs of breasts there."

Rothstein understands the propriety and practicality of Playboy's double standard, though she considers it incorrect in principle. She thus follows the pattern set by male peers, who lament softcore's sexist patterning while acting within its strictures. The difference is that Rothstein accepts this inequity in compensation: it reinforces ideas basic to her sense of gender superiority. "Women are not as turned on by pure voyeurism," she claims, for they prefer "something a little more complicated" (qtd. in Eby 3; see Jaehne 15). Because *WSP* satisfies this yearning for narrative, it does not matter that its spectacle is biased toward "male-defined eroticism." That she and other women do not care overmuch about this sort of equality only confirms their sexual complexity (Eby 4).

Here the ideas of Jane Juffer and Backstein form an intriguing addendum. If the diegetic feminization compensates Martin and Rothstein for visual inequity, it seems to spur Juffer and Backstein to view that inequity less clearly. *Contra* Rothstein's own admissions, these scholars claim that *WSP* transcends the visual inequity typical of the softcore serial. "In contrast to *Red Shoe* and to most adult cable programs," Juffer asserts, "*Women* regularly shows as much of the male body as the female" (*Home* 224). Though Backstein notices that *WSP* lacks penises, she concurs with Juffer by quoting her on this point (312–13). *WSP does* sexualize males, aligning this objectification with female viewpoints. And like *RSD*, *WSP does* go beyond the norm in providing sculpted male bodies. But this hardly amounts to *regular visual equality*. In *WSP*, female nudity is far more on display than male. It is possible that Juffer has formed this misimpression not only on the basis of the profemale diegesis but also on that of *WSP*'s ostensibly all-female team—that is, on that of the female-authenticity rhetoric manipulated by Rothstein, Playboy, and Showtime.[13] Throughout *At Home with Pornography: Women, Sex, and Everyday Life* (1998), Juffer stresses the importance of women's having access to production, so her investment in a positive evaluation of *WSP* is perhaps suspect.

Such reactions offer industrial incentives to maintain the inequity of the spectacle. They also offer incentives to fortify the inverse inequities of the diegesis. Both trends would seem to feed the masochistic pattern of male identification to which Linda Ruth Williams alludes (*Erotic* 352). If female viewers can leave a softcore narrative feeling empowered, as Martin implies, male viewers are unlikely to do the same. It is intriguing that these interlocking, gender-specific, narrative-number biases have only become more overt in the softcore serial as budgets have fallen. Though it makes sense that producers have packed later, less aspirational serials like *Nightcap, Hotel Erotica,* and *The Best Sex Ever* with more sex to overcome lower values, it is less commonsensical that post-*RSD* plots have at the same time become more bluntly misandristic. But that is precisely what has happened. This misandry has not made the subgenre less proper.[14] *If this subgenre teaches anything, it is that misandry does not transgress postfeminist ideas of propriety; unlike misogyny, it may be used as a defensive shield.*

Post-*RSD* serials have tended to comply with Martin's most pressing narrative concerns[15]—and, in a parallel trend, have reinforced visual inequities. Often, the creation of increasingly proper postfeminist narratives has entailed supplementing narrative biases already evident in *RSD*. To wit, Martin praises *RSD* for positioning its female subjects as active voyeurs in many installments, of which there are sixty-seven. Consider "Runway" (1993), an *RSD* featurette that centers on a fashion model (Amber Smith) who inverts the objectification that structures her work life by encouraging Miguel (Daniel Blasco), a working-class immigrant, to sample her experience by modeling for her.[16] But "Runway" is typical of *RSD* and its successors in that it skews toward male objectification and nudity mainly in diegetic and intellectual senses. Thus, in its climactic spectacle, the hero is surrounded by a bevy of naked models more exposed than he.

RSD and its successors have been less equivocal in embodying another element of the King paradigm that Martin deems praiseworthy. According to Martin, "the common stereotype of female overidentification with image and narrative" has yielded an image of women as susceptible, infantile consumers needful of paternalistic censorship to protect them from inappropriate cultural forms, including those involving rape (46). But if women easily differentiate reality and fantasy, it is wrong to place "prescriptive" limits on female desire, including rape fantasies (56). Martin thus applauds *RSD* narratives for bolstering the idea that women have no trouble negotiating the fantasy-reality divide. Of course, not every *RSD* featurette agrees with Martin on this. As noted in chapter 5, "Auto Erotica" ends with the heroine chanting, "Was he real, or did I make him up?" Still, Martin's point is mostly valid and is even more applicable to *RSD*'s successors.

Witness "Locked Up" (1995), an *EC* featurette whose heroine (Raelyn Saalman) trades letters with a man who she assumes is a prisoner. Their correspondence fuels her *noir*-inflected fantasies of dominance; having lost a spouse, such fantasy is therapy. This patently sympathetic use of fantasy is disrupted when her "pen" pal reveals a plan to visit her. But the heroine's anti-erotic anxieties go for naught. In a closing twist, the man turns out to be not a dangerous ex-con but a dapper warden with a British accent. As in many featurettes—*Hot Line*'s "The Brunch Club" (1996) offers another sterling example—the point is clear. Women not only distinguish fantasy from reality but manifest distinct erotic reactions based on the plane on which they perceive themselves. The more feminized and aspirational the serial, the more didactically it underlines this postfeminist truism. Hence *WSP* has a notable investment in it. For instance, in "Mind's Eye" (1997), the heroine (Holley Chant) clarifies and reclarifies this point in two enclosing voiceovers, which both assert that "[w]hat I want in my fantasies, the scenarios that excite me, aren't necessarily what I would get with a man I wanted to share my life with."

Besides reinforcing elements of the *RSD* narrative paradigm that Martin identifies as profemale, post-*RSD* serials have also modified elements that Martin identifies as antifemale. According to Martin, these include King's use of a male commentator, Jake, who punishes women "every time they put on the red shoes in what he deems is an inappropriate heterosexual relationship" (55). Though Martin is right about Jake, what she could not realize from her temporal vantage is that his commentaries would, as Backstein discerns, grow more detached and ironic over the course of the series. Juffer's critique also overlooks Jake's principal function. Like Max (James Spader) in *White Palace* (1990), this character is a pervasively feminized emblem of male heterosexual commitment. To eliminate him is to purge a source of narrative richness and to censure a major heterosexual fantasy whose ownership by "real" women is implicit not only in a serial like *WSP* but in more consistently female-produced genres like romance fiction and soap opera. Thus Martin has herself placed a "prescriptive" limit on the fantasies that women might entertain. Her proempowerment position cannot countenance the idea that women might enjoy watching fictive men judge fictive women.

Putting these points aside, it is fascinating to note how fully later examples of the subgenre have corrected *RSD* in this regard. In shows that either feature or imply a host—including *EC, Hot Line, WSP, Intimate Sessions, Hotel Erotica,* and *The Best Sex Ever*—such a figure is neither male nor judgmental. What remarks these hosts offer are rarely salient, limited to affirmation or arousal. Indeed, even *EC*'s unclad Jacqueline and *WSP*'s buttoned-up Interviewer, who both recall Jake,[17] avoid commentary. This development is in accord with other elements of the subgenre, which has steadily abolished any physical or psychological threat associated with a female's active donning of the "red shoes" of desire. In that sense, the subgenre represents the farthest reach of an antimisogynistic process initiated by classical sexploitation. This consumerist tendency toward postfeminist tolerance and empathy has simultaneously afforded the subgenre further opportunities for female objectification. Although *WSP*'s host is a notable exception, the hosts of *Hot Line* (Tanya Roberts) and *The Best Sex Ever* (Angela Davies) are highly sexualized. *EC*'s ever-naked Jacqueline is the logical culmination of this trend.

Post-*RSD* serials also provide qualified "improvements" in diversity. Though still dominated by white, middle-class, female heterosexuals, compared to other softcore subgenres, the softcore serial offers a strikingly diverse cast of characters.[18] In *EC*, an episode like "The Games People Play" (1994) portrays a casual group of six friends, three of whom are nonwhites and all of whom are of equal diegetic significance. The later serial *Intimate Sessions*—which was financed by New City under Marilyn Vance's Ministry of Film label, a corporate softcore label that coproduced *EC*—includes several multiethnic featurettes, including "Celeste" (1998) and "Elena" (1998). In "Celeste," the white protagonist (Caroline Key Johnson) is involved in a relationship with a black man (Alan Foster) that temporarily expands into a *ménage à trois* with another white woman (Landon Hall). In "Elena," the three principals (Letrica Cruz, Al Cruz, J. T. Pontino) are Mexican Americans, with the plot focusing on a father-daughter relationship. That other serials supply comparable examples demonstrates the imprecision of referring to *WSP* as a multicultural "exception" (308), as Backstein has—though she is correct in that *WSP* is the most reliably diverse serial and the one most likely to address minorities through identity-specific stylization. On the whole, however, *WSP*'s treatment of diversity resembles that of other softcore serials, which habitually adopt nonoppositional postures that most often result in assimilationist, melting-pot depictions of diversity—*or* in the eroticization of diversity as "the exotic." The one area in which *WSP* adopts a relatively critical posture *vis-à-vis* its own diversity is in its depiction of female same-sex sexuality. Though this factor may seem adversarial, it is more compellingly viewed as a function of the comfortable sexism that pervades the subgenre's narratives.

By "assimilationist," I imply the softcore serial's aforementioned reluctance to "confront the interconnected oppressions of race and gender." Many post-*RSD* serials are more diverse than *RSD* but no more critical; gender and sexuality are still deployed as essentialist qualities submerging other forms of difference. Projansky suggests that such mechanisms are characteristic of postfeminist forms (73–74, 87–88). In popular works, minority figures seem present mainly to enable, in Celia Lury's words, "communication between white people" (190). Thus Projansky helps contextualize how a featurette like "Celeste" can focus on an interracial trio in which two white women vie for the sexual attention of a black man without *once* alluding to race—an omission that is nothing if not characteristic of the subgenre. Of the above featurettes, "Elena" comes closest to a critique. It attempts a credible depiction of a Mexican American family and involves the messy breakup of a Chicana and her white boyfriend (Ed Lee Johnson). But even here there is a curious reticence. Though "Elena" implies that this breakup is motivated by racism, the diegesis avoids exploration of this possibility, with Elena repeatedly dismissing her boyfriend's evident disrespect by reference to alcohol intake.

Despite its greater diversity, *WSP* follows the pattern. In Julie Dash's "Grip Till It Hurts" (1997), a multicultural group of female subalterns confirms its savvy at film production—and at negotiating the sexual hazards of the workplace. But the fact that the four major figures include two positive black men (including a director) and two negative black men (including a producer) muzzles the critique, which goes no further than to say that some men are unprofessional "womanizers" while others are sensitive and professional. Diversity is more central in *WSP* featurettes such as "The Lucky Bar," "Angel from the Sky," "Sophie Shpoorickey's Night of Love," "La Limpia," and "Voodoo" (all 1997). Like "Elena," these episodes construct detailed, stylized images of the everyday lives of minority women, lives inflected by diverse heritages. But if the multicultural stylization apparent in these featurettes makes them less assimilationist than is typical, it does not make them any more adversarial. These featurettes at most posit undeveloped hints that a heroine's ethnic background has adversely affected her love life. And it is *far* more likely for such details to be eroticized than politicized. Thus "Elena" imagines a milieu in which copulation occurs in a kitchen, with a classic "Latin lover" purveying spicy food and spicy sex. Such diegetic processes sustain cultural stereotypes, "exoticizing" ethnic details in all of the above *WSP* featurettes. Even more subtle effects inform other featurettes, as when, in "Motel Magic" (1997), an anonymous black male with dreadlocks is twice used to deliver magical dishware.

Most arresting is the use of the exotic to structure an entire featurette. In "Voodoo," a repressed, light-skinned black doctor (Daphne Duplaix) is "awakened" by a dark-skinned black researcher with dreadlocks (Leroy Edwards). She is thereafter disturbed by dreams in which seminude black dancers in white shifts palpate each other to jungle rhythms. It is slowly revealed that her love object has cast a spell on her, confirming him as a beneficent practitioner of voodoo: he is a witch doctor to her medical doctor. This scenario hinges on specific racial images and invokes conceptual "bundles" limned by Dyer (*Matter* 141–61) wherein whiteness (here *lightness*), rationality, and asexuality oppose blackness, irrationality, and sexuality. That the traditional valuations of these groupings have been reversed, such that the former are neutral and the latter virtuous, does not make them less stereotypical—though the dialogue, in a familiar pattern, avoids race.[19] This scenario also traffics in a backlash stereotype—for women, professional success connotes dysfunction and "bitchiness"—that has been a constant of the softcore serial since King routinized it in *RSD*. Like King's career women, the heroine of "Voodoo" just needs hot sex to improve her life and mood.

That Rothstein would approve such scripts is predictable. She wrote *Delta of Venus,* an Anaïs Nin adaptation directed by King that features interracial spectacle of a buff West African whose clairvoyance has "voodoo" appeal. Accordingly, *Delta of Venus* has been criticized for perpetuating King's "bad habit of using lesbians, gays, prostitutes, and nonwhites as exotic accents; they lend a touch of artsy kink that never endangers the main characters' respectable heterosexuality" (Elias 64). It is instructive that this survey neglects King's signature "exoticism." His middle-class heroines often objectify lower-class white heroes in a way that fetishizes class and gender difference, positioning them not just as objects but as cultural "others." That such a dynamic has escaped attention is unremarkable given that American cultural studies, unlike its British opposite, has never lavished as much attention on the politics of class as on those of gender and race. Thus Martin is able to celebrate King's signature motif as progressive (50). If, then, Martin has avoided the exotic in a class context, she has also avoided it in a racial context. Though Martin alludes to the limitations of *RSD*'s assimilationist depictions (56), she omits that by 1994 *RSD* had a record of relegating minorities to supporting roles exploited for their exotic-other status. It is possible that she has avoided this topic—which is relevant to her "Taboo as Turn-on" section (50–52)—because in this context her feminist imperatives conflict with the larger imperatives of multiculturalism. Martin promotes a vision of female fantasy unconstrained by external influence; she also advocates responsibly diverse depictions. It is worth speculating that she banishes the exotic from her analysis because it highlights the difficulty of reconciling such imperatives.

The closest Martin comes to critiquing *RSD*'s use of the exotic is her complaint that the serial places same-sex contact in a heterosexual framework such that it becomes "just another spicy alternative" rather than "a political or emotional question for the female heroine" (52). She is correct. If *RSD* departs from low, pornographic convention in the style and detail with which it treats the girl-girl number—which feminists have historically reviled for its heterosexual underpinnings and lack of realism—it does not radically remodel this sexploitation motif. It is here that Rothstein's serial seems least superficial. Even "Kat Tails" (1997), a *WSP* featurette that retains a heterosexual scheme, frames its same-sex climax as no mere dalliance. Keenly stylized, "Kat Tails" concludes with an emotional epiphany through which the heroine (Trista Delamere) positions her encounter with a lesbian (Kelly Galindo) working for a peep-show operator as a necessary act of female self-revelation. "To know it"—and by "it," the heroine means her sexual self—"I had to find my mirror. What I saw was *lovely.*"

Like so many closure devices in the subgenre, this epiphany is premised on male deficiency: the heroine bemoans the fact that she did not know basic things about herself like the softness of her lips because no man had told her. But it is telling that even an episode that removes the heterosexual frame still depends on misandry for impetus and closure. Consider "Room 1503," which conveys the separatist view that for women same-sex encounters are preferable *because* they do not involve men. Two pointed elements lead to this misandristic proposition. First, the featurette begins in a bar where cloddish, territorial men try and repeatedly fail to pick up the presumably heterosexual heroine (Lisa Welti). Second, in articulating postcoital same-sex delight, this heroine stresses that sex with a man "is very different than this . . . I'm usually the passive one. I usually have to wait for the man. It's like I'm not afraid to be myself with you." The heroine's point is indirectly expressed by spectacle that self-consciously foregrounds mutual pleasure as intermingled with what Backstein calls "warm girl talk" (312), which is distinct from a "hotter," more pornographic "dirty talk." The heroine's insight would seem identical to that of "Kat Tails" except for the twist. The entire scenario amounts to role-playing within a committed lesbian relationship. The misandry that at first seems incidental is a ritualized component of this couple's sex life.

In dispensing with the exotic, "Room 1503" establishes itself as a credible and "correct" attempt to depict same-sex contact. But in its reliance on a simplified misandry, its feminist correctness overlaps with a nonsubversive, postfeminist propriety that sexploitation has rigidly upheld in the contemporary era. Here it is worth stipulating that despite their female authorship, the same-sex segments of "Kat Tails" and "Room 1503" do not exist apart from sexploitation traditions. The idea that the male-authored girl-girl number always amounts to an unrealistic, throwaway scene involving minor characters with peroxide hair and silicone breasts is an ahistorical view that can only be based on a limited knowledge of texts. Such scenes exist in profusion, but more upscale depictions exist in profusion as well. In fact, the misandristic bias informing "Kat Tails" and "Room 1503"—namely, that girl-girl sex is more tasteful, sensitive, and *lovely* than boy-girl sex—is a normalized assumption of the feminized, aspirational sexploitation long purveyed by male directors like Metzger, Sarno, Jaeckin, King, Alexander Gregory Hippolyte, and Tom Lazarus.[20] Given softcore's historical desire to elevate itself above "mere porn," this motif's ubiquity is logical, as is its deployment in prestige hardcore by Candida Royalle and Andrew Blake (O'Toole 194–95)—and in prestige nighttime soaps like Showtime's *The L Word*. Traditionally, this motif has been popular because it highlights female nudity. Thus the irony underlying the condescension of "Room 1503": the feminized diegesis collaborates with the masculinized bias of the spectacle, dispensing with any possibility of male display. The softcore serial has again "fixed" a patriarchal flaw identified by Martin in a way that accentuates female nudity.

In valorizing *WSP*'s profemale narrative, Juffer and Backstein do not identify the condescension and occasional hostility toward men that typify the *WSP* worldview. But their indirect references to this antipathy suggest that, like Rothstein, they view such sexism as broadly proper and narrowly correct. Indeed, after falsely asserting *WSP*'s freedom from visual bias, Juffer specifically condones the show's presentation of women "in the role of teachers, instructing men on how to give women greater sexual pleasure" (*Home* 224)—and on both points, Backstein indicates her agreement with Juffer (313). But here again, an ahistorical view is misleading. According to Juffer, the tutor-heroine of *WSP*'s "The Bitter and the Sweet" (1997) "enhances other women's real sexual lives by instructing a young man how to better pleasure women" (*Home* 224). Though "The Bitter and the Sweet" is undeniably biased toward women, the understanding that Juffer takes from this episode is not historically distinctive and cannot be meaningfully assigned to a female essence encoded in the piece by *WSP*'s female producers. As a sexploitation motif, the female sexual tutor is foregrounded in many serials and has been a standard sexploitation device since the classical era. A notable juncture in the postfeminist evolution of this motif is the divide between *Emmanuelle* and *Emmanuelle 2: The Joys of a Woman* (1975).

Though Jaeckin's original now seems incorrect *and* improper in its paternalistic vision of a heroine whose erotic education is dominated by males, Francis Giacobetti's sequel shifts control to Emmanuelle herself, yielding a depiction whose misandry remains current. In the 1980s, this feminized motif was incorporated by openly pornographic sexploitation comedies (*Young Lady Chatterley II*) and by less pornographic ones (*My Tutor*). In such films, older women tutor younger men in the "art" of female pleasure. Thus, when the softcore serial adopted the motif, the beneficence of the tutor was underscored by educational metaphors, as in *Love Street*'s "Grading on a Curve" and *The Best Sex Ever*'s "Homework" (2002). Hence, "Grading on a Curve" ends with a twist already predictable in 1995. Rather than reproving her boyfriend's former "tutor" (Kendra Tucker) as the audience is led to expect, the woman (Elisabeth Imboden) who is the "beneficiary" of her instruction thanks the tutor instead.

I do not mean to overstate the offensiveness of this sexist motif. It is typically couched in a gentle idiom blending the maternal with the paternalist—which makes it an improvement on the bondage-and-brutalization misogyny offered by classical subgenres. But this inverted paternalism does betray fixed condescensions and double standards. Consider that vehicles like *My Tutor* and "Grading on a Curve" often involve teenage males in high school. Could a correct *or* proper subgenre be fabricated from a motif in which male teachers instruct their female charges in the tender art of fellatio, while justifying themselves via the altruistic thought that they are improving the experience of unknown boyfriends? It is a ludicrous contemplation. But this motif has occasioned even more expansive double standards. In *Nightcap*, the tutor figures as a metaphor for the role heterosexual women *should* play in the lives of their partners. The men of "Illicit Affairs" (2000) and "Everyone Has a Price" (2000) are uncivilized children needful of reform. In the former, this misandristic perspective motivates an extended, passionate oration greeted by sisterly huzzahs, adding a new inflection to Backstein's "warm girl talk."[21] In both featurettes, the give-him-a-dose-of-his-own-medicine pedagogy deployed by the heroines offers a rationale for getting them out of their clothes, indicating another way in which feminized narrative biases collaborate with masculinized visual biases in this subgenre. Most striking is that the necessity of "civilizing" one's man acts as an ethical catchall that gives the heroine unquestioned license to cheat and lie.

The softcore serial departs from its celebration of female agency in one notable respect: it often resorts to art-world scenarios in which women serve as passive muses. As chapter 3 notes, the artist-model motif has a long sexploitation lineage, figuring in classical exploitation (see *The Naked Venus*), in contemporary sexploitation (see *Delta of Venus*), and everywhere in between. This durability is understandable. It confers aspirational cachet and offers justification for denuding "Venus." Still, its presence is peculiar in a postfeminist subgenre, for it empowers a male subject. Even in *EC*'s "Model Situation" (1995)—a featurette that subverts the more passive constructions of featurettes like *Love Street*'s "Galatea's Wish" (1994) and *EC*'s "The Painting" (1995)—the heroine's agency is confined to the imaginary. Only *WSP* resists these reactionary dynamics. *WSP*'s treatment of this device is, then, one of the few instances in which the program's female bias does not augment the exposure of female bodies in the spectacle and one of the few ways in which its feminist intonation diverges from broader trends. Apparently, in other serials, this motif has retained its prefeminist inflection because its traditional gender dynamic cannot be reconfigured without forfeiting its traditional visual utility—and because producers have calculated that the aspirational feminization encoded in such scenarios is *enough*. After all, the stereotypical artist subject who objectifies a muse as a prelude to fucking her is a feminized male with long hair and Euro-sensibility who articulates an aesthetic of female beauty. But the subtext of this flattering gentility is a sacrifice of female subjectivity. The softcore serial is, then, more likely to abandon its female-agency ethic than its female-nudity imperative. At times, such a sacrifice leads to the alignment of the softcore serial's perspective with a misogynistic ethic that openly patronizes women, thus "resisting" the misandristic norms typical of the subgenre. This type of condescension is, for instance, on brazen display in "Galatea's Wish." It is as if the platitudinous aestheticism of such vehicles—complete with their incoherent rejection of consumer materialism—releases them to vent a kind of misogyny far more common in prefeminist sexploitation. Plainly, these misogynistic scenarios are sexist and superficial. In a generalized sense, then, they conform neatly with the subgenre's larger trend toward misandry, which likewise combines sexism with superficiality.

"Exploitation films present serious problems for feminists," Pam Cook wrote in 1976 (123). Given that the softcore serial offers relatively inoffensive, female-friendly, and "naturalised" versions of the "myths" so clear in the classical sexploitation films of which Cook speaks (124), this subgenre may present more subtle yet no less serious problems. And now it is clear why. Sexploitation has steadily synthesized feminist ideas into its postfeminist "propriety." This trend has been most comprehensive in the softcore serial, an aspirational subgenre inspired by a Showtime hit, *RSD*. Despite this absorption of feminist ideas—and *because* of it—the subgenre has remained rife with gender-based double standards and images. Its most decisive double standard is spectacle that inordinately commodifies female nudity. Though this profitable bias could be presented as exploitive, similarly "pro-sex" biases have been so normalized by postfeminist popular culture that they are today rarely presented as hostile to women, least of all when couched in hyperfeminized mainstream forms like the softcore serial. Indeed, the subgenre's secondary bias—as encoded in postfeminist strategies that cater to women diegetically and stylistically—is the commercial guarantor of such inequity. Any style of critique with a fixed investment in feminine stereotypes may be inequipped to detect these sexist dynamics, which are difficult to discern in part because variations on them are everywhere operative in postfeminist culture.

This concern is not new. Since the 1980s, feminists have warned of the allure of a qualified turn toward traditional femininity. If critics like Read, Projansky, and Hollows are correct, "postfeminist feminism" often mirrors postfeminist culture: its essentialist embrace of femininity corresponds to a declining rigor *vis-à-vis* gender itself. Ergo, the slackening apparent in the movement from Martin's relatively critical posture to the more optimistic stances of Juffer and Backstein may gloss a larger academic receptiveness to the most characteristic strategies of the softcore serial.

"Our core audience will not accept anything that's not completely moronic and sexist."
—*Star Struck*

The Softcore Public
A Cult of Bad Faith?

I. SILENCE AND MUTILATION

Much of this study depicts contemporary softcore as a system of self-conscious texts rooted in an equally self-conscious "middle" industry situated uncertainly between hardcore and theatrical Hollywood. The benefit of this perspective is that it lavishes attention on the two elements principally responsible for the genre's peculiar coherence: its narrative-number dichotomy and the anxious industrial maneuvering that this sexualized structure has habitually precipitated. Unfortunately, this focus on texts and producers has tended to marginalize the softcore public, a clear apprehension of which is crucial to an overall softcore concept. The self-conscious patterns of omission, abjection, and distortion that distinguish softcore reception are, in fact, so of a piece with patterns discernible at other generic levels that studying this public yields a compelling argument for holistic conceptions of film genre generally.

However, these patterns of negation also frame the softcore public as a singularly difficult object of analysis. I make no pretense of presenting an exhaustive or scientific sociological study of the softcore audience. In the absence of reliable survey data, I focus instead on the interpretive habits of those segments of the audience that have publicized their consumption. This distinction between an *audience* and a self-proclaimed *public* may seem obvious, but clarity is mandatory here. In most contexts, the failure of an individual to publicize group membership would not of necessity entail suspicions of evasion and bad faith. If a fan of classic Westerns kept his obsession to himself, such would not by itself suggest that he was anxious or even *hiding*. But since every level of softcore shows traces of anxiety, reticence does raise suspicion; in this genre, consumer silence seems to assume a surplus intentionality. Doubtless, suppositions of this sort are in many if not most cases unwarranted, but as will become plain, they are not baseless.

Consider that silence is arguably the most salient way in which the contemporary softcore industry has marketed its products. In theatrical contexts, the discursive activity of consumers is spurred in part by the promotional exertions of producers and distributors, which provide consumers with a preliminary basis for their own readings, evaluations, and generic repositionings (Sandler 202; Altman 44–46). Yet in softcore, producers and distributors outside the cult nexus do not devote much energy to promotion. There are reasons for this reticence. Major cable and video distributors prefer producers to adopt an under-the-radar stance that allows entry into crucial outlets. Corporate softcore in particular has discouraged discussion, which could entail pornographic classification, thus jeopardizing distribution. Of course, this strategy often backfires, not only muzzling confab but also confusing genre-literate consumers hunting for softcore, cash in hand. Especially in chains like Blockbuster and Hollywood Video, the industry's under-the-radar approach—along with the fact that neither chain cordons softcore into an "adult" section—forces consumers to rely on rudimentary cues to predict a text's genre and contents.[1] But condemning such practices as hypocritical or inept would only conceal how it all *works:* discreet or deceptive producers have made feminized, values-oriented softcore films that have achieved mainstream reach through values-oriented chains, whose discreet or deceptive policies have acted as the guarantor of this market penetration. In turn, these policies have worked to consumer advantage in at least two major respects. As Jane Juffer asserts, a "bright, well-lit," family-friendly Blockbuster is such an "innocuous and easy site" that even "mothers with little time" can rent softcore there, all without the stigma of "going into a 'porn section'" ("No Place" 55). Industrial discretion and generic ambiguity also work to the advantage of consumers who would rather not admit even to themselves that they are renting "porn."

Which is to say that this industrial strategy may help individuals negotiate a set of intricate, internal contradictions that resemble what Jean-Paul Sartre has defined as "bad faith" or self-deception. In my research, I have talked to producers as well as consumers who have resisted calling fully dichotomous softcore "porn" or even "softcore." Typically, they would not, or could not, reconcile the dominant devaluation of "pornography," which they accept, with their manifest approval of a genre that they enjoy in various ways for various reasons. Hence, after one discussion—whose omissions and evasions made it seem like a *non*-discussion—my interlocutor stopped renting a popular form of softcore. Our conversation had repositioned those vehicles beyond his ideological limits. Rather than revalue the term "pornography" in a more flexible manner reflective of the harmless pleasure that he had taken from softcore, this consumer distanced himself from the object of his pleasure. According to Sartre, individuals in the thrall of bad faith convince themselves that they cannot live by their own beliefs, preferences, and values due to reasons beyond their control (*Being* 86–116). Pressured by ideologies that make it convenient to avoid asserting their idiosyncrasies (Coombes 1), such individuals reject the implications of their existential freedom. The reluctance of the softcore industry to talk about its products is, among other things, a tacit recognition that many consumers would sooner refuse its products than remold their attitudes in conformity with their pleasure. For the softcore industry, then, silence and obfuscation make better economic sense than the kind of ideological confrontation that begins with straightforward classification.

Despite these muzzlings, a softcore conversation has emerged as one concomitant of the post-1995 Internet explosion, which roughly coincided with the maturation of the industry. Though softcore has long had a marginal presence in print fanzines such as *Psychotronic Video,* the Internet has dramatically enlarged awareness of this genre. Today, many Internet sites provide forums for discussing softcore (though only a self-conscious few self-identify with the genre). Ironically, this expanding discursive fabric has made it possible to gauge the silences that still enmesh the genre. Such lacunae have a gendered character. Both men and women are susceptible to the ideologies that restrict and devalue softcore, but it appears these pressures have affected them unevenly. Though cable softcore in particular has a large female viewership, women are less likely than men to register their responses to softcore—and when they do, they prefer the most mainstream response sites. These intriguing phenomena dovetail with dispositions noted by scholars working on cult networks. But because it is difficult enough to follow the softcore conversation as manifest, I have limited my speculations about these and other silences, concentrating on the most salient and *present* responses.

For sake of clarity, I have organized the sites that register this online response to softcore into three categories. In the first category are relatively small "outsider" review sites that fit into a much larger cult network. These sites include The Joe Bob Report and b-independent, among scores of others. The second category is devoted to definitively mainstream "user review" sites such as IMDb and Amazon. The third and most pertinent category focuses on sites wholly devoted to softcore such as Softcore Reviews and This Is Sexy?[2] Though these consumer-oriented areas all evince a populist, nonacademic sensibility, each one is a specialized category that represents a distinct demographic and articulates a distinct taste regime. Though it is not possible to bestow the same level of detail on each of these categories, I will discuss the broadest distinctions among them, reserving the most scrutiny for the third category—and, more specifically, for Softcore Reviews, a forum that offers intriguing continuities and discontinuities with sites that identify themselves less problematically with the cult nexus.

Despite the minutiae distinguishing these sites, the responses they generate are dominated by some striking patterns. It is critical to bear in mind that the softcore public mainly comprises fans who verify their predilection for the genre by regularly returning to it. Still, even when they explicitly intend to celebrate softcore, these fans tend to delegitimize it via their application of condescending disclaimers. More characteristic yet is their bias toward partial interpretations that diminish or deny one part of softcore's narrative-number dichotomy so as to privilege another, a practice that at times verges on textual amputation or mutilation. These tendencies are rooted in anxieties attached to the genre's dichotomous structure and correlate with patterns visible in the response to other pluralistic softcore media. Reception theorist Mark Jancovich has, for instance, detected comparable patterns among *Playboy* readers ("Placing" 2–4). Interpreters of both forms of softcore insist that the "truth" of these mixed, middlebrow media inheres either in their "respectable" materials (narrative segments in the films, essays and fiction in the magazine) or in their "illegitimate" erotic materials (sexual numbers in the films, pictorials in the magazine). Though these responses to contemporary softcore are not always tantamount to bad faith, they routinely tend in that direction. Many responses conform to Sartrean definitions in that they implicitly value softcore's "impure," dichotomous nature even as they explicitly devalue, diminish, or deny that nature.

The negational style peculiar to softcore reception is disclosed most tellingly by comparison with the oppositional advocacy of cult audiences. The softcore advocate avoids the aggressive, self-assured rhetoric of "outsiders" praising low, cult texts or of "insiders" praising high, elite texts. Outsider and insider alike mystify their tastes via terms like "masterpiece" and "genius." But the softcore advocate shuns sacralizing terms, at most praising a film *qua* softcore in practical, utilitarian language that recognizes the genre's eroticism and even its craftsmanship but rarely its artistry—as if to imply that as a commercialized, affective genre softcore is *intrinsically* inartistic, one that can aspire to Entertainment but not Art. This self-effacing rhetoric is distinctive in that it dispenses with essentialist terminology but only as a meek gesture of "good taste" that recognizes a "higher" claim on such terms. As in responses to *Playboy*, this middling inferiority may come across as a self-conscious tic. The evaluation policy of Softcore Reviews reduces softcore vehicles to a single sexual criterion, "steaminess," partly out of anxiety that judging softcore according to broader criteria could only result in the site's appearing pretentious, blind, or otherwise foolish. Apparently, what Jean-Claude Chamboredon once said of photography may also be said of softcore: advocating this particular medium "means condemning oneself to a practice that is uncertain of its legitimacy, preoccupied and insecure, perpetually in search of justifications" (129).

It is likewise revealing that softcore anxiety subverts cult confidence in areas of overlap such as cult softcore. Softcore materials present cult commentators with special dilemmas that problematize their carefully cultivated (albeit mostly nominal) oppositionalism. This dynamic is crucial in that it isolates the decisive significance of antisex attitudes and antimasturbatory norms in particular. My assumption is that two far-reaching ideological influences have conditioned softcore abjection: aesthetic elitism and an even broader anticonsumerism. Both of these hierarchizing imperatives limit and devalue consumer-oriented sexual expression. A pornographic form like softcore is uniquely susceptible to these devaluations. Because one of its "target audiences . . . is absolutely guys who want to masturbate" (Linda Ruth Williams, *Erotic* 243), it represents, on one hand, a radical violation of neo-Kantian values privileging "disinterested" modes of aesthetic contemplation and, on the other, a challenge to traditional family values that valorize heterosexual monogamy. Softcore also flouts codes of quality. Its frequently low values—which are "low" insofar as they fail to conform to arbitrary technical standards established by classical Hollywood—exemplify one way of breaching a traditional elitism. But as Jeffrey Sconce first noted a decade ago, cult fans have had little trouble endorsing low-budget films that flaunt low values (380–87). Indeed, "trash" fans often use these "failures" as the basis for anti-Hollywood manifestos, which may be as elitist and as self-important as any highbrow diatribe. Such interpreters have also had little trouble reconciling their "reverse elitism" with other cult "impurities" (Sconce 382), like the blatant commercialism of a low-budget industry that churns out genre pieces and the reliance of this industry on affective spectacle. But when these impurities combine with the autoerotic import that attends pornographic sexualization, cult commentators are more prone to incertitude, self-consciousness, and contradiction.

Bad faith, it should be noted, is not necessarily "bad." Though I embrace the utility of *mauvais foi*, I reject the early Sartre's snobbish, hence logically untenable and practically dishonest, construction of this term along with his antideterministic view that individuals are uniformly free to transcend contradiction and self-deception. One would expect Pierre Bourdieu, whose more deterministic, sociological premises are basic here, to offer an antidote to this Sartrean condescension. Such is not the case. The tone of Bourdieu's rhetoric reinforces the snobbery historically implicit in terms like *culture moyenne* ("middlebrow culture"). Personally, I have zero desire to add to the anxiety already entangling the softcore genre through any insinuation that its self-consciousness, which is nothing if not *useful,* proves that its texts and fans "really" are inferior. *They are not:* for neither they nor anything else has intrinsic value.

II. PICTURES OF RAINCOAT MEN, NOT YOU

> "Show me a girl who doesn't masturbate, and I'll show you trouble waiting to happen."
> —*FAST LANE TO MALIBU* (2000)

Before turning to these response categories, it helps to consider the generic implications of an archaic but oddly durable consumer stereotype: the image of the porn consumer as the furtive and disreputable "raincoat man." This figment is a legacy of porn's theatrical heyday, when the audience for classical sexploitation and classical hardcore first emerged in the cultural imagination as a group of "dirty old men in semen-spotted black raincoats who frequent[ed] sex theatres" (Turan and Zito 219).[3] One would expect this grindhouse image to have receded in an age in which porn consumption has become pervasive and overwhelmingly private, but the raincoat man is a surprisingly current pejorative. Though it tells us more about the stability of antimasturbation norms than the demographic and sartorial realities of contemporary audiences, it offers insights into absences that structure softcore textually and contextually.

This low-other imagery of a "brigade" of "poor suckers," in Karen Jaehne's phrasing (12), and "zombies," in Gertrud Koch's (151), was never honest. As early as the 1970s, research had emerged suggesting that this image distorted the realities of actual porn audiences, who reportedly mirrored society in age, ethnicity, and education (Turan and Zito 220; see 219–22). The stereotype was further corroded by porno-chic. By 1975, film critic Wayne Losano could presume that times had changed: "The old audience, stereotyped into raincoat carrying old men, has been replaced by a more varied group. Young people, women, and respectable-looking middle-aged couples are appearing with increasing frequency" (136). This vogue did not endure. The less permissive 1980s hastened the return of the old pejoratives—as did the 1991 arrest of Pee Wee Herman (Paul Reubens) for masturbating in a Florida theater (Linda Williams, "Second" 165; Linda Ruth Williams, *Erotic* 256, 273n11). Technology played a decisive yet ironic role in this wholesale restigmatization. Cable and video have made porn consumption a domestic experience, democratizing its audience—meaning that the idea of the porn consumer as a low other has become even more dishonest. But because porn spectatorship has become invisibly private, this image has reemerged unchallenged. When updated at all, it has only proved more pathetic, as when Tom Lazarus points to "some guy in a motel in Toledo with his pants around his ankles" as the reality of Playboy's pay-per-view audience (Andrews, "Personal" 27). Despite this image's incompatibility with the demographics of cable and video,[4] privacy has made it possible to view the porn consumer as a déclassé slob unlike oneself. In that sense, the raincoat-man image foments bad faith.

One does not have to read deeply into this stereotype to discern its masturbatory import. ei Cinema's Michael Raso makes this explicit in confirming that his company's films are often "geared to—fine, I call it 'the raincoat brigade,' other people call it 'the jerk-off crowd'—which basically is saying we produce a lot of films specifically for men to masturbate to" (Andrews, "Lesbian" 31–32). The logic of this imagery is that the men who masturbate to sex films are failed men. Lonely, untidy, and unproductive, these men lack prestige and social graces. Antimasturbatory pejoratives are also applied to women but are today embodied in less abject terms. The raincoat man seems to be the cinematic equivalent of the aging romance novel reader who reads pulp novels well into the night, substituting autoeroticism for heterosexuality.[5] Through negative association, these two images imply a common failure to conform to socioaesthetic ideals. Each stereotype links dubious classes of aesthetic objects (sex films, romance novels) to dubious classes of subjects (older males who inhabit skid row areas, unmarried older women). Most pertinently, each stereotype insinuates the dubious, flagrantly interested uses to which said subjects put said objects (masturbation, autoerotic fantasy).

One should not overstate such comparisons. The public man in his loose, dirty raincoat is more seedy and menacing than the private woman snug in her clean, bourgeois bed. This difference reflects the genteel prejudice that men are "naturally" less hygienic than women, a stereotype reinforced here by the squalid arenas visited by sexploitation's original clientele and by the "ballooning and squirting mechanics" of the male genitalia, as Alan Soble puts it (*Sex* 67). But this difference also reflects cultural patterns in the expression of antimasturbation norms, which have since the sexual revolution regulated female masturbation less stringently than male. According to Thomas Laqueur, this change was effected by second-wave feminism, which validated clitoral masturbation as the "truth" of female sexuality and as the path to self-sufficiency (74–82; see O'Toole 373n15). Before feminism's second wave—and since onanism emerged around 1712 as "the evil doppelgänger of modernity" (Laqueur 419)—post-Enlightenment norms had painted male and female onanism in similarly bleak, repressive terms.[6] The harsh negativity of the raincoat-man image indicates what is obvious: masturbation, "at once most vanilla and most politically incorrect of sexual acts" (Dyer, "Idol" 109), has never been rehabilitated on a similar scale for heterosexual men.[7]

Feminism's rehabilitation of female masturbation was embraced by classical sexploitation and was in fact in accord with trends already apparent in it. As far back as burlesque, films in the softcore lineage had favored female imagery with positive autoerotic resonance. At the advent of sexploitation, fairly explicit female masturbation sequences became a staple, often with a male observer serving as an audience stand-in. But as the classical era wore on, the female masturbator was increasingly portrayed *as* the observer figure. This alteration was one of many ways in which sexploitation maximized female spectacle. Apart from vehicles like *Mondo Rocco* (1970) that were specifically geared to homosexual audiences, male observer figures seldom exhibited autoerotic signals, much less masturbated. Because there was obviously no similar injunction against framing the female observer in the act of masturbating, she could supplement a number's sexual imagery rather than merely serve as a detached and peripheral exemplar of audience desire. On the other hand, it was perhaps in the latter capacity that the female version of this device was most significant. After all, the implication of the female observer-masturbator was that the sexploitation audience was to some extent composed of autoerotic females (see Linda Ruth Williams, *Erotic* 340–41), a progressive notion that sexploiteers fostered in part because it conferred legitimacy.

By co-opting feminist ideas about masturbation's revolutionary value for women but continuing to spurn or ignore its value for men, sexploitation has developed into one of the areas of contemporary culture that evinces the starkest sexism in its masturbatory attitudes.[8] In the rare instances in which soft vehicles refer to male masturbation, they construct it as a symbol of male futility.[9] Often such symbolism reinforces a low, burlesque ethos, as in Chuck Vincent's sex-coms or Seduction Cinema's carnivalesque. Though this anti-erotic, anticonsumerist comedy antedates by two millennia the post-Enlightenment hysteria limned by Laqueur, it is now complicit with the same. (Consider that the raincoat man has done double duty as a target of Aristophanic derision and as a focus of "productivist" fearmongering.) Today, most middlebrow forms of sexploitation, including corporate and aspirational softcore, avoid this low comedy and rarely depict male masturbation graphically. By contrast, these postfeminist forms still routinely lend female masturbation an affirmative mystique, positioning it as a quintessentially erotic and "serious" activity, not as grounds for fear or embarrassment.

The upshot of these developments is the negation that structures and strictures contemporary softcore. Directors view male masturbators as a core constituency; indeed, male consumers on mainstream sites like Softcore Reviews attest that masturbation is a normalized though not necessarily habitual aspect of their home viewing experience. And there is much evidence that the flow of spectacle is synchronized to a masturbatory logic. Of one film, Linda Ruth Williams has speculated that, though there is too much spectacle "for even the most energetic onanist to keep up with," the unevenly paced "scenes come in bursts, presumably because the average length of self-pleasuring stretches beyond the duration of one individual scene" (*Erotic* 45). Williams has also noted how the shift to private technologies, which has had "massive implications for how we understand the role of the viewer in the production of cinematic meaning," abets masturbators not only through privacy but through the enhanced controls that VCRs and DVD players offer, including freeze frames, slow-mos, replays, and skips (*Erotic* 257; 175–76, 256). *In* the texts themselves, male masturbation occasionally figures as humiliation, but mostly it does not figure at all. Thus it shapes softcore positively and negatively and qualifies as a "structuring absence" in Dyer's sense—for male masturbation is quite definitely an issue that a softcore "text cannot ignore, but which it deliberately skirts round or otherwise avoids, thus creating the biggest 'holes' in the text" (*Matter* 105).

Female masturbation, by contrast, seems to qualify as a *contextual* absence. Though softcore films indefatigably affirm female autoeroticism—and though anecdotal evidence suggests that women employ softcore to autoerotic ends[10]—and though postfeminist norms support female openness on this subject—the genre's female viewers are nevertheless relatively reticent as a group and specifically silent on masturbation. Despite consumerist trends supportive of female openness, the antisex, anticonsumerist norms that have traditionally placed gender-specific pressure on women to deny or downplay interest in porn and masturbation may remain operative (see Lopez and George 275–88). This silence is so pervasive that one might almost think that the raincoat-man pejoratives that have long attended softcore demonize female, not male, masturbation.

III. FROM JOE BOB TO AMAZON

Jeffrey Sconce's 1995 *Screen* article "'Trashing' the Academy: Taste, Excess, and an Emerging Politics of Cinematic Style" remains the most cited piece of scholarship on the aesthetics and ideological postures of cult film networks, which he calls "paracinema." Sconce frames paracinema as a "counter-aesthetic turned subcultural sensibility devoted to all manner of cultural detritus" (372). Cult has not only established a grassroots base in fanzine discourse but has also penetrated academia, where its adversarial tastes and politics challenge canonical criteria (Sconce 373–77). Yet paracinematic discourse has links to elite discourse. Drawing on cultural studies scholars like John Fiske, Sconce observes that trash aesthetics and elite aesthetics "situate themselves in opposition to Hollywood cinema and the mainstream US culture it represents," with "the paracinematic community often adopt[ing] the conventions of 'legitimate' cinematic discourse in discussing its own cinema" (381). These convergences lead paracinema to invoke an ironic "reverse elitism" marked by aggression (Sconce 382).

Since the appearance of Sconce's article, the cult film network has expanded dramatically through the Internet, prompting many savants to weigh in on its processes. Feminists have proved influential, with scholars like Joanne Hollows and Jacinda Read providing recent pieces that limn the masculinized nature of these subcultures. (Compare Hollows's "The Masculinity of Cult" [2003] to Read's essay, "The Cult of Masculinity" [2003].) Today, most scholars concur that the "oppositionality" claimed by cult fandom is nominal. Picking up on gender and class identities posited by Sconce (375), Jancovich et al. observe that these fans "are largely middle-class and male, and their oppositionality often works to reaffirm rather than challenge bourgeois taste and masculine dispositions" (2). Feminists in particular have shown how cult mechanisms serve status-quo purposes and, in the process, exclude women (Feasey 183), all while failing in the larger culture to confer anything but a "nerdish failed masculinity" (Read 68). On the other hand, as Nathan Hunt has pointed out, it is mainly within discrete subcultures that the insider's "trivia" functions as cultural capital. Hunt adds a crucial insight in verifying that such esoteric information is neither a useless form of "trivia" nor, *contra* Henry Jenkins, a transcendent act of resistance (185). Such information is instead a locally useful form of capital that may confer various distinctions on its user (Nathan Hunt 198).

The small cult discourse on contemporary softcore provides an adjunct to these comments, for it reveals inconsistencies in its speakers' adversarialism. Before exploring this, I should situate softcore *vis-à-vis* cult discourse. Contemporary softcore has virtually no place in the large academic discourse on cult, which reflects the fact that the genre has but a minor place in cult itself (Linda Ruth Williams, *Erotic* 295). By contrast, classical sexploitation—the supergenre that almost seems as successful for "cult smut" distributors like Mike Vraney's Something Weird Video as it was for the original sexploiteers—has established a purchase in cult discourse and is rapidly establishing one in the academic discourse on cult. This contrast is predictable given classical sexploitation's promotion of itself as a terrain of nonpareil transgression—an identity with appeal not only for cult fans but also for academics schooled in modernist rhetoric—and given the genre's distance from more current genres in time, visual style, and sensibility.

Contemporary softcore has affected the "zine" world most often when circulated by labels that emphasize subgenres in the cult nexus (horror, sci-fi, comedy, etc.). Studios in this cult softcore category, like Seduction Cinema, the now-defunct Surrender Cinema, and American Independent Productions, reside outside the corporate softcore orbit in that they stress video distribution over cable and cultivate an alternative, youth-oriented demographic that targets fans who attend cult conventions. Seduction is intriguing insofar as it has embraced classical sexploitation, whose titles it rereleases and even remakes. More intriguing is that the contradictions that have affected other softcore sectors have left their mark on Seduction, whose founder, Raso, is loathe to admit that his movies qualify as "porn" despite his admission that they have been geared to male masturbation (Andrews, "Lesbian" 31–32, 34–35). This anxiety is pertinent to his desire to nudge ei Cinema, Seduction's parent, toward horror. For several years, he pursued this goal by linking the studio's fortunes to a single "cult" actress, Misty Mundae, who hopes to cross from sex films into horror films. If Mundae is successful in this maneuver, the company that so tirelessly promoted her will have enhanced its own cult credentials.

The cult forums that discuss the output of such companies do at times realize the juvenilia predicted by some feminists. Witness Joe Bob Briggs of The Joe Bob Report, whom James Naremore has referred to as an "ersatz good old boy" and a "carefully constructed persona who enjoys redneck camp" (161). In his newspaper column, long-running premium cable show, and Internet site, Briggs has for several decades reviewed sexploitation films, including Seduction titles like *Gladiator Eroticvs* (2001) and *Play-Mate of the Apes* (2002); he has also surveyed classical sexploitation films and the tendencies of contemporary cult producers like Roger Corman, Andy Sidaris, and Lloyd Kaufman. Briggs's signature is to count breasts and other body parts and to wield crude homespun neologisms like "fu" and "aardvark," a practice marking him as a forerunner of macho folk stylists in other media like sports radio's Jim Rome.

But it would be wrong to position Briggs as a "natural" effusion of this cult-sex territory, which is also covered by more sophisticated voices at sites like b-independent (Allen Richards), Cold Fusion Video Review (Nathan Shumate), SexGoreMutants (Alan Simpson), Horror Express (Scott Davis), and Cinebizarre ("Chris" "Main Policy"). Often doubling as compact cyberbazaars, these interactive sites, which typically contain message boards and chat spaces, are run by highly educated men who perceive themselves as cult curators, propagating and hawking distinctive tastes in a recognizable cult rubric. Though they traffic in misogynistic texts, they frequently reject or qualify texts that violate their own postfeminist indices of good taste or good business. For instance, when confronted by Bill Hellfire's faux-snuff films starring Mundae, b-independent's Richards worries about the audience for female strangulation segments that stretch to twenty minutes—and struggles to find a redemptive reading that allows him to avoid a condemnatory posture in conflict with his official valorization of indie filmmaking (*Strangler* 1).

Richards's anxiety is indicative of the dilemmas faced by other critic-merchants who, when confronting softcore texts, struggle to maintain their adversarial composure. Though he has never been the hardcore advocate of excess and "badfilm" described by Sconce (385–91), Richards has fabricated an oppositionalism from a set of "illegitimate" tastes. But cult-sex films subvert his consistency along with his certitude, encouraging him to voice middlebrow values antithetical to an adversarial stance. That this dynamic places him in an uncomfortable position is suggested by his delicate response to the faux-snuff film. He can condemn neither asphyxiation imagery nor the fans who consume it, for doing so would violate his nonjudgmental ethos and link him to the postfeminist genres and proprieties that, as Read notes, are depicted as "uncool and unhip in cult movie criticism" (61). Yet his undeniable revulsion confers a mainstreamness that limits his adversarialism. Nathan Hunt argues that cult fans want to differentiate "themselves from the 'phantom menace' of the mainstream consumer" (198), who is the feminized figment against which they style self-consciously discerning personae (Hollows, "Cult" 46–48; Read 56–57). But time and again, sexual materials reduce the distance between these twin illusions. Witness Richards's review of *Hellcats in High Heels* (1997), where he admits to being "as vanilla as it gets, suburban to the core" (1). Though such disclaimers hardly offer a seamless outsider identity, they are a predictable "muddle ground" for critics aiming to dissociate themselves from masturbatory stereotypes.

Cult reviewers are very sensitive to these pejoratives, which evoke the failed-male imagery that, as Read verifies, is often applied to the "nerdish" cult fan. In pop culture, such fans are depicted as sex-starved geeks, which is to say compulsive masturbators. Cult softcore usually offers the critic "alibis" allowing him to disavow or otherwise avoid this issue. But as the sex scenes get longer, yielding texts that approach hardcore ratios, reviewers like Richards begin to squirm, for they are forced to confront two questions:

Why are the numbers so long? What is a viewer to *do* with them? Contemporary hardcore is rare on cult sites in part because its utility is so difficult to deny. However, when hardcore has the patina of age—see Something Weird's juxtaposition of stags, loops, and classical hardcore alongside its other cult materials—this variety of porn is more easily defended as just another ironic consumer pleasure, as it has become more opaque and less obviously masturbatory. (Frances Ferguson has lately written that if "it doesn't feel contemporaneous, it isn't pornography. Pornography brooks no stance involving historical distance" [152].) But by distancing himself from masturbation, the cult critic undermines his oppositionalism by signaling his conformity with a pivotal mainstream ideology. As Laqueur puts it, in a post-Freudian world, one's rejection of "masturbation track[s] precisely one's willingness to go with the flow of the civilizing process" (74). The lesson in this is that it is cool to cast oneself as a cultural other so long as that other is not wearing a semen-spotted raincoat. Unless cult critics learn to accept the risks of a masturbatory aesthetic whose style of "authenticity" is to subvert the neo-Kantian and anticonsumerist prejudices that structure American culture, then the softcore two-step will continue to corrode their careful illusions of oppositionality.

Richards verifies how difficult it is to stop dancing. At times, he almost condones masturbation. He begins his review of *Hellcats* by noting that such a text is graded "by how well it turns you on." But Richards then equivocates, asserting that *Hellcats* "isn't about making the audience hot and heavy, but it is about arousal" before denying that the audience is "meant to be turned on" and closing with the safe view that *Hellcats* "is about finding the art in sexual deviance" (1–2). In other reviews, Richards exemplifies the dynamic noted by Jancovich. He prioritizes one part of the softcore dichotomy over the other, usually favoring narrative over spectacle. Indeed, it is with relief that he waxes rhapsodic anent the complexities and polished values of Seduction offerings by Terry West (whose roots in comic art provide his work with cult credibility [see Simpson 1–2]) and Tony Marsiglia (who borrows highbrow devices from David Lynch [see Scott Davis 1–2]). Though Marsiglia's films include lengthy, explicit numbers, his *outré* aspirationalism offers Richards a diversion from questions of utility. Here it is also notable that Internet technology may spur cult anxiety and incoherence. Because e-zines are so interactive, many cult critics must regularly respond to antiporn fans—and their understandably anxious responses to such fans are distinctively contradictory. For example, when answering fans who question his inclusion of softcore on an otherwise "legitimate" site like b-independent, Richards alternates between using the value-laden concept "erotica" as a defense of his sexual taste and undermining the very same concept, as when he points to the final arbitrariness of any attempt to elevate "an erotic feature" to the status of art as opposed to that of "mere pornography" (*Witchbabe* 1).

The responses generated by cult sites supply fascinating comparisons with those generated by mainstream sites like Amazon and IMDb. These distinctions owe much to the distinctions among the sites themselves. Cult sites are organized by an individual or coterie of individuals who advance their agenda by winnowing the films they review. Though these cult sites include chaotic, demotic discussions, such forums focus on the films critiqued on site and thus represent extensions of an idiosyncratic taste regime. By contrast, the primary voices on Amazon and IMDb do not represent a narrow aesthetic, for their reviews may derive from any of the vast diversity of film products that they sell (Amazon) or track and classify (IMDb). Rather than bonding with like-minded fans or performing the role of cultural gadflies, these amateur critics attempt to fill the journalistic role of the reviewer in the press. Their "user reviews" usually begin with a plot summary that is often prefaced by a "spoiler alert" (a courtesy to readers who might not want to learn too many plot details) and end with an evaluation that warns consumers away from irredeemable dreck or informs them of rewarding choices. Though these sites rarely offer the tribal *communitas* of cult sites, they may seem more welcoming to female respondents for this reason, with their unthreatening anonymity supplemented by secure corporate backing. Given how common it has become to contribute amateur reviews to such sites—many sources attest that the amateur review has become a blunt economic force, especially in book publishing (e.g., Tawa 1–2)—this combination of anonymity and familiarity has made such sites popular with consumers who share Richards's urge to opine on softcore but lack his identification with paracinema.

Cult oppositionalism differentiates these response engines in most cases but less consistently in the case of softcore, which elicits a halting traditionalism from a cult reviewer like Richards much as it does from the broad demographic sampled by Amazon and IMDb. Though the diversity of softcore reception is astonishing, familiar patterns may be discerned within it.[11] The realistic ideals established by classical Hollywood narrative figure as the cinematic standard by which users tend to interpret and evaluate contemporary softcore, with reviewers virtually always privileging one aspect or other of the narrative-number unit. As a result, three principal response paradigms are generated, each of which devalues softcore. A large category of response either ignores the spectacle or downplays it (often treating it as an accident or "mistake"). This type of response almost always results in a caustic review. A second major type of response correctly notes that the film under review has a "mixed," dichotomous character and rates it according to how well it "overcomes" this hybridity by delivering complexity and values on a par with films in related Hollywood categories. A positive review is thus contingent on the size of a film's budget and on how well the film, in the reviewer's estimate, integrates narrative and number.[12] Reviews in this category tend to be negative, for they often juxtapose softcore thrillers and big-budget erotic thrillers, softcore action films and big-budget action films, and so on. This is not a game softcore can "win."

But even when the deck is stacked in softcore's favor, the genre still cannot win. Consider that the third and largest response category identifies the softcore feature as One of Those Movies—a form of genre literacy that is often tantamount to the condescending belief that the film is not a Real Movie—and rates it as such. This premise may eventuate in positive valuations depending on the film itself but also on whether the viewer has a taste for "Skinemax" films and applies genre-specific criteria to them.[13] Ergo, reviewers often construct "special" standards that allow softcore films to earn "artificial" affirmations. This type of user review occasionally notes the value of such a film as a "couple's aid," stressing the film's sexual utility in an acceptable way.[14] But even when affirmative assessments result, these reviews are so replete with disclaimers and reductions that they rarely fail to belittle softcore (and, by extension, the user's own taste). It is not hard to recognize why. Traditional Hollywood criteria may retain their *a priori* privilege even in rating schemes that do not directly implement them. In this economy, the big-budget narrative is still the measure of cinematic value and "reality."[15]

During my research, I culled almost a thousand capsule reviews from IMDb and Amazon. While these sites do not provide anything close to precise, reliable demographic data, they do suggest trends that correlate with the above patterns. Respondents usually identify themselves as male under forty-five, with a significant minority self-identifying as female; contemporary softcore has, then, generated a broader female response on these mainstream sites than on cult sites. Though the gender data provided by these user reviews are incomplete and unreliable, IMDb provides an intriguing service that attaches gender- and age-based profiles to its rating system (a simple one-to-ten scale in which ten is ideal). These data roughly correspond to the ratios inferable from the user reviews themselves, with women seemingly comprising between 15 and 20 percent of softcore respondents. Given the many factors that may dampen female Internet response to such materials, it may be surmised that the actual percentage of female softcore fans is higher and, as some critics report, approaches 50 percent for cable-oriented subgenres.[16] An intriguing implication of the IMDb system is that when rating softcore male voters may implement traditional criteria more rigidly than female voters. Highly feminized, aspirational softcore often achieves high ratings from females but not males, as if this higher-end "erotica" in effect crosses into Real Movie territory for many women but not men. These men may give such a movie a low rating *whether they like it or not* because it remains in their minds an illegitimate pleasure, One of Those Movies, due to its structure, imagery, and personal utility. Here it is worth recalling that the most aspirational forms of softcore, including the mid-budget softcore thriller and the softcore serial, impart the misandristic lesson that male sexuality is neither good nor complex. Male viewers might denigrate such vehicles because they feel attacked by them—or, in a more masochistic pattern, because they view said vehicles as an extension of the "bad" male sexuality demonized *in* said vehicles. Supporting the latter position is the fact that men give only slightly higher marks than women to lowbrow films like *Femalien* (1996), *Bikini Summer III* (1997), and *Play-Mate of the Apes* (2002), with average ratings remaining low enough (below five) to imply that neither constituency views them as Real Movies. Given that male users across the Internet shower praise on this type of softcore, their negative evaluations of it seem to reflect an anxiety inclining toward bad faith.

IV. THE CASE OF SOFTCORE REVIEWS

Founded in 2000 during the heyday of corporate softcore and still the most specialized softcore Internet site, Softcore Reviews verifies that anxiety remains central to softcore reception even at a site geared to celebrate the genre through positive evaluation. Like many user reviews on IMDb and Amazon, Softcore Reviews makes it possible for softcore films to earn high ratings (again, on a one-to-ten scale).[17] But its policies do not provide representative accounts of what the genre is or what its fans want. Instead, such statements graph the site's self-conscious evasions of the kind of attacks launched against defenders of other middlebrow pornographies like *Playboy*. "Commonsense" detractors have positioned *Playboy*'s fiction and reportage as "a mere 'gloss' or 'window-dressing' that is designed to legitimate the magazine and divert attention from the 'pornographic' materials" (Jancovich, "Placing" 3). *Playboy* readers who focus on the articles have thus been mocked as pretentious, foolish, dishonest, or just dull. Softcore Reviews shows that it feels an analogous anxiety about focusing on softcore narrative; this anxiety is inflamed by its project of rating and ranking specific films. Like most sites devoted to "genre films," Softcore Reviews wants to perform these tasks but cannot do so straightforwardly, for the site collectively recognizes Bourdieu's point that if "[t]aste classifies" it also "classifies the classifier" (*Distinction* 6). The site thus reflects a common fear that elevating "inferior" tastes above their stations can only render one foolish.

Softcore Reviews employs two tactics for evading mockery. First, it preemptively mocks its own project. Thus it laughs at its task of rating softcore when it directs its users "to read our standards (ha!) in full" ("FAQ" 2). But its more intriguing tactic is to create a demarcation between softcore and "legitimate" genres such that granting a particular softcore feature a high rating cannot be read as a claim that it "really" merits this rating in a field that also contains Real Movies, including Serious Films. This tactic insulates the reviewer from ridicule but also inadvertently reinforces the claims of highbrows and of various antiporn factions. To create this divide, Softcore Reviews reduces softcore to sex and nudity, indicating that the genre's essence resides "in" its numbers. This reduction, which it frames as mere common sense, justifies its manner of reception: "We watch for the sex and nudity, plain and simple" ("FAQ" 2). Even here, the site mocks itself preemptively, as when it sarcastically refers to its main criteria, "nudity" and "steaminess," as two "highly complex levels" ("How We Rate" 1).

By privileging the numbers, Softcore Reviews attempts to institutionalize a broad evaluative mutilation ("FAQ" 2). This is a futile gesture, for it is impossible to enact a policy that directs reviewers to deprioritize diegetic segments that often comprise more than 50 percent of a film's running time. Predictably, the site's reviews devote almost as much space to the diegesis as to the spectacle. Given that the site's criteria for rating the "steaminess" of a film's spectacle involve complexity, acting technique, and general credibility, the reviewers' failure to embody the site's policies marks a tacit admission that the qualities that appeal to fans in the numbers are not fully distinct from those in the narrative. And of course, it is not strange to think that softcore narrative might enhance softcore number and vice versa. A central tenet of Linda Williams's *Hard Core*—that "[n]arrative informs number, and number, in turn, informs narrative" (130)—is an item of faith among softcore fans and producers, with estimates of quality traditionally tied to this integration. Indeed, Softcore Reviews' attempt to rip these elements apart ignores a probability borne out by its own reviews: despite the disclaimers and reductions, softcore fans appear to value the softcore film at least as much for what it *is* (a dichotomous, narrative-number construct featuring inexplicit sex and nudity that aspires to a measure of realism and diegetic complexity) as for what it is *not* (a narrative-heavy, conservative Hollywood blockbuster or a spectacle-heavy, fully explicit hardcore video).[18] Hence, fans of both sexes testify that they are fans of the genre because the softcore dichotomy offers a combination unavailable in Hollywood or hardcore.[19]

From a generic perspective, then, Softcore Reviews' most telling characteristic is its lower-middlebrow rhetoric, which is characterized by bawdiness, defensiveness, and double talk. This distinctive tone, which is present in sexploitation discourse as far back as the burlesque era, is clearly discernible in its policy statements:

> We are not so foolish as to think that people watch these movies for the cinematography, storyline, or the editing, although all of those elements can certainly help to make a softcore film succeed. ("FAQ" 2)

> Softcore movies . . . can hardly be criticized as "serious" film (although we think the genre has some bona fide talent on both sides of the camera), [but] we do think that it's fair to critique a softcore erotic movie based on its levels of nudity and the realism of the sex being depicted. If these qualities can lend themselves well to an interesting story or good character development then even better, but we can hardly care about that stuff when Lorissa strips down to her g-string panties and starts rubbing herself. I mean, c'mon! ("How We Rate" 1)

Though they do not strictly adhere to these policies, reviewers do reflect their rhetorical style, offering cautiously measured claims. The essentialist superlatives ("masterpiece," "excellence," "artistry," "genius") that are *de rigueur* in almost every sector of review culture are thus muted. It is rare for reviews to depart from a mildly ironic or practical tone. On the few occasions in which reviewers strive to convey a sense of real cinematic distinction, they usually revert to double talk before the end of the review. To wit, in his review of *Word of Mouth* (1999), "Mick" initially praises the film by suggesting that it does not belong to a genre that is, it seems, shoddy by definition:

> Those whose taste in softcore runs on the cerebral side will find lots to like about *Word of Mouth,* an intelligent and *very* hot film that rises far above traditional "B" movie standards. Hell, to even call this a "B" movie would be misleading; you'll find no amateurish acting, no razor-thin plot, and no scrimping on the production values. What you will find is a well made and captivating little sex-o-drama that slowly draws you in and turns you on unlike any other movie I've seen in quite a long while. Yeah, I liked this one. I liked it a lot. (1; Mick's italics)

Because *Word of Mouth* so clearly is of the genre—the film is, after all, richly "steamy"—Mick must back away even from this qualified flattery. He does this, first, by anointing *Word of Mouth* "the *Citizen Kane* of softcore," a compliment that looks considerably more timid once its context ("all those Shannon Tweed 'thrillers'") is stipulated (2).[20] That the reviewer's closing praise is more ribald signals that it is even more reserved. "At the very least,"

Mick concludes, "this flick will get your attention, and not simply by dangling tits in your face" (2).

The rhetorical humility in evidence on Softcore Reviews is neither antiessentialist nor fallibilistic, for its restraint is a gesture of lower-middlebrow deference that consents to the aesthetic ideology informing current cultural hierarchies. Nor is this rhetoric, in its bawdiness, more liberated than that expressed in other sectors; Mick's "dirty talk" is, after all, a weak substitute for a discussion of masturbation. One consequence of the site's self-conscious reductivism is that it simultaneously overstates *and* understates the genre's affective quality. By pretending to reduce softcore to sex, the site indicates that its reviewers are concerned with sexual titillation above all else; it reinforces this implication through its descents into good-natured lewdness. But the logic of its conformity with the mainstream is that it cannot confront this erotic utility head-on and thus largely ignores it. Not even the naughtiest mainstream reviewer invites confusion with the raincoat man. Conversely, this style does effectively differentiate Softcore Reviews from cult sites dominated by a more bombastic rhetoric that attacks the academic canon even as it mimics aspects of academic elitism. But as noted above, cult softcore prompts cult critics to adopt a similarly contradictory and halting style. This subtle concordance implies that Softcore Reviews may not be so far from the cult nexus after all.

For fans, the distinction between Softcore Reviews and a cult forum is perhaps nominal, for it fills functions filled by sites like b-independent and SexGoreMutants. By providing fans with a populist space to discuss a stigmatized genre, Softcore Reviews allows them to "come out," to confess their affection for a genre that many were not sure could be classified as such until they visited the site. Through a combination of policies, reviews, interviews, message boards, links, and VCR alerts, Softcore Reviews has gone further than any other softcore site in forming an interactive community. This tribe has reached consensus on contemporary "classics," whose exemplars are most consistently held to include *Play Time, I Like to Play Games, Friend of the Family* (1995), *Femalien, Word of Mouth, House of Love,* and *Forbidden* (2001), and on contemporary icons, most of whom are actresses (Shannon Tweed, Shannon Whirry, Julie Strain, Gabriella Hall, Lisa Boyle, Monique Parent, Maria Ford, Catalina Larranaga, Tracy Ryan) or aspirational directors (Zalman King, Alexander Gregory Hippolyte, Mike Sedan, Tom Lazarus). Plus, the site has established insider trivia and commonplaces like "R means return to shelf"—a truism routinely invoked in the message spaces and a reflection of Softcore Reviews' official castigation of edited, R-rated softcore as "an abomination" ("FAQ" 3). The message boards are active and *highly* substantive and have featured regular visits by influential industry figures. Consider that in 2004, one topic to have garnered heated interest was viewer perception of the genre's sexism and racism; consequently, during his back-and-forths with fans, longtime MRG casting director Robert Lombard came in for rough treatment over his role in reinforcing softcore's "whiteness." Interestingly, by 2005, Lombard had been so fully absorbed into the tribe that members of the forum rallied to his defense when a respondent perceived as an "outsider" launched an extended attack on his casting practices, blaming him for the decline of softcore.[21]

Considering that these spaces indicate that softcore's audience is more diverse than its films indicate, such viewer-producer interactions may prove significant insofar as they represent a partial reversal of corporate softcore's traditional disconnect from its audience. My informal surveys suggest that these online fans represent what sociologists describe specifically as a "neotribe," whose fluid membership is formed not by relatively stable identity categories like gender, race, or class but by "a multitude of individual acts of self-identification" (Lury 251). The majority of these "chatty" fans are males between twenty and fifty.[22] Though many describe themselves as middle-class, educated, white, and straight (a group that seems to divide evenly in marital status), most respondents do not fit all these categories at once, with significant numbers identifying themselves as working-class, African American (most prominent among the ethnicities mentioned), and gay. Moreover, the men who responded to my queries implied, albeit self-consciously, that masturbation is a regular if not requisite part of their viewing routine.[23] The female presence on Softcore Reviews is more muted, and the questions that I posted for women mainly drew responses from men.[24] Still, a consistent female presence exists on the site, where it is welcomed without the caveats noted by cult scholar Rebecca Feasey (182–83). Recent contributions by female voices on the Softcore Reviews message boards included a comparison of what women take from gay porn versus what men take from girl-girl scenes. Another centered on one fan's fetish for semiconsensual rape scenes—and her hatred of nonconsensual scenes.[25] Yet another addressed the dearth of male nudity. And still another concerned a female moderator's decision to censor the comments of a male participant who had a history of incivility; in performing this conversation maintenance, she conferred with her male peers, eliciting their full support.[26]

In the end, Softcore Reviews cannot be classified as a cult entity. Its rejection of cult adversarialism is in part a function of its identification with mainstream culture. In this respect, the site has much in common with corporate softcore, the strain of softcore that it embraces most consistently. This self-identification with the mainstream, which may at first seem ironic, is the reason its abjection and bad faith are so deeply rooted. (What is more deeply ironic is that the genre's increasing flirtations and conflations with hardcore have reinforced the site's sense of itself as a mainstream entity during a moment in which the genre is clearly edging away from the mainstream.[27]) Naturally, such identifications, in tandem with the civility they entail, have enlarged this community by encouraging diversity, which includes a salient female presence. But by the same token, these democratizing impulses have counteracted the elitist, exclusionary processes through which cult entities tend to define themselves. At the most, then, Softcore Reviews is a cult of anxiety and bad faith whose meekness dictates that its users can never form a "cult" in today's ironically conventionalized oppositional sense.

My assumption is that the softcore audience, vast segments of which are so private as to remain imperceptible, conforms to the patterns notable at Softcore Reviews and other sectors of the softcore public. As long as producers channel doubts about the genre's legitimacy into new texts, it is difficult to imagine how any part of this negative-feedback loop could be altered. In this circle of contempt, filmmakers denigrate the softcore audience, despite the fact that they continue to produce softcore. In turn, the softcore public denigrates the filmmakers who produce softcore, despite the fact that it continues to consume softcore. And they all denigrate themselves. Economics plays a decisive role in this acerbic loop, with softcore's low (and shrinking) budgets reinforcing the genre's low (and shrinking) prestige. But even if the softcore industry were to somehow return to the comparative largesse of the early 1990s, it seems likely that competition would eventually enforce a new cycle of austerity that would gradually renew these tendencies toward anxiety and bad faith. Only a radical, durable liberalization of cultural attitudes regarding art, sexuality, and their utilitarian intercession might spark the change requisite to raise softcore's self-esteem. I hardly see it coming.

Corporate Softcore and Its Discontents
Weightlessness and Weightiness at Playboy Enterprises

Corporate softcore makes a curious object of analysis. The studios that have produced this strain of softcore and the distributors that have financed it are mostly faceless, unreachable entities like MRG and New City.[1] These companies have routinized their film products so that they flow freely through the broadest channels available. As a result, the corporate paradigm has since its emergence around 1994 been a patently "mid-middlebrow" aesthetic that cultivates not correctness *per se* but an inoffensive propriety. It strives, it seems, to leave no impression at all. Though this Hollywood-based aesthetic has accumulated *de rigueur* motifs—the smooth jazz, the slick business settings, the upscale McMansions—it is this unfluctuating *weightlessness* that best captures corporate softcore's negative identity. Studios in this area have accordingly avoided self-promotion. Whereas aspirational and cult producers often submit their work for review and foster, no matter how unconvincingly at times, a sense of distinction, corporate purveyors have shunned such tactics.[2] These producers seem abashed, as if their work were unworthy of criticism. Ironically, their negative procedures have spawned a cinema that is in its semiadvertent way as resistant to analysis as more elite texts.

The key to this self-effacement is corporate softcore's openly pornographic format. Though not as conservative as corporate softcore, aspirational softcore is fairly traditional in its assumptions and stylistics—and it, too, has sought wide distribution. But whereas corporate softcore makes little effort to hide its softcore dichotomy, aspirational softcore attempts to elevate itself by blurring its dichotomy. Such ambition is encoded in its use of the soft style and its more complex deconstructions of the art-porn distinction. It is also encoded in aspirational softcore's more subtle integrations of diegesis and spectacle, which cause the narrative-number dichotomy to recede. By contrast, corporate softcore simply deflects attention from its format by making itself as placidly weightless as possible. On one hand, its visual style is defined by a flat realism that avoids the elaborate, expensive aestheticization popularized by Zalman King. On the other, its narrative is defined by thematic heterogeneity. Corporate softcore embraces cultural pieties—which is to say *all* of them, and seemingly at once—as if to compensate for the central impiety of its format. The more subtle effect of this disparate traditionalism is to engender a system of mutually nullifying significations that in turn contributes to the aforementioned weightlessness. Neither exactly random nor exactly intentional, these textual practices are instead a logical function of a nakedly pornographic form produced by a conservative industry desirous of an under-the-radar stance.

It feels odd to suggest that one studio has made a distinctive contribution to this strategically unimpressive category. Yet that is the task of this chapter, which discusses Playboy Entertainment's corporate softcore model in the context of its corporate parent, Playboy Enterprises. The films made by Mystique and Indigo, Playboy's all-but-identical softcore labels, are shiny, happy, and defiantly superficial; they are also peculiarly *right*. This *je ne sais quoi* surely has something to do with Playboy's high-gloss finish and its basic competence relative to its lower-budget peers. But it also has something to do with company history. Over the past twenty-five years, Playboy has grown increasingly bland and, well, *corporate* as the company's iconoclastic founder and his philosophy have been relegated to the sidelines. Though the company still adheres to the premises of Hugh Hefner's "fun morality," it has marginalized the hectoring didacticism of Hefner's prefeminist consumerism. If "the heart of *Playboy*'s success," as Jack Stevenson puts it, "is that it took the guilt out of sex" (165), Playboy is today more guilt-free, more *secure*, for its avoidance of ideology as such—in part because its postfeminist consumerism poses little threat to feminists and conservatives. The aim of Playboy corporate softcore is to realize a similarly guiltless, anti-ideological posture through visual and thematic practices that foment its peculiar weightlessness. The pluralist, self-canceling embrace of cultural pieties evident in Playboy films is not just a moral compensation for what some might consider dubious materials. It is also corporate softcore's elaborate manner of having *all* the pieties so as to have no single Piety—and none of the burdens, including the distribution obstacles, that might accompany the emergence of a clear and consistent viewpoint.

Corporate Softcore and Its Discontents | 207

The following chapter has three parts. The first is an overview of Playboy's role in sexploitation cinema as it relates to Playboy's television operations and the emergence of corporate softcore. The premise of the section is that the decline of this paradigm at Playboy is a function of Playboy TV's recent tendency toward harder-core content. The next two sections discuss corporate softcore's soft, weightless realism as outlined above. In the first of these, I detail corporate softcore's visual and narrative practices, examining them in their most routinized forms. In the final section, I focus on the work of Tom Lazarus, a "dissident" filmmaker whose relatively "hard" and "weighty" auteurism led him to invert basic elements of corporate softcore practice. In his quartet of Playboy films, Lazarus exhibits a complex visual style exuding an idiosyncratic aspirationalism; moreover, Lazarus unifies his ideational content such that it endorses a consistent moral viewpoint and controls his stylistic heterogeneity. Lazarus's departures from corporate softcore convention not only underscore the peculiar difficulties of a filmmaker who would preserve his creative vision within a fairly low-budget corporate system. They also signal the end of corporate softcore production at Playboy and the increasing ascendancy of a harder, "purer," reality-based aesthetic at Playboy TV.

I. PLAYBOY AND SEXPLOITATION CINEMA

Playboy Enterprises, it might be said, is the Ezra Pound of pornography: the imprint of Hefner's company is so pervasive that one strains to imagine the history of the field without it. Though best known for the men's magazine that still bears its name, Playboy has exercised a robust influence in many sectors, sexploitation cinema in particular. Indeed, the magazine had a formative impact on sexploitation. Russ Meyer derived crucial inspiration for *The Immoral Mr. Teas*—which, as the first nudie cutie, spearheaded classical sexploitation—from his experience as a *Playboy* photographer. According to David Frasier, "in content and theme *Teas* is a literal translation of what [Meyer] had been doing for *Playboy*, a movie version of the girlie magazine" (qtd. in Schaefer, *Bold* 338).[3] As dramatized by *Star 80*, Playboy has also shaped sexploitation in that its Playmates have historically parlayed their appearances in the magazine into low-budget roles (Turan and Zito 222; Linda Ruth Williams, *Erotic* 292–93). Meyer and David Friedman helped establish a *Playboy*-to-sexploitation pipeline, casting models like Lorna Maitland and Connie Mason. Producers like Roger Corman, Chuck Vincent, Alan Roberts, Paul Thomas, and Andy Sidaris, all active in the classical era, carried this practice into the contemporary period, with Sidaris bluntly exploiting Playboy prestige.[4] This pipeline of mostly unskilled talent has yielded many minor celebrities synonymous with softcore's post-1990 renaissance.[5] Most august among them is former Hefner protégée and 1982 Playmate of the Year, Shannon Tweed.

The company has also influenced sexploitation through the Playboy Channel, which since its 1982 inception has operated on subscription and pay-per-view bases.[6] Though affiliated with cinematic projects throughout the classical era, Playboy has been more active in this area since the formation of its cable and satellite operations. The wherewithal driving this activity sustained sexploitation through the cultural, economic, and technological transitions of the 1980s. Without it, directors like Vincent and Roberts would not have supplied American markets with sexploitation vehicles that occasionally included fully softcore projects like *Young Lady Chatterley II*, which was funded by Playboy alone and premiered on its channel prior to being licensed to premium cable. In supplying itself with programming, Playboy has operated in diverse genres, many of which have lent themselves to video and cable distribution. Besides softcore features and serials,[7] the company has financed sexploitation variants of game shows, call-in shows, reality shows, music videos, and exercise videos; it has also worked in unique formats like the video centerfold and the sex instruction video for couples. Of the feature forms, the video centerfold is most abundant. These slick yet inexpensive, nonnarrative vehicles far outnumber Playboy's contributions to corporate softcore.

Playboy TV has always been slanted toward sexual content. Consisting entirely of such content, the video centerfold is suited to this medium; thus the Playboy Channel's original marketing line was "[w]e take the staples out of the centerfold" (qtd. in Mair 84). It is worth speculating that the channel might have configured itself along the "classier," more pluralistic lines of HBO or Showtime had they not established their upscale niches first. After all, premium cable is in some ways closer to the original *Playboy* model than is Playboy TV.[8] Playboy TV has been unable to duplicate *Playboy*'s stolid respectability because it has had to remain harder than premium cable while simultaneously jockeying with harder-core channels. In its resulting fluctuations between hard and soft—including its post-2000 trend toward greater explicitness, as spurred in part by Playboy Entertainment's acquisition of Spice and harder-core channels[9]—Playboy's flagship channel has in a sense found itself in the reactive position of *Penthouse*, which as of 2003 featured at least one hardcore pictorial per issue. Indeed, the style and explicitness now available on Playboy TV has much in common with the style and explicitness of *Penthouse*.[10] *Playboy* the magazine, however, has had the option of ignoring harder competitors. Recently, it has focused its attention on "lad" magazines like *FHM* and *Maxim,* neither of which fully exposes breasts. Ergo, *Playboy* has chosen to update its lifestyle appeal without transforming the quantity or explicitness of its nudity.[11]

Corporate softcore has long been among Playboy TV's most restrained formats and has thus grown more out of place there over the last five years. But from 1994 to 2000, it presented a less obvious contrast with most Playboy programming, making the company's activity in the genre understandable. And that activity *was* significant. After the success of its Cameo films, Playboy adopted the corporate softcore paradigm on a broad scale in 1995, when it began producing and distributing softcore features under the Mystique label, which by 2000 it had phased out in favor of the identical Indigo label.[12] The competitiveness of this glossy, budget-conscious model was proved not only by its own Cameo brand but by other purveyors like CPV and New City, which often achieved a polished look at a lower cost than midbudget specialists like Axis and Prism.[13] Thus Playboy's routinization of its corporate model—from 1995 to 2002, its labels accounted for more than seventy films—contributed to softcore's coalescence as a middle industry *and* its deflationary evolution. Early in the decade, the genre's underpinnings had been loose, indistinct from those of the nonpornographic industry, so it was a fairly costly subsector. Though the softcore thrillers put out by Axis Films were bluntly softcore—seldom true of earlier erotic thrillers—the studio's practices often resembled those of Hollywood minors and midbudget independents. To wit, unlike current labels, Axis depended on players with SAG credentials.[14] These "crossover" practices resulted in expenses that, though below Hollywood standards, were astronomically high by today's softcore standards, when MRG is struggling to finance 16mm thrillers shot in less than a week at a cost under $130,000 and is moving to cheaper, shot-on-video projects for pay-per-view (Lombard, "Casting" 5).[15] Playboy budgets, by contrast, ranged from $300,000 to $325,000 between 1998 and 2002.[16] Playboy reports that it made ten softcore films in 2000 alone (*Annual Report* 12), earning $12 million in video sales in 2001. Given that the latter figure does not account for cable sales—besides airing on Playboy TV, these films have been licensed by HBO, Showtime, and pay-per-view[17]—the profit potential of such productions was once clear. But by 2003, Playboy had closed its Indigo division.

Playboy supplanted the first-wave of contemporary softcore labels by rolling out its line of lower-budget, openly pornographic films, so it was perhaps inevitable that its own brands would be rendered obsolete by cheaper labels with younger, harder sensibilities. Studios like MRG adapted to emerging necessities by slashing costs and values. Others, like Rosebud and Sapphire, were formed by producers who accomplished the same feat—

albeit on a smaller, less durable scale—after leaving soon-to-be defunct labels such as Surrender and Indigo. These start-ups and "one-offs" retained components of corporate softcore's glossy, pluralistic appeal. By contrast, nimble players like Seduction Cinema departed from this model altogether, verifying the new viability of cult softcore. But like Axis before it, Playboy refused to alter its formula. Indigo writer Leland Zaitz suggests that this reluctance points to internal and external pressures:

> Playboy Entertainment spent a lot of money buying harder-core TV channels, and just built a huge new state-of-the-art studio facility, so the budget had to be trimmed dramatically.[18] Indigo made movies for a much bigger budget than most of the other companies producing softcore movies. We took pride in making a better product, but in the end, I guess it wasn't financially feasible to continue making movies of that caliber. I was chagrined that there wasn't an attempt made to at least try to make the movies for less, but I guess in the end, no one was really excited about producing a product of much less quality. (2)

Zaitz indicates a curious ambivalence. Playboy stopped producing softcore films because it could no longer afford its former values. Though rivals like MRG were licensing 16mm simulation films featuring hardcore stars to HBO and Showtime, Playboy did not respond to the downward pressure with cheaper features of its own. Why it did not is a mystery. Playboy's aversion to downscale content applied *only* to simulation features, for before closing Indigo, it had embraced such content on its flagship channel and the channels it bought from Vivid. Moving to cheaper, lower-brow features would then have made fiscal and programming sense. The answer to this riddle seems to be that Playboy views its 35mm films in the same way it views its magazine.[19] In these media, which it has distributed via the broadest outlets (Blockbuster, Borders, HBO), the company perceives the deflationary, porny models of its rivals as harmful to its core franchise.

II. VARIETIES OF WEIGHTLESSNESS

The strategic superficiality of corporate softcore results from two interlocking mechanisms: a bright, simplified visual realism and a complex, disunified thematic pluralism. Though this section focuses on the latter, the style is worth examining first, for it provides telling contrasts with softer, more aspirational modes and harder, more dogmatically realistic ones. Playboy style also resembles classical Hollywood style. Bruce Crowther argues that classic *noir* stands out against its Hollywood backdrop because flat, unimaginative lighting characterized studio films. Though skilled, Hollywood cinematographers "were inhibited from experimentation and had to confine themselves to delivering what the studio wanted" (61). This production model led to innocuous lighting that underscored an "unspoken rule that every penny the moguls spent had to be visible on screen." Playboy, with "its reputation for strict control," has enacted a similarly routinized process (Linda Ruth Williams, *Erotic* 293). Playboy softcore has thus been typified by flat lighting that brightens every facet of the frame, culminating in what Linda Ruth Williams calls "the bland over-illuminated DTV 'look'" (*Erotic* 419). This "studio style" departed from the expressionistic, antirealistic surfaces that dominated the aspirational softcore of the early 1990s. Late Playboy softcore in particular evinces little interest in soft-focus female fantasy, seldom replicating the oneiric signatures of King and Hippolyte. Not surprisingly, this nonviolent cinema also reduced its reliance on the noirish chiaroscuro of the softcore thriller, a subgenre Playboy rarely emulated persuasively. Such trends indicate a point that also applies to corporate softcore shot elsewhere: the corporate "look" is defined by the realistic transparency that is abandoned when directors "elevate" softcore through feminized aspirationalism. Indeed, if Playboy corporate softcore evokes any form, it is soap opera. But this sudsy realism is a *type* of softening, as is the limpid, all-American good cheer that is its existential counterpart. Everything seems visible, but the details are missing. The edges—the unhappy blemishes, all the "dirty" bits—have been cropped or airbrushed.[20]

Whereas Playboy's visual aesthetic is characterized by homogeneity, its thematic approach is characterized by heterogeneity. Ironically, both effects contribute to the same condition: weightlessness. Corporate softcore's thematic heterogeneity reveals itself most vividly through tensions between the narrative and spectacle and through contradictions manifest within the narrative itself; similar tensions may be observed across corporate softcore texts. Corporate softcore deflects the pornographic implications of its spectacle by embracing socially acceptable ideas, many of which center on the workplace. Among the advantages of this staple setting is that it is easily linked to softcore's staple virtues: a consumerist materialism *and* a more traditional "productivism." Though these virtues overlap, they also conflict. The ethic of consumption suggests the prefeminist "male fun" for which Playboy was first known, while the older ideology of production sanctions the middle-class breadwinner ethic that, as Barbara Ehrenreich notes (44–51), was the ethos against which Hefner rebelled to win a readership. This consumerist/anticonsumerist tension is corporate softcore's *sine qua non,* for it organizes a cluster of subordinate oppositions, including Sex-Love, Bachelorhood-Family, and Porn-Art. By embracing both terms of this master opposition, Playboy embraces all these themes, including Porn, which causes it the most anxiety. In true "pop" fashion, corporate softcore at Playboy says that it is *all* good. But Playboy softcore does recognize that these themes vary in acceptance. Thus it endorses them with a specificity that reflects whether they are "guilty pleasures" or cultural pieties. Though Hefner founded his company on consumerist values, Playboy softcore directly promotes such values only in its minimal marketing; it promotes them somewhat less directly in its spectacle. But in the narrative, Playboy does not exude the old Hefner confidence in male consumption. Instead, Playboy narrative reserves its direct, didactic energy for safe, anticonsumerist pieties.

In a sense, then, the most public, visible components of Playboy's vertically integrated empire are in greater conformity with softcore "good taste" than they were in Hefner's heyday, the early days of the sexual revolution. According to pornography theorist Peter Michelson, softcore "celebrates social order": "In fact, [soft-core's] pornographic character is only approved insofar as it associates itself with elevated cultural sentiments. The two staples of this social elevation are, again, wealth and power. And soft-core . . . focuses extravagantly on both. But naked wealth and power border on the obscene, so they need to be made presentable to 'civilized' society" (51). Michelson's logic explains some of the shifts evident in Playboy's output. Playboy has moderated its prefeminist consumerism to appease opponents on the left and right. Before the advent of Christie Hefner's corporate presidency in 1982, Playboy evinced antifeminist and misogynistic sentiments more often than today, eliciting the ire of Gloria Steinem, Susan Brownmiller, and so on (Juffer, *Home* 208–13). Since then, it has made itself more female-friendly by dropping the antifemale rhetoric that was one bludgeon in Hefner's assault on middle-class life (Ehrenreich 42–48). And the company has tempered its antipathy to monogamy and marriage. These postfeminist shifts do not reflect a core change. The company still idealizes naked women; it still glorifies unfettered men. But these shifts do represent a significant rhetorical shift. If Playboy still hawks consumerist values, it has lately had the good taste and the business savvy to drop its self-righteous "philosophy." The company has in fact dispensed with its old insistence on rhetoric and ideology *as such*. This adjustment has been crucial in the development of corporate softcore and its weightless, postfeminist consumerism.

Such conversions may be viewed in microcosm by looking at Playboy's shifting use of its initial persona: the frolicsome "playboy." Though the consumerism implicit in this image has always lent Playboy cachet, as a corporate emblem the jet-setting male came to seem too naked, too obscene, and has required ongoing renovation to retain its place in the postfeminist mainstream. As a result, corporate softcore at Playboy has relied on swinging heroes fraught with a chirpy sensitivity. Such hybridity amounts to a

figure 22. The "swinging Playboy male" as reimagined in the video-box art for a corporate softcore drama, *The Model Solution* (2001). © Indigo Entertainment and Playboy Entertainment, 2001.

corporate effort to avoid direct endorsement of hedonism. In dramas like *Hollywood Sins* (2000) and *The Model Solution* (2001), these composite heroes are rich executives who ooze heterosexual allure but who are insulated from censure by a fully incoherent feminization. Consider the hero played by Sebastien Guy in *The Model Solution*. According to the video box copy, this good-natured rake has it all, including "a modeling agency, beautiful girlfriends, and fabulous wealth [. . .]." Though he expresses his "playboy lifestyle" through routine debaucheries with female underlings, he manages to remain an upstanding professional, not to mention a female fantasy who exudes warmth and romantic empathy. It is, indeed, typical of Playboy pluralism that the diegesis implies his unproblematic accommodation of all these personae. Granted, the Playboy hero's traditional values are privileged through their position as "the last word." Hence, in *Hollywood Sins'* closing voice-over, the talent agent protagonist (Hal Hutton) brightly asserts that "money, power, and sex mean very little without the hidden talent of love." But Playboy heroes are not Zalman King heroes; they do not "change" over the course of their plots. They are instead static contradictions who embody conflicting gender traits throughout. Another type of hero is discernible in the studio's sex comedies. In adopting the trappings of the buddy film, a number of these films—*Fast Lane to Malibu* (2000), *Fast Lane to Vegas* (2000), and *Hollywood Sex Fantasy* (2001) among them—recall genres as chronologically disparate as the nudie cutie and the teen sex-com. But even in his most macho, juvenile phases, the contemporary Playboy hero displays a synthetic postfeminist charm, lending him a propriety distinct from that of his original incarnation.[21]

Because of Playboy's larger history, corporate softcore at Playboy is a shade more male-oriented than corporate softcore at MRG and New City. But this should not suggest that the company is out of sync with the larger sexploitation trend toward female protagonists. Its postfeminist heroines have dominated films in an array of subgeneric fields, including the soapy drama (*Passion's Peak* [2000]), the romantic comedy (*Talk Sex* [2001]), the erotic thriller (*I'm Watching You* [1997], *I Like to Play Games Too* [1998], *Forbidden Highway* [1999]), the horror film (*Embrace the Darkness II* [2001]), and even the witchcraft film (*Sexual Magic* [2001]). Most common is the corporate drama in which heroines overcome professional obstacles, drawing on feel-good, girl-power friendships to conquer villainous female bosses (*Staying on Top* [2001]). Like Playboy heroes, then, Playboy heroines are composite figures who embody not only soft, feminized traits but all the elements of "toughness" categorized in James Beggan and Scott Allison's recent *Journal of Popular Culture* article on Playboy Playmates (796–818). Indeed, if anything, Playboy is more uniformly positive in its treatments of its heroines. Though these women often fuck where they work (*Corporate Fantasy* [1999]), their ethics are never in doubt, so they rarely exhibit the paradoxes of the heroes. In the end, these heroines reconfirm their middlebrow values by discovering love in the same milieu (*Personals 2: casualsex.com* [2001], *Perfectly Legal* [2002]).

These weightless films are least convincing when they adapt the heavy, violent gestures of dark, stylized genres. For example, despite its gothic ambience, *Embrace the Darkness II* effects a well-scrubbed vivacity mainly because its vampire heroine (Renee Rea) exemplifies a classic Playboy type, the girl next door. Playboy's softcore ethos is more natural in a corporate *mise-en-scène*. Its soap opera realism[22] also lends itself to an even more conservative format, the domestic drama as exemplified by films like *Close Enough to Touch* (2001). *Close Enough* adapts its look and scenario from an early contemporary softcore domestic drama, *Friend of the Family* (1995). A durable fan favorite, *Friend* is notable in that its variance from erotic-thriller norms represented on its release a departure for Axis, which produced the film jointly with emerging corporate purveyor New City. That the film influenced Playboy's brand of corporate softcore and *Close Enough* in particular is further indicated by the fact that its writer-director, Edward Holzman, has since then accumulated dozens of Playboy credits.

One of *Close Enough*'s obvious borrowings is its use of a neglected housewife (Parent as "Scarlet Johansing"). *Friend* inherited this figure from earlier Axis films like *Carnal Crimes* and *Secret Games*, but unlike them, neither *Friend* nor *Close Enough* uses this character's adultery as a trigger for traditional erotic-thriller violence, an adjustment suited to Playboy's later, lighter, more consumerist touch. Instead, both films broaden the diegetic and spectatorial focus to encompass an entire family and feature late adolescents (and their "sexy" friends) struggling to separate themselves from parental values and dysfunctions. The quotidian, seemingly transparent realism of these films is thus "sudsier" than the visual style of Axis's softcore thrillers, whose suburban milieus often conflict with their *noir* mannerisms. Both films are dominated by sequences shot in daytime indoor settings—the kitchen and dining room as well, of course, as the bathroom and bedroom—though the light is rarely natural. The result is a flat, "overilluminated" surface that matches the films' family-oriented consumerism.

Remade by Playboy, the aspirational Axis scenario becomes more conservative. This difference is highlighted by variations in otherwise identical systems of themes, motifs, and relations. Both films feature daughters (Montana [Lisa Boyle] and Suzanne [Brandy Montegro] respectively) whose prodigality is manifest in sexual rebelliousness and sons (Josh [Will Potter], Neal [Jason Schnuit]) whose prodigality is manifest in artistic rebelliousness. Both sons negotiate pressure exerted by their fathers (Jeff [C. T. Miller], Jason [Bobby Johnston]) to attend law school. In *Friend,* Josh aspires to direct films; in *Close Enough,* Neal aspires to paint. In both, older "mystery women" (Elke [Shauna O'Brien], Elaine [Riley Jordon]) enter their lives and urge them to forego pecuniary motives. Montana and Suzanne, by contrast, are advised to temper self-destructive tendencies, renew family ties, and initiate healthy heterosexual liaisons. These gender-traditional plots impel sons toward professional worlds, promoting male autonomy, while impelling daughters toward more emotional domestic spheres. Economic ambition devoid of creative spark is depicted as cold, vapid, and worthless; the idealistic antimaterialism of each son is valorized. Sexual rapture apart from love and family is depicted as devoid of worth; the rebellion of each daughter is hence devalued. As these respectably ready-made values are conveyed by sexualized, commercialized films, only brief contemplation is requisite to reveal them as illogical—and as attempts to drape each film's pornographic character in the safest of pieties.

What makes *Close Enough* more conservative than *Friend* is its demonization of porn. Both films use art subplots to motivate numbers. In *Friend*, Josh's arc is to elide art and sex. Elke advises him to humanize his art by eroticizing his cinematography, offering herself as the subject of a nude montage. In *Close Enough*, the analogous scenario is lent a pejorative spin. In its diegesis—though *not* its spectacle, which embraces its theme with bright Playboy cheer—the film depicts Suzanne's participation in the production of slick, softcore material as a betrayal of her aspirations and one index of her confusion. The implication is that two degrees of separation divide her situation as a porn model from that to which her brother Neal aspires. Even if Suzanne were "a real model" in a "legit" industry, she would still be debased by commercialism. By contrast, at the start of the film, Neal already has a "real" job as a paralegal in his father's firm. His trajectory, then, is to further elevate himself by histrionically rejecting his father's "hollow" materialism during his ascetic makeover into a tortured, talented loner. In other words, *Close Enough* uncritically opposes art and porn, denigrating the latter through a received wisdom that frames sex and money as equally dirty. The incoherence of this perspective is betrayed by its inconsistencies. *Close Enough* urges the fortification of domestic ties everywhere *except* in Neal's arc, wherein an artistic piety (the pure-autonomy imperative) trumps family piety. The strongest evidence that the diegesis can muster in support of Neal's elevation is his acquisition of the external accessories "necessary" to his aestheticism: the motorcycle, the rakish wardrobe, and so on. *Close Enough*'s most basic tension, then, is the blunt conflict between its consumerist spectacle and its anticonsumerist pieties. This tension is, in turn, most fully amplified through the film's simultaneous development of a pornographic structure and an antipornographic viewpoint.

In their divergent treatments of the art-porn dichotomy, these films reflect a crucial difference between aspirational and corporate forms. A transitional film, *Friend* adopts a liberal stance by blurring the distinction. It does not condone porn *per se*, but it does imply that films with strong erotic content may qualify as a salutary art, making it possible to view *Friend* as having a like merit. Thus *Friend* adopts an aspirational, upper-middlebrow perspective, one that in registering an implicit defense of its own nature is susceptible to charges of pretentiousness. *Close Enough* evades this charge but becomes stunningly contradictory in the process. Unlike aspirational softcore, corporate softcore prefers to avoid dramatizing the art-porn opposition because it prefers its porn "straight up" but cannot openly endorse a theme that it recognizes as one of our culture's enduring impieties. Ergo, when corporate softcore does handle this theme, it treats it exuberantly in the spectacle only to demonize it in the narrative. That corporate softcore shuns the porn theme suggests that its producers may view this "solution" as too contradictory even for a form defined by contradiction. (Consider that *Close Enough* backs into this material by following its *Friend* prototype.) Indeed, this tension is so overt that it threatens to disrupt the weightlessness cultivated through such incoherence.

In most Playboy vehicles, these tensions are less overt but still readily apparent on reflection.[23] Witness *Hollywood Sex Fantasy*, which critiques the banality of Hollywood and lauds the sincerity of regional theater. Here again, Playboy pluralism leads to disparate combinations that yield illogical, dishonest postures—and weightlessness. *Hollywood Sex Fantasy* focuses its satire on a particular type of Hollywood film, the buddy film *qua* blockbuster sequel ("Space Buddies II"), despite the fact that it is itself a buddy film, and one that would in a sense love to *be* a blockbuster sequel. In this respect, the film's antimaterialism approaches the paradox of *Close Enough*'s antisoftcore attitudinizing. Though *Hollywood Sex Fantasy* expends energy indulging a Tinseltown fantasy, it ends by highlighting the costs of celebrity—and *also* by highlighting the costs of noncelebrity. Further, its celebration of regional theater is far more ambivalent than the thin veneration of neo-expressionist painting in *Close Enough*. In the end, Zaitz's script critiques the playboy lifestyle but embraces it; skewers Hollywood superficiality but admires it; and lampoons regional theater but applauds it.

This complex superficiality is not random. Playboy has systematically favored the weightless vision that such thematic disunity effects.[24] Evident as early as 1991 at CPV, a similar dynamic has also informed the works of major corporate softcore purveyors like New City and MRG. Besides a bright, flat realism and a frank softcore structure, what distinguishes corporate softcore is its catholic embrace of middling values, *all* of them, and its abandonment of any pretense of unifying irreconcilable opposites. The result of this self-canceling system is an unthreatening, guilt-free ethos that exudes consumerist optimism even as it strives to satisfy a complex consumer desire for traditional *and* untraditional values. In this sense, the weightless effects of corporate softcore resemble the contradiction-based "defects" that Tania Modleski—in a segment of *Loving with a Vengeance* (1982) that is influenced by Pierre Macherey—interprets as "'indispensable informers'" that point "to the active presence of conflicts at the borders of [popular] works" (111; see 110–13).

III. SAUSAGE AND DISSIDENCE AT PLAYBOY

In remodeling Playboy's corporate paradigm, Tom Lazarus altered its soapy nature, nudging it toward the nontheatrical art film, the hardcore feature, and reality television. He relied on two strategies. First, he invented a grainy, lo-fi, *cinéma vérité* grammar for his films, which integrate film and video as a function of his signature format, the mock documentary. Second, he controlled their thematics, reducing Playboy's trademark pluralism. *Word of Mouth* (1999), *House of Love* (2000), *Voyeur Confessions* (2001), and *The Exhibitionist Files* (2002) are all fairly didactic—but whereas corporate softcore is *multiply* didactic, the Lazarus quartet generates a coherent attitude toward a single sexual problem. Relative to corporate softcore, these moody, weighty features are "harder-core," insofar as the term connotes a fairly explicit idiom and an unusual commitment to craft. Thus they stand out against Playboy softcore much as *noir* stood out against classical Hollywood.[25] Lazarus's reality program *7 Lives Xposed* (2001 on), which employs devices first deployed in his quartet, creates less contrast with its Playboy TV peers than his films create with other corporate softcore features. As a result, Playboy's accommodation of Lazarus's softcore dissidence may be read as a local victory over homogenization *and* a somewhat less heartening prediction of Lazarus's aesthetic co-optation after the decline of corporate softcore at Playboy.

Lazarus indicates in interviews and in *Secrets of Film Writing* (2001) that he aims for the autonomy of the auteur. He therefore expresses ambivalence toward his industrial place. Having "toiled in the mainstream world of television movies," Lazarus today wants to direct major Hollywood films and has already written the theatrical hit *Stigmata* (1999; "Q&A" 1). But just as he has reservations about television, he has problems with Hollywood's puritanism and reliance on the "ever-boring 'studio style' of masters, over-the-shoulders and tight shots" (Andrews, "Personal" 29). He has no problem with porn—he is among a tiny cadre of directors who applies the term to his own softcore output—which is why he turned to sex films in the 1990s. Given its underutilization as a "fertile canvas for intelligent . . . human stories," porn offered him ample opportunity for pursuing his vocation ("Q&A" 1). But he was foiled in his attempt to sell his "odd, borderline" vision to Universal, and his appeal to Vivid collapsed even more quickly ("Q&A" 1). That he would turn almost interchangeably to Hollywood and hardcore makes sense, given his openness and background (he has extensive experience in low-budget educational films). Lazarus's taste for hard over soft makes equal sense, given his respect for explicitness and his disdain for "soft-focus fluff" (Andrews, "Personal" 27).

In his appeal to Universal, Lazarus signals a willingness to cede some control in return for the predictable values that corporate entities, including Vivid, can deliver. This is crucial in sexualized genres because of a tendency to skimp "on anything creative that has to be worked on along the way," which Lazarus refers to as the it's-good-enough-for-porn principle (Andrews, "Personal" 28). The premise of his attempt to work within Playboy constraints is that during the creative process he will through Wellesian force of will bend "uninspired financiers and unimaginative filmmakers" to his vision (Andrews, "Personal" 32). Certainly, he has succeeded in establishing more play than Playboy directors like Holzman, Kelley Cauthen, John Quinn, and Robert Kubilos—though not as much as he might have established had he risked "toiling" for a less corporate studio. (Hence, whereas a cult softcore filmmaker like Tony Marsiglia presses into avant-garde territory, Lazarus never gets that far, remaining by inclination and necessity within Hollywood traditions.) These dynamics have led to a love-hate relationship. Though he evinces polite gratitude that Playboy has indulged him at all, he also mocks its limitations. In illustration of what he has endured at Playboy, Lazarus supplies a droll anecdote:

> I once presented a rough cut to Playboy. It was filled with a potpourri of film styles: black and white, solarization, slow motion, color saturation, high contrast black and white—all attempts to present different ways of presenting the "real." The man in charge of production called me after the rough cut—as a freelance writer-director, I was not in the screening—and he said, "Tom, if we were sending this to Sundance, it would be perfect. But we're not. We make sausages here. Make it sausage." Pretty inspiring marching orders, eh? (Andrews, "Personal" 28)

Though a bit phallic for softcore, "sausage-making" is an apt metaphor in that it pinpoints the absence of idealism critical to the corporate softcore process.

Lazarus's unwillingness to accede to such a process may be situated as a rejection of corporate and aspirational conventions. Though he has no familiarity with softcore beyond his perusal of a few Playboy "sausages" that "totally sucked" ("Q&A" 2), his contempt for it is rooted in antipathy for King's slick, antirealistic aspirationalism. Thus he has long urged Playboy to aim for "more realistic depictions of sex" by adopting anti-Zalmanesque tactics: "No soft lens, dissolves, non-linear love scenes. I was a proponent of realistically filming the sex act—long uncut sequences, with sync sound and lots of dirty talk" ("Q&A" 2). Such realism is more "believable, and therefore erotic." It is also more unified, he insists, and therefore aesthetic. These claims are more arguable than he lets on, but to his credit, he admits that his methods are motivated by the practical. Hence, he notes that the mock-doc format is "cheap and makeable," allowing parsimonious use of Playboy's "minuscule budgets" as a result of "[f]ewer lighting needs, more production time, less asking unskilled actors to act" (Andrews, "Personal" 27, 28). This format also furnishes Playboy with ready-made hooks, for it combines the popularity of reality television with the allure of "the webcam-house school of pornography" (Andrews, "Personal" 27). Most personally, it has offered Lazarus a cinematic identity: "I felt there was a niche that could be carved out in the world of softcore in the area of realistic or faux documentary presentation of softcore sex. Zalman King had created a niche for himself as a lush, erotic storyteller. I wanted my own niche" ("Q&A" 2).

Predictably, Lazarus's view of softcore is itself fuzzy. Though Playboy softcore is relatively realistic, he makes no distinction between its weightless vision and the softer, more antirealistic modes typical of aspirational forms. His favored idiom is not without softcore precedent. Its grungiest motifs have been deployed in softcore thrillers, stripper flicks in particular. And his mock-doc style has a precursor in Mike Sedan's influential *Married People, Single Sex* franchise (Juffer, *Home* 226–28). Though Sedan's recent work (*Hot Desires* [2002]) tends toward the corporate, he pioneered the softcore mock-doc in the first installments of his *Married People* series (1993, 1995). In shifting between black-and-white interviews and color dramatizations, these moody melodramas anticipate Lazarus devices. Further, shortly before Lazarus arrived at Playboy, ex-Axis director Hippolyte took a hyperrealistic, anti-Zalmanesque approach in the short-lived series *The Profession* (1998). Hippolyte claims that Playboy ditched his series because it was too far from *Red Shoe Diaries* (Linda Ruth Williams, *Erotic* 280–81)—but this "failure" may still have paved the way at Playboy for Lazarus's use of a similar idiom. Finally, it bears repeating that Lazarus's style has no monopoly on reality. When pressed, he admits his style is "as manipulative as other filmmakers' fantasy style" (Andrews, "Personal" 30). But this nuance is often drowned out by his more naïve claim that his style is in some ahistorical sense "'real-er' looking" than other styles—and by his contempt for "manipulated, over-produced, dissolve-riddled, non-linear-because-they're-afraid-to-deal-with-sex-head-on, soft-focus fluff" (Andrews, "Personal" 30, 27).

The stridency of Lazarus's hostility toward this Zalmanesque idiom is, perhaps, a function of his experience.[26] Especially in his first films, he uses the soft style that he derides. (Such imagery may have remained over his objections; this seems most likely in the case of *Word of Mouth,* which often resorts to soft lenses.) But what makes Lazarus distinctive is that he often uses lo-fi devices to soft-focus ends. At other times, he uses such devices as a way of combining softcore distinction with hardcore allure.

An arresting example of lo-fi traditionalism emerges in *House of Love*'s fourth number, which acts as a narrative-spectacle pivot (Andrews, "Convention" 20–22). *House of Love* focuses on Melinda (Catalina Larranaga), a documentarian whose feminist inclinations inform her initial contempt for her subject: prostitution at a high-end brothel. Her rigid sex-negative attitudes predictably yield to a more flexible, postfeminist perspective. This conversion is predicated on an increasing familiarity with the brothel, as capped in the seventh and concluding number by her orgiastic sampling of its "wares." The rudiments of this plot are generic staples, with Melinda's crossing-the-line trajectory a *de rigueur* softcore trope. What distinguishes *House of Love* is its gradual development of this arc. The fourth number foreshadows the seventh via the seduction of Melinda's soundman, Peter (Peter Gaynor), by Rosemary (Tracy Ryan). Like Emmanuelle, Rosemary is linked to aesthetics and beauty: she is a frustrated painter; she considers prostitution an art; and she recognizes that her beauty makes her an idealized figure. The fourth number reinforces this link by accenting her extraordinary beauty, the effect of which evokes the classical sublime: it enchants Peter as prelude to paralyzing him. The key to conveying this sublimity is a complex stylization. By combining "old, grainy stock found in the back of Indigo's refrigerator" with tight, softly backlit close-ups and slow, circling camera work (Andrews, "Personal" 30), Lazarus evokes an ethereality similar to that achieved by soft-focus technicians from Struss to Jaeckin. In other words, though this affordable, low-resolution scene "was shot purposely gritty," it refers to traditional beauty and aims for it, an aspiration reinforced by the classical score that accompanies this imagery throughout its trifold deployment. (This sequence is also recycled for an erotic overture to the film used in the initial credits and for Melinda's masturbation fantasy in the fifth number.)

Though this idiom is neither hard-edged nor notably realistic, it evinces hardcore subtleties. Hard-edged techniques are often employed for their "dirtiness," an erotic criterion that Lazarus links to lo-fi, hardcore stylistics and low, hardcore content like sex toys, sex talk, erections, and ejaculate. Such motifs form an important part of the realism to which he aspires, so it is predictable that several are manifest in the above scene (*viz.*, Rosemary's synchronous dirty talk and the service that she performs for her disabled onlooker [she jerks him off]). Though not shown, the erect penis is invoked in this and other sequences,[27] modifying their softer, more traditional aspects.

A similar interplay emerges through Lazarus's differentiation of the three low-res styles that open *Word of Mouth*, which also stars Larranaga and focuses on prostitution. The grainy, sepia-toned stills that accompany the opening credits represent the first style. These fragmented close-ups of Torri

Figure 23. The dark, self-reflexive promotional art for Tom Lazarus's first Playboy film, *Word of Mouth* (1999), suggests the director's departure from corporate softcore convention. © Mystique Films and Playboy Entertainment, 1999.

(Larranaga), the heroine *qua* prostitute, impart an impressionistic effect that aspires to the same ideal beauty for which Lazarus aims in the aforementioned *House of Love* sequence; such graininess also decreases the explicitness, another traditional soft-focus effect. Midway through the credits, Lazarus switches to soft lenses and live-action shots of the heroine's breasts as she dons a filmy chemise. Here the color imagery is ultratraditional in that its low-res shimmer is devoid of graininess, suggesting diffusion filters, shallow focus, or out-of-focus footage (the look is *that* soft). As in *House of Love*,

Figure 24. *House of Love* (2000) reinforced Lazarus's status as a corporate softcore "dissident." © Indigo Entertainment and Playboy Entertainment, 2000.

these sequences balance soft motifs with harder ones, which again include dirty talk and the prostitute's masturbation of her john. Before Torri finishes her trick, a third style is introduced: documentary footage of Torri, who is interviewed about the experiences visualized in the second set of images, thus situating the latter as a product of her recollection. The lo-fi verisimilitude of this video footage includes flat, bright light and low resolution. That this look emerges as the film's standard of cinematic objectivity justifies its contrast with the softer dramatizations of Torri's memories. The latter are slowly revealed as fluid, self-serving projections of male fantasy.

All of which suggests that Lazarus's low-resolution, hyperrealistic stylization evinces a greater functional overlap with traditional soft focus than the filmmaker has let on. In his second pair of films, Lazarus realizes his manifestos most fully by giving his hyperrealistic documentary footage a more prominent position, which effectively displaces the lush, antirealistic motifs that recur throughout *Word of Mouth*. A thematic shift is of equal import: the twin fetishes that unify *Voyeur Confessions* and *The Exhibitionist Files* make Lazarus's video footage and his allusions to amateur porn the more germane. That he was impelled along this lo-fi trajectory by dwindling resources as well as by his own auteurism is suggested by his observation that shoots at Playboy fell from twelve to eight days between 1999 and 2002, a decline in accord with larger industry patterns (Andrews, "Personal" 28).

The infusion of documentary footage into the spectacle enhances structural unity. This unity, which foments the Real Movie effect that Playboy's corporate softcore pluralism undercuts, has long been the filmmaker's aim. "I don't write movies that have sex scenes," Lazarus asserts. "I write sex movies. Big difference" ("Q&A" 5). Such a distinction is logical given that all four Lazarus films focus on a single sexual "problem" and generate their erotic spectacle from situations linked to it. Thus, all four thematically integrate narrative and number. Indeed, his second two films are so well integrated that their narrative-number dichotomies recede. On the other hand, if anything, the stylistic differentiation noted in his first two features—which broadly restricts documentary footage to the narrative, while allowing softer effects to pervade the spectacle—amplifies the narrative-number dichotomy. Though *Voyeur Confessions* betrays its budgetary constraints more fully than its predecessors, its overall production value is boosted by the visual unity that Lazarus achieves in integrating lo-fi, "objective" video into the sex itself, a tactic that maximizes spectacle but radically disrupts number.

Voyeur Confessions follows Lisa (Larranaga), a researcher videotaping interviews with three male voyeurs and several female acquaintances. The film's complex grammar divides into five principal looks, all of which aspire to objectivity even when highlighting subjectivity. The dramatizations of Lisa at home and at work provide the master realistic look. Though their lighting is subdued, these segments resemble Playboy's typical realism in their flat stability. Related to this idiom is a more subjective, handheld effect whose main deviation from the master look is its shakiness. Alternating between interior and exterior points of view, this style evokes the partiality of Lisa's perception—but because its drab lighting resembles that of the master style, it remains fairly objective. The third style, mock-doc footage of the interviewees and later of Lisa herself, is the most objective look; it is characterized by bright lighting and low resolution. Sequences of this sort are intercut with passages dramatizing the interviewees' most *outré* memories, which exemplify the fourth and most stylized vision. Alternating between color and black and white, this grainy, shaky, fractured look resembles the style of Lisa's perspective. Its greater stylization evokes the greater furtiveness of these memories as well as their more distant, mediated character. The fifth and final mode, voyeur-cam footage, is also located in the memories of Lisa's subjects. Such squalid footage of "images stolen from life" includes sex illegally taped in restrooms and hotels. Because it represents video that the voyeurs have repeatedly re-viewed, its porny, lo-fi style strays from the stylization (though not the furtiveness) of the other reconstructions of memory, exemplifying a dark variation on the low-tech objectivity of the interview footage.

Voyeur Confessions contains only two sequences that resemble the distinct sex numbers normalized by Playboy and corporate softcore. These segments, in which Lisa has sex with her boyfriend (Christopher John Kapanke) and with her boss (Jack Lincoln), are integrated with the diegesis—and since they adopt the flat-yet-furtive handheld idiom that distinguishes Lisa's subjectivity, they work well with Lazarus's visual fabric. Moreover, the voyeur memories are delivered in fragmented snippets in conformity with Lazarus's *cinéma vérité* logic. Their breathy aestheticization does not, then, reduce to a ready-made soft focus. In aiming at a "classier" form of unity, Lazarus has dispensed with softcore's most traditional mode of aspirationalism. Unlike *Word of Mouth*, *Voyeur Confessions* contains no aspirational "fluff" in its spectacle.

In calling Playboy films "anti-sex" ("Q&A" 2), Lazarus hints at the standoffishness in the company's hesitance to confront porn head-on in films like *Close Enough*. Similarly, corporate softcore avoids plots that focus on the sex industry or on sexual dysfunction, two staples of sexualized genres from classical hardcore to the erotic thriller (Linda Williams, *Hard* 128–52; see Linda Ruth Williams, *Erotic* 335, 348). Of the "sexily" titled Playboy films named here, only *Talk Sex* focuses on sex—and it does so in a romantic-comedy manner that aims from the outset to reconcile sex and love. Corporate softcore avoids sex-besotted scenarios for the same reason it avoids porn: they disrupt its bright, sanitized consumerism. They are also superfluous given its acceptance of its pornographic format. The rationale for such plotting is that it supplies diegetically coherent spectacle. In departing from corporate softcore, Lazarus has logically returned to such scenarios. If pressed, this tactic not only yields spectacle that makes narrative, thematic, and stylistic sense, it also suppresses the softcore dichotomy.

One function of this tight sexual focus is that it lends softcore an involute, self-referential quality. In this regard as in many others,[28] Lazarus is an exception in that he has bluntly embraced this symbolic dimension of his work. Consider *House of Love,* his cheeriest film as well as the one in which he most clearly allegorizes his position as an ambitious filmmaker working for Playboy. What distinguishes Lazarus is his view that the limits on softcore's aesthetic potential are extrinsic (historical, cultural, industrial). The genre may be pornographic, but it is not intrinsically inartistic: "I think softcore can be smart, dirty, funny, challenging, visually and audibly interesting . . . it's like any other genre of filmmaking. It's what you bring to it . . . what your aspirations are. In softcore, my aspirations are to create art" (Andrews, "Personal" 29). This is not to deny that Lazarus would rather work elsewhere. If he had the chance to direct in more respected genres, he would, mainly because doing so would supply greater creative resources (Andrews, "Personal" 32). In this regard, Rosemary's situation in *House of Love* parallels Lazarus's situation at Playboy. A frustrated painter, she has turned for work to an upscale, corporate sector of the Hollywood sex industry—one that constrains her creativity even as it provides her with resources and outlets. Like Lazarus, she embraces her new field, which she views as an aesthetic challenge. For this "pretension," fellow call girl Pamela (Kelli McCarty) mocks her, derisively labeling Rosemary "the princess." Later, Pamela's self-doubt infects Rosemary, leading to a deflated sequence in which she admits she is "just a call girl." But Rosemary soon regains her buoyant determination to be a remarkable prostitute. It takes little insight to decode this arc as a gloss on the director's own. *Contra* many sex-film auteurs (Metzger, Jaeckin, King, Hippolyte, Marsiglia, etc.), Lazarus admits that he is "just" a pornographer. Honesty, however, need not deter aspiration.

Unlike *Close Enough* and other corporate softcore films, *House of Love* adopts a loosely aspirational posture by reducing the thematic gap between art and sex. *Word of Mouth, Voyeur Confessions,* and *The Exhibitionist Files* do the same, albeit more darkly. The rigid sexual focus of these films is critical to their moral consonance. *Word of Mouth* develops a coherent cynicism toward prostitution that is tantamount to a self-reflexive cynicism toward art. Their implication is that artists may be as manipulative, evasive, and subtly malign as Torri. *Voyeur Confessions* develops a similarly self-reflexive cynicism toward voyeurism. Most intriguing is its depiction of one voyeur as an aesthete corrupted by a sense of beauty that he equates with truth. Not unlike Oscar Wilde or Vladimir Nabokov, Lazarus distances himself from aesthetic corruption by critiquing a corrupt aesthete. Through his vision of Christopher B. (Kevin Bravo), Lazarus makes an ethical distinction between the synthesis of aestheticism, art, and porn in which he himself traffics and the pathological kind that leads Christopher to wire an apartment complex with secret cameras so as to supply himself with illicit amateur porn (think *Peeping Tom* [1960] and *Sliver*). The diegesis punishes this voyeur but not before letting him speak, revealing the pious terms in which he justifies his invasions of privacy. Unsurprisingly, he invokes the same "aesthetic bliss" rhetoric that the narrator of Nabokov's *Lolita* (1955) uses to justify pedophilia. Christopher routinely ascribes to his voyeurism a beauty and a truth that surpasses quotidian understanding and hence suspends quotidian morality: "The things that I remember from my life are the things that I saw. What most people might call dirty things I call beautiful things. Those are the images that shaped me. Listen, it's the moments in life with truth. Those are the images that turn me on. Stealing images from life is my life." In *House of Love,* Lazarus manipulates his visual rhetoric much as Christopher manipulates his verbal rhetoric: both justify marginal sexual practices by identifying those practices with mainstream pieties like beauty and truth. But unlike Christopher and other eroticized apostles of aesthetic amorality in film and literature (cf. Wilde's Lord Henry), Lazarus does not conflate such fuzzy pieties with morality. In the end, the Lazarus documentarians endorse *outré* practices like prostitution and voyeurism only in a qualified way, always stipulating that any sexual practitioner who transgresses middling values like consent and emotional balance constitutes a social threat.[29]

Given the relative safety of this vision, it is almost baffling that Lazarus presents such a contrast with his fellow Playboy directors. Consider that in *Voyeur Confessions*' closing monologue, Lisa observes, "I'm not gonna say I don't miss [voyeurism's] rush, but it's an even better rush being in a loving relationship." Such moral traditionalism notwithstanding, the Lazarus quartet is the antithesis of corporate softcore in that it absolves certain sexual impieties as a function of its development of a unified viewpoint. Corporate softcore, by contrast, either avoids or demonizes such practices, partly out of an executive anxiety that such careful distinctions might be misconstrued. Instead, it opts for weightless contradictions and only indirectly endorses consumerist impieties. Given Lazarus's aspirations, his rigid thematic consistency and post–*Word of Mouth* preference for strict moral clarity may appear simplistic and incompletely modernist—but a clear view of his *oeuvre* requires placing that work in the context of the strategic mishmash that studio production at Playboy has otherwise conditioned.

The uncut versions of the corporate softcore features that have recently aired on Playboy TV confirm that Playboy filmmakers were moving toward a harder-core aesthetic when Indigo shut down. But unlike Lazarus's films, an unrated feature like *Perfectly Legal,* which routinely depicts unsimulated masturbation complete with labial movement, had not significantly modified its glossy, pluralistic piety and was no closer to the lowbrow confessional realism now *de rigueur* on Playboy TV programs like *Night Calls* (1995 on), *SXTV* (2001 on), and *The Extreme Truth* (2003 on), as well as on Lazarus's scripted reality show, *7 Lives Xposed.* Playboy TV has not embraced Lazarus's auteurism; indeed, this vision is not clearly discernible in the filmmaker's own show. Playboy TV has, however, embraced his reality aesthetic, including his taste for hardcore raunch, unvarnished sex, and mock documentary. In these serials, much as in the edited hardcore airing beside them, the sex is often unsimulated but still inexplicit. Flaccid or semi-erect, the penis makes guest appearances on these programs and is often invoked through references to masturbation and semen (Andrews, "Personal" 29, 31). In "Sexposé" (2003), an episode of *Night Calls,* a masturbator dedicates his "load" when calling the show, while in the first episode of *7 Lives Xposed*'s 2004 season, a glass of "jizz" is passed about as a trophy in the house's voyeuristic warfare. Playboy TV, it seems, has decided that Lazarus is right, that "softcore is pretty much a dinosaur" ("Q&A" 4). Its flagship channel has thus curtailed its on-again, off-again strategy of mimicking the middlebrow pluralism of its print precursor, a strategy in which corporate softcore had a central place. In so doing, it has co-opted Lazarus's talents, pressing them into the service of larger corporate strategies minus all the "arty farty" details that discomfited executives intent on making "sausage" ("Re: it's Tom Lazarus" 1).

Is corporate softcore permanently extinct at Playboy TV? Assuming its continued abeyance, what ideologies will replace its conflicting pieties? Playboy materialism is as prominent as ever. More intriguing is the network's evolving treatment of gender, race, and sexual orientation. Though corporate softcore rarely critiques (though often reflects) social imbalances, its postfeminist consumerism has acted as a check on the misogyny, racism, and homophobia that permeated classical sexploitation. Will the network's drift toward déclassé content remove such checks, or will its "corporateness" continue to mute these impolitic strains? Recent Playboy programming proves equivocal. However lowbrow, the empowered sexual woman remains a fixture at Playboy TV—except in the sex-and-music formula of *Buckwild* (2003–4), which disempowers its females in accord with the slick, hip-hop misogyny typical of MTV, VH1, and BET. (Predictably, Playboy TV promoted *Buckwild* by trumpeting it as the first Playboy show aimed at a black audience.) Moreover, in the finale of the third season of *7 Lives Xposed,* Slide, a white character affecting hip-hop mannerisms, provides a moment of spectacle through a violent spasm of homophobia that supplements his routine misogyny (e.g., he typically applies terms like "bitch-whore" to the women with whom he fornicates, as if such locutions were terms of endearment). This outburst is normalized as a voyeuristic pleasure akin to any other provided by the wired-house concept.[30] While these instances of impropriety may prove isolated, their larger normalization may leave Playboy's audience longing for the golden age of corporate softcore—and its bright, weightless civility.

"From Skin to Scream"
Evolution and Elevation at a Cult Softcore Label

If late-night cable is famous for the softcore thrillers and softcore serials often made by corporate softcore labels, the vast home video market has generated a greater diversity of cinematic forms. Yet this direct-to-video segment of the contemporary nontheatrical market has not consistently fostered fully softcore content—despite the fact that sexploitation content is viewed as a commercial necessity in many areas of home video, especially the cult-film nexus of low-budget horror and comedy. One explanation for this quirk is that whereas corporate vehicles usually focus on sex alone, cult vehicles divvy up their resources between two significant sources of spectacle, that is, female nudity and something else, with the nonsexual spectacle often privileged. Cult sexploitation labels like Roger Corman's Concorde–New Horizons have thus proliferated, while cult softcore labels specializing in vehicles with fully dichotomous, narrative-number structures have proved comparatively rare. As the successor to Torchlight at Charles Band's Full Moon Pictures, Surrender Cinema was once the most reliable label in this cult softcore category, contributing the "cult classic" *Femalien*, a notably explicit sci-fi sex-com. On the other hand, as a West Coast label, Surrender had industrial overlaps with corporate softcore, often culminating in textual resemblances to the same.

Thus far, the same has not proved true of Seduction Cinema. Seduction is the cult softcore label of ei Independent Cinema (or ei Cinema),[1] a New Jersey studio entrenched "in the world of 'low-brow' fan culture (fanzines,

Figure 25. A frame enlargement showing the alien protagonist of Surrender Cinema's cult softcore hit *Femalien* (1996). *Femalien* is widely credited with introducing a new explicitness into contemporary softcore cinema. © Full Moon Pictures and Charles Band, 1996.

film conventions, memorabilia collections, and so on)" that Jeffrey Sconce has identified with the "paracinematic sensibility" (373). From 1999 to 2004, ei Cinema made at least two dozen examples of its trademark Seduction vehicle, the softcore spoof, producing more than fifty features in all in that span. Most were shot on high-definition video for under $50,000, with budgets approaching $200,000 for 16mm "prestige" films like *Lord of the G-Strings* (2003).[2] ei Cinema has also accrued affiliate labels like Retro-Seduction, which rereleases classical softcore features and featurettes from the 1960s and 1970s, occasionally pairing them with ultracheap remakes starring Seduction regulars Misty Mundae, Julian Wells, and Darian Caine. Most recently, ei Cinema has begun producing nonsoftcore horror like *Screaming Dead* (2004), *Bite Me!* (2004), and *Shock-O-Rama* (2006) under its Shock-O-Rama imprint, which had formerly been used as a distribution label for films made outside the studio.

This production slate is complemented by the machinery that Michael Raso, Seduction's forty-two-year-old chief, has constructed to promote it. Unlike corporate softcore, which does not stress promotion and has largely ignored its fans, cult softcore evinces its classical lineage through vigorous, interactive publicity. Seduction is no exception. Raso advertises Seduction via slick poster art that doubles as box cover art (or vice versa), perpetuating sexploitation's most traditional promotion. He also markets the studio's output through less traditional media. ei Cinema has achieved notoriety in the cult world by dint of its presence at expos like the Chiller Theater convention and relationships with major fanzines like *Fangoria* (which sponsors Chiller Theater) as well as a legion of smaller forums, including e-zines. Raso also publishes a glossy fanzine, *Alternative Cinema,* which lavishes attention on ei Cinema and offers articles devoted to larger cult contexts. In addition, Seduction sells itself through its Web sites and, crucially, the many extras it packs into its DVDs, including trailers, insider interviews, behind-the-scenes documentaries, and deleted scenes. These editions are packaged with variants of each film (rated and unrated versions, or, in Retro-Seduction's case, originals and remakes) as well as CD soundtracks and promotional pamphlets. Of these materials, the interviews, documentaries, and pamphlets are notable for the increasingly specialized manner in which they have attempted to manipulate the reception of Seduction features. Collectively, these tactics may be viewed as relocating the "carnivalesque ballyhoo" that Eric Schaefer has identified as integral to the promotion and reception of classical exploitation (*Bold* 4). Though Raso and his minions cannot always recapture this bygone carnival atmosphere via public screenings at conventions and theater premieres, they can seek to transfer it to the private sphere, there simulating it via Web sites, fanzines, and DVD extras.

Besides maximizing fan contact, ei Cinema's marketing has resulted in an industrial transparency unmatched in contemporary softcore. This window reveals an idiosyncratic studio whose texts have rapidly recapitulated developments associated with early cinema, classical exploitation, and classical sexploitation, all of which prioritized spectacle over narrative. Seduction's development may be clarified by analyzing its most salient distinction strategies. In its first stages, these centered on its "lesbian" (or girl-girl) imagery and its low synthesis of body comedy, formal parody, and political burlesque. Since then, Seduction has developed a star system in which one actress far outshines the rest; has cultivated its sexploitation roots; and has mimicked auteurs like David Lynch. These three later strategies represent incremental steps toward the realization of Raso's twofold aim: to transform ei Cinema into a financially solid, low-budget company that specializes not in comic turn-ons but in more "elevated" chills. In this connection, softcore sex has once again been framed as a somewhat embarrassing if wholly indispensable means to an end. Moreover, the studio's evolution "from skin to scream" has been marked not only by a trumpeted move toward horror but also by a quieter expansion of its distribution of softcore and harder-core fetish material.

I. THE SEDUCTION TRICHOTOMY:
Transformation, Recapitulation, Distribution

The original Seduction Cinema paradigm, first embodied by the 1999 spoofs *Titanic 2000* and *The Erotic Witch Project*, contains three principal components: sketch comedy, girl-girl numbers, and narrative spoofs. Because ei Cinema, which Raso founded in 1994, is a grassroots company, this paradigm—which supplants softcore's traditional narrative-number dichotomy with a trichotomy of sorts—was pieced together rather haphazardly by a mostly male group of friends interested in television and low-budget films. In this cult subsector, comedy came first, for Raso and his fellow filmmakers, several of whom attended film school in New York and New Jersey, had grown "up making goofy skit comedy for cable access on local cable":

> Seduction Cinema is "Meadowlands Showcase" with nudity. The entire Seduction Cinema group wrote skit comedy for a New Jersey–wide variety show called "Meadowlands Showcase." This was the foundation of all of our films to follow. I produced cable TV spots during the day and then pulled all-nighters to produce a monthly show. Every member of the group was technically trained as writer, producer, director, and in some cases, editor. I bicycled the finished show throughout New Jersey and distributed it to any cable station in the country that would play it. We did it for a good five years—1988–1993. No pay. Didn't care. We just had an intense drive to create. It was a dream. We had an audience. We had fan mail. If someone told me then that all we needed was naked women, I would have blushed. (Andrews, "Lesbian" 35)

By 1996, Raso and his colleagues had realized somewhat grudgingly that comic instincts alone would not guarantee the viability of a studio producing feature-length films in cult-horror genres, which was their long-term ambition. As a result, they founded the Seduction label on an idea that "started out as nothing more than 'sex sells.'" Formally, this meant that Seduction would make horror comedies, reflecting the studio's cult ambition as well as its cable background, and it "would just inject seven- or eight-minute sex scenes into them. Sometimes those scenes would fit with the story, sometimes they would not" (Andrews, "Lesbian" 35). The result of this new paradigm was ei Cinema's first feature, *Caress of the Vampire* (1996). Produced specifically for Chiller Theater, the unfinished *Caress* unexpectedly gained distribution via LA-based Ventura Marketing and the Playboy catalogue. Having "stumbled upon . . . this market strictly by accident," Raso and his cadre began shooting new features like *Vampire Seduction* (1998),[3] the first produced for the Seduction imprint (Andrews, "Lesbian" 32).

These bluntly masturbatory films, which ei Cinema expected to appeal "to one man in a room" (Andrews, "Lesbian" 32), are all but devoid of plot.[4] They oscillate between skit comedy and female spectacle with little to link them. But Seduction gained its current identity in its next phase when Raso and company added another element, the parody of mainstream blockbusters, to Seduction's repertoire, lending spoofs like *Titanic 2000* and *The Erotic Witch Project* a "parasitic" narrative tissue with which to bind the other elements.[5] Still, Seduction required experience and budget growth for its films to become more naturalistic and unified. The parodic textures of *Mistress Frankenstein* (2000), *Gladiator Eroticvs: The Lesbian Warriors* (2001), *Witchbabe* (2001), and *Play-Mate of the Apes* (2002) contain an increasingly organize spectacle, but through this period integration remained "sketchy" at best, yielding only threadbare illusions of reality.

Raso soon pressed for a new phase in which the parodic diegesis would motivate both the sex and the comedy, rendering skit comedy superfluous:

> In sitting down with the writers, I might say, "Hey, can we stop doing skit comedy? Can we sort of evolve the characters into a relationship so the sex sequences are even remotely believable?" If we stuck with our old formula of skit comedy with burlesque—it was almost like a burlesque show of the dancing girls and a bunch of guys doing goofy skits—I think it would get very tired very fast. (Andrews, "Lesbian" 35)

These initiatives resulted in two Seduction spoofs of 2003, *Lord of the G-Strings* and *SpiderBabe*, which evince higher values than their predecessors, including enhanced naturalism, special effects, and especially integration. *SpiderBabe*'s simulation of the setting of its model, *Spider-Man* (2002), is more realistic than that of its predecessors as director Johnny Crash was able to shoot on location in New York. Plus, the film all but dispenses with skit comedy. That said, Seduction has not fully abandoned its trichotomous tendency. *G-Strings* flashes its original humor through comic sketches that feature the scatological body comedy of Seduction vets John Fedele and Michael Thomas. Recent and upcoming spoofs such as *Sexy American Idle* (2004), *The Sexy Adventures of Van Helsing* (2004), *The Girl Who Shagged Me* (2005), and *Kinky Kong* (2006) verify the label's continued investment in skit comedy. But even a patently lowbrow, trichotomous film like *American Idle* is more unified than its precursors, for it motivates its variety show format through its central spoof of *American Idol* (2002 on). The structural integration of ei Cinema's most upscale line of films is even more apparent. The latter features often eliminate skit comedy while making efforts at narrative synthesis such that softcore dichotomies recede into sexploitation unities. First visible in Tony Marsiglia's films for Seduction, including *Dr. Jekyll and Mistress Hyde* (2003), *Sin Sisters* (2003), and *Lust for Dracula* (2004), this production trend has lately culminated in Brett Piper's *Screaming Dead* and *Bite Me!*, which flaunt sexploitation sensibilities but not narrative-number formats. Brand-new releases like "New York Wildcats" (2005),[6] *Lust for Laura* (2005), *Sinful* (2006), and *Chantal* (2006) reinforce this dramatic accent, further marginalizing Seduction's reliance on trichotomous structures.

Considering that these developments parallel significant moments in film history, Raso's reference to burlesque is apt. According to David Bordwell et al., classical studio practices worked to give primacy to narrative causality and realistic illusion, unifying and diminishing the spectacle contained in Hollywood films. These production trends, which culminated in what Bordwell labels "the classical Hollywood style," marked a departure from early cinema, whose texts and modes of reception were episodic and weighted toward spectacle. Tom Gunning has referred to early cinema as a "cinema of attractions," an exhibitionist industry reliant on comic and erotic spectacle (57). But after 1917, even Hollywood genres that flaunted early cinema's overt vaudevillian and carnivalesque heritage were "tamed" by the consistent imposition of narrative illusion. Thus, as Bordwell notes, even in Hollywood vehicles like "the films of the Ritz Brothers, Abbott and Costello, and the Marx Brothers, the vaudeville skit or comic dialogue rests within a relatively unified narrative. The backstage musical encouraged interpolated songs and dances while still maintaining an ongoing causal chain" (Bordwell et al. 71). In Schaefer's account, classical exploitation capitalized on Hollywood's diegetic restrictions by offering viewers untamed spectacles, providing continuity with early cinema and the older exhibition circuits from which it derived. In nonnarrative subgenres like burlesque, this heritage was pronounced, with mostly female striptease juxtaposed with mostly male stand-up. Though classical sexploitation presents a break with exploitation (*Bold* 337–39), the former perpetuates exploitation's episodic, exhibitionist character. Witness Russ Meyer's *The Immoral Mr. Teas*, a nudie cutie in which burlesque nudity and sight gags are only loosely organized by the diegesis. More upscale, plot-oriented treatments emerged, but sexploitation's burlesque heritage remained intact, as verified by spectacle that resists full integration. In classical softcore, this populism was apparent in the comic costume epics produced by David Friedman's EVI or Harry Novak's Boxoffice International. Although softcore spoofs like *The Erotic Adventures of Zorro* and Novak's *The Secret Sex Lives of Romeo and Juliet* have fairly coherent narratives, their large casts and stress on slapstick betray an adherence to a populist spectacle rooted in the traditions of early cinema.

Seduction's spoof-oriented, carnival-style softcore is similar to that of EVI and especially Boxoffice in that it has the same trichotomous tendencies.[7] But the broader picture is what intrigues me. Though Seduction first stressed burlesque spectacle (mostly male slapstick, mostly female nudity), it has enhanced its illusionism and varied its spectacle in a development that recapitulates film history (the move from early cinema to classical Hollywood) and that of classical sexploitation more narrowly (the move from nonintegrated forms to integrated ones). Here it should be kept in mind that these parallel historical sequences are neither progressive nor teleological. Classical Hollywood was not "intrinsically" superior to earlier or alternative modes, nor has it proved to be an "end." It is also instructive that the renewed stress on sex and other forms of spectacle that has distinguished contemporary Hollywood was influenced by the profits of low-budget classical genres, including hard and soft porn (see Lewis).

By the same token, even as ei Cinema has moved toward a Hollywood model, the company has never abandoned spectacle and remains more likely to distribute cheap, lower-middlebrow spoofs consisting mainly of spectacle than fully middlebrow films largely devoid of it. Economics have encouraged ei Cinema to stratify its products into two broad tiers. The company's cheapest, most downscale products are distributed by its Video Outlaw (faux-snuff, "badfilm") and After Hours (fetish, harder-core films) labels, which complement its *relatively* upscale Seduction and Shock-O-Rama imprints. Though I focus on the latter, neglecting the existence of the former would reproduce the myopic view typical of studies that have focused on the history of the most elite and expensive genres to the exclusion of "lower" ones. All of these products are aimed at distinct niches and play specialized roles in support of the studio's solvency. Like MRG, ei Cinema is only able to survive through a tech-oriented flexibility that embraces downscale forms and the emerging niches in which they now thrive, including pay-per-view and video-on-demand. Even in the cult nexus, such forms exist in hierarchies that dovetail with those of the larger culture. Hence, as Harmony Wu has suggested, hardcore porn is still at the bottom, where it looks "up" at softcore and, arching its figurative neck further, at nonpornographic horror (85–87). These classed formations explain why Raso has so volubly aimed ei Cinema at horror while denying the pornographic character of his softcore films and remaining comparatively reticent about his most downscale lines (Andrews, "Lesbian" 34–35). ei Cinema's prestige projects are specifically designed to raise the company's cultural profile and broaden its distribution into more mainstream fields.

For a cult softcore studio that eschews corporate softcore's more proven under-the-radar approach, ei Cinema has been notably successful in the home video market. It claims to have sold five hundred thousand copies of its films in just two years (2002–3) through retail outlets like Borders, Virgin, Best Buy, Tower, Sam Goody, and FYE and rental outlets like Blockbuster, Hollywood Video, and Movie Gallery (Fine 2). Even in 2005, when major chains were stocking fewer softcore titles, ei Cinema managed to keep movies like *The Girl Who Shagged Me* on Hollywood Video's new release shelves. ei Cinema has also licensed *Gladiator Eroticvs, Play-Mate of the Apes, G-Strings,* and *SpiderBabe* to premium cable, which has heretofore been dominated by corporate softcore. This stress on distribution has played a central role in the evolution of Seduction and, recently, Shock-O-Rama. Consider that ei Cinema has pursued realism across its lines in accord with its distribution targets. Raso tellingly (and *incorrectly,* politically speaking) equates realism not only with skillful acting and substantive plots but also with heterosexual spectacle:

> A lot of foreign territories have eluded us because some countries will not accept girl-girl situations throughout a movie. And many cable channels do not want a strictly lesbian film, a strictly girl-girl production. The people in control—the gatekeepers of these markets—we sit down and talk to them and say, "This is who we are, this is what we do, and our films are very popular in this market. Why can't we market our films to a certain television station or to Japan or to some other foreign territory?" Typically, their feedback is, "your storylines are not realistic enough," or, "your sex scenes are all girl-girl and this specific market does not cater to that." (Andrews, "Lesbian" 33)

It seems unlikely that ei Cinema will pursue distribution to the point of homogenizing Seduction "into" corporate softcore.[8] Raso has said that Seduction will rely on girl-girl imagery to satisfy established markets, deploying its "realistic" (heterosexual, narrative-oriented) ventures to advance into new markets.[9] *G-Strings* indirectly makes this point in a ludic segment marking the collision of opposing categories of spectacle: epic violence and girl-girl imagery. In an interchange fraught with implications *vis-à-vis* Seduction's direction, warriors led by General Uptight (Peter Quarry) happen upon two white-clad women in a "lesbian" clinch on a field to host a battle between the forces of good and Sourasse's "Dork" army. Uptight warns the women of the "manly" adventure to engulf them, but they pooh-pooh him. "Well, silly, it's not four o'clock yet," Benadryl (Anoushka) notes. "You're ten minutes early." "So if you don't mind," her partner (Allanah Rhodes) adds, "we're going to finish up here before your little battle." "Well,

Figure 26. This DVD art for *Lord of the G-Strings* (2003) demonstrates Seduction Cinema's stress on exploitation-style art and its heavy promotion of the women it trumpets as "contract players." Used courtesy ei Independent Cinema.

it's going to be a really *epic* battle," Uptight pleads, deflated. He and his warriors then beat an ogling retreat, signaling Seduction's ongoing allegiance to girl-girl imagery.

Before analyzing the distinction strategies characteristic of ei Cinema's recent initiatives, it is worth considering how the company has manipulated the "accidental" sexism of its original formula. According to Raso, the "fact that our sex scenes are mostly of the girl-girl variety—or that the comedy routines tend to be composed of a lot of guys—was not a result of a creative process. It was a practical process" (Andrews, "Lesbian" 32). On one hand, Seduction's mostly male ensemble had a background in low comedy; on the other, the women cast for its first productions "did not want to do scenes with men but felt very comfortable doing scenes with other women." Seduction has subsequently used each of these twin sexisms to offset criticism associated with the other. For example, in insisting that feminists have never criticized Seduction's girl-girl imagery, Raso points to the carnival spirit of comedies that frequently resort to dancing gorillas: "We produce many erotic comedies. They are 'silly.' Most women . . . see it as entertainment" (Andrews, "Lesbian" 32). Conversely, the deeper seriousness of such comedy may also be accented so as to deflect criticism of the sex. Cultural scholars have linked the carnivalesque to political subversion (e.g., Stallybrass and White 12–16), a reading that the Seduction formula encourages. Though hardly encoded for revolt, Seduction films sneer at power, exuding a scattered subversiveness in mockery of any character who represents officialdom. Such humor often lampoons repressive sex attitudes; hence the mayor (Fedele) in *Witchbabe* is satirized as a social and sexual fascist. Seduction's girl-girl imagery may thus be linked to elements conveying "legitimate," that is, nonsexual, meanings. As a result, cult reviewers have on occasion received Seduction comedy more solemnly than one might expect (e.g., Richards, *Witchbabe* 1).

That the mayor in *Witchbabe* may be read as a homophobic slur implies something else about carnival: politically, it is unreliable, for it irrepressibly burlesques both left and right. Thus the Seduction formula is likely to seem incorrect regardless of viewer politics. *Play-Mate of the Apes,* for instance, juxtaposes mockery of Charlton Heston's pro-gun attitudes with mockery of Bill Clinton's sexual peccadilloes.[10] In this respect, the aspirationalism ascribed to girl-girl imagery may for some elevate Seduction features by countering the gay jokes, fart jokes, and masturbation jokes of the burlesque. Though not a typical soft-focus label, Seduction recognizes the cultural value historically tied to this type of spectacle. Several of its films (*Witchbabe,* the *Roxanna* remake [2002], *The Erotic Diary of Misty Mundae* [2005], *Curious Obsessions* [2006]) soften their girl-girl sequences, achieving the video equivalent of filter effects. These "aesthetic" tactics provide contrasts with the low, masculinized depictions located elsewhere in the films. *Mistress Hyde* even manipulates the positive values encoded in "lesbian" stylization to motivate a cynical twist undercutting the viewer's acculturated expectation that this postfeminist imagery signifies Hallmark-card virtue. But Seduction has mostly used girl-girl spectacle to reinforce plots that empower women and humiliate men, as in the "warring spectacle" of *G-Strings.* "Because we're in a genre that still tends to be more lesbian or girl-girl," Raso notes, "women have dominant roles in our movies; they're the central characters, and if anything, the male figure is a buffoon or a comedic sidekick, someone who is there specifically for laughs" (Andrews, "Lesbian" 32). Seduction's blend of male comedy and female nudity resembles the nudie cutie, wherein the "depleted male" is a disempowered buffoon who poses no threat to the higher females he ogles (Schaefer, "Burlesque"). Seduction's girl-girl formula updates the nudie cutie for a postfeminist era by refining, subjectifying, and empowering females such that their virtues offset "indecent" elements of the spectacle gendered male. In a brief interval, then, the studio has recapitulated a complex set of gender progressions basic to softcore history.

II. THREE CATEGORIES OF CULT SOFTCORE DISTINCTION

If the original Seduction model developed accidentally, the way in which ei Cinema marketed that paradigm quickly grew calculated. By 2001, it had begun sponsoring a female star system oriented around Misty Mundae, a promotional strategy that evolved from the studio's girl-girl biases and its links to the cult film nexus. ei Cinema's deliberate strategies have also been exemplified by its careful cultivation of its sexploitation heritage and its encouragement of an arthouse sensibility among its directors. These related trends have culminated in reverential, allusive parodies of works bearing elite mannerisms, including sexploitation "classics" like *Swedish Wildcats* (1972) and more recent art films like *Mulholland Drive* (2001).

After inaugurating its line of spoofs, ei Cinema began promoting its actresses as "contract players" in a nostalgic evocation of classical Hollywood ("Profile" 2). But this studio-based system has not reinforced Seduction's links to Hollywood so much as to the cult nexus, which has since the 1980s celebrated "scream queens" like Linnea Quigley, Brinke Stevens, and Debbie Rochon in *Scream Queens, Femme Fatales, Draculina,* and other fanzines.[11] Seduction's system marks another contrast between corporate softcore—which has ceased to pay any actresses like semicelebrities (Lombard, "Casting" 5)—and cult softcore. ei Cinema has remodeled this cult paradigm with vigor. As clarified by "Misty Mundae: From Skin to Scream" (2004), one of ei Cinema's more polished promo-documentaries, the studio views the success of its "starlet" as crucial to establishing its labels as credible cult-horror brands.[12] If Mundae succeeds in evolving from "skin chick" to "scream queen," the studio with which she is identified may effect a similar transition, enhancing its cult credentials in the process.[13]

Darian Caine was among the first anointed a cult celebrity at ei Cinema. Caine serves as the heroine of *Mistress Frankenstein* and *Gladiator Eroticvs* and provides the upturned face that is the Seduction logo. But by 2002,

Mundae had clearly supplanted Caine as Seduction's main icon, with Julian Wells figuring as the principal supporting star in the ei Cinema system. After her feature role in *Gladiator Eroticvs,* Mundae starred in heroine-driven vehicles like *Misty Mundae: Mummy Raider* (2002), *SpiderBabe, The Seduction of Misty Mundae* (2005), *The Erotic Diary of Misty Mundae, Sinful, The Girl Who Shagged Me, Chantal,* and many others. She also amassed production credits, with ei Cinema distributing her remake of Nick Phillips's *Lustful Addiction* (2002), her "semi-autobiographical" *Confessions of a Natural Beauty* (2003), and even her experimental 16mm, black-and-white featurette, "Voodoun Blues" (2004). This Misty-centric slate has contributed to ei Cinema's move into dramatic forms and has yielded a corporate output that bears increasingly mainstream and postfeminist traits.

That said, extrafilmic promotions have most clearly defined Mundae's cult of celebrity. Mundae is the focus of many ei Cinema documentaries, including "From Skin to Scream" and *Misty Mundae: Girl Seduction* (2003), a compilation of "archival" shorts from her no-budget years with fetish-oriented Factory 2000. Founded by Bill Hellfire, Mundae's former mentor, Factory 2000 once occupied a distinct sector of the New Jersey cult film subculture, but its links to ei Cinema proliferated after Raso chose Mundae to spearhead his market strategy. (Indeed, Raso purchased Factory 2000 in 2002.) Mundae is also the focus of pamphlets like "Profile: Misty Mundae" (2), a bio piece accompanying ei Cinema's "New Releases" catalogue for winter 2004. What is more, ei Cinema sponsors MistyMundae.com, a Web site that includes a fan club, and Mundae has served as the face of the company at conventions, interviews, and other events. The rhetorical thrust of these promotions is fairly uniform. According to ei Cinema, Mundae has a rare "star quality"—as the narrator of "From Skin to Scream" claims, "it is called, simply, stardom"—that is grounded in her looks, talent, and intelligence.

Not surprisingly, Seduction lavishes more attention on Mundae's appearance than her other qualities, deploying a descriptive rhetoric that stresses simplicity, nature, and authenticity to situate her as a "natural beauty," or, more colorfully, a "doe-eyed beauty oozing girlish naïveté" ("Profile" 2). Such rhetoric is a self-referential staple of Mundae-driven vehicles. In *Bite Me!* her character looks at herself in a mirror and laments, "Maybe I should get a boob job . . . they don't look like stripper tits. They're not the kind that guys like." This dialogue is a joke for insiders; ei Cinema producers *do* believe that men like Mundae's physique. At the same time, it points to the ambiguity of her youthful, girl-girl image, whose Pre-Raphaelite pallor and flower-child formlessness appeals not just to heterosexual men but to women as well. On the other hand, Mundae's girlishness has also allowed Seduction to avoid challenging mainstream culture, which tolerates a poly-

Figure 27. A production still from *SpiderBabe* (2003), a higher-end spoof from Seduction Cinema. Used courtesy ei Independent Cinema.

morphous sexuality among young women more readily than it tolerates the same among older women or men of any age.[14] But most crucially, Mundae's "simplicity" has allowed ei Cinema to stake a niche distinct from that of corporate softcore. "Her normality," as Raso puts it, "deviates from the classic softcore image as portrayed by late-night cable programmers. She's not bleached blonde, her hair isn't teased, she doesn't have fake breasts. She's natural. The folks at *Penthouse* and *Playboy* would not see her as acceptable, but that would be missing the point. She's wildly popular because we're presenting her as she really is" (Andrews, "Lesbian" 33). The irony is that Seduction underscores this aspect of Mundae's appeal by co-opting the *Playboy* tag, deploying "girl next door" as a shorthand in contexts that distinguish her from the type of actress who populates *Playboy* and corporate softcore ("Profile" 2). Seduction's promotion of Mundae may thus be viewed as a subset of Seduction's marketing of its own cult-indie roots, a strategy tapping a preexisting ideology that privileges independent filmmaking, high or low, over the "sanitized" forms of corporate filmmaking that dominate Hollywood and television. In sum, Mundae's cult of celebrity represents a most supple distinction strategy, one through which Raso has sought to encapsulate the distinction of an entire company. "I think that, in Misty's case," he notes, "what's old is new. It's apparent that we at Seduction Cinema go back to basics. When I say 'basics,' that's what Misty's appeal is" (Andrews, "Lesbian" 33).

Mundae has been acting in fetish films like the recent asphyxiation release *Flesh for Olivia* (2002/2006) since she was eighteen, so the freshness-and-naïveté rhetoric that now encases her has the smell of an exploitation con—as does Raso's alignment of ei Cinema, which has distributed Factory 2000 titles under its After Hours label, with such qualities. It is inarguable, though, that Mundae easily personifies the retro appeal that ei Cinema has ascribed to her, making her a "natural" for its Retro-Seduction insignia. This facility is striking in the promotional art that accompanied Retro-Seduction's 2001 rerelease of Joe Sarno's *Inga*—perhaps because *Inga*'s original star, Marie Liljedahl, whom Mundae has supplanted in the DVD art, projected a naïve image that led her to multiple appearances in *Playboy*. Fortifying what is in cult contexts a prestigious link to Liljedahl is Mundae's star turn in *The Seduction of Misty Mundae,* a patently aspirational, Raso-directed update of Sarno's awakening-sexuality classic that was shot in 2001 but released in 2005. Most intriguing is that Mundae's character in this straightforwardly realistic feature is called "Misty Mundae" (her aunt [Julian Wells] is given the "Inga" sobriquet), as if to stress that the actress is identical to her girl-next-door incarnations.[15]

Along with Nick Phillips (a.k.a. Steve Millard),[16] Sarno is one of two old-school sexploiteers around whom ei Cinema has built its Retro-Seduction label. Having moved into a market dominated by Something Weird, ei Cinema now distributes a growing line of classical features and featurettes, a practice that provides another key component of the studio's cult image. By 2005, this line had expanded to include an impressive array of archival peeps and loops. ei Cinema has distinguished this line of rereleases by lavishing resources on the films of Phillips and Sarno, as measured by the quality of Retro-Seduction's DVD transfers and the reverential attitude of its bonus materials, including commentaries, archival footage, and remakes. With Sarno, ei Cinema has extended this "homage" strategy by luring the octogenarian from retirement in 2003 to direct one last, low-budget film, *Lust for Laura*, under the auspices of its Retro-Seduction label.

Like Mundae, Phillips and Sarno represent recognizable values and tastes. It is instructive, then, to consider what ei Cinema's decision to focus resources on these two sexploiteers says about the company's direction. On first glance, these contemporaries seem very different. The Phillips films remade by Retro-Seduction in 2001 and 2002 (*Lustful Addiction, Roxanna*

[1970], and *Pleasures of a Woman* [1972]) were marginal sexploitation vehicles produced for grindhouse exhibition. They flaunt low mannerisms and values, including nonsynchronous sound, which led to the wry yet screechy voice-overs that are among the most memorable aspects of Phillips's work. These dour films assert their solidarity with a pornographic heritage and their own production milieu. By contrast, Sarno's work has crossover appeal, as verified by *Inga*'s breakout success on its American release in 1968. Even in his harder-core features, Sarno evinces a feminized, upper-middlebrow sensibility indicated by his ability to wring stylish production values from diminutive budgets; his consistent stress on female psychology in both narrative and number; and his reverence for an auteurist, art film tradition once dominated by Ingmar Bergman.[17] Still, closer inspection reveals that Phillips and Sarno converge in ways that betray ei Cinema's market logic. Both filmmakers stress girl-girl spectacle, conforming to an ei Cinema signature. And both evince the aspirationalism to which ei Cinema now links its own ambitions. Though Phillips's *Roxanna* expresses these aspirations through less mainstream practices than Sarno's *Inga*, in many cult niches, the grungy, avant-garde "authenticity" of the former is not necessarily a commercial detriment. Conversely, given the crossover respect generated by Sarno's work, it is obvious that ei Cinema's redoubled emphasis on his work since 2003 signifies another phase in the company's ongoing effort to tweak its cult appeal so as to edge into broader markets.[18] It is also instructive to consider what these filmmakers do *not* represent, namely, low, spoof-oriented burlesque. Had ei Cinema merely hoped to extend its established blend of masculinized comedy and feminized sex into classical contexts, it could have focused on the many directors and studios identified with such comedy.[19] Its decision to focus instead on classical softcore of a distinct style and gravity implies a deliberate strategy to link itself to a "serious" sexploitation heritage. ei Cinema's newly elite bearing is, in short, a meaningful departure for a company with roots in populist comedy.[20]

What has not changed is ei Cinema's excavation of cinema's past. Cult is defined by its nostalgic mechanisms—which means that, unlike corporate softcore, cult softcore recognizes that it *has* a history. As ei Cinema helps push softcore into its shot-on-video future, it seems only more likely to fetishize its theatrical, shot-on-film past. Thus a recent release called *Curious Obsessions* eroticizes a "possessed" home theater projector—which turns itself and others on—as much as the "two luscious young women" who watch the "purring" machine projecting "hot, classic stag loops" and "unspooling reels of 16mm file" ("Studio News" 2).[21] ei Cinema's signature expression of this nostalgia is, of course, parody. Spoofs of mainstream hits and reverential remakes of neglected "classics" both qualify as forms of parody. In *A Theory of Parody* (1985; see 43–68), Linda Hutcheon argues that

Figure 28. A 2006 sales catalogue for Retro-Seduction Cinema. Used courtesy ei Independent Cinema.

satire is "extramural" in that it points outside art to human vices or follies that the satirist targets for ridicule. Parody is more "intramural," inward, and self-conscious in that it only requires conscious imitation of one text by another. If parodic imitation *may,* as in burlesque, involve ridicule, it does not demand it and may incline toward reverence. According to Hutcheon, this value-neutral character is what has made parody so attractive to post-modernists, whose yen for self-reflexive, intertextual forms does not necessitate satire's didactic and judgmental purposes. Hence, ei Cinema's more recent parodic strategies suggest a move toward a "purer" parody, one that is just as likely to result in affirmative allusions to preexisting forms as to mocking burlesques of them. In this maneuver, ei Cinema embraces a dual mechanism recognizable in many cult forums: it distinguishes its idiosyncratic taste and thus its cult identity both through the objects of its disgust and through the objects of its admiration.

ei Cinema's decision to endorse Phillips's low, pornographic efforts is curious given Raso's soft-pedaling of similarly downscale efforts distributed by After Hours and Video Outlaw. The patina of time and distance is crucial here, for it invests otherwise "indefensible" materials with a nostalgic elevation that is nothing if not anachronistic. (Of course, Phillips could be defended by reference to the psychedelic avant-gardism that to varying degrees informs films like *Roxanna*, but a similar rhetoric could be applied to the underground films that Hellfire has made for Factory 2000.) In a sense, this low patina has licensed ei Cinema to be as humorless, squalid, fetish-oriented, and *inexpensive* as possible in its first three remakes of Phillips's work. All that is required is the maintenance of a "properly" self-conscious attitude toward the newly respectable original. Another curiosity lies in the fact that Sarno's market utility is his crossover appeal, which suggests his mastery of qualities valued by the postfeminist mainstream—yet Sarno is today used to help ei Cinema distinguish itself from the same amorphous entity.

Interestingly, ei Cinema's recent remakes have evinced more polished values than those visible in its first three remodelings of Phillips's work. Given Sarno's middlebrow appeal and his extensive collaborations with the studio, ei Cinema's comparatively elaborate treatment of its cabaret featurette "New York Wildcats," Johnny Crash's stylish, shot-on-video remake of Sarno's *Swedish Wildcats*, was to be expected. Somewhat more surprising is that the studio would lavish higher values on its 16mm remake of Phillips's *Chantal* (1969). This remake's rigid aestheticization is attributable to Tony Marsiglia, a director with a distinctive role as ei Cinema's resident auteur. Marsiglia's auteurism, which is characterized by control, intertextuality, and experimentation, has been sharply promoted by ei Cinema and represents a significant addition to its distinction strategies, one that complements its star system and its classical library. ei Cinema's marketing of Marsiglia signifies a logical move beyond the elitism informing its commodification of its classical roots. Not only has Marsiglia allowed ei Cinema to further pursue its repackaging of this cult past, he has also allowed it to establish credible links to elite modes of contemporary indie filmmaking with cachet beyond the cult nexus.

To a lesser extent, ei Cinema has adopted this auteur approach before. As writer-director on films like *Witchbabe* and *G-Strings*, Terry West has been prominent in ei Cinema's coverage of its own directors, for his background in underground comics lends him cult prestige. However, Marsiglia's aestheticist sensibility has proved more useful to ei Cinema's move into new genres and niches. This sensibility is grounded in technical acumen and a knowledge of film history, two qualities visible in the experimental film

Ashes and Flames (1998), which Marsiglia produced under the name Anthony Michael Kane prior to working with ei Cinema. Of course, the studio is not the only one to benefit from this collaboration. ei Cinema has afforded Marsiglia the opportunity to write, direct, and cut his own films, all without financing them. "Who," Marsiglia asks, "would have that kind of freedom in Hollywood?" (2). In this vein, it helps to consider the differences between Marsiglia's experience at ei Cinema and Tom Lazarus's at Playboy. The directors are comparable in that both have enjoyed the status of reigning auteur at their respective labels. But whereas Marsiglia's cult label has encouraged his antirealism, Lazarus's more corporate label first discouraged his hyperrealism and squelched promotion of it, treating such stylization as an impediment to Playboy's production of "sausage." Of course, it is possible to go too far with this contrast, which might yield the complacent valorization of indie filmmaking that has distorted not just cult contexts but academic discussions of the same. Indeed, there is an obvious sense in which Seduction *is* a "corporate" softcore label: its parent is a for-profit corporation that places restrictions on its employees, maintaining final say on casting, titles, and trailers. Still, such compromises seem relatively limited. Marsiglia's loyalty and affection confirm that Seduction is open to the creative "excess" of its directors, in part because the cult nexus has historically treated such excess as a salable commodity.

Similar treatment is apparent in ei Cinema's promotion of Marsiglia. As noted, ei Cinema has from its inception provided extras with its DVDs so as to supplement perceptions of consumer value—even if these extras at first consisted of little more than records of "the cast eating baked ziti" (Andrews, "Lesbian" 31). The first wave of Seduction extras reinforced a sense of fun, defusing resistance to its least polished films by situating them in the carnival context most likely to afford viewer enjoyment. As ei Cinema's films grew more sophisticated, its extras evolved in tandem. Marsiglia's *Dr. Jekyll and Mistress Hyde* and *Lust for Dracula* and Piper's *Screaming Dead*—works that presumably require less external "support" than Seduction's initial spoofs—include intricate, polished extras that manipulate the framework for reception and, in the process, articulate the narrative of ei Cinema's "progressive," skin-to-scream transformation. In Marsiglia's case, these extras focus on his aestheticism as proof that ei Cinema fosters art film talent rather than merely recovering such talent, as in Sarno's case. The documentaries and interviews that accompany *Mistress Hyde* thus underscore Marsiglia's desire for control over all aspects of production. He is depicted as an intense director who constructs careful shots and studiously advises the principal actresses, who then testify to his Flaubertian drive for perfection ("the director had us do the most insignificant scenes ten times").[22] The actresses also position the film and its maker by stressing *Mistress Hyde*'s allusions to Lynch, *Mulholland Drive* in particular. These promotional tactics dovetail with references to Marsiglia's taste for a noirish antirealism that favors nonlinearity and ambiguity, suggesting his experimentalism. In sum, these extras elevate Marsiglia by deploying the same aestheticism that Toby Keeler's *Pretty as a Picture: The Art of David Lynch* (1997)—a more "legitimate" but no less partisan documentary filmed on the set of *Lost Highway* (1996)—deploys to elevate Lynch.

Perhaps the strongest index that ei Cinema is revising its exploitation style is that its hype of *Mistress Hyde* undersells the film's links to *Mulholland Drive*.[23] Mundae and Wells indicate that Marsiglia's debt to Lynch is limited to broad themes and styles, but the dense Lynchian textures of his film suggest otherwise. Though its title implies yet another pornographic spoof of the Robert Louis Stevenson classic, *Mistress Hyde* is closer to a dramatic parody of *Mulholland Drive* (and to a lesser extent of *Lost Highway*). This relation perpetuates ei Cinema's reliance on intertextuality while applying its newly reverential attitude to elite contemporary classics (as opposed to limiting such treatment to older sex classics like *Inga* and *Roxanna*). Enriching this relation is that Lynch is himself a postmodernist who favors dense intertextuality—and dense sexuality. In *Mulholland Drive*, this duality results in extensive references to *doppelgänger* films like Bergman's *Persona* (1966), whose bisexuality Lynch expands into imagery with a pornographic, girl-girl intonation. It is, then, possible to "justify" Marsiglia's market-driven expansion of Lynch's bisexual imagery into the full-blown softcore structure of *Mistress Hyde* by pointing to Lynch's analogous expansion of Bergman's imagery.

Mistress Hyde's main resemblance to *Mulholland Drive* inheres in its romance, which involves two women who undergo psychosexual shifts, literally becoming different people during the *doppelgänger* plot. As in *Mulholland Drive*, this oneiric, nonlinear story line involves an acting theme and eventuates in destruction and revenge, revealing an initial mirage of bisexual love to be just that. These diegetic echoes are augmented by precise reconfigurations of Lynch's distinctive lighting, music, imagery, and dialogue. Some remodelings refer specifically to *Lost Highway*, as in Marsiglia's close-ups of Mundae's lips, which recall close-ups of Alice (Patricia Arquette), Lynch's blonde *femme fatale*. Others refer to *Lost Highway* and *Mulholland Drive* at once, as in Marsiglia's use of ostentatious wigs and blue, flickering light to mark metamorphosis.[24] But like the plot's erotic ellipses, Marsiglia's technical borrowings mostly remodel *Mulholland Drive*. In *Mistress Hyde*'s soundtrack, Marsiglia often resorts to a nostalgic ditty that unmistakably mimics Linda Scott's 1961 rendition of "I've Told Every Little Star" as used by Lynch. Marsiglia's stylized compositions also evoke *Mulholland Drive*. A striking red postcoital shot alludes to the blue postcoital shot of Betty (Naomi Watts) and Rita (Laura Elena Harring) in which the latter chants the word *silencio*.[25] Specific moments of the script—which, though credited to Bruce Hallenbeck, was broadly reimagined during shooting by Marsiglia—are manipulated to similar ends. To wit, in the red-tinted sequence, Wells's character claims, "I've never even done this before." The wording and false naïveté of this line recreate Betty's "Have you ever done this before?" which serves as a wide-eyed prelude to her initial tryst with Rita.

Because Raso's aim has been to create a solid base from which to make horror films, it is intriguing that Marsiglia's lush, allusive softcore—which is gothic but rarely formulaic or plot-heavy—now has a featured place at ei Cinema.[26] This positioning is attributable to the fact that Marsiglia evinces great continuity with the company's spoof-oriented past—and it hasn't hurt that he is comfortable with girl-girl sex. But for a clear view of ei Cinema's evolution, it is crucial to recognize that Marsiglia has moved away from softcore dichotomies in films like *Chantal* and *Sinful*.[27] Thus his work represents continuities with ei Cinema's past output *and* sharp breaks with the same. This duality is especially apparent in his nascent project to remake *Frankenstein* for Shock-O-Rama. Predictably, Marsiglia plans to lend this project an arthouse conceit foregrounding form and style. Shot *sans* dialogue, "it will let the theme rely only on the imagery" (Marsiglia 2). In an earlier phase, Seduction produced the lo-fi comedy *Mistress Frankenstein*—which includes a television antenna doctored with tin foil as a lab prop—so this new ei Cinema project may in the end provide not only a new variant on an enduring myth but also an ironic commentary on the company's transformations.

The above transformations have yielded other notable ironies as well. Though now integrating "straight sex" into its spectacle, ei Cinema has retained its preference for girl-girl imagery. Maintaining this imagery while moving toward dramatic modes that incline toward avant-garde horror and excess has made it possible to move further beyond the postfeminist limits that have shaped corporate softcore and, to a much lesser extent, cult softcore.[28] But if ei Cinema is edging toward the greater variety of the classical era, it is also edging toward a greater misogynistic potential. Whereas an early film like *Mistress Frankenstein* treats its "evil lesbians" ludically, later ones like *Mistress Hyde* and *Lust for Dracula* adopt a darker attitude toward the same device, often combining it with the bondage imagery that also figures in *Screaming Dead*. Though it would be a mistake to read these films as misogynistic—Marsiglia and Piper actively deflect this—the use of violence in highly sexualized contexts always risks such readings. This hazard is ironic given that the studio's girl-girl bent is rooted in part in Raso's desire to indulge actresses like Mundae, who dislikes heterosexual sequences.[29]

Another irony is economic. Though ei Cinema has been inflationary, reinvesting earnings and often increasing budgets, in softcore's larger scheme it has played a deflationary role. With its ultralow budgets, it has contributed to the competition that has encouraged the use of 16mm and video and that has eliminated both low-budget corporate softcore labels (like Indigo at Playboy) and low-budget cult softcore labels (Surrender at Full Moon) that once adhered to a 35mm paradigm. Corporate softcore label MRG has played a similar role by slashing budgets, filming highly routinized softcore thrillers on 16mm (one of which, *Young and Seductive*, stars ei Cinema "contract player" Julian Wells), and embracing shot-on-video procedures. But the contrasting outcomes of these trends at MRG and ei Cinema suggest that similar equipment, shooting schedules, and budgets do not entail similar products. For ei Cinema, 16mm shoots that last about a week and cost upwards of one hundred thousand dollars signify prestige, health, and upward mobility, enhancing formal exuberance rather than sapping it, as seems the case at MRG.

Given its lo-fi origins, ei Cinema's current position as a player in the cult film nexus may itself seem ironic. But its brief history suggests this status is the result of a set of rapid yet incremental adjustments to its original and more accidental identity. Since 1999, ei Cinema has changed from a studio stressing a burlesque formula of sketch comedy and girl-girl spectacle into a more narrative-oriented cult softcore company that lends its most strident marketing to dramas, horror films in particular. In this skin-to-scream "elevation," it has recapitulated transformations identified with earlier moments in film history. Besides enhanced realism and prodigious promotion, ei Cinema's most significant strategies today include the celebration of an in-house star system based on cult scream queens; the recycling of its classical sexploitation roots; and the promotion of auteurist tendencies among its filmmakers. If ei Cinema continues to develop and expand while maintaining its idiosyncratic use of parody, its various labels may one day establish a precedent that reverses the deflationary slide into explicitness and homogenization that has recently typified many segments of the softcore industry.[30]

Baring flesh just doesn't get you noticed the way it used to.
— *Chicago Tribune columnist Steve Chapman on the 2003 Victoria's Secret fashion show (31)*

Conclusion

Whither Softcore?

My favorite response to the Janet Jackson affair was a full-page appliance ad in the *Chicago Tribune* on 14 December 2004. Against a teal backdrop, two Siemens "xTronic" ranges sit side by side. The oven on the viewer's left is wide open, revealing a succulent turkey. The tagline: "our apologies to anyone offended by our exposed breast" (Siemens 17).[1] Only an ingenious culture, I reasoned, could use sex to sell stoves. And only an inspired culture could use an oven door to simulate a "wardrobe malfunction" and a roast turkey to signify a woman's breast. (Her *right* breast, at that.)

More than a year later, the effects of the Jackson imbroglio seem no less impressive—consider that the Siemens ad appeared ten months after the 2004 Super Bowl show that spawned it—but much less inspired. The litany of headlines about indecency fines, self-censorship, and unintended consequences is instead numbing. This durability testifies to a fact broadly recognized in early 2004 but not today: the FCC crackdown was planned in advance of Janet and Justin's epochal tango, and this federal choreography has yet to malfunction.[2] Congressional legislation to increase fines for broadcast networks was in place before the Super Bowl took place on 1 February 2004. The FCC had levied its first indecency fine—against a San Francisco television station that had shown a penis—on 27 January 2004. Moreover, former FCC chairman Michael Powell, pressured by Congress and the mass e-mail campaigns of the Parents Television Council (Shields 1), had warned the cable and satellite industries in the weeks prior to the Super Bowl.

Figure 29. A telling sign of the cultural penetration of the Janet Jackson affair: an ad for Siemens stoves. © Siemens and *The Chicago Tribune*, 2004.

Figure 30. Janet Jackson's notorious "wardrobe malfunction" may have contributed to contemporary softcore's current decline. © CBS and MTV, 2004.

Indeed, the FCC's actions and widening threats might be viewed as the most publicized component of a strategy to "sanitize" the culture that also included the Justice Department's resumption of obscenity prosecutions in 2003, its first major effort in a decade, and the solicitor general's attempt in 2004 to smash the impasse blocking the enforcement of the Child Online Protection Act (Singer 1, 16; "Time" 10). Given all this, then, the infamous "wardrobe malfunction" is shown for what it was: a high-profile, high-impact opportunity that a reformist government had prepared for and did not miss.

What intrigued me in February 2004 and still fascinates me a year later is how this contrived brouhaha would affect softcore. Such interest is more than a scholar's filmy conflation of a breast-induced upheaval and a breast-heaving genre. Softcore, it bears repeating, is not as hardy as hardcore. In the past, it has proved uniquely susceptible to shifts in economics and cultural temperament. It was softcore that retreated after the *Miller v. California* ruling in 1973; softcore that remained absent through the reactionary 1980s; and softcore that reemerged as the Justice Department scaled back anti-obscenity prosecutions in the early 1990s. Now this middling genre is uncharacteristically off-center and thus more fragile. Since launching my project in 2002, I have had occasion to watch softcore, corporate softcore in particular, as it has withered into a less fruitful form. Though the genre's renewal in the 1990s was rooted in an upscale, midbudget paradigm, this always-deflationary genre has flirted with hardcore for so long that its downscale, ultra-low-budget identity is today equivocal. Given America's repressive climate—to which Linda Ruth Williams has ascribed Hollywood's current unwillingness to treat sexual themes and imagery in a frank, substantive manner ("No Sex" 1–6; *Erotic* 37, 245)—the markets may soon render this type of softcore expendable as well.

And they may already have. Recently, I revisited the home video outlets that from 2002 to 2004 supplied my study with much of its material. I was struck by softcore's recession. The most mainstream outlets registered the most drastic contraction. Hollywood Video was carrying no new softcore releases, and Blockbuster was carrying but one—and that one had been produced in 2003. How this diminished presence relates to politics is not clear, but the fact persists that a year earlier those same shelves were replete with new softcore releases. Of course, video distribution is not as crucial in this respect as cable and satellite distribution, for the production slates of the corporate softcore studios that yet comprise the largest segment of the industry remain contingent on the needs of premium cable and pay-per-view. The premium networks are decisive insofar as they provide a much wider distribution base than pay-per-view; if softcore is to move upscale again, premium cable is still the most likely context for it to do so. Though the softcore licensed by HBO and Showtime has long been shifting downscale, these entities still pay comparatively high licensing fees and continue to avoid the harder, shot-on-video content that has become *de rigueur* even among studios like MRG and New City, which have been increasingly reduced to scrabbling after pay-per-view dollars—and, in consequence, producing ever more explicit, low-end material.

But a move upscale is hardly in the works. Premium cable is licensing fewer new vehicles and perhaps playing fewer old ones as well. Since 2001, corporate softcore production has dropped sharply. This decline has many determinants, including "softness" in the German market that has offered the most reliable international distribution for American softcore companies from Axis to MRG. But the cardinal factor has been cable's appetite, which has diminished to the point that MRG casting director Robert Lombard had by February 2005 yet to schedule any 16mm films for the coming year, with his slate slanted toward "porny" serials and shot-on-video features, some showing the elongated numbers indicative of pay-per-view distribution.[3] One quirk in this trend is that, over the past five years, cable has aired more softcore than ever due to the programming needs stimulated by its extensive multiplexing. Most of this content has not been new, for cable has always relied on reruns—though it now appears that even this reliance on old material is shifting. Over the first months of 2005, the premium cable networks appeared to be airing fewer TVMA-rated vehicles at later hours than during a comparable period a year before. These softcore vehicles have mainly been running on nonflagship channels; Cinemax's MoreMAX channel has, for example, been airing softcore in disproportionate quantities. Even within cable's established nocturnal framework, then, softcore seems to be in retreat—and increasingly contained and "ghettoized." Neither HBO nor Showtime has responded to inquiries about these patterns, so I do not want to classify what might be a scheduling blip as a full-blown "trend." But suffice it to say that any further decrease in cable's appetite could have an outsize impact on a fractured industry.

There is reason to surmise that cable might elect to wean itself from softcore, at least temporarily. In February and March 2004, the mainstream media were abuzz with speculation that Powell might try to enlarge the FCC's jurisdiction. Expanding on comments made before the Jackson affair, Powell complained to legislators that network TV was not responsible for 85 percent of television's effluence, most of which flowed from cable (Smith and Simon 13). Though the networks share links with cable, including corporate ownership (e.g., Viacom owns CBS, Showtime, and MTV), network executives shifted the blame. Not only had the CBS halftime show been produced by MTV, they asserted, but the networks' disposition toward racy fare had been spawned by competition with cable, whose edgiest programs were fostered by an antiquated regulatory regime that held the networks to higher standards than nonbroadcast entities (John Cook 13). Spooked by Powell's threats and by Congress's receptiveness to the same, the industry responded with peace offerings. Shortly after a Senate committee narrowly defeated new decency standards for cable in March 2004, National Cable and Telecommunications Association president Robert Sachs announced that companies representing 85 percent of the nation's subscribers had agreed to offer free channel-blocking gear so subscribers without cable boxes could customize their "dial" ("Cable" 12). Having resisted earlier calls to let subscribers buy "a family-friendly tier," the industry offered a compromise with a smaller downside for operators. The question now is whether softcore might become a similarly marginal offering in a bid to insulate the risqué spectacle of hits like *The L Word*. It is not hard to imagine that Viacom might pressure Showtime to make "good-faith gestures" by using more R-rated softcore and less softcore overall, pushing what it does use to later slots on less prominent channels.

But should anyone care what happens to softcore? Not necessarily. After all, if the genre did disappear, history would probably repeat: following a hiatus, it would revive in a reconfigured form and format. Despite its inferiority complex, softcore offers a narrative-spectacle synthesis that consumers, male and female, are willing to pay for, so it is unlikely that a consumer culture would permanently eradicate it. But because the divide between "decent" and "indecent" is a softcore line, it strikes me that free speech advocates and anyone who opposes federal sexual repression should be curious as to the fate of the genre's current edition. For as it happens, softcore qualifies as indecent material—which is not illegal but is proscribed from public airwaves between 6 A.M. and 10 P.M.—*far* more predictably than hardcore qualifies as obscenity.

That said, the decency-indecency line is still not a simple one. Judging by Powell's construction of FCC policy, "indecency" is an extremely subjective standard contingent on nuanced questions of structure, context, and expectation:

> For material to be indecent in the legal sense it must be of a sexual or excretory nature and it must be patently offensive. Mere bad taste is not actionable. Context remains the critical factor in determining if content is legally indecent. Words or actions might be acceptable as part of a news program, or as an indispensable component of a dramatic film, but be nothing more than sexual pandering in another context. (29)

Despite this formulation's considerable fuzziness, it fits softcore rather neatly. More than its emphasis on female nudity, softcore's narrative-number dichotomy confirms that the genre "panders" to "low" sexual tastes. Indeed, this impulse is a generic priority that typically works against narrative unity, such that softcore canoodling may seem anything but "an indispensable component" of the drama. Contextual factors also play a role here. Consider that premium cable is under no legal obligation to exhibit its most sexualized programming after 9:30 P.M. That the industry has traditionally done so proves not only that it is a good citizen, so to speak, but that it recognizes the FCC's decency standards—and that it has a clear idea about which genres violate them.

The self-consciousness that structures softcore indicates that this heterosexist genre longs to be decent but "knows" that it is not. Yet how elaborately it has tried to cover its naked indecency! Even amid the shock and disorder of the classical era, the forms that evoke its current spirit offered a tolerant, consumerist counterpoint to the transgressions of sexploitation. In the contemporary era, softcore has expressed its *anti*-antisocial posture through a comprehensive feminization that correlates with the genre's most distinctive textual qualities: its middlebrow aesthetics and lush romanticism; its middling, postfeminist ideology, including a female-friendly narrative bias tied to a socially acceptable misandry; and its tendency to suppress sexual violence, especially rape, even in subgenres dependent on sexual violence. This feminization is at once cause and consequence of softcore's stress on female subjectification, the steady expansion of which has "collaborated" with mechanisms favoring female nudity.

By itself, the middling ethos implicit to softcore feminization might seem to be an uncomplicated expression of postfeminist propriety. But since this propriety is steeped in self-consciousness and therefore tied to processes of negation, abjection, and bad faith, it is far more than that. It is also a tacit acceptance of antisexual assumptions operative in Powell's smug construction of "indecency." In softcore, these regressive essentialisms work in tandem with aesthetic ideology and with a multitude of class, sex, and gender stereotypes (and less obviously with stereotypes that center on race) to demean, diminish, and restrict popular sexual expression, including softcore itself. Defined broadly, this genre is thus typified by an under-the-radar stance that demonstrates that its producers, distributors, and consumers "know their place"; by its self-effacing modes of reception, which certify that softcore sex renders even cult audiences squeamish; by its relentless evasion of the "pornography" classifier; by its structuring absences, which at the textual level include the penis, male masturbation, male same-sex contact, and male-identified rape fantasy; and by its "corporate" taste for a stylistic and intellectual weightlessness largely fabricated from cliché, superficiality, and contradiction.

Must this genre exude embarrassment? As a broad, commercial field—and in the absence of a new sexual revolution—probably. While writing this study, I have often daydreamed that a well-funded, liberated auteur might embrace softcore's constraints rather than feeling *compelled* to work within them, spurring an NC-17 vogue in defiance of softcore history and received ideas of legitimacy. This is a fairly implausible fantasy—auteurs are as allergic as anyone to overt pornography and more allergic than most to the middlebrow—but not an impossible one. Why can't softcore have its Quentin Tarantino? This auteur's apostasy would confirm not that softcore is intrinsically inartistic but that it is comparatively difficult, hence peculiarly rich. But not even in fantasy could I imagine that a "softcore chic" inspired by this individual could have anything more than a marginal impact on a sprawling form. As long as cultural commissars continue to define sex as a low, indecent pleasure, and as long as corporate distribution schemes continue to reflect this very *human* abnegation, fans must continue to consume abjection along with their tub scenes, lace scanties, and soft-focus romance.

I wish them well. In a culture compelled to sublimate sex into turkeys and other, less appetizing objects, people must take joy as they can.

Notes

NOTES TO PREFACE

1. In July 2005, shortly after *Soft in the Middle* was accepted by The Ohio State University Press's outside readers, the release of Linda Ruth Williams's book *The Erotic Thriller in Contemporary Cinema* dramatically altered the condition of "softcore studies." As the first survey of theatrical and nontheatrical erotic thrillers, Williams's study is also the first extended treatment of contemporary softcore, for Williams considers the nontheatrical erotic thriller (or "direct-to-video erotic thriller," in her phraseology) tantamount to softcore. Luckily, though our books overlap, they are not redundant. Williams focuses on the erotic thriller, whose development she traces through Hollywood. In looking at softcore thrillers, she focuses on vehicles of a single budgetary paradigm—which, as she admits, became more or less obsolete after 1996. *Soft in the Middle,* by contrast, offers the first comprehensive survey of contemporary softcore, a multiform genre whose history I trace mainly through non-Hollywood traditions. My study thus examines a variety of pornographic forms, including a softcore subgenre that emerged in the 1960s. Though chapter 6 is devoted to the softcore thriller, it presents this category as one softcore subgenre among many. Further, it presents the "midbudget" model on which Williams concentrates as one phase of a subgeneric sequence that has continued to unfold as of 2005, albeit in ever-cheaper forms. But make no mistake: Williams's contribution to softcore studies represents an unprecedented resource. Because Williams's combination of prodigious research and academic reliability makes her book unique in the field, it was crucial that *Soft in the Middle* draw on her study—even if I had to scramble to make that happen. Ultimately, it is to the reader's benefit that the chapters that follow refer often to *The Erotic Thriller in Contemporary Cinema.*

2. These first names all refer to a single softcore personality, Susan Featherly, who has also performed under the aliases Marie West, Michelle Turner, and Jen Dike. Such a tactic is hardly uncommon. Tracy Ryan, for example, has performed under at least twice as many pseudonyms.

3. In his interview with Linda Ruth Williams, softcore director Jag Mundhra refers to his cinematography and editing as "very modular" (*Erotic* 327). Mundhra learned to shoot each sex scene using three lenses: tight, wide, and long. Because each version was of the same duration, he could easily substitute one scene for another when conforming to the level of explicitness mandated by a given market.

4. In January 2004, Cinemax repeatedly aired the same softcore thriller starring Richard Grieco under two different titles, *Sexual Predator* and *Dangerous Desires*. (Released in 2001, this film has also been marketed as *Last Cry*.) When previewing the film under the latter title, Cinemax programmers made matters more befuddling by erroneously supplying credits from an entirely different thriller, *Tomcat* (1993), which is subtitled *Dangerous Desires* and which also stars Grieco. In a similar practice, I have witnessed the same softcore feature rented under multiple titles in the same retail outlet.

5. These compilations have their home on pay-per-view but occasionally run on premium cable. In February 2004, Showtime aired the Pat Siciliano compilation *Behind Closed Doors* (2002), whose narrative frame was shot on video and processed in Filmlook but whose recycled numbers were shot on film. As of 2005, these supercheap vehicles represent one of few growth areas for studios like MRG.

NOTES TO CHAPTER 1

1. Although softcore features are increasingly shot on video, the vast majority discussed here were shot on 35mm or, somewhat less frequently, 16mm. Thus I mostly refer to softcore as a film genre.

2. As Linda Ruth Williams quips, "films such as *Hidden Obsession, Naked Obsession* and *Blindfold: Acts of Obsession* may as well have called themselves 'Erotic Thriller 1,' 'Erotic Thriller 2' and 'Erotic Thriller 3' for all the distinction the title gives as a designator of individuality" (*Erotic* 9).

3. "In the 1930s," Roger Corman explains, "when attendance began to drop, the studios lured audiences into theaters with two-for-one double bills. The 'A' movies featured stars like Clark Gable; B's were made quite fast and inexpensively with either new contract players seeking to rise to the A's or fading older stars. The B's were also a minor league for untested writers, directors, and producers and there was no shame or stigma attached to B moviemaking" (36). See also Naremore (140–66) and Schaefer (*Bold* 44–47, 49–51, 53, 56–59).

4. My uses of "classical" ultimately follow the example of Bordwell, Staiger, and Thompson. I resort to this term reluctantly, for I do not mean to obscure Schaefer's usage, which hinges on detailed parallels between classical exploitation and classical Hollywood. But at this point, using "classical" to denote an earlier, more established period, style, or mode of exhibition is almost obligatory in film studies; witness Williams's deployment of the term in referencing the "classical" hardcore of the 1970s and early 1980s in the updated *Hard Core* (1999; see 296). (See also Schaefer ["Gauging" 22n6.]) Thus I apply the term as necessary to distinguish low-budget antecedents from post-1980 successors.

5. *Surrender*'s demise was also a function of the larger decline of its parent company, Full Moon Pictures.

6. Most narrowly, "art film" refers to imports like Roger Vadim's . . . *And God Created Woman* (1956) and Louis Malle's *Les Amants* (1958) that gained American notoriety after World War II on an expanding arthouse circuit. (See Wilinsky; Neale ["Art Cinema"]; and Schaefer [*Bold* 331–7].) But the term clearly has a wider application. Consider that for

more than twenty years, mid- to low-budget American films like *Love Letters* (1983), *Talking Walls* (1987), and *Delta of Venus* (1995) have existed on the nontheatrical (direct-to-video and less reliably direct-to-cable) peripheries of sexploitation, offering an art-sex synthesis with deliberate arthouse appeal. As the sexuality of these American art films rarely achieves softcore density (although *Anthony's Desire* [1993] proves that exceptions exist), their artiness is their most distinguishing trait, with plots habitually conforming to romantic clichés. Thus "tortured" men paint, photograph, and fornicate with "muses" in *Twogether* (1992), *Wildly Available* (1996), *Luscious* (1999), and so on.

7. Rothstein collaborated with King on *Delta of Venus,* but she is best known for producing the aspirational Showtime serial *Women: Stories of Passion* (1997) with Playboy backing.

8. On the term "postfeminist," see Phoca and Wright, Kim (321), Projansky (66–89), and Hollows (*Feminism* 190–203).

9. See Linda Ruth Williams (*Erotic* 342–53). These comments should not suggest that such "empowerment" withstands scrutiny (often it does not) but that the genre makes consistent gestures in this direction.

10. The flaccid penis could fortify softcore realism if it had a presence in the passive spectacle, where nudity is not directly related to sexual action. Passive nudity forms a large part of softcore spectacle, but such imagery focuses on women getting dressed or undressed, taking showers, etc. Men do these things, too—but one would hardly suspect that from softcore representations.

NOTES TO CHAPTER 2

1. Softcore's abject cultural status is in many respects comparable to that of other feminized forms such as romance fiction and soap opera. See Modleski (*Loving* 11–13).

2. See Michael Wilmington's review, "[*When Will I Be*] *Loved* Needs More Than Soft Porn to Satisfy" (1).

3. That is, Linda Ruth Williams. In a very useful passage, Williams notes that softcore has a hybrid, neither-fish-nor-fowl status that "pleases no one and everyone" (*Erotic* 270; see 269–71). She is most perceptive in alluding to the overlap between softcore's bivalent devaluation and a related devaluation of femininity, which has also been critiqued "for being both oversexed and insufficiently sexual."

4. It would not be too difficult, for instance, to frame a pervasively sexualized film like David Lynch's *Lost Highway* (1996) as a "dilution" of preexisting styles *or* as a commercial venture governed by financial motives *or* as a descent into the pornographic. But the film is unlikely to be examined in such lights, for Lynch has aligned it with privileged codes—*noir* stylization, experimental auteurism, autotelic aestheticism—whose masculinized "purity" suppresses critical recognition of the film's quotidian purposes and practices.

5. See Linda Ruth Williams's interview with Hippolyte *qua* Gregory Dark (*Erotic* 280).

6. "[P]ornography is not literature," Marcus blithely asserts, for literature possesses "a multitude of intentions, but pornography possesses only one" (278).

7. This method of reducing the pornographic to a single sexual intention so as to demean it as Pure Porn inverts art for art's sake, which elevates the artwork to Pure Art by pretending that a single artistic intention impels it—and which therefore dismisses messy, historical multiplicities as illusions.

8. *Deep Throat* reportedly grossed $600 million on an initial investment of just $25,000 (Caro 1).

9. Laurence O'Toole makes a similar point, quoting Camille Paglia's assertion that liberated women were "bawdy in [their] speech" prior to feminism's "horrible retreat into puritanism since the sixties" (32).

10. Schaefer, for example, provides instances of males and females alike evincing liberationist sentiments in the context of 16mm simulation films ("Gauging" 15–16).

11. Robin Morgan's slogan "[p]ornography is the theory, and rape the practice" was included as fact in the Meese Commission Report (qtd. in Linda Williams, *Hard* 16). For an acerbic reading of the shortcomings of antiporn scholarship, see Alan Soble's *Pornography, Sex, and Feminism* (2002).

12. David Begelman has reported that the Hollywood studio Columbia picked up the X-rated *Emmanuelle* for distribution only after he noticed "that the lines outside theaters showing the film in Paris 'were comprised of 75 to 80% women.' 'We would have had no interest in the film if its appeal was totally to men,' mused Begelman. 'Then it could be taken as pornographic'" (qtd. in Lewis 228; see also Jaehne).

13. Feminization is now crucial to the video game industry's "upscale" strategy. See "Programmers" (1–2).

14. See Jancovich ("Naked" 2–5) and Juffer (*Home* 2–3) on feminism's stress on hardcore transgression.

15. Bourdieu neither takes a simplistic attitude toward the middlebrow nor expresses a straightforward highbrowism. After all, his sociological approach to aesthetics is an antiessentialist project that *undermines* highbrowism by emphasizing that disinterestedness, like aesthetic distinction generally, is a practical tool deployed by social beings never removed from the world of quotidian experience. Nevertheless, in both *Photography: A Middle-brow Art* (1965) and *Distinction* (1979), Bourdieu consistently makes linguistic choices that imply identification with elite culture. Thus, in arguing that "[w]hat makes middle-brow culture is the middle-class relation to culture—mistaken identity, misplaced belief, allodoxia" (*Distinction* 327), Bourdieu is making the antiessentialist point that the middlebrow as such is an effect of lived relations rather than of "objective" taste distinctions. Yet the negative wording that permeates this passage and much of *Distinction* conveys an opposite view. This "creeping" essentialism is not intentional but rather an almost ineluctable linguistic function of dealing with the middlebrow concept at all.

16. Greenberg focuses on the middlebrow in "The State of American Writing" (1948; *Collected* 254–57). For another influential essay, see Russell Lynes's "Highbrow, Lowbrow, Middlebrow" (1949; *Tastemakers* 310–22, 331–33).

17. "Softcore" and "soft focus" are so tightly linked that it is worth noting that not all softcore is soft focus.

18. Strong evidence of this link is supplied in the form of the Struss Pictorial Lens, which, as Kristin Thompson points out, was "originally created for [Karl Struss's] delicately hazy still photographs of the early decades of the century" but was by 1916 being used by art directors to lend cinema the same "poetic" appeal (Bordwell et al. 288). Another piece of evidence offered by Thompson was that filmmakers often adopted soft-portraiture techniques for character close-ups even when relying on the standard, high-contrast style through the rest of their films, suggesting that pictorialism influenced discrete cinematographic effects and disrupted continuity (Bordwell et al. 289).

19. Vieira defines "pre-Code Hollywood" as falling "between March 1930, when the Production Code was adopted, and July 1934, when it was amended and enforced" (6).

20. Consider that Cecil B. DeMille's *The Sign of the Cross* (1932), which was shot by soft-focus innovator Karl Struss, contained all four elements, including a tub scene in

which Claudette Colbert bathed in asses' milk up to her nipples and an orgy scene culminating in "Dance of the Naked Moon," which reviewer Martin Quigley condemned upon the film's release as "'that lesbian dance'" (qtd. in Vieira 107).

21. Though *Playboy* and *Penthouse* have appealed to distinct tastes, with *Penthouse* positioning itself as "harder" and less uptight than *Playboy* (Jancovich, "Placing" 4, 7), neither magazine has straightforwardly identified itself with the low—though *Penthouse* has moved in that direction. *Hustler* claimed the low as its territory in part by rejecting the "Vaselined lenses" of its more upscale rivals (Kipnis 131).

22. Qtd. in "Chris" Rev. 2. This observation is repeated by Tons May (149).

23. Though this sounds like the kind of easy pronouncement often found in reviews, it is borne out by facts. Significant American directors other than King—Alan Roberts, Alexander Gregory Hippolyte, etc.—have acknowledged the impression that *Emmanuelle* made on their soft-focus softcore. See chapters 4 and 6.

24. As the case of Karl Struss indicates, film has a long history of photographers who have transitioned into cinematography and brought their soft styles with them. During the sexploitation era, soft photographers—including Francis Giacobetti, who directed *Emmanuelle 2: The Joys of a Woman* (1975), as well as Jaeckin—often migrated to sexploitation from fashion. Even in hardcore, soft focus has been identified with fashion's feminized cachet and not infrequently realized in girl-girl numbers. "In the soft-focus image system of porners like [former fashion photographer] Andrew Blake," Laurence O'Toole asserts, "there's nothing more beautiful, elegant or sophisticated than the sight of two gorgeous women languorously amusing each other" (195).

25. Emmanuelle's fellow characters often refer to her as Beauty incarnate, implying her metaphysical import.

NOTES TO CHAPTER 3

1. I mean no disrespect by this term. I have opted for "empowered babe" over more neutral phrases—like "super-assertive woman" and "aggressive positive heroine," which refer to the same sexploitation type (Pam Cook 125–26)—because it pinpoints this heroine's fetishized, heterosexualized construction. For similar reasons, I often choose "girl-girl number" over the neutral term "same-sex number" and over the inaccurate term "lesbian number" (which is seldom appropriate in softcore contexts).

2. Early stags or "smokers" like *A Free Ride* (a.k.a. *A Grass Sandwich,* variously dated 1915 and circa 1917–19 [Linda Williams, *Hard* 61]) feature explicit male and female nudity and hardcore encounters. Though available for private consumption, these shorts were mainly exhibited in bordellos and other illicit, though tolerated, public gatherings of men (Linda Williams, *Hard* 73–76; Stevenson 9–13; Lennig 40).

3. Drawing on Kevin Brownlow's book *Behind the Mask of Innocence* (1990), Jack Stevenson discusses "the softcore 'nudie,'" a series of "humorous and playfully intended" sketches that in the 1920s formed part of the "Kodascope Home Movie Library" for 16mm home projection (8). Other products for private consumers included 16mm "art studies," which featured "full-frontal nudity as well as the caveat that they were 'produced for the exclusive use of artists and art students'" (Schaefer, "Gauging" 7). As Eric Schaefer notes, by the mid-1930s, these nonnarrative shorts were being sold to the "middle- and upper-middle-class families" who bought 16mm equipment from Kodak and Bell and Howell ("Gauging" 7).

4. Schaefer's work on the nudist film and the burlesque film has so deeply influenced

my understanding of this phase of softcore's genealogy that the debt requires formal recognition here.

5. What makes *This Nude World* unsettling today is not its spectacle, which includes female frontal nudity, but the fact that nudism's anti-urban, antimodern rhetoric has fascist overtones.

6. Schaefer has recently admitted to viewing "the transition from exploitation to sexploitation as a gradual process, not so much as the paradigm shift as it has been characterized. Burlesque is the most apparent through-line from classical exploitation to sexploitation" ("RE: Thanks," 31 Mar. 2).

7. The square-up is a defining feature of classical exploitation. This "prefatory statement about the social or moral ill the film claimed to combat" indicates, according to Schaefer, "the tension between education and titillation within exploitation" (*Bold* 69, 71). Through this device, exploitation made "a modest stab at respectability" while pointing the viewer to the specific appeal of the spectacle.

8. For commentary on the straitened production values of burlesque films, see Schaefer (*Bold* 56, 80–83).

9. Schaefer notes that a few exceptional burlesque films include a "hobbled narrative" (*Bold* 82).

10. The burlesque film is not the absolute origin of these motifs; it is instead a nexus through which these motifs have been transferred to contemporary softcore. Indeed, several of these motifs are discernible as early as Eadweard Muybridge's motion studies (see Linda Williams, *Hard* 37–43).

11. The usage of these comic symbols is classed and gendered, traditionally connoting a low, masculine "indecency." They are thus rare in feminized, middlebrow forms like contemporary softcore.

12. For example, see David Friedman's *The Adventures of Lucky Pierre* (1961). Among other borrowings, *Lucky Pierre* recycles Meyer's central conceit of a man who imagines he can see women naked.

13. See the Teas-like hero of Carl Monson's *Please Don't Eat My Mother* (1971), which spoofs Roger Corman's *The Little Shop of Horrors* (1960). This film's *Playboy*-reading protagonist (Buck Kartalian) routinely peeps on young lovers during lunch, at which time he makes feminized autoerotic gestures.

14. *. . . And God Created Woman* showed sexploiteers like Meyer and Metzger the forms that might succeed in arthouses and grindhouses alike, so its biases are notable. In particular, the Dionysian sexuality of Vadim's childlike heroine Juliette (Bardot) is linked not only to animals but to black characters who share her "primitive" energy. This sexuality is cordoned off—and the white, patriarchal order she threatens restored—when her husband beats her at the end of the film. Juliette greets this violence with a masochistic smile.

15. As symbolized by Lorna's fantasy of topless go-go dancing in anonymous urban environs.

16. Schaefer points out that the vice film crime boss becomes a monstrous "other," and a threat to middle-class women in particular, through his foreign birth (*Bold* 259; see 254–65).

17. As a fossil of Weiss's "roadshow days" in exploitation, the *Olga* voice-overs pay "lip service to being socially redemptive," as Bill Landis and Michelle Clifford put it, but imply an awareness that the films are "an excuse to supply the viewer with captions for the S&M caricatures" (12).

18. Page is even spuriously named in the credits of *Body of a Female*.

19. In respects anticipating Katt Shea's *Stripped to Kill* franchise and its softcore progeny (see Linda Ruth Williams, *Erotic* 362–63, 370–74), *Mantis in Lace* focuses on a stripper heroine who kills her lovers while on LSD. Though the film has a clear narrative-number structure, it integrates its sex with violence and with post–*Blood Feast* gore. (*Love Toy* also integrates its sex with violence.)

20. This unreleased film would spark feminist outrage when producer Allen Shackleton appended a new ending to it, releasing it as the notorious *Snuff* (1976). See Johnson and Schaefer (40–59).

21. Responsibility for the rape is shunted onto Forrest Barker, the victim's boyfriend. This is intriguing in that Barker is also a softcore director whose ineptitude is conveyed in a line that undercuts the film's efforts to deflect its abjection: "He's all right for nudies, but I wouldn't let him touch anything else."

22. As the rapist—again played by Alderman, albeit in a consistently villainous role—steps away from his young victim, the camera pans her bloody groin in a grotesque proof of her former virginity.

23. Actress Nina Hartley reports that, in hardcore features, rape scenes "were passé by 80, 81," thus obviating many antiporn complaints (qtd. in O'Toole 46). See Linda Williams (*Hard* 165–66).

24. In the commentary to Something Weird's *The Secret Sex Lives of Romeo and Juliet* DVD (2002), Novak claims that *Romeo and Juliet* cost two hundred thousand dollars, a figure so lofty it seems unreliable. See Rotsler (55).

25. Cleopatra's final "it" clearly refers not just to rape but to the pleasure she took from it. It seems, then, that Linda Williams's thesis in *Hard Core* is applicable to classical softcore, which uses semiconsensual rapes "to solicit what it can never be sure of: the out-of-control confession of [female] pleasure" (51).

26. But as Richard Dyer reminds us, comedy subverts the status quo, including masculinity, only to reinforce its "naturalness" in the end (*Matter* 117). It is predictable, then, that Zorro's masculinity, unlike Diego's effeminacy, is never explicitly undercut—as if swords, masks, and black capes were naked nature.

27. *The Agony of Love* (1966) parodies this motif through its heroine's stony expression. This self-conscious usage demonstrates how entrenched the motif was in sexploitation prior to *I, a Woman*'s American release.

28. *Bibi: Confessions of Sweet Sixteen* (1974; a.k.a. *Baby Love* and *Girl Meets Girl*) demonstrates that in using the awakening-sexuality model Sarno did not *always* avoid negative, medicalized closure devices like nymphomania. For an exemplary use of addiction metaphors, see Nick Phillips's *Roxanna* (1970), which offers extreme, intentionally avant-garde distortions of the facial motif.

29. For example, *Butterflies* depicts a German marquee advertising Claude Chabrol's *Der Schlachter* (1970).

30. Metzger's *Score* (1972) provides a rare and rebellious (albeit utopian and antirealistic) exception in that its happy-go-lucky liberalism smiles on boy-girl "swaps" and even on boy-boy swaps.

31. Numerous exceptions to this generalization exist. See, for example, *Abigail Lesley Is Back in Town* (1975), a somber film whose mixture of suburban adultery and awakening sexuality ultimately tends toward the positive.

32. Especially prolific in the early 1970s, when a slew of examples issued from New World—see Jack Hill's *The Big Doll House* (1970) and *The Big Bird Cage* (1972), Gerry de Leon's *Women in Cages* (1971), and Jonathan Demme's *Caged Heat* (1974)—the women-

in-prison film has seldom had a softcore format. Though it offers constant spectacle, this plot-oriented subgenre is all but devoid of men and is tame in its sexuality, with its staple images including group showers and bondage. Its contributions to the softcore lineage have thus been marginal and were perhaps most crucial in the 1980s, when sexploitation had been winnowed to a few hardy, inexplicit vehicles. (See *The Concrete Jungle* [1982], *Chained Heat* [1983], and *Reform School Girls* [1986].) That said, the women-in-prison subgenre is intriguing in that it is a rigid form that has long pitted a dominatrix femininity against an empowered-babe femininity. It is also one of few subgenres that mandates an antipatriarchal subtext. The stock types whose sadistic inclinations are officially or unofficially sanctioned, including the warden, the warden's enforcer, and the tough favored prisoner, access their power through patriarchal sources located "on the outside." The more sympathetic women who band together for a "breakout" form radical if rudimentary sisterhoods that oppose the "inauthentic" internal matriarchies whose power is an extension of male domination. For this reason, the subgenre necessitates a protofeminism and rarely rewards male dependence. By the same token, its patterning is politically incoherent. Why the obligatory breakout if the outside merely reconfigures the patriarchal institutions that confront the empowered babe on the inside—while dissolving the solidarity that she enjoys there? Though Corman productions invoke "revolutionary" imagery and rhetoric (*viz.*, *The Big Bird Cage*), they do not grapple with basic subgeneric dilemmas such as this.

NOTES TO CHAPTER 4

1. This type of "promotion," in which a heroine supplants a hero as protagonist, occurs in *Hollywood Hot Tubs 2: Educating Crystal* (1989), sequel to Vincent's *Hollywood Hot Tubs* (1984); *Picasso Trigger* (1988), sequel to Sidaris's *Hard Ticket to Hawaii*; and many other sexploitation series.

2. Dubbed the year of the "wandering X" by *Variety*, 1970 was crucial in that it "saw CARA raising the R age limit from sixteen to seventeen in order to absorb previous X-rated content into the R category. R-rated films, once 20 per cent of CARA's categorisations, now made up 37 per cent of its rating" (Sandler 206). Within four years, that figure would rise to 48 percent, where it remained through 1999 (Lewis 188).

3. Divestiture was one of the principal factors informing sexploitation's rapid diversification after 1960. It is thus predictable that Hollywood's renewed investment in exhibition in the 1980s would have an exaggerated impact on this vulnerable cinematic category. See Schaefer (*Bold* 327–28, 330). See also Stevenson (47).

4. Indeed, Sherman is still at it, having recently negotiated with ei Cinema to rerelease old Independent-International titles like *The Naughty Stewardesses* under the Retro-Seduction imprint.

5. Though often preferable to the irritations of Hollywood financing, such arrangements still held pitfalls for independent producers. For example, when financing *Hard Ticket to Hawaii* and *Picasso Trigger*, Sidaris "did not have the time or the money to go through [the studio] process," so he put together a "pre-license deal with Lorimar for video and TV rights" (Sidaris and Sidaris, *Bullets* 18). The pre-license fees would be paid on delivery of the films, with production funds coming from a bank loan and Sidaris's own company, Malibu Bay Films. But there was a significant drawback: Sidaris had to use his home as collateral (19). For explanations of the basics of independent feature-film financing, see Squire.

6. See MRG's "Company Profile" (1–3).

7. Though Reagan is recalled for his family values, including his antiporn ethic, his main sexploitation legacy resulted from his probusiness, antiregulatory stance. Though Reagan-era deregulation sharpened Hollywood's competition with sexploitation, further marginalizing it as a theatrical form, this deregulatory imperative also stimulated cable growth, yielding new sexploitation niches.

8. Robert Lombard confirms that Blockbuster still conditions the practices of MRG ("Casting" 6); a similar impact was once visible at Playboy. Since its acquisition by Viacom in 1994, Blockbuster has mirrored premium cable in that it has gradually tolerated more explicitness by increasing its distribution of "the more palatable genres of erotic thrillers [and] cable erotic series turned into videos" (Juffer, "No Place" 55). Blockbuster has also quietly increased its distribution of unrated material, allowing it to technically avoid vitiating its policy against NC-17 films. (On this policy, see DeGeorge [189] and Lewis [292].) In the late 1990s, Blockbuster grew more active in subsidizing softcore. It is the owner of the softcore label Ambrosia and the distribution imprint DEJ—shadowy brands listed in the credits of *many* softcore videos carried by Blockbuster. Today, Blockbuster is stocking fewer softcore new releases. If this trend represents a return to a strict construction of its family values policy, the result could be a death blow to an already moribund industry.

9. Thus feminized sexploitation has not been sham, but it *has* been a position of safety—for it appears to be the type of sexploitation least likely to stoke the paternalism that *still* leads advocacy groups like the Parents Television Council to frame cable sex as a threat to women, children, and decency.

10. "Home video has been the key to our survival," says Corman (228). Falling prices did not allow video to emerge as a true rival to cable until 1983, but the industry stretches back to the 1970s. In 1977, Charles Band, who later ran Full Moon, helped pioneer the cult video market by founding his Media Home video label.

11. Cult softcore has been airing on premium cable with growing frequency. Over the past decade, Fred Olen Ray has directed many softcore films under the name "Nicholas Medina" for American Independent Productions, including its popular *Bikini* movies (*Bikini Airways* [2002], *Bikini a Go Go* [2004], *The Bikini Escort Company* [2004], etc.). These cheap softcore comedies have played cable, as have Seduction films. But cable softcore has for the most part remained slanted toward more middling "corporate" formulae.

12. See, for example, Ray's art for *Hollywood Chainsaw Hookers,* which features two women in lace scanties brandishing prodigious chainsaws (187). The tag line: "They charge an arm and a leg!"

13. Cable did occasionally produce its own teen sex-coms, sometimes in partnership with Hollywood; e.g., *Private Resort* (1985) is a TriStar vehicle. (TriStar was founded in 1983 as a Columbia-HBO partnership.)

14. Although X- and R-rated "edited hardcore" does not qualify as softcore by my criteria, in the early 1980s its iconography did resemble that of "true" softcore more than currently. Many of the radical divergences from film and narrative paradigms that hardcore now routinely displays had not yet evolved.

15. "M&G's" is industry shorthand for the nonsynchronous "moans and groans" dubbed over numbers.

16. Vincent's films abound with images of covert female dominance: women manipulate men by performing falsely submissive or maternal roles. In *Sex Appeal,* the hero is fooled by a pair of "nurturers" who turn out to be dominatrices and a "gentle" hooker

(Candida Royalle) who knocks him out and steals his money.

17. *Student Affairs, Wimps,* and *Hollywood Hot Tubs* are all overtly self-referential. *Sex Appeal*'s title refers to a book-within-the-film entitled "Sex Appeal" written by "Mark Eubell," which is a variant of Vincent's "Mark Ubell" pseudonym. (In the credits of *Sex Appeal,* for example, Mark Ubell shows up as editor.) Further, Mark Eubell is a character in *Sex Appeal* who is a sexploitation director planning to direct an X-rated film based on the hero's life as filtered through a series of "Playhouse" stories.

18. The imagery of empowered babes in leather scanties penetrating male enemies complements and inverts the rape spectacle. This inversion is acknowledged in *Barbarian Queen II* when the archmisogynist Hofrax is captured by the matriarchal rebels and threatened with castration and anal penetration.

19. These heroines, who are not exactly the same, were both played by the recently murdered Lana Clarkson.

20. The Sidarises are reportedly at work on a new film, *BattleZone Hawaii.*

21. *Malibu Express,* for example, reportedly cost five hundred thousand dollars during the mid-1980s.

22. Sidaris often intentionally subverts his heroes' masculinity by subverting sex-com tactics. In *Malibu Express,* the hero repeatedly claims to have been raped by his female admirers. In *Hard Ticket,* the hero (Ronn Moss) is feminized by his M&G's. (Sidaris helpfully informs us in his commentary that "the woman . . . normally is the screamer.")

23. In her *Picasso Trigger* comments (2001), Arlene Sidaris notes that "there's nothing wrong with opening the door and finding Steve Bond there." She later classifies Bond's physique "a post-production asset."

24. Here Sidaris is well within sexploitation tradition in that his claim is simply untrue. (Witness the interminable gore of the climactic *Hard Ticket* sequence in which Speir's character becomes a parody of the slasher's victim-hero.) But because he is a postfeminist sexploiteer, Sidaris *soft-pedals* his films as often as he exaggerates them. Thus, to counter the view that his films are ultraviolent, he often claims of a given scene that it is "the bloodiest scene we've ever shot" (as he asserts of the booby-trapped Frisbee sequence in *Hard Ticket*). He also wants his viewers to believe that he shows only villains getting torn apart—but his films force him to admit otherwise. His paternalistic assertions also run counter to the rape and bondage imagery and anachronistic rape humor of *Malibu Express* and *Hard Ticket.*

NOTES TO CHAPTER 5

1. Collaborating on this screenplay was King's wife, Patricia Louisianna Knop, who shares many credits with King. Two of his daughters, Chloe King and Gillian Lefkowitz, have also worked with him extensively. This family influence bears comparison to the aspirational-sexploitation partnerships formed by Radley Metzger and Ava Leighton and by Joe Sarno and Peggy Steffans-Sarno.

2. Of these films, King directed the first three and produced and cowrote the fourth, *Lake Consequence,* which longtime *Red Shoe Diaries* collaborator Rafael Eisenman directed.

3. King has also put his stamp on hardcore. See, for example, Andrew Blake's *Hidden Obsessions* (1992) or Michael Ninn's *Sex* (1994).

4. Because King has drawn directly on many of the art film directors who once influenced Metzger and Sarno, his cinematic lineage should not be reduced to its sexploita-

tion genealogy. For instance, King has cited Bernardo Bertolucci, among other European auteurs, as a strong influence (Kleinman 2). But though King claims no knowledge of Metzger, he is familiar with his classical sexploitation precursors and has even expressed respect for Russ Meyer—albeit while differentiating his own vision from Meyer's dirty-movie credo (Armstrong 4–5). This delicate differentiation is another way in which King recalls Metzger (see Turan and Zito 66–74), who distinguished himself from Meyer in the same way.

5. King has mostly resigned himself to the invective. "Everything I do gets bad reviews," he laments. "I think critics have just made up their minds" (Armstrong 5). Elsewhere, King vents an antipathy for critics that recalls Metzger (see Turan and Zito 68–70). "I think they're a bunch of idiots," he tells Softcore Reviews (Sibert 3).

6. King's lyrical shots of corporate buildings located somewhere-in-LA—see, for example, *RSD* featurettes like "Safe Sex," "Double Dare," and "Jake's Story" (all 1992), all of which use the same shot of clouds speeding past a corporate facade—have been routinized by corporate softcore labels.

7. The similarities are manifold. Though Lynch is more experimental, both aspire to an auteur status linked with an oneiric, eroticized neo-*noir* stylization. The directors' musical preferences are similar as well, with Angelo Badalamenti's lush, Lynchean orchestrations stressing a lyric form of jazz only slightly edgier than George Clinton's scores for King. (King's positioning of the *Red Shoe Diaries* soundtrack also evokes Lynch's eroticized marketing of the *Twin Peaks* soundtrack.) Given that the two filmmakers have drawn on the same marginal Hollywood players, including Sherilyn Fenn and Sheryl Lee, the overall resemblance is compelling. Indeed, *Boxing Helena* (1993), a Fenn vehicle directed by Lynch's daughter, confirms that "diluted" versions of the Lynch aesthetic are indistinguishable from the King aesthetic.

8. That the *ChromiumBlue.com* (2002) pilot aspires to the condition of a music video is indicated by its thick visual style as well as by its MTV-inspired use of nondiegetic inserts that promote the names of songs and recording artists at the start of each musical piece. It is instructive, then, that even this King score intersperses its up-tempo orchestrations with heavy doses of smooth jazz.

9. Jane Juffer argues that women's literary erotica attempts to claim aesthetic value and to distinguish itself from pornography by foregrounding its own literariness (*Home* 105–6).

10. The Desire formula has recently allowed for an initial sexual encounter between hero and heroine midway through the narrative; this scene is followed by conflicts blocking another, resolving sexual encounter that functions as the dénouement. Sexualization is otherwise limited to the kind of oblique descriptions of the heroine's conflicted psychosexual states that Cohn has described. For reference, see Sheri Whitefeather's *Cherokee Baby* (2003) and Julianne MacLean's *Sleeping with the Playboy* (2003).

11. The exception is *Delta*, whose heroine is an Emmanuelle-like seeker. That *Delta* strays further from romance than other King films is predictable, for like Jaeckin's *Story of O* (1975), it adapts highbrow erotica. It is also King's most self-conscious film. He uses Nin's story to explore his conflicts as a director who values himself as a visual poet—but whom the world often devalues as a pornographer.

12. That I focus on *noir* and romance does not indicate the lesser importance of the woman's film here. After all, the middle female–low male dynamic central to King's work has a traditional place in classic melodrama like Douglas Sirk's *All That Heaven Allows* (1955). On the other hand, classifying King's work as "erotic melodrama," as Linda Ruth

Williams proposes (*Erotic* 390), may underrate the noirishness of King's features, separating them from the softcore thrillers that King so heavily influenced—and that, as Williams admits, also resemble both romance and the woman's film.

13. In *9½ Weeks,* John (Rourke) talks while eating, a lowbrow mannerism duly noted by the middlebrow heroine (Kim Basinger). In *Wild Orchid,* Wheeler (Rourke) rides a Harley, dresses with a rakish sloppiness, and presents himself as an outcast. Both characters have risen above impoverished upbringings.

14. For example, early in *Wild Orchid,* Emily (Carré Otis), a fledgling lawyer assigned to Brazil, is excited by the "exotic" spectacle of two naked black "natives" coupling roughly in a dilapidated hotel.

15. Relative to King's *noir*-romance hybrid, erotic thrillers that lean toward misogynistic *noir* prescriptions are less likely to stress disgust in their "conflictual fusion." Though sexploitation thrillers like *Naked Obsession* (1990) exemplify Stallybrass and White's ideas, their masculinized formulae accent a noirish anxiety that tends toward fear, not class-oriented distaste. My assumption is that middlebrow feminization encourages more misandristic, disgust-oriented depictions. Supporting this point are the highly feminized softcore thrillers of the early 1990s that adhere more closely to King's *noir*-romance hybrid than to a neo-*noir* model. Thus heroine-driven films like Jag Mundhra's *The Other Woman* (1992) depict their eroticized heroines as suspended between disgust and desire. A significant exception to this rule is Jane Campion's *In the Cut* (2003), in which the heroine (Meg Ryan), an English teacher and aspiring poet, is fascinated and disgusted by the many low males whom she encounters, including two detectives. (One of these men turns out to be her romantic interest [Mark Ruffalo], the other a misogynist killer [Nick Damici].) Though studiously *noir* in sensibility (see Linda Ruth Williams, *Erotic* 418–20), Campion's midbudget art film features many discernibly middlebrow traits that dovetail with and predict the persistent foregrounding of the female protagonist's disgust. Such traits include the film's emphasis on class, its stylization and literary accent, and its monolithic equation of masculinity with lowbrow animality.

16. King's occupational divisions are worth considering here. A successful architect, Jake is initially the most rarefied character. As an interior decorator, the heroine Alex (Brigitte Bako) has a more domestic role suggestive of her concern with psychological interiors. Her suicide disrupts Jake to such a degree that he can no longer function as an architect, instead becoming obsessed with sentimental details. In other words, Jake falls into a "middle" existence, becoming a variation on Alex herself. By contrast, Tom easily withstands Alex's death, preserving his unsentimental, anti-intellectual masculinity.

17. A sexy Hollywood production replete with smooth jazz, *White Palace* may have influenced the *RSD* feature. (The latter was produced in 1990, the same year that *White Palace* enjoyed its successful theatrical run, but did not air on Showtime until 1992.) As a traditional female fantasy of love, commitment, and security, Max (James Spader), the hero of *White Palace,* closely resembles Jake. Max is financially secure and emotionally loyal to his dead wife; he even wears a trench coat similar to the one immortalized by Jake in the *RSD* serial. Max is also elaborately feminized; consider that the camera focuses on his orgasmic face during oral sex. The class implications of *White Palace* likewise recall *RSD*.

18. Strangely, the dog in *Two Moon* (who resembles Stella in *RSD*) prefigures the two male principals of the *RSD* feature. The dog's character is named "Tom"; the dog is credited as "Jake."

19. Besides confirming his internalized sense of abjection, the ponderous revelation

Notes to Chapter 5 | 271

that the wealthy, controlling Rourke hero had a difficult childhood links him to the romance hero. "Romance fiction," Cohn notes, "treats the hero's past with a good deal more emotional respect than the heroine's. It is somehow taken as a given that heroines may have been orphaned, impoverished, jilted. But when these calamities occur to the valued and valuable hero they carry significant emotional weight" (48).

20. Cohn asserts that the rise in popularity of Harlequin romances has mirrored feminism's second-wave development, thus indicating a postfeminist link between the economic anxieties encoded by romance and the economic uncertainties that women discerned in feminism. "Paradoxically," Cohn writes, "the promise of feminism carried a considerable threat, undercutting traditional gender relations, particularly in regard to courtship, and thereby putting women in jeopardy of failing in the marriage market" (10).

21. As *A Place Called Truth* (1998) verifies, King has continued to depend on the low male even in his later features. *RSD* episodes in which low males captivate middlebrow females include "Just Like That" (1992), "Runway" (1993), "Night of Abandon" (1993), "Kidnap" (1993), "Burning Up" (1993), "In the Blink of an Eye" (1993), "The Game" (1994), "Like Father, Like Son" (1994), and "Hard Labor" (1996).

22. This sequel is faithful to King's romance prescriptions in its focus on a middlebrow female (a successful urban model) and a low male (an unsuccessful rural artist). True to form, the heroine (Melinda Clark) "rescues" the feminized hero (John Clayton Schafer) from his own economic innocence.

23. The *RSD* serial regularly opposes romantic mystery to quotidian love. In "Jake's Story" (1992), for example, the heroine (Sheryl Lee) writes to Jake that "the hardest thing for anyone to give up is their mystery. But if you love someone, really love someone, you have to make that choice."

24. The *RSD* serial often weaves the consumerist illusion that it is possible to synthesize mystery-based romance and everyday life such that relationships like those enjoyed by Alex and Tom may continue in perpetuity. (See "You Have the Right to Remain Silent" [1992].) Though this untraditional happy ending is more consistent than *Two Moon*'s traditional happy ending, it is no more convincing.

25. King's symbolic gestures function as part of the literariness through which he positions his work as middlebrow. Like the shopworn titles of *RSD* episodes, these gestures often come across as simplistic or simply hackneyed. (For example, after cheating on Jake, her fiancé, the heroine of the *RSD* feature returns home and literally plays with fire.) Still, such negative valuations do not alter the fact that King has encoded his texts with an aspiration to a quintessentially serious, literary form of meaning.

26. Another way to read April's decision is to view it as her self-liberation from a domineering grandmother.

27. The *ChromiumBlue.com* pilot contains a similar shower scene complete with penises.

28. The King *oeuvre* frequently conflates disparate varieties of sensuality, taste, and consumption. For example, see the tame sadomasochism of the food-sex scene in *9½ Weeks*, or the many episodes of *RSD* in which edibles enhance sexuality, including "The Cake" (1994).

29. After all, King's self-obsessed heroines are never concerned with the plight of women as a political class.

30. *ChromiumBlue.com* does not sacrifice traditional romance altogether. This project retains a love-besotted male (Shane Brolly) as a continuity device and a female fantasy.

But it also retains an adventurist heroine (Erica Prior) whose central action is to spurn traditional romance in favor of sexual freedom.

31. *RSD*'s hypersexuality allowed it to give fuller body to the themes of gender-bending and bisexuality that had been present in King's narratives as early as *9½ Weeks*. This may be one reason that such themes begin to impinge on the foreground in *A Place Called Truth* and the *ChromiumBlue.com* pilot. In any event, such foregrounding seems to be linked to the comparative failure of these late features to succeed in a mainstream, post-feminist marketplace overwhelmingly geared to heterosexual eroticism.

32. As Martin explains (44), the red shoes represent a liberated form of female sexual desire.

NOTES TO CHAPTER 6

1. In *The Erotic Thriller in Contemporary Cinema,* Linda Ruth Williams offers a valuable corrective by devoting half her book to "direct-to-video" erotic thrillers, an area she deems synonymous with "softcore" (249–50). But if Williams renders one *relatively* inexpensive form of mainstream nontheatrical erotic thriller *more* visible, she may reinforce the invisibility of the subgenre's least expensive forms. The reason for this is that she focuses on softcore thrillers of a single fiscal and historical moment, the one I refer to as the "midbudget" paradigm. Thus her account tapers off after the gradual collapse of Axis Films in the mid-1990s. As I verify here, the softcore thriller has had a dynamic and continuous history through 2005.

2. The hardcore erotic thriller or "hardcore thriller" exists outside the patently mainstream distribution channels (premium cable, major rental chains, etc.) that supply my parameters. That said, this subgenre has an intriguing place in the larger picture given hardcore's industrial links to softcore and the hardcore thriller's ultimate position as the erotic thriller's most sexualized variant.

3. There is one formal rationale for stressing the softcore thriller's place in sexploitation's contemporary succession. In the 1960s, violent forms like the roughie and kinky capitalized on the success of tame, masculinized nudie cutie comedies. In turn, early classical softcore films like William Rotsler's protoerotic thriller *Mantis in Lace* integrated their numbers with the violence of their immediate sexploitation antecedents. The parallel with contemporary sexploitation is arresting. In the 1980s, tame, masculinized sex comedies again dominated sexploitation, with subgenres blending sex and violence proliferating as the decade progressed. The most prominent of these, the nontheatrical erotic thriller, had the most sex and led back to softcore. But these cyclical resemblances should not lull critics into simplifying salient industrial differences dividing the eras, especially contemporary sexploitation's decade-long reliance on Hollywood models—which was an ironic by-product of Hollywood's post-Code tendency to emulate the spectacle-based formulae that had enriched lower-budget producers during the 1960s (see Lewis).

4. According to IMDb.com, these films cost $14 million and $49 million, respectively—and grossed $320 million and $353 million worldwide. See Linda Ruth Williams (*Erotic* 2).

5. *Fatal Attraction* has spawned persistent sexploitation motifs like sink sex and elevator fellatio as well as blatant rip-offs like *Body Chemistry* (1990). *Basic Instinct* has inspired myriad softcore titles (e.g., *Animal Instincts* [1992]) and influenced the performances of many sexploitation *femmes fatales* (see, for example, Sharri Shattuck in

Notes to Chapter 6 | 273

Dead On [1993] and Maria Ford in *Showgirl Murders* [1995]).

6. Linda Ruth Williams provides broader sections on both films and adroitly discusses the controversies that shaped their public receptions—subjects for which I unfortunately have no space. On *Fatal Attraction,* see Linda Ruth Williams (*Erotic* 48–56, 177–87); on *Basic Instinct,* see Linda Ruth Williams (*Erotic* 163–67, 187–89, 222–30).

7. Walter Kendrick explains pornography's censorship and historical marginalization in terms of the cultural myth of "the Young Person." It is instructive, then, that while the theatrical erotic thriller often places children at the center of its moralistic schemes—a trend duplicated by just-shy-of-softcore sexploitation thrillers like *Body Chemistry*—the softcore thriller depicts a childless world.

8. That this sequence is specifically engineered to underscore Dan's motivation for adultery is indicated by the use of an analogous sequence in *Unfaithful.*

9. I say "approximation" because in the early 1990s "true" softcore sexploitation typically had a bit more sex than *Basic Instinct,* with seven or eight numbers a standard minimum.

10. See McQueen and Linda Ruth Williams ("No Sex" 4). The majors believe that sexualized films will flow through disparate markets most readily if they include sex-negative moralism and graphic violence. The erotic thriller is thus one of few forms in which a "Hollywood ending" is depressing. See Lewis (223).

11. See Linda Ruth Williams ("No Sex" 1–6).

12. Similarly, Linda Ruth Williams documents a "'trickle-up' as well as a 'trickle-down' effect" between theatrical and nontheatrical erotic thrillers (*Erotic* 12; 12–14).

13. As Naremore notes (140–43), the Hollywood "Bs" of the 1940s and 1950s favored *noir* for its affordability. There is, then, irony in sexploitation's latter-day efforts to siphon the prestige "in" *noir* style. That these "siphonings" represent a self-conscious distinction strategy is confirmed by the fact that in the early 1990s nontheatrical studios like Prism explicitly identified themselves as the successors to the midbudget mode of "B" production that Hollywood had abandoned by 1960. See Naremore (162).

14. *In Dangerous Company* (1988) typifies the equivocal sexism that has shaped sexploitation *noir.* In this film, a secondary character voices the misogyny felt by the stoic hero (Cliff DeYoung): "You know what's wrong with this country today, Blake? Women control fifty percent of the money and one-hundred percent of the pussy." As the film's default worldview, this sort of misogyny indirectly softens the monstrousness of the *femme fatale* (Tracy Scoggins), giving her another tool with which to manipulate the hero: "It's not my fault I look the way I look. Guys have been following me home since I was thirteen—and using me and abusing me and lying to me. You think you were the only person to ever suffer?"

15. Corman's company has specialized in sexploitation *noir.* See Odette Springer's documentary, *Some Nudity Required: The Naked Truth Behind Hollywood's B-Movies* (1998).

16. *I Like to Play Games* was also important in that it and other films put out under the Cameo label—including *Play Time* (1994), another of softcore's few cult classics—signaled the final crystallization of a distinctive middle industry that specialized in low-budget (i.e., sub-$400,000) corporate softcore. Within two years, this slick paradigm had rendered midbudget softcore thrillers obsolete.

17. Like IMDb, Linda Ruth Williams supplies a 1990 date for *Carnal Crimes,* but it is not clear whether this is a production date, a German release date, or an American release date. To the best of my knowledge, all other sources indicate that Axis released the film in America in 1991.

18. The necessity of keeping "the women in front of the camera," as Walter Gernert puts it, prompted Axis to make its heroines "as complex as [it] could," as Andrew Garroni puts it (qtd. in Linda Ruth Williams, *Erotic* 65).

19. If Hippolyte borrowed from King, King may have returned the favor by making Hippolyte's trademark character, the bored housewife, the centerpiece of his 1992 *noir*-romance hybrid, *Lake Consequence*. And of course, more than anyone else, King capitalized on (and reinforced) Hippolyte's example through his *Red Shoe Diaries* serial (1992–99), whose episodes typically have softcore formats.

20. Naremore places nontheatrical thrillers in the "one-and-a-quarter- to two-million-dollar range" (161). It is safe to say that most fully softcore thrillers fell into the bottom of this range. The "million or less" figure quoted by Linda Ruth Williams is a reasonable estimate of the average cost of the midbudget softcore thriller (*Erotic* 8; see 285, 291–92, 311, 323). As Gernert and Garroni verify, the midbudget market was in decline in the mid-1990s (Linda Ruth Williams, *Erotic* 71–72), making films like Axis's *Body of Influence 2* (1996), whose cost has been estimated at $1.2 million, increasingly rare.

21. In a subsection aptly entitled "Women's Stories and Lousy Husbands," Linda Ruth Williams anticipates many of my claims about Axis Films and the softcore thriller's postfeminist feminization (*Erotic* 342–53). Equally useful is the fact that throughout her book Williams discusses midbudget films examined here, including *Night Rhythms* (350–51), *Night Eyes* (337–38), *Carnal Crimes* (43–44), *Animal Instincts* (336–37), *Secret Games* (339, 344–45), and *The Other Woman* (314–15, 347–48).

22. That the career woman has been the most common protagonist across contemporary softcore owes much to *Red Shoe Diaries,* the King serial that often centers on frustrated working women. See chapter 7.

23. By the mid-1990s, softcore thrillers had stopped taking it for granted that work and femininity conflict, so today's professional heroines no longer automatically grapple with gender insecurities.

24. Evidence of this backlash is common on Internet sites like Softcore Reviews and This Is Sexy?

25. For insight into these pressures, see Linda Ruth Williams's interviews with Gernert and Garroni (*Erotic* 69–73) and with Mundhra (*Erotic* 323). The first interview is significant in that Gernert and Garroni stress that changes in distribution were crucial in eliminating midbudget studios like Axis (see 71–72). Not to be forgotten in this connection was Hollywood's growing domination of the home-video market in the mid-1990s. As Barbara Boyle notes (in Squire 176), the "growth of home-video revenue in the early 1980s had a great and positive impact on independent financing and distribution because a significant percentage of a movie's budget could be secured by an advance from licensing home-video deals, in effect subsidizing independent filmmaking. . . . It took years for studios to decide to cut out the middleman and build their own home-video divisions, at which point separate advances for home video rights declined as U.S. distributors required all rights in all formats." This shift appears to have had a particularly adverse impact on independent softcore producers in the midbudget bracket.

26. Within Mainline, MRG is considered the "softcore" division and Magic Hour the "mainstream" division. At least occasionally, Magic Hour produces bigger-budget films like the *Wild Things* sequels, suggesting a high-end stratification within Mainline's line of nontheatrical erotic thrillers.

27. Between 1999 and 2002, Playboy's Indigo label spent from $300,000 to $325,000 on its low-budget, 35mm, corporate softcore. (See chapter 9.) Since MRG was making

16mm corporate softcore vehicles for less than half the cost, Playboy's decision to close its Indigo unit was predictable.

28. See Lombard ("Re: tiny addendum" 1–3). Like Torchlight, a new label headed by an old rival (New City), MRG is also now shooting sixty-minute softcore vehicles for about fifty thousand dollars, using three- to four-day shoots and thirty- to forty-page scripts. These very explicit simulation features are long on sex and short on narrative and are intended mainly for pay-per-view distribution.

29. The softcore-only actresses reacted unhappily to softcore's increasing flirtation with hardcore, for it destabilized their economic position and made it more difficult for them to displace their abjection onto those in a "lower" form. This middlebrow frustration is evident in Shauna O'Brien's response to a question about whether "the lines between hardcore and softcore are being blurred or crossed": "Yes, absolutely the lines are being blurred. It's just like when *Penthouse* magazine started adding fist-fucking to their lovely array of features. I for one had no more interest in being a part of that magazine" (Kennerson 3).

30. These porny gestures include head-wagging (during oral sex), butt-swatting (a light sadie-max effect), and positions like the reverse cowgirl. A sonic dimension previously confined to hardcore is the ball-slapping effect added to MRG sequences depicting doggie-style penetration. For reference, see Eric Gibson's *Wicked Temptations* (2001) or Madison Monroe's *Love Games* (2001), *Erotic Obsessions* (2001), and *Dangerous Pleasures* (2002). Another porny element of recent MRG fare is the frequent use of "blank sex," a long number used to open a film. This front-loading immediately declares a pornographic intent and imparts a distinctive diegetic opacity in that nothing is known of the amorous figures.

31. An upscale variation on MRG's hidden *femme fatale*, which Linda Ruth Williams calls "a retrospective *femme fatale*," has a presence in the higher-end *Wild Things* franchise (*Erotic* 100). For example, *Wild Things: Diamonds in the Rough* (2005), the third installment of the series, hides two *femmes fatales* and contains three *femmes fatales* in all. Because this film was produced by Mainline/Magic Hour/MRG executives Marc Greenberg, Richard Goldberg, and Marc Bienstock, it seems quite possible that this film's upscale, elaborately motivated incarnation of the hidden *femme fatale* was shaped not only by the big-budget original but also by an intracorporate "trickle up"—which is to say, by MRG's downscale, comparatively unmotivated incarnation of the hidden *femme fatale*.

32. See *Sex, Secrets, and Lies* (2002)—which is not to be confused with *Sex, Secrets, and Betrayals* (2001).

33. In the classical era, 16mm softcore films had somewhat comparable effects. See Schaefer ("Gauging" 3–26).

NOTES TO CHAPTER 7

1. In making this point, I do not mean to suggest that the misapprehension of softcore is limited to feminist critics. Indeed, as chapter 8 details, outside the academy, softcore reception is defined by patterns of distortion that cannot be fully organized by gender attitudes. Alternatively, antiessentialist feminist critics like Linda Ruth Williams have supplied very perceptive treatments of softcore gender biases. Regrettably, Williams has not yet published on the softcore serial itself, though that may soon change.

2. The most telling link is industrial. The softcore serial has been an integral part of

the softcore industry that coalesced in the mid-1990s and has thus been produced by the same companies that have produced softcore features. Like the feature, the serial began as crossover aspirational softcore but was later dominated by corporate softcore studios, including MRG, Playboy, New City, etc. By contrast, cult softcore studios like Seduction, which depend on home video distribution and whose lower-middlebrow depictions are less feminized than aspirational and corporate producers, do not produce in this area.

3. Critics like Martha Nochimson have celebrated soap opera by constructing its apparent lack of closure—a trope devalued for its link to "bad" classical Hollywood—as a function of its televisual "femaleness." As antiessentialists like Laura Stempel Mumford have noted, this ahistorical approach is guilty of many theoretical and empirical errors. I have tried to avoid similar errors by stressing that "women's genres" and "women's media" are not *essentially feminine* but instead *elaborately feminized* by producers and receivers who have operated under the influence of historical constructions of femininity.

4. See, e.g., *WSP*'s "Room 1503" (1997) and "Kat Tails" (1997) and *Hotel Erotica*'s "Screwed Up" (2003).

5. Consider that a single *RSD* featurette, "Auto Erotica," uses solarization, saturated color, black and white, grainy and soft-focus imagery, slow motion, voice-over, montage, jump cuts, discontinuity editing, and abrupt sonic disruptions—all to invent audiovisual parallels for the heroine's psychosexual disintegration.

6. Theaters initiated this use of the short decades ago. A current analogue is provided by Playboy TV, which rounds out its time slots with numbers detached from edited hardcore (i.e., inexplicit yet nonsimulated) features.

7. As of 2004, Showtime had eight different schedules: Showtime, Showtime Women, Showtime Showcase, Showtime Beyond, Showtime Extreme, Showtime Next, Showtime Too, and Showtime Family Zone.

8. For a description of the three rating systems still in use on pay cable, see Juffer (*Home* 208).

9. This trend has recapitulated the deflation visible across contemporary softcore. An MRG insider who wishes to remain anonymous has quoted the average licensing fees paid by HBO/Cinemax in 2004 as having been between $70,000 and $85,000 per featurette, with Showtime paying far less. Though no direct equivalence between licensing fees and production budgets may be assumed, it is clear that aspirational shows like *RSD* and *WSP* could not have been supported by similar economies.

10. HBO once aired softcore serials like *Strangers* (1996) but rarely does so as of this writing—though the subgenre still has a presence on Cinemax. Instead, HBO offers sex documentaries like *Real Sex* (1992 on), *Taxicab Confessions* (1995), and *G-String Divas* (2000). These confessional shows combine the mainstream appeal of reality television with the alternative sexualization of the softcore serial.

11. See the unanswered posting from "debbie" at http://www.sreviews.com/forum/viewtopic.php?t=1211.

12. Diana Russell rightly defines as "sexist" any form "in which women are consistently shown naked while men are clothed" and/or "in which women's genitals are displayed but men's are not" (49). But Russell is not exactly *demanding* more penises. Moreover, her logic is not that common.

13. Unlike Backstein, Juffer indicates no knowledge of Playboy's involvement. This omission highlights a serious problem in her method: she treats the cable networks as

direct producers rather than noting the intercession of outside labels that put distinct imprints on films. Acknowledging this intercession would complicate the clear-cut, male-female distinction that she makes between Playboy TV and premium cable. Consider that much of the corporate softcore that Playboy has produced for exhibition on its own network has also been distributed through premium cable, which Juffer depicts as profemale.

14. See Projansky on the marginalization of men in much postfeminist discourse (67, 84–86).

15. I am not suggesting any direct correlation. Martin's comments are indicative of larger feminist discourses of which postfeminist softcore producers have demonstrated varying degrees of awareness.

16. Besides "Runway," *RSD* featurettes like "Double Dare" (1992), "You Have the Right to Remain Silent" (1992), "Accidents Happen" (1992), "Liar's Tale" (1993), "Night of Abandon" (1993), "Burning Up" (1993), and "Strip Poker" (1996) supply fine examples of this female-voyeurism motif. That the motif's gender slant has been maintained by subsequent softcore serials is indicated by *EC*'s "The Business Trip" (1995), *The Best Sex Ever*'s "The Peeping Thompsons" (2002), and scores of others.

17. Jake participates in the sexual spectacle of only one featurette, "Jake's Story" (1992).

18. Softcore's deflationary decline has contributed to a reduction in the ethnic diversity of recent serials.

19. That the two "doctors" have a common interest in breast cancer is the subgenre's way of signaling their common virtue. For the hero, this detail is crucial, for it counteracts any anxiety attached to his exotic trappings. More counterintuitive and idiosyncratic is that "Voodoo" integrates several sex sequences with visual references to cancer and tumors. For another *WSP* featurette in which breast cancer factors into a self-consciously female-friendly trajectory, see "The Bitter and the Sweet" (1997).

20. Sarno's *Butterflies* (1974) provides a perfect but not at all singular example of postfeminist classical softcore that constructs lesbian sexuality as more sensitive and refined than "phallic" heterosexuality; it even cuts back and forth between a girl-girl encounter and a boy-girl encounter so as to reinforce the distinction. That said, neither classical nor contemporary softcore has to be overtly "postfeminist" to reflect this common assumption about girl-girl imagery. It is not surprising, then, that the narrator of Nick Phillips's *Fancy Lady* (1971), a comparatively lowbrow Uschi Digart vehicle, claims that "lesbian love is considered perverse, but none can deny that it is delicate—and in this delicacy, a certain beauty is to be found." Nor is it surprising that Seduction Cinema, a comparatively downscale current producer, has an outsize investment in this type of spectacle. On "lesbian" sexuality in Metzger's cinema, see Gorfinkel (37–38). For treatments of the contemporary girl-girl scene, see Tricia Jenkins (491–504) and Linda Ruth Williams (*Erotic* 196–210). See also Barbara Lee's documentary, *Girls Kissing Girls* (2003).

21. The misandristic excess of this oration is worth recording in full: "You know what? The hell with them. You know, I am fed up. Why is it that we have to suffer every time? But it always ends up this way: dissatisfaction. And who is it that causes us to have so much humility to them? Men. Tell me honestly, Nikki—who are our seducers, our betrayers, our most faithless friends, and our worst enemies? Men. Who might as well steal every ounce of joy right at the beginning of our lives to dishonor us? And who else is it that turn our hearts into bitterness and emptiness and despair? Men. And who when we're older and we're not so pretty any more—who is it that chooses to make a mockery of our grief?"

NOTES TO CHAPTER 8

1. See Juffer ("No Place" 55). Early in my research, I often rented just-shy-of-softcore sexploitation by mistake. Sexploitive art and taglines are not in themselves telling; even chaste Hollywood films deploy them. Differentiation is most difficult among erotic thrillers. Because cable segregates softcore into late-night slots and offers a variety of descriptors, industrial reticence causes fewer snafus there.

2. Two categories of softcore site that I have excluded here are "celebrity" fan groups like Shauna O'Brien Nation (e.g., <http://movies.icq.com/groups/group_details?gid=12024439>) and Web pages devoted to icons like Shannon Tweed (<http://www.angelfire.com/film/shannontweed/>) and a multitude of lesser figures like Kelli McCarty (<http://www.kellimccarty.com/>). Grassroots softcore discourse often revolves around actresses, so these categories should be considered in more expansive treatments.

3. For mentions of this stereotype, see Linda Williams (*Hard* 99); Johnson and Schaefer (51–52); and Gorfinkel (30–31). This image is also present in elite texts like Philip Roth's *Portnoy's Complaint* (1969).

4. According to Laurence O'Toole, some twenty million Americans had access to porn subscription channels in 1998 (165)—and by then, many times that number enjoyed access to premium channels like Cinemax, Showtime, and the Movie Channel. By itself, Showtime had a subscribership of some 22,300,000 in 1999 (Backstein 305); HBO's numbers have always been much higher than its archrival's.

5. Softcore typically views female masturbation as serious and straightforwardly erotic—but not when it filters this autoeroticism through the image of the romance reader. For instance, *Personals 2: casualsex.com* (2001) employs this stereotype as a cautionary example when the protagonist (Beverly Lynne) is advised by her eventual lover (Christopher John Kapanke) that if she does not "get back in the game" she will find herself "at home with six cats reading romance novels every night."

6. Schaefer has noted the exquisite irony of classical exploitation's antimasturbation tradition (see *Bold* 35, 129), as demonstrated by early features like *The Solitary Sin* (1918).

7. One aspect of second-wave feminism—"the antipornography, and arguably antisex, campaign associated with Catharine MacKinnon"—actively reinforced prevailing stigmas by referring to male masturbation as a "rehearsal for real sexual aggression" (Laqueur 80). This attack represents a departure from contemporary trends. In the past, masturbation's adverse effects were often described in clinical and grisly terms, but now it is rare for people "to say exactly what's so bad about masturbation" (Kipnis 179; 178–88). The shame is mostly expressed through silence. See Kendrick (88–91), Marcus (19–20), and O'Toole (299–302).

8. This sexism is more consistent than in heterosexual hardcore, which traditionally depicts men masturbating within a "couples" framework as a way of inducing the all-important "money shot."

9. A crucial early example of the corporate aesthetic, *Play Time* (1994) offers a significant exception to this generalization. Though *Play Time* recognizes the cultural stigmas associated with male masturbation, it approaches the subject with the same sympathetic gravity with which it approaches female masturbation.

10. This point is borne out by the fourth section of this chapter (see note 24). A number of commentators, including Linda Ruth Williams, take it for granted that women masturbate to softcore, but comparatively little evidence is attached to these assumptions

(see, e.g., *Erotic* 265, 275n29).

11. One trend among amateur critics is toward objectivity. "Users" like "David Brown" and "Smooth B." have contributed scores of detailed responses to IMDb and other sites. Such detail curtails contradiction and condescension, making such reviews relatively reliable. Indeed, this level of detail makes these critics more reliable than many academics, who have typically referred to softcore in glancing and evaluative ways. Janet Staiger has argued that "'[u]ntutored' readings are just as real and material in their effects as 'tutored' ones and may, indeed, be considerably more influential" (48). Detail-oriented amateur critics suggest that "untutored" readings may be more accurate than "tutored" ones as well.

12. Consider one "positive" response to Anne Goursaud's midbudget, straight-to-video, aspirational softcore thriller *Poison Ivy 2* (1995): "I don't think it was just a soft core porn movie, I believe all the nudity had a reason that was directly associated to the plot" ("Good" 1). In this view, which uses traditional criteria, narrative unity allows a film to transcend porn. Softcore is thus construed as a form whose illegitimacy results from a failure to subordinate number to narrative.

13. All five IMDb comments on MRG's *Sensual Friends* (2001) exemplify this paradigm. Each indicates that the film is "that" type of movie and must be rated according to "a different set of scales" ("User" 1). But then the evaluations range from three qualified affirmations ("a 10/10 on a Erotic film scale"; "NOT BAD AT ALL"; and "[l]aughable movie, but excellent erotica" ["User" 1, 1, 2]) to one hatchet job ("the worst Skinemax flick I have ever seen . . . 1/10 even on the Skinemax scale" ["User" 2–3]).

14. That softcore fans are more likely to admit using the genre as a couple's aid than to admit using it as a masturbation aid appears to isolate the influence of anticonsumerist or "productivist" ideology, which demonizes sexual activity outside committed heterosexual relationships, from that of aesthetic elitism, which denigrates any affective or utilitarian consumption of art. Outside elite contexts, antimasturbation norms place a more direct restriction on honesty on this issue than neo-Kantian norms of disinterestedness.

15. "Not bad for softcore," a response to *Friend of the Family* (1995), explains the essentialist rationale of such a response: "Let's be honest, one does not watch a movie such as this for the intellectual kind of stimulation. It is softcore porn, and is closer to that genre than film . . . most importantly, its structure is segregated into sex scenes with filler space between them to fake a movie format. A good softcore movie has many great sex scenes, and somewhat entertaining if imbecile filler space" (2). This odd reasoning is not unusual. It views Hollywood narrative as the measure of cinematic reality, with any attempt to fuse narrative and number constituting a pretentious if entertaining attempt to fake a Real Movie. In other words, because the numbers *are* there, the narrative is not *really* there. This logic also assumes that nonnarrative hardcore is the measure of pornographic reality. Softcore is, then, hardcore in false (and skimpy) Hollywood clothing.

16. Even if these estimates were (unaccountably) accurate, they would not offer a reliable breakdown of the softcore audience. All they would indicate is that a significant portion of that audience is female—with the ratio likely skewing more toward females than these sites suggest. For many years, studies have indicated that women tend to be less voluble and direct than men in contributing their opinion in a variety of institutions (Frazer and Frazer 206–8, 213–14; Fishman 11–22), so it would be surprising if this were not true even in a comparatively anonymous institution like the Internet. That it *is* true of these sites is suggested by IMDb's breakdowns for movies loosely considered examples of the contemporary woman's film—*Pretty Woman* (1990), *Thelma and Louise* (1991),

Titanic (1997), and *How Stella Got Her Groove Back* (1998)—all of which skew toward male voters, sometimes by three-to-one margins. (For example, as of 18 July 2004, *How Stella* had generated 575 male votes against only 270 female votes [http://pro.imdb.com/title/tt0120703/ratings].)

17. After I drafted this chapter in 2004, Softcore Reviews redesigned its Web site—and changed its rating system from a ten-point to a five-star scale. However, the logic of the rating system did not change. At the same time, Softcore Reviews removed links to its "FAQ" and ratings criteria from its home page—but these resources, which on last check were modified only slightly, may still be accessed through the URLs or alternative URLs in my Works Cited. All quotations refer to the original pages.

18. That Softcore Reviews feels pressured to justify its taste for this middle genre in terms of hardcore (Real Porn) as well as in terms of Hollywood (Real Film) is indicated on several policy pages. For example, "FAQ" features the heading, "Why a site dedicated to softcore movies? Isn't hardcore better?" (1).

19. David Loftus indirectly supports this view in *Watching Sex* (2002). His surveys suggest that men want the same qualities from "porn" that women want from "erotica." Besides sex and nudity, men favor "credibility, realism, and overall quality"—i.e., "good writing, characterization, decent acting, 'realistic' characters, and a natural progression of events" (Loftus 29). According to Loftus, the most notable objects of male disgust could "be summed up in a word, 'unreality'" (30). Other common dislikes include violence, scatology, degradation, chauvinism, genital close-ups, and shoddy finish (Loftus 30–44).

20. This "compliment" is omitted from the version of this review posted on the redesigned Softcore Reviews.

21. For this diatribe, see "Robert Lombard (Rant)" (http://sreviews.com/forum/viewtopic.php?t=1204).

22. This survey consisted of questions posted on the site's message boards; a review of the contents of all of the site's message boards; and e-mail correspondence with a number of willing fans.

23. For a sample, see "The Softcore Audience" (http://sreviews.com/forum/viewtopic.php?t=547).

24. I have gathered more secondhand details on female autoerotic reception than firsthand details. A similar effect is evident in Loftus's surveys, which yielded frequent male statements on a female partner's usage of erotic films; for example, one respondent notes that "mainstream films with erotic content" helped acclimate his wife to porn, who began masturbating to hardcore as well as to "softer" films like *Basic Instinct* (179). Because this evidence is so unreliable, I have formed no fixed conception of female uses of the genre.

25. See "Rape Scenes that 'Victims' enjoy in it" (http://sreviews.com/forum/viewtopic.php?t=913).

26. See, e.g., "Feversteamgirl" (http://sreviews.com/forum/search.php?search_author=feversteamgirl).

27. This complex relational process is reinforced by the presence on the site of industry insiders like Syren and Lombard, who use "mainstream" as a relative term for differentiating softcore from hardcore—a tendency that has encouraged fans on the site to apply the term "mainstream" to softcore and to their own taste for it. But a more detached perspective clarifies that the presence of these crossover figures testifies to softcore's present flow away from the mainstream, a current that has naturally tugged fans with it.

NOTES TO CHAPTER 9

1. Top executives at MRG—including Marc Greenberg, reportedly the "king" of the industry—have ignored my repeated interview requests. Influential producers with ties to other corporate softcore studios (e.g., Pat Siciliano) have done the same. My inability to access this tier has been a disappointment, for I subscribe to the Marxist view that it is "the direct relation of the owners of the conditions of production to the direct producers, which reveals the innermost secret, the hidden foundation of the entire social construction" (Marx 1). On the other hand, such closedness is itself a crucial part of the corporate softcore story.

2. See Lazarus's comments on Playboy's "official" antipathy to reviews (Andrews, "Personal" 28).

3. Jack Stevenson concurs, arguing that "*Teas* was heavily influenced by the new *Playboy* magazine mentality, and it unspooled like a series of *Playboy* centrefolds come to life" (165). See also Turan and Zito (31).

4. Sidaris proudly enumerates his Playboy links, including his attendance at "over 50 parties and functions at [Hefner's] Playboy Mansion" (Sidaris and Sidaris 11). More pertinently, Sidaris has used twenty-three Playmates in his films (Sidaris and Sidaris 101). Friedman notes that "[b]eing a *Playboy* playmate in [the early 1960s] conferred a minor national celebrity status" that a sexploiteer might treat as "something salable" (337). Sidaris recognized this point as early as *Stacey* (1973), which starred Playmate Anne Randall, and has relied on it ever since.

5. On the other hand, some enormously talented actresses have used *Playboy* as a platform—and at least one, Sharon Stone, later achieved superstardom. Stone is distinctive in that she used *Playboy* as a way *out* of "the B-movie ghetto," not as a way into it. See Linda Ruth Williams (*Erotic* 195; 226).

6. As a full-blown network, the Playboy Channel is now referred to as Playboy TV.

7. Playboy's Alta Loma label has produced *Women: Stories of Passion* and *Passion's Cove* (1999–2001).

8. For example, premium cable divides its programming into "day-parts," reserving its sexual content for nighttime slots. This day-night axis resembles *Playboy*'s division between sexual and nonsexual materials.

9. The enhanced security of Playboy TV's digital technology influenced its purchase of harder-core channels and its own increasing explicitness (Christie Hefner 2–3). Given the litigation Playboy has faced over its scrambling, this factor should not be neglected when discussing Playboy TV's fluctuating explicitness.

10. Recent *Penthouse* pictorials evince various styles and levels of explicitness. Some integrate solo-girl inexplicitness with grainy realism and low motifs like urination (e.g., Gordon 59–76; Ward 87–95); others integrate soft focus with hardcore penetration (Wachter 107–23). In its softcore pictorials, then, *Penthouse* has used a "dirty," realistic aestheticization to position itself as harder-than-*Playboy*. In its more risqué hardcore pictorials, it has used impressionistic aestheticization to position itself as softer-than-*Hustler*.

11. Hugh Hefner asserts this point in "Hugh Hefner: Playboy Enterprises" (2). See also Juffer (*Home* 210).

12. Besides the umbrella designation "Eros," Playboy has used various labels for its films. It has made occasional use of the "Playboy" name, as with the Pat Siciliano

production *Passion Lane* (2001). It has also used the old Cameo label for *Hot Club California* (1999) and *Forbidden Highway* (1999), perhaps because viewers associate it with the popular mid-1990s titles (*Play Time, I Like to Play Games, The Affair* [1995], *Watch Me* [1996], etc.) that helped establish the viability of corporate softcore.

13. The corporate softcore model lent itself to big business. As early as 1994, CPV had thirty-eight employees, a "substantial production slate," and annual sales of around five million dollars (MRG 3).

14. On current corporate softcore casting practices, see Softcore Reviews' interview with MRG casting director Robert Lombard. Lombard stresses the equity of softcore's pay scales: "No one has dollar power in this genre!" ("Casting" 5). This has not always been true. As Lazarus recalls, under prior cost structures, Playboy made some "softcore features with mainstream semi-name actors and actresses. They found the added star power and expense didn't add to the 'box office'" (Andrews, "Personal" 28).

15. Playboy features have historically operated on a low- to midbudget scale. In 1985, the studio set the budget for Alan Roberts's *Young Lady Chatterley II* at $270,000; the film came in at $310,000 (Roberts 2). The Playboy Channel also financed cheaper films with lower values. In the early 1980s, it recruited Vincent to produce ten films for one million dollars (Ford 2). Never completed, this deal did yield *Preppies* (1982).

16. My source for these figures has asked to remain anonymous.

17. Playboy's diverse distribution net has helped to moderate the explicitness—and to effect the glossy, guilt-free weightlessness—of its corporate softcore. This Playboy TV content never shifted as far toward hardcore as other Playboy TV content because its producers had to account for the constraints of divergent markets.

18. Christie Hefner alludes to this new studio complex (3).

19. In its *2000 Annual Report,* Playboy promotes its softcore features much as it promotes its print division, that is, as the safest, most upscale, most mainstream components of the company (see 6–12).

20. The visual aesthetic of Playboy's corporate softcore has an analogue in the retouched realism of *Playboy* pictorials, which have been criticized as "'sanitized' and 'plastic'" (Jancovich, "Placing" 4).

21. Brian McNair argues that "1980s New Man," who offered a newly feminized stereotype of masculinity, "was less the by-product of feminism or gay rights than an update of 1950s *Playboy* man" (*Striptease* 158). As my discussion indicates, similar "updates" were taking place *within* Playboy—but in Playboy's case, feminism was doubtless the central cultural determinant informing this renovation.

22. Several Playboy regulars had daytime gigs; e.g., Kelli McCarty has played Beth on *Passions* (1999 on).

23. Other scholars have noticed these tensions. Juffer alludes to them in referring to *Damien's Seed* (1996), one of Holzman's Playboy projects, as "a mass of contradictions" (*Home* 216).

24. Lazarus verifies that Playboy executives discouraged anything but a disunified vision (Andrews, "Personal" 28). They also encouraged disunity by spending little on scripts. As the former director of development for Indigo, Zaitz observes that for Playboy it was enough to recruit scriptwriters capable of formulating sex scenes that followed from the narrative "without it seeming wholly implausible" (2). By observing that a writer's agent might earn "a few hundred dollars" (6), Zaitz indicates that Playboy paid at most a few thousand dollars for scripts (assuming an agent's percentage of 10 percent). "There is only so much money available for a softcore erotic script," Zaitz asserts (6).

"That's just the fact of the matter." A process that barely rewarded basic narrative-number integration was even less likely to reward thematic unity. Instead, Playboy used outside writers to doctor scripts "as necessary"—a studio practice notorious for introducing incoherence.

25. One might with equal justice say that Lazarus's films stand out against the Playboy norm much as films like Haskell Wexler's *Medium Cool* (1968)—which, as Robert Allen and Douglas Gomery note, initiated the trend of using "a verité 'style' (hand-held camera work, location shooting) to lend a documentary feel to a scripted, fictional film" (237)—once stood out against the Hollywood norm. For more on *cinéma vérité*, see Allen and Gomery (215–41).

26. Lazarus's rhetoric is so hostile to soft-focus stylization that it resembles the rhetoric characteristic of highbrow denunciations of middlebrow "interlopers" like Metzger, Jaeckin, and King.

27. The film's third number ends with an inexplicit simulation of the money shot. Thus its unconventional focus is the orgasmic male face, not the orgasmic female face. See Andrews ("Convention" 19–20).

28. In *Voyeur Confessions* and *The Exhibitionist Files,* Lazarus diverges from the corporate softcore norm by depicting unpleasurable sex (and by using actresses that do not conform to Playboy's visual ideals). With few exceptions, corporate softcore depicts sex as enjoyable. Bad sex may exist offscreen but not on. Indeed, as in MRG's *Exposed* (2001), even those who sleep with people they despise do so not because they are coerced but because they enjoy the act. See Andrews ("Convention" 15–16).

29. Three out of four of these documentarians initially represent a detached, amoral objectivity. (Melinda of *House of Love* is the exception; she is initially a feminist caricature clouded by sex-negative moralism.) This objectivity is conspicuous in the second pair of Lazarus films, in which Lisa is aligned with a strong, scientific discourse of truth, which Michel Foucault has referred to as *scientia sexualis,* and which implies moral detachment (57; Linda Williams, *Hard* 3–4). The documentarians' impartiality is qualified sexually *and* morally when they cross over, in effect, from *scientia sexualis* to *ars erotica.* This outcome suggests Lazarus's insight that the moral impulse is just as seductive as the sexual impulse that it restrains.

30. In defense of *7 Lives Xposed,* Lazarus has consistently pressed for diversity in his depictions. The show is notable for its multicultural cast and its depictions of male homosexuality and transgender characters.

NOTES TO CHAPTER 10

1. In June 2006, this company announced that it was changing its umbrella name from "ei Independent Cinema" (or "ei Cinema") to POPcinema."

2. See Andrews ("Lesbian" 34). Shot-on-video features in this genre can be *very* inexpensive. Director Donald Farmer reports in his DVD interview that *An Erotic Vampire in Paris* (2002), which stars Misty Mundae and was picked up for distribution by ei Cinema, cost under $8,000 to shoot. Additionally, Raso has confirmed that *The Sexy Adventures of Van Helsing* (2004), a recent Seduction Cinema "quickie," cost under $20,000 to produce (1).

3. *Vampire Seduction* is now available as an extra on the *Sexy Adventures of Van Helsing* DVD (2004).

4. That Seduction aims its films at heterosexual men has only been reinforced as it has

added men to its spectacle. Only rarely are these men sculpted and idealized sex objects. Raso and his colleagues thus seem to agree with cult softcore veteran Jim Wynorski, who argues that "guys at home drinking beer [don't] want to see five good-looking studly guys in a movie. They want to see themselves in the movie" (Springer).

5. See Buscombe (27). To prove his point that audiences stubbornly "require a story of sorts," causing producers reliant on pornography's "ultra-low budgets" to "steal" story lines from elsewhere, Edward Buscombe points to the Seduction Cinema titles *Erotic Witch Project* and *Play-Mate of the Apes* (27).

6. Johnny Crash's featurette "New York Wildcats" was produced in 2002 but not released until 2005, when it was used as an "extra" on the Retro-Seduction DVD rerelease of Joe Sarno's *Swedish Wildcats* (1972). ei Cinema often releases projects years after completion to ensure a steady flow of product.

7. Unlike EVI and Boxoffice International, Seduction's carnivalesque relies on a grossout aesthetic that it shares with Troma, which also shares its populism. The motif that captures this populism at all four companies is the crowd sequence—which, in softcore vehicles, is often realized through orgies.

8. Mark Jancovich et al. note that "[n]ew media such as video, cable, satellite and the internet ... threaten the sense of distinction and exclusivity on which cult movie fandom depends" ("Introduction" 4). Harnessing these disparate media may also threaten the distinction on which cult producers depend. But thus far, Seduction has maintained its characteristic idiosyncrasy even when moving into new forms and markets.

9. To satisfy divergent retailer guidelines, Seduction placed a new emphasis on narrative in *G-Strings*. As director-writer Terry West notes, "the executive producers were looking for a really meaty story and wanted something where you could cut the stronger sexual content out and still have a movie. I've been working pretty much with the basic formula that Seduction has used for years, so it took a little bit of acclimation" (qtd. in Hallenbeck, "Lord" 42). The film was thus released in multiple versions, including an unrated version and two R-rated versions (the tamer of which is entitled *Lord of the Strings*).

10. In this respect, the pornographic tradition represented by Seduction's carnivalesque is very old—much older, in fact, than the largely apolitical type of pornography characteristic of the post-*Playboy* era. "Not until the nineteenth century did grossly sexual and excremental references lose their satirical aura," Walter Kendrick asserts (42). Until then, such "references were abusive, funny, and low."

11. Unlike corporate labels, cult sexploitation labels have commodified their actresses in the same way, with formulations like "the Women of Troma" and "the Women of Surrender" identifying this trend. What distinguishes Seduction is the tenacity with which it has promoted a single actress.

12. Particularly intriguing is the way in which this documentary builds to the clip from *Screaming Dead,* the Piper film that this extra accompanies, in which Mundae's character lets loose an iconic horror scream during a bondage sequence. The documentary points to this scream as visual proof that Mundae has made a successful transition from softcore to horror. Inadvertently, however, this sequence accents one of the continuities between sexploitation and horror: though both genres prefer female spectacle, both contain mechanisms for shifting the visual focus from the female body to the "frenzied" female face.

13. By autumn 2005, when this manuscript went to press, Mundae's "exclusive" contract with Seduction had expired, and the actress was performing for low-budget horror

companies under the name Erin Brown. Still, even then, Raso was linking his company's distinction-oriented transformation to the actress's performance in unreleased ei Cinema films like *Chantal* and even in unshot projects (see Waltz 1–2)—meaning that the company remained dependent on the "aura" that it fashioned for her.

14. ei Cinema plots usually imply that its girl-girl heroines are being *girlish,* that is, experimenting with alternative sexualities but not openly endorsing them. See, for example, *SpiderBabe.*

15. IMDb erroneously cites "Erin DeWright" as Mundae's birth name. As the owner of the Mundae name, ei Cinema has vigilantly protected the identity of its trademark actress.

16. ei Cinema most often spells Millard's "Nick Phillips" pseudonym as "Nick Philips." I have opted for the former spelling because it seems most common in other sectors. The "Nick Phillips" designation is, incidentally, just one of Millard's many false names.

17. See Sarno's *The Indelicate Balance* (1969), which is a close imitation of the Bergman style during the *Through a Glass Darkly* (1961) period. That Retro-Seduction would rerelease this particular film, which is driven by dialogue rather than spectacle, is instructive of its perception of Sarno's appeal.

18. Retro-Seduction has most recently produced Sarno's *Lust for Laura*; rereleased lavish editions of *The Seduction of Inga* (1969/72), *The Indelicate Balance, Swedish Wildcats,* and *Abigail Lesley Is Back in Town*; and released two Sarno remakes, *The Seduction of Misty Mundae* and "New York Wildcats." Retro-Seduction also lists myriad Sarno titles on VHS. In press releases, Raso has stressed the director's cachet, praising his films as "timeless works of art" that exude "thematic complexity and richness of characterization" (qtd. in Faoro and Fine 2).

19. In 2005, Retro-Seduction rereleased *The Naughty Stewardesses* (1973) and *Blazing Stewardesses* (1975). Directed by Al Adamson and produced by Sam Sherman, *Blazing Stewardesses* contains a spoof narrative, tame sex spectacle, and burlesque comedy, notably by the Ritz Brothers. The presence of the Ritz Brothers in a sexploitation film rereleased by Retro-Seduction marks the convergence of three spectacle-based traditions. All that said, however, this sort of trichotomous spoof is an exception among Retro-Seduction's rereleases.

20. By 2005, Retro-Seduction had begun acquiring the rights to Doris Wishman films, including *Hideout in the Sun* (1960) and *The Prince and the Nature Girl* (1965). Given its elevation strategies, ei Cinema's acquisition of Wishman's work—which has been accorded "elite" status in many academic quarters (see, for example, Bowen, "Doris Wishman")—makes sense.

21. *Curious Obsessions* integrates grungy classical footage from authentic peeps and loops with softer contemporary footage; hence this film-video hybrid represents a new phase in ei Cinema's parasitic commodification of its sexploitation past. What I find most intriguing about the shot-on-video frame narrative is the way in which it actively sexualizes the physical components of the "archaic" projector and of the film that circulates through it.

22. Though useful to the studio, Marsiglia's aestheticism is not a studio construction. That he has managed to reconcile this persona with softcore necessities offers a neat proof of Jean-Claude Chamboredon's view that the commercial virtuoso must be "driven by the pure intention to be an artist" (149).

23. Marsiglia also refers to *Mulholland Drive* in his very loose remake of *Chantal,* which is about a Candide-like ingenue (Mundae) who fails as a Hollywood actress,

descending into the Hollywood sex industry instead. Further, *Chantal* and two other recent Marsiglia projects on 16mm, *Lust for Dracula* and *Sinful,* allude to an array of elite filmmakers, including Hal Hartley and Stanley Kubrick.

24. Marsiglia's metallic corridor remodels the "psychogenic" hallway scene near the end of *Lost Highway.*

25. Lynch's postcoital sequence in turn recreates a famous shot from *Persona.* See Andrews ("Oneiric" 36).

26. See *Seduction Cinema: Erotica 2005* for a clear example of Marsiglia's featured position at ei Cinema.

27. Because of this transition, Raso is able to applaud Marsiglia in the *Lust for Dracula* DVD commentary much as he elsewhere applauds Mundae: as a personification of the "elevations" transforming ei Cinema.

28. Marsiglia, for example, relies on bizarre sexual violence, including rape. In *Lust for Dracula,* a fifty-thousand-dollar film on 16mm, Mina Harker (Mundae) is raped by Jonathan Harker (Wells), who is referred to as a man yet played by a woman. Unlike most rape scenes in contemporary softcore, this one implies heterosexual penetration but still carefully mediates the act itself. The use of females in ostensibly male roles (Caine plays Dracula) also allows Marsiglia to maximize female objectification without fully sacrificing heterosexual themes.

29. Mundae's dislike of boy-girl numbers is corroborated in interviews (e.g., Hallenbeck, "Confessions" 19–20). This disinclination in effect bars her from corporate softcore, where casting agents have increasingly expressed impatience with the "Do's and Don'ts" of would-be actresses (Lombard, "Casting" 2–3).

30. It is worth remembering that many other filmmakers at many other companies have been thwarted in their efforts to "elevate" their respective studios and hence the softcore genre itself. To cite just one instance, consider Alexander Gregory Hippolyte, who in his interview with Linda Ruth Williams laments that while at Axis he had "hoped the company would elevate itself to a different . . . not 'elevate,' that sounds like sort of a moralistic judgement, but *transition* into a variety of other things, and it never did. I had hoped that we would make erotic thrillers sometimes, just softcore movies sometimes, sometimes horror movies, different kind of genres. Very specific genre-oriented movies, but having the company develop a number of things" (*Erotic* 281; Williams's italics). Clearly, ei Cinema has already realized important aspects of Hippolyte's dream, albeit at lower budgetary levels than Hippolyte was used to at Axis. The question now is whether Raso can nudge ei Cinema's idiosyncratic, multifaceted softcore model into higher economic brackets.

NOTES TO CONCLUSION

1. "We know you weren't expecting it," reads the sly caption at the bottom (Siemens 17). "But now that you're staring at it, you have to admit that you've never seen one quite so perfect."

2. See Bauder (15); James (1); Jones and Cook (9); Smith and Simon (13); "FCC" (21); "Cable" (12).

3. Between 2001 and 2004, HBO and Cinemax "went from licensing 30" films from MRG per year "down to 15 down to 12" (Lombard, "Industry Insider" 2). Because of such declines, MRG and New City stress shot-on-video features for pay-per-view distribution. The cheapest vehicles—shot in three days for about $50,000—are reportedly quite

explicit, with long numbers and little dialogue. New City's new Torchlight label (not to be confused with the defunct Full Moon brand) produces videos using scripts that are, at thirty to forty pages, *half* as long as corporate softcore's former eighty- to one-hundred-page standard. MRG has also converted its older, less explicit thriller—the 16mm category produced for about $130,000—to video procedures. Costing up to $80,000, this new model indicates the obsolescence of 16mm production at MRG. By February 2005, MRG had scheduled seven of these thrillers for production over that year.

Film- and Videography

The list below contains information on every feature-length film or video mentioned above. It also contains a small number of entries for contemporary softcore features *not* mentioned above; these clarify significant patterns in the softcore industry that I have not had space to discuss in detail. Space constraints have also compelled me to make distinctions among various types of entries. Entries that refer to quoted texts include the fullest source information—and though this list does *not* include an entry for every softcore featurette mentioned in *Soft in the Middle,* it does supply exact source information for any featurette cited extensively or quoted directly. I have also provided *relatively* full information on any film or video that clearly qualifies as *contemporary* softcore. Identified by the familiar "SC" tag, the entries on these productions contain data on directors, writers, producers, performers, production studios, distributors, and release dates (generally the date of first release, if known). Entries on features outside the contemporary softcore category or mentioned only in passing supply less documentation, with a rudimentary title-director-date scheme providing my template. Finally, I have opted for the most relevant names and titles, indicating alternate designations only as seems helpful. (Please note that ei Cinema features released in the second half of 2006 may appear under the company's new umbrella name, "POPcinema," as well as under one of the company's subsidiary brands, which have remained intact.)

9 Songs. Dir., writ., prod. Michael Winterbottom. 2004.
9½ Weeks. Dir. Adrian Lyne. Writ., prod. Zalman King. 1986.
Abigail Lesley Is Back in Town ("*Abigail Leslie Is Back in Town*"). Dir., writ. Joe Sarno. 1975. Retro-Seduction (ei Cinema), 2005.
Accidental Stripper. Dir. Woquini Adams. Prod. Pat Siciliano. Dir. phot. Howard Wexler. Perf. Myla Leigh, Danny Pape, Susan Hale. Rosebud (Silhouette), 2003. SC.
The Adult Version of Jekyll and Hide. Dir. Byron Mabe. Prod. David Friedman. 1971.
The Adventures of Lucky Pierre. Dir. Herschell Gordon Lewis. Prod. David Friedman. 1961.

The Affair. Dir. Danny Taylor. Prod. Sonya Burres ("Samantha Kash"). Casting Lori Cobe. Perf. Raelyn Saalman, Will Potter. Cameo (Playboy), 1995. Orion, 1996. SC.
The Agony of Love. Dir., writ. William Rotsler. Prod. Harry Novak. 1966.
Alley Tramp (a.k.a. *I Am a Woman*). Dir., prod. Herschell Gordon Lewis. 1966.
Altar of Lust. Dir., writ., prod. Roberta Findlay. 1971.
Les Amants. Dir., writ. Louis Malle. 1958.
American Pie. Dir. Paul Weitz. 1999.
. . . And God Created Woman. Dir. Roger Vadim. 1956. American release, 1958.
Andromina: The Pleasure Planet. Dir. Darren Moloney. Writ. Louise Monclair. Prod. Pat Siciliano. Exec. prod. Charles Band. Perf. Susan Featherley, Flower Edwards, Susan Hale, Griffen Drew, Tre Temptor, Mike Roman. Surrender (Full Moon), 1999. SC.
Animal Attraction: Carnal Desires. Dir. Eric Gibson. Prod. Debra Nichols. MRG, 1999. Metropolis (Spartan), 2003. SC.
Animal House. Dir. John Landis. 1978.
Animal Instincts. Dir. A. Gregory Hippolyte (a.k.a. Gregory Dark). Writ. Georges des Esseintes. Prod. Andrew Garroni. Exec. prod. Walter Gernert. Casting Lori Cobe. Perf. Shannon Whirry, Maxwell Caulfield, Delia Sheppard, Jan-Michael Vincent, David Carradine, Bobby Johnston. Axis (Academy), 1992. SC.
Animal Instincts: The Seductress (a.k.a. *Animal Instincts 3*). Dir. Gregory Hippolyte. Writ., prod. Andrew Garroni. Exec. prod. Walter Gernert. Perf. Wendy Schumacher, James Matthew, Jacqueline Lovell. Casting Lori Cobe. Axis (A-Pix), 1995. SC.
Another Language. Dir. Edward Griffith. 1933.
Anthony's Desire. Dir., writ., prod. Tom Boka. Prod. Michelle Jaffe, Zsuzsa Fontner. Perf. Douglass DeMarco, Mihaella Stoicov, Gwen Somers. Tom Boka Productions, 1993. SC.
Ashes and Flames. Dir. Anthony Michael Kane (a.k.a. Tony Marsiglia). 1998.
"Auto Erotica." SC featurette. Dir. Zalman King. Writ. Ned Bowman. Exec. prod. King, Patricia Louisianna Knop, David Saunders. Perf. Caitlin Dulany, Nick Chinlund. Showtime, 1992. *Red Shoe Diaries 4: Auto Erotica.* Unrated VHS anthology. Republic, 1994.
Bad Company. Dir. Damian Harris. 1995.
Bad Girls from Mars. Dir. Fred Olen Ray. 1989.
Barbarian Queen. Dir. Héctor Olivera. Writ. Howard Cohen. Exec. prod. Roger Corman. Perf. Lana Clarkson, Katt Shea. Rodeo (Concorde), 1985. R-rated DVD. Concorde–New Horizons, 2003.
Barbarian Queen II: The Empress Strikes Back. Dir. Joe Finley. Writ. Howard Cohen. Exec. prod. Roger Corman (uncredited). Perf. Lana Clarkson. Triana (Concorde), 1989. R-rated DVD. Concorde–New Horizons, 2003.
Bare Deception. Dir. Eric Gibson. Writ. Steve Martel. Prod. Debra Nichols. Exec. prod. Marc Greenberg. Perf. Tane McClure, Daniel Anderson, Michelle Von Flotow, Brad Bartram ("Brad Bartman"). R-rated VHS. MRG (Ambrosia/Blockbuster), 2000. SC.
Bare Witness. Dir. Kelley Cauthen. Prod. Marc Laurence, Ralph Portillo. Exec. prod. Marc Greenberg, Angie Everhart, Daniel Baldwin. Casting Robert Lombard. Perf. Everhart, Baldwin, Catalina Larranaga. R-rated VHS. Magic Hour (Columbia TriStar), 2002. SC.
Basic Instinct: The Original Director's Cut. Dir. Paul Verhoeven. Writ. Joe Eszterhas. Prod. Alan Marshall. Perf. Sharon Stone, Michael Douglas, Jeanne Tripplehorn. Unrated VHS. Carolco, 1992. Live Home Video, 1993.
Beach Babes 2: Cave Girl Island. Dir. David De Coteau ("Ellen Cabot"). Prod. Karen Spencer. Torchlight (Full Moon), 1995. Cult Video, 1998. SC.

Beach Babes From Beyond. Dir. David DeCoteau ("Ellen Cabot"). Prod. Karen Spencer. Perf. Don Swayze, Joe Estevez, Joey Travolta, Burt Ward, Sarah Bellomo, Tamara Landry. R-rated VHS. Torchlight/Full Moon (Paramount), 1993. SC.
Behind Closed Doors. SC compilation. Dir. Stephanie McLellan. Writ. Clark Winslow. Prod. Pat Siciliano. Casting Robert Lombard. New perf. Kira Reed, Houston, Samantha Phillips. IMP Development, 2002. TVMA. Showtime. 23 Feb. 2004.
Behind the Green Door. Dir., prod. Mitchell Brothers. 1972.
Belle de Jour. Dir., writ. Luis Buñuel. 1967.
Beverly Hills Vamp. Dir., prod. Fred Olen Ray. 1988.
Bibi: Confessions of Sweet Sixteen (a.k.a. *Girl Meets Girl: The Erotic Adventures of a Student Abroad* and *Baby Love*). Dir. Joe Sarno. Perf. Marie Forsa. 1973.
The Big Bird Cage. Dir., writ. Jack Hill. Exec. prod. Roger Corman. 1972.
The Big Doll House. Dir. Jack Hill. Exec. prod. Roger Corman. 1970.
Bikini A Go Go. Dir. Fred Olen Ray ("Nicholas Medina"). Perf. Beverly Lynne, Jay Richardson, Danny Pape, Nikki Fritz. American Independent, 2004. SC.
Bikini Airways. Dir. Fred Olen Ray ("Nicholas Medina"). Perf. Jay Richardson, Regina Russell, Brad Bartram. American Independent, 2003. SC.
The Bikini Escort Company. Dir. Fred Olen Ray ("Nicholas Medina"). Perf. Beverly Lynne, Jay Richardson, Michelle Bauer, Brad Bartram. American Independent, 2004. SC.
Bikini Summer III: South Beach Heat. Dir., writ., prod. Ken Blakey. Perf. Heather-Elizabeth Parkhurst. Shadow Mountain (PM Entertainment), 1997. SC.
Bite Me! Dir., writ. Brett Piper. Exec. prod. Michael Raso. Perf. Misty Mundae, Julian Wells, Michael Thomas. R-rated DVD. Shock-O-Rama (ei Cinema), 2004.
"The Bitter and the Sweet." SC featurette. Dir., writ. Valerie Landsburg. Prod. Maricel Pagulayan, Tracy Paddock, Randy Rowan. Exec. prod. Elisa Rothstein. Perf. Rothstein, Beth Broderick, Jennifer Edwards, Peter Jason. *Women: Stories of Passion.* Alta Loma (Playboy), 1997. TVMA. Showtime. 8 Mar. 2004 (2:30–3 A.M.).
Blazing Stewardesses. Dir. Al Adamson. Prod. Samuel Sherman. 1975.
Blindfold: Acts of Obsession. Dir., writ. Lawrence Simeone. Prod. Ronnie Hadar. Perf. Kristian Alfonso, Judd Nelson, Shannen Doherty. Saban (Libra), 1994. SC.
Blood Feast. Dir., writ., prod. Herschell Gordon Lewis. Prod., writ. David Friedman. 1963.
Blue Movies. Dir., writ. Paul Koval, Ed Fitzgerald. Prod. Maria Snyder. Perf. Larry Poindexter, Lucinda Crosby, Larry Linville. R-rated VHS. Blue Partners (Academy), 1988.
Body Chemistry. Dir. Kristine Peterson. R-rated VHS. Concorde–New Horizons (Columbia), 1990.
Body Chemistry 4: Full Exposure. Dir. Jim Wynorski. Writ. Karen Kelly. Prod. Andrew Stevens. Exec. prod. Roger Corman. Perf. Stevens, Shannon Tweed, Larry Poindexter, Stella Stevens. Concorde–New Horizons, 1995. SC.
Body Double. Dir., writ., prod. Brian De Palma. 1984.
Body Heat. Dir., writ. Lawrence Kasdan. 1981.
Body of a Female. Dir., prod. Michael Findlay, John Amero. 1965.
Body of Evidence. Dir. Uli Edel. Prod. Dino De Laurentiis. 1992.
Body of Influence (a.k.a. *Indecent Advances*). Dir. Gregory Hippolyte. Prod. Andrew Garroni. Exec. prod. Walter Gernert. Perf. Shannon Whirry, Nick Cassavetes, Richard Roundtree, Monique Parent, Anna Karin. Unrated VHS. Axis (Academy), 1993. SC.
Body of Influence 2. Dir., writ., prod. Brian Smith. Prod. Andrew Garroni. Exec. prod. Walter Gernert. Perf. Jodie Fisher, Daniel Anderson, Landon Hall. Axis (A-Pix), 1996. SC.
Boogie Nights. Dir., writ., prod. Paul Thomas Anderson. 1997.
Boxing Helena. Dir., writ. Jennifer Lynch. Perf. Sherilyn Fenn. 1993.
"The Brunch Club." SC featurette. Dir. Rob Spera. Writ. Laura Francis. Prod. Mark Lasser.

Exec. prod. Marc Greenberg. Music Nicholas Rivera. Perf. Alan Andrews, Mimi Cochran. *Hot Line.* Magic Hour/MRG, 1996. TVMA. Cinemax. 31 Jan. 2004 (10:40–11:10 P.M.).
Butterflies. Dir. Joe Sarno. Prod. Chris Nebe. Perf. Marie Forsa, Harry Reems, Eric Edwards. Monarex. 1974. Unrated VHS. Retro-Seduction (ei Cinema), 1998.
Caged Heat. Dir., writ. Jonathan Demme. Prod. Roger Corman (uncredited). 1974.
Camille 2000. Dir., prod. Radley Metzger. 1969.
Candy Stripe Nurses. Dir. Alan Holleb. Prod. Julie Corman. Exec. prod. Roger Corman. 1974.
Caress of the Vampire. Dir., prod. Frank Terranova. 1996.
Carmen, Baby. Dir., prod. Radley Metzger. 1966.
Carnal Crimes. Dir. Alexander Hippolyte. Prod. Andrew Garroni. Exec. prod. Walter Gernert. Perf. Linda Carol, Martin Hewitt. Unrated VHS. Axis (Magnum), 1991. SC.
Carrie. Dir. Brian De Palma. 1976.
"Celeste." SC featurette. Dir. Marilyn Vance. Prod. Ladd Vance. Exec. prod. Marilyn Vance. Perf. Caroline Key Johnson, Alan Foster, Landon Hall. *Intimate Sessions.* Ministry of Film (New City), 1998. TVMA. MoreMAX. 11 Jan. 2004 (10:40–11:05 P.M.).
Chained Heat. Dir., writ. Lutz Schaarwächter. Dir. phot. Mac Ahlberg. 1983.
Chantal. Dir. Nick Phillips (a.k.a. Steve Millard). 1969.
Chantal. Dir., writ. Tony Marsiglia. Exec. prod. Michael Raso. Perf. Misty Mundae, Julian Wells, Darian Caine. Seduction (ei Cinema), 2006.
Cheerleaders' Beach Party. Dir., prod. Alex Gotein. Writ. Chuck Vincent. 1978.
Cherry Hill High. Dir., prod. Alex Gotein. 1977.
ChromiumBlue.com. Dir. Zalman King. Dir., writ. Scott Sampler. Prod. Frank Huebner. Exec. prod. Zalman King. Perf. Erica Prior, Shane Brolly, Summer Attice. Carousel (Ambrosia/Blockbuster), 2002. R-rated pilot (first four episodes of serial).
Citizen Kane. Dir. Orson Welles. 1941.
Close Enough to Touch. Dir. Jamie Scabbert. Writ. Romy Hayes. Prod. Jennifer Byrne. Exec. prod. Kelley Cauthen. Perf. Jason Schnuit, Bobby Johnston, Tracy Ryan, Monique Parent ("Scarlet Johansing"), Sebastien Guy, Jack Lincoln. Indigo (Playboy), 2001. R-rated feature. Cinemax. 10 Jan. 2004. SC.
Conan the Barbarian. Dir., writ. John Milius. Exec. prod. Dino De Laurentiis. 1982.
The Concrete Jungle. Dir. Tom DeSimone. 1982.
Confessions of a Natural Beauty. Dir., writ. Misty Mundae. Prod. Michael Raso. Dir. phot. John Fedele. Perf. Mundae, Darian Caine, Ruby Larocca. Seduction (ei Cinema), 2003. SC.
Corporate Fantasy. Dir. Charles Randazzo. Writ. Garrett Clancy, Catalina Larranaga. Prod. William Burke. Exec. prod. Edward Holzman. Perf. Tracy Ryan ("Tracy Smith"), Larranaga, Susan Featherly. Mystique (Playboy), 1999. SC.
Cruising. Dir., writ. William Friedkin. 1980.
Curious Obsessions. Dir., writ. John Bacchus. Writ., exec. prod. Michael Raso. Perf. Bethany Lott, Jackie Stevens. Seduction (ei Cinema), 2006. SC.
The Curse of Her Flesh. Dir., writ., prod. Michael Findlay ("Julian Marsh"). Prod. Roberta Findlay ("Anna Riva"). Riva Marsh Productions (American Film Distributing). 1968. Unrated DVD. Something Weird, 2003.
Damien's Seed. Dir., writ. Edward Holzman. Ed. Kelley Cauthen. Perf. Jacqueline Lovell, Shauna O'Brien, Kira Reed. Mystique (Playboy), 1996. SC.
Dangerous Pleasures. Dir. Madison Monroe. Writ. David Ciesielski. Prod. Debra Nichols. Exec. prod. Marc Greenberg. Casting Robert Lombard. Perf. Jacy Andrews, Collin Hughes, Burke Morgan. MRG, 2002. TVMA. The Movie Channel. 15 February 2005. SC.

Deadly Weapons. Dir., prod. Doris Wishman. 1973.
Dead On. Dir. Ralph Hemecker. Writ. April Wayne. Prod. Stu Segall. Perf. Shari Shattuck, Tracy Scoggins, Matt McCoy. Unrated VHS. MetToy (Orion), 1993. SC.
Deathstalker. Dir. John Watson. Writ. Howard Cohen. Exec. prod. Roger Corman. 1983.
Deep Jaws. Dir. Perry Dell. Prod. Manuel Conde. 1976.
Deep Throat. Dir. Gerard Damiano (a.k.a. Jerry Gerard). 1972.
Delta of Venus. Dir., prod. Zalman King. Writ. Elisa Rothstein, Patricia Louisanna Knop. Music George Clinton. Perf. Audie England. Unrated DVD. New Line, 1995.
The Devil in Miss Jones. Dir. Gerard Damiano. 1972.
The Diktator. Dir. Perry Dell. Prod. Manuel Conde. 1974.
Disclosure. Dir., prod. Barry Levinson. Writ., prod. Michael Crichton. 1994.
Double Agent 73. Dir., writ., prod. Doris Wishman. 1974.
Dressed to Kill. Dir. Brian De Palma. 1980.
Dr. Jekyll and Mistress Hyde. Dir., writ., prod. Tony Marsiglia. Prod. Michael Raso ("Michael Beckerman"). Music Don Mike. Perf. Misty Mundae, Andrea Davis, Julian Wells. Unrated DVD. Seduction (ei Cinema), 2003. SC.
Ecstasy. Dir. Gustav Machaty. 1933. American release, 1934.
"Elena." SC featurette. Dir. Marilyn Vance. Writ. Karol Silverstein. Prod. Ladd Vance. Perf. Edward Johnson, J. T. Pontino, Letrica Cruz. *Intimate Sessions.* Ministry of Film (New City), 1998. TVMA. MoreMAX. 11 Jan. 2004 (10:15–10:40 P.M.).
Emanuelle in America. Dir. Joe D'Amato. 1976.
Embrace the Darkness II. Dir. Robert Kubilos. Prod. Jennifer Byrne. Exec. prod. John Quinn. Writ. April White, Ed Gorsuch. Perf. Renee Rea, Catalina Larranaga, Jezebelle Bond. Music Herman Beeftink. R-rated VHS. Indigo (Playboy), 2001. SC.
Emmanuelle. Dir. Just Jaeckin. Writ. Emmanuelle Arsan. Dir. phot. Richard Suzuki. Prod. Yves Rousset-Rouard. Perf. Sylvia Kristel, Alain Cuny, Daniel Sarky. English version (dir., writ. Paulette Rubinstein). Trinacra, 1974. X-rated VHS. RCA/Columbia, 1984.
Emmanuelle 2: The Joys of a Woman. Dir. Francis Giacobetti. Prod. Alain Siritzky. 1975.
The Erotic Adventures of Zorro. Dir. Robert Freeman. Dir., prod. William Allen Castleman. Writ., prod. David Friedman. Perf. Douglas Frey, Bob Cresse, John Alderman. EVI. 1971. Unrated VHS. Something Weird, 2000.
The Erotic Diary of Misty Mundae. Dir., writ. Helen Black. Dir. phot. John Fedele. Prod. Michael Raso. Perf. Misty Mundae, Anoushka, Darian Caine, A. J. Khan. Unrated DVD. Seduction (ei Cinema), 2005. SC.
Erotic Obsessions. Dir. Madison Monroe. Writ. April White, Edward Gorsuch. Prod. Debra Nichols. Exec. prod. Marc Greenberg. Perf. Griffen Drew, Flower Edwards, John Crown, David Usher, Collin Hughes. MRG, 2001. TVMA. Cinemax. 25 Jan. 2004. SC.
An Erotic Vampire in Paris. Dir. Donald Farmer. Perf. Misty Mundae, Tina Krause ("Mia Copia"), William Hellfire. Unrated DVD. Artschiv (Seduction/ei Cinema), 2002. SC.
The Erotic Witch Project. Dir. John Bacchus. Prod. Michael Raso ("Michael Beckerman"). Perf. Darian Caine, Laurie Wallace. Unrated DVD. Seduction (ei Cinema), 1999. SC.
The Exhibitionist Files. Dir. Tom Lazarus. Writ. L. L. Thomaso (a.k.a. Tom Lazarus). Prod. Jennifer Byrne. Exec. prod. Kelley Cauthen. Perf. Catalina Larranaga, Rife Urquhart. Unrated VHS. Indigo (Playboy), 2002. SC.
The Exorcist. Dir. William Friedkin. 1973.
Exposed. Dir. Clinton Williams. Prod. Debra Nichols. Exec. prod. Marc Greenberg. Perf. Julia Kruis, Jezebelle Bond, Samuel Iam. MRG, 2001. SC.
Fallen Angels. Dir., prod. Alexander Gregory Hippolyte ("Gregory Dark"). 1985.
Fancy Lady. Dir. Nick Phillips (a.k.a. Steve Millard). Writ., perf. Uschi Digart ("Uschi

Digard"). 1971. Unrated DVD. Retro-Seduction (ei Cinema), 2006.
Fascination. Dir., prod. Chuck Vincent. 1980.
Faster, Pussycat! Kill! Kill! Dir., writ., prod. Russ Meyer. 1966.
Fast Lane to Malibu. Dir. Kelley Cauthen. Writ. Leland Zaitz. Prod. Jennifer Byrne. Music Nicholas Rivera. Perf. Steve Curtis, Tracy Ryan, Renee Rea, Kira Reed, Susan Featherly ("Marie West"), Nikki Fritz, Stephen Harvard. Indigo (Playboy), 2000. SC.
Fast Lane to Vegas. Dir. John Quinn. Writ. Leland Zaitz. Prod. Jennifer Byrne. Exec. Prod. Kelley Cauthen. Perf. Steve Curtis, Tracy Ryan ("Tracy Angeles"), Renee Rea, Tera Patrick, Kelli McCarty, Flower Edwards. R-rated VHS. Indigo (Playboy), 2000. SC.
Fast Times at Ridgemont High. Dir. Amy Heckerling. 1982.
Fatal Attraction. Dir. Adrian Lyne. Prod. Stanley Jaffe, Sherry Lansing. Perf. Michael Douglas, Glenn Close, Anne Archer. R-rated VHS. Paramount (Paramount Home Video), 1987.
Fatal Instinct. Dir. Carl Reiner. 1993.
Female Chauvinists. Dir. Jay Jackson. 1975.
Femalien. Dir., writ. Cybil Richards (a.k.a. Sybil Richards). Exec. prod. Pat Siciliano, Charles Band. Perf. Jacqueline Lovell, Vanessa Taylor ("Venesa Talor"), Everett Rodd, Kathleen Mazzotta. Unrated DVD. Surrender (Full Moon), 1996. SC.
Femme Fatale. Dir., writ. Brian De Palma. 2002.
Flesh for Olivia. Dir., writ. William Hellfire. Prod. Michael Raso ("Michael Beckerman"). Ed. Johnny Crash. Perf. Misty Mundae, Darian Caine, Julian Wells, A. J. Khan, Dean Paul. Factory 2000, 2002. After Hours/Seduction (ei Cinema), 2006. SC.
Forbidden. Dir. Robert Kubilos. Writ., prod. Eric Mittleman. Perf. Renee Rea, Tracy Ryan, Jason Schnuit. Sapphire Films (New City), 2001. SC.
Forbidden Highway. Dir., prod. Kelley Cauthen. Writ., prod. April White. Perf. Kira Reed, Mia Zottoli, Tracy Ryan, Francis Cobert. Cameo (Playboy), 1999. SC.
Forbidden Sins. Dir. Robert Angelo. Prod. Michael Feifer. Exec. prod. Marc Greenberg. Casting Robert Lombard. Music Herman Beeftink. Perf. Shannon Tweed, Amy Lindsay. Magic Hour (Columbia TriStar), 1998. SC.
French Peep Show. Dir. Russ Meyer. Prod. Peter DeCenzie. 1952.
Friend of the Family. Dir., writ. Edward Holzman. Writ. April Moskowitz. Prod. Andrew Garroni. Exec. prod. Walter Gernert. Perf. Lisa Boyle, Shauna O'Brien, Griffen Drew, C. T. Miller, Raelyn Saalman, Will Potter. R-rated VHS. Axis/New City (Triboro), 1995. SC.
"Galatea's Wish." SC featurette. Dir., writ. Thomas Patrick Smith. Prod. Dana Middleton. Exec. prod. Marc Greenberg, Jennifer Marchese. Perf. Michelangelo Kowalski, Allison Lewis, Lisa Verlo. *Love Street.* CPV, 1994. TVMA. Showtime. 18 Jan. 2004 (1:45–2:15 A.M.).
"The Games People Play." SC featurette. Dir. Peter Gathings Bunche. Writ. Barbara Parker. Prod. Ladd Vance. Exec. prod. Alan Bursteen, Marilyn Vance. Perf. Landon Hall, Bobby Johnston, Griffen Drew, Barak Schurr. *Erotic Confessions.* Vol. 4. Ministry of Film (New City), 1994. TVMA. MoreMAX. 7 Jan. 2004 (10–10:18 P.M.).
Gaslight. Dir. George Cukor. 1944.
The Girl Next Door. Dir. Luke Greenfield. 2004.
The Girl Who Shagged Me. Dir. Tom Moose. Writ. Andy Sawyer. Exec. prod. Michael Raso. Perf. Misty Mundae, Anoushka, Rob Taylor. Unrated "Super-Sexy Edition" DVD. Seduction/Viscera (ei Cinema), 2005. SC.
Girls Kissing Girls. Dir., writ., prod. Barbara Lee. 2003.
Gladiator Eroticvs: The Lesbian Warriors. Dir., writ. John Bacchus. Prod. Michael Raso ("Michael Beckerman"). Perf. Darian Caine, Misty Mundae, John Fedele. Seduction (ei Cinema), 2001. SC.

"Grading on a Curve." SC featurette. Dir. Jennifer Marchese. Writ. Laura Glenning-Nagle. Prod. Carla Diamond. Exec. prod. Marc Greenberg. Perf. Kendra Tucker, Elisabeth Imboden, Timothy DiPri. *Love Street.* TVMA. CPV, 1994. Showtime. 27 Jan. 2004 (2:35–3:05 A.M.).

"Grip Till It Hurts." SC featurette. Dir., writ. Julie Dash. Exec. prod. Elisa Rothstein. Perf. Siena Goines, Bonita Brisker, Lawrence LeJohn. *Women: Stories of Passion.* Alta Loma (Playboy), 1997. TVMA. Showtime. 14 Feb. 2004 (2:50–3:20 A.M.).

The Happy Hooker. Dir. Nicholas Sgarro. Perf. Lynn Redgrave. 1975.

The Happy Hooker Goes Hollywood. Dir. Alan Roberts. 1980.

Hardcore. Dir., writ. Paul Schrader. Prod. John Milius. 1979.

Hard Hunted. Dir. Christian Drew Sidaris. Prod., writ. Andy Sidaris. Prod. Arlene Sidaris. 1992.

Hard Ticket to Hawaii. Dir., writ. Andy Sidaris. Prod. Arlene Sidaris. Dir. phot. Howard Wexler. Perf. Hope Marie Carlton, Ronn Moss, Dona Speir. 1987. R-rated DVD. Malibu Bay, 2001.

Hellcats in High Heels. Dir. Justice Howard. 1997.

Hidden Obsession. Dir. John Stewart, 1992.

Hidden Obsessions. Dir. Andrew Blake. 1992.

Hideout in the Sun. Dir. Doris Wishman. 1960.

Hot Tub California. Dir. John Quinn. Writ. Leland Zaitz. Casting Anna Camille Miller. Exec. prod. Edward Holzman. Perf. Tracy Ryan, Angela Davies, Mia Zottoli, Al Wise. Cameo (Playboy), 1999. SC.

Hollywood Chainsaw Hookers. Dir., writ., prod. Fred Olen Ray. 1987.

Hollywood Hot Tubs. Dir. Chuck Vincent. Writ., prod. Mark Borde. Perf. Jewel Shepard. 1984.

Hollywood Hot Tubs 2: Educating Crystal. Dir. Kenneth Raich. Writ., prod. Mark Borde. Perf. Jewel Shepard. 1989.

Hollywood Sex Fantasy. Dir., prod. Kelley Cauthen. Prod. Jennifer Byrne. Writ. Leland Zaitz. Perf. Catalina Larranaga, Kelli McCarty, Flower Edwards, Jack Lincoln, Zak Harding, Tracy Ryan ("Tracy Angeles"). R-rated VHS. Indigo/Playboy (Universal), 2001. SC.

Hollywood Sins. Dir., prod. Edward Holzman. Prod. William Burke. Perf. Hal Hutton, Kim Dawson, Tracy Ryan, Mia Zottoli. R-rated VHS. Mystique (Playboy), 2000. SC.

"Homework." SC featurette. Dir. Lucas Riley. Prod. Marc Laurence, Diane Cornell. Exec. prod. Marc Greenberg. Perf. Angela Davies, Ava Vincent, Lane Anderson. *The Best Sex Ever.* TVMA. MRG, 2001. Cinemax. 9 Jan. 2004 (11:20–11:50 P.M.).

Hot Desires. Dir., prod. Mike Sedan. Prod. Chanda Fuller. Casting Robert Lombard. Perf. Eddie Jay, Chrissey Styler ("Kara Styler"), Kristin Kowalski. Hawaiian One, 2002. TVMA. Showtime. 25 Feb. 2004. SC.

House of Lies. Dir. David Stanley. 2001.

House of Love. Dir. Tom Lazarus. Writ. L. L. Thomaso (a.k.a. Tom Lazarus). Prod. Jennifer Byrne. Exec. prod. Kelley Cauthen. Perf. Tracy Ryan, Catalina Larranaga, Kelli McCarty, Peter Gaynor, Kira Reed, Paul Logan, Susan Featherly ("Marie West"), Mark Pellegrino ("Henry Taggert"). Unrated VHS. Indigo/Playboy (Universal), 2000. SC.

How Stella Got Her Groove Back. Dir. Kevin Rodney Sullivan. Writ. Terry McMillan. 1998.

I, a Woman. Dir. Mac Ahlberg. 1966. American release, 1968.

I Am Curious (Yellow). Dir. Vilgot Sjöman. 1967. American release, 1969.

The Ice Storm. Dir. Ang Lee. 1997.

I Like to Play Games. Dir. Moctezuma Lobato. Writ. David Keith Miller. Prod. Nick Zuvic, Vivian Mayhew. Music Herman Beeftink. Perf. Lisa Boyle, Ken Steadman, Jennifer

Burton. R-rated VHS. Cameo/Playboy (A-Pix), 1994. SC.
I Like to Play Games Too. Dir., writ., prod. Edward Holzman. Writ. David Keith Miller. Prod. William Burke. Casting Anna Camille Miller. Perf. Maria Ford, Bobby Johnston, Kim Dawson, Catalina Larranaga. Unrated DVD. Mystique/Playboy (Image), 1998. SC.
I Spit on Your Grave. Dir., writ., prod. Meir Zarchi. 1977.
Illegal in Blue. Dir., prod. Stu Segall. Writ. Noel Hynd. Perf. Stacey Dash, Dan Gauthier, Tammy Parks. Unrated VHS. Stu Segall Productions (Orion/MetToy), 1995. SC.
"Illicit Affairs." SC featurette. Dir. David Nicholas. Prod. Diane Cornell. Exec. prod. Marc Greenberg. Perf. Tane McClure, Kim Dawson, Daniel Anderson. *Nightcap.* MRG, 2000. TVMA. MoreMAX. 15 Jan. 2004 (9:40–10:10 P.M.).
Illicit Dreams. Dir. Andrew Stevens. Writ. Karen Kelly. Prod. Ashok Amritraj. Perf. Stevens, Shannon Tweed, Stella Stevens, Michelle Johnson, Rochelle Swanson, Joseph Cortese. Unrated VHS. Amritraj/Stevens (Republic), 1995. SC.
Ilsa, She-Wolf of the S.S. Dir. Don Edmonds. 1974.
I'm Watching You. Dir. Blain Brown. Prod. William Burke. Exec. prod. Edward Holzman. Perf. LoriDawn Messuri, Jacqueline Lovell. Mystique (Playboy), 1997. SC.
The Immoral Mr. Teas. Dir., writ., phot. Russ Meyer. Prod. Peter DeCenzie. Perf. Bill Teas, Ann Peters. 1959. R-rated VHS. Russ Meyer Films, 1996.
In Dangerous Company. Dir., prod. Ruben Preuss. Perf. Tracy Scoggins, Cliff DeYoung. R-rated VHS. Preuss Entertainment (Forum Home Video), 1988.
In Love. Dir., writ. Chuck Vincent. 1983.
In the Cut. Dir., writ. Jane Campion. 2003.
In the Realm of the Senses. Dir., writ. Nagisa Oshima. 1976.
Indecent Behavior. Dir. Lawrence Lanoff. Exec. prod. Marc Greenberg, Richard Goldberg. Perf. Shannon Tweed, Jan-Michael Vincent, Ken Steadman. Magic Hour (WEA), 1993. SC.
Indecent Behavior II. Dir. Carlo Gustaff. Exec. prod. Marc Greenberg, Richard Goldberg. Perf. Shannon Tweed, James Brolin, Rochelle Swanson, Craig Stepp, Nikki Fritz. Magic Hour (Atlantic Group), 1994. TVMA. Showtime. 4 Feb. 2004. SC.
Indecent Behavior III. Dir. Kelley Cauthen. Prod. Marc Laurence. Exec. prod. Marc Greenberg. Perf. Shannon Tweed, Doug Jeffery, Griffin Drew. Unrated VHS. Magic Hour (Warnervision), 1995. SC.
The Indelicate Balance. Dir. Joe Sarno. 1960.
Inga. Dir., writ. Joe Sarno. Perf. Marie Liljedahl. Cannon/Inskafilm, 1967. Cinemation, 1968. Unrated DVD. Retro-Seduction (ei Cinema), 2001.
Inn of the Red Dragon (a.k.a. *Red Dragon*). Dir. Brad Armstrong. Perf. Asia Carrera. 2002.
Intimacy. Dir., writ. Patrice Chéreau. 2001.
Intimate Moments (a.k.a. *Madame Claude 2*). Dir. François Mimet. 1981.
Invasion of the Bee Girls. Dir. Denis Sanders. Sequoia (Centaur), 1973.
Jade. Dir. William Friedkin. Writ. Joe Eszterhas. Perf. Linda Fiorentino, Angie Everhart. 1995.
"Jake's Story." SC featurette. Dir. Michael Karbelnikoff. Writ. Ed Silverstein. Exec. prod. Zalman King, Patricia Louisianna Knop, David Saunders. Perf. David Duchovny, Sheryl Lee. Showtime, 1992. *Red Shoe Diaries 4: Auto Erotica.* Unrated VHS anthology. Republic, 1994.
Janie. Dir. Roberta Findlay. 1970.
Jaws. Dir. Steven Speilberg. 1975.
"Kat Tails." SC featurette. Dir., writ., prod. Maricel Pagulayan. Writ. Larra Anderson. Exec.

prod. Elisa Rothstein. Perf. Trista Delamere, Kelly Galindo. *Women: Stories of Passion.* Alta Loma (Playboy), 1997. TVMA. Showtime. 27 Feb. 2004 (12:30–1:00 A.M.).

Killer Looks. Dir., writ., prod. Paul Thomas ("Toby Phillips"). Prod. Steven Hirsch. Casting Lori Cobe. Perf. Sara Suzanne Brown, Janine Lindemulder, Michael Artura. Unrated VHS. Cinnamon (Imperial), 1994. SC.

Kinky Kong. Dir., writ. John Bacchus. Dir. phot. Brett Piper. Exec. prod. Michael Raso. Perf. Darian Caine, Jackie Stevens, Sabrina Faire. Seduction (ei Cinema), 2006. SC.

The Kiss of Her Flesh. Dir., writ., prod. Michael Findlay. Prod. Roberta Findlay. 1968.

Lake Consequence. Dir. Rafael Eisenman. Writ., prod. Zalman King. Prod. Avram Butch Kaplan. Perf. Billy Zane, Joan Severance, May Karasun. Zalman King Company (Showtime), 1993. R-rated VHS. Republic, 1993.

The Little Shop of Horrors. Dir., prod. Roger Corman. 1960.

"Locked Up." SC featurette. Dir. Peter Gathings Bunche. Writ. Sahara Riley. Prod. Ladd Vance. Exec. prod. Marilyn Vance. Music Herman Beeftink. Perf. Raelyn Saalman. *Erotic Confessions.* Vol. 3. Ministry of Film (New City), 1995. TVMA. MoreMAX. 14 Jan. 2004 (10:40–11 P.M.).

Lord of the G-Strings: The Femaleship of the String. Dir., writ. Terry West. Prod. John Bacchus, Michael Raso ("Michael Beckerman"). Perf. Misty Mundae, Darian Caine, A. J. Khan, Michael Thomas, John Fedele. Unrated DVD. Seduction (ei Cinema), 2003. SC.

Lorna. Dir., writ., prod. Russ Meyer. Perf. Lorna Maitland, Hal Hopper, James Rucker, Mark Bradley. Eve Productions, 1964. Unrated DVD. Ventura, 2003.

Lost Highway. Dir. David Lynch. 1996.

Love and Bullets. Dir., prod. Veronica Hart (a.k.a. Jane Hamilton). 2004.

Love Camp 7. Dir. R.L. Frost. Writ., prod. Bob Cresse. 1968.

Love Games. Dir. Madison Monroe. Writ. J. L. Conners. Prod. Debra Nichols. Exec. prod. Marc Greenberg. Casting Robert Lombard. Perf. Venus, Paul Johnson, Flower Edwards, Sebastien Guy ("Scott Duke"). MRG, 2001. TVMA. Showtime. 20 Mar. 2004. SC.

Love Letters. Dir., writ. Amy Jones. Prod. Roger Corman. 1983.

Love Toy (1968). Dir., prod. Doris Wishman ("Louis Silverman").

The Lover. Dir., writ. Jean-Jacques Annaud. 1992.

Lover's Leap. Dir., prod. Paul Thomas ("Toby Phillips"). Perf. Sara Suzanne Brown, Craig Stepp, Dawna MacLaren. R-rated VHS. Cinnamon/Panther (Rocket), 1995. SC.

"The Lucky Bar." SC featurette. Dir. Adele Bertei-Cecchi. Prod. Shelly Strong. Exec. prod. Elisa Rothstein. Perf. Cece Tsou. *Women: Stories of Passion.* Alta Loma (Playboy), 1997. TVMA. Showtime. 9 Mar. 2004 (2–2:30 A.M.).

Luscious (a.k.a. *Vivid* [1997]). Dir., writ. Evan Georgiades. 1999.

Lust for Dracula. Dir., writ. Tony Marsiglia. Exec. prod. Michael Raso. Perf. Andrea Davis, Misty Mundae, Julian Wells, Darian Caine. Unrated director's cut. Seduction (ei Cinema), 2004. SC.

Lust for Laura. Dir. Joe Sarno. Prod. Michael Raso. Perf. Isadora Edison, John Fedele, A. J. Khan, Chelsea Mundae. Retro-Seduction (ei Cinema), 2005. SC.

Lustful Addiction. Dir. Nick Phillips (a.k.a. Steve Millard). 1969.

Lustful Addiction. Dir., writ., perf. Misty Mundae. Prod. Michael Raso ("Michael Beck"). Perf. Ruby LaRocca, Darian Caine. Retro-Seduction (ei Cinema), 2002. SC.

Malibu Express. Dir., writ., prod. Andy Sidaris. Dir. phot. Howard Wexler. Perf. Sybil Danning, Darby Hinton, John Alderman, Michael Andrews, Brett Clark, Linda Wiesmeier. R-rated VHS. Malibu Bay Films (MCA Home Video), 1984.

Mantis in Lace (a.k.a. *Lila: Mantis in Lace*). Dir. William Rotsler. Prod. Harry Novak. 1968.
The Mark of Zorro. Dir. Fred Niblo. Writ. Johnston McCulley. Writ., prod., perf. Douglas Fairbanks. 1920.
Married People, Single Sex. Dir., writ., prod. Mike Sedan. Perf. Chase Masterson, Josef Pilato. Miklen (Triboro), 1993. Rated R. Showtime. 19 Mar. 2004.
Married People, Single Sex II: For Better or Worse. Dir., writ., prod. Mike Sedan. Casting Lori Cobe. Perf. Craig Stepp, Monique Parent, Kathy Shower, Julie Strain, Tamara Landry, Tane McClure. Triboro, 1995. SC.
Marsha, the Erotic Housewife. Dir., prod. Don Davis. Perf. Marsha Jordan. Hollywood Cinema Associates. 1970. Unrated VHS. Something Weird, 2001.
Medium Cool. Dir., writ. Haskell Wexler. 1968.
"Mind's Eye." SC featurette. Dir., writ. Deirdre Fishel. Prod. Maricel Pagulayan. Exec. prod. Elisa Rothstein. Perf. Rothstein, Holley Chant, Joey Gian. *Women: Stories of Passion.* Women/Alta Loma (Playboy), 1997. TVMA. Showtime. 12 Mar. 2004 (2:05–2:35 A.M.).
Mirror Images. Dir. Alexander Gregory Hippolyte. Writ. Georges des Esseintes. Prod. Andrew Garroni. Perf. Delia Sheppard, Julie Strain, Jeff Conaway. Axis (Academy), 1991. SC.
Mirror Images II. Dir. Gregory Hippolyte. Perf. Shannon Whirry, Sara Suzanne Brown, Lauren Hays. Axis (Academy), 1993. SC.
Mistress Frankenstein. Dir. John Bacchus. Prod. Michael Raso ("Michael Beckerman"). Perf. John Fedele, Darian Caine, Debbie Rochon. Unrated DVD. Seduction (ei Cinema), 2000. SC.
Misty Mundae: Girl Seduction. Promotional documentary. Dir. William Hellfire. Dir., prod. Michael Raso ("Michael Beckerman"). Factory 2000/Seduction (ei Cinema), 2003.
Misty Mundae: Mummy Raider. Dir. Brian Paulin. Writ. Bruce Hallenbeck. Exec. prod. Michael Raso. Perf. Misty Mundae, Darian Caine. Seduction (ei Cinema), 2002. SC.
Model Lust. Dir. Frederick Morehouse. Writ. Connie Milton. Prod. Pat Siciliano. Dir. phot. Howard Wexler. Perf. Juliana Kinkaid, Diana Espen, Glen Meadows, Holly Hollywood, Mary Carey. Rosebud/Silhouette (New City), 2003. SC.
"Model Situation." SC featurette. Dir. Peter Gathings Bunche. Writ. Rick Bitzelberger. Prod. Ladd Vance. Exec. prod. Marilyn Vance. Music Herman Beeftink. Perf. Landon Hall, Mark Dalton. *Erotic Confessions.* Vol. 3. Ministry of Film (New City), 1995. TVMA. MoreMAX. 14 Jan. 2004 (10:25–10:40 P.M.).
The Model Solution. Dir., prod. Edward Holzman. Writ. L. Douglas Zajec. Perf. Sebastien Guy ("Scott Duke"), Jason Schnuit ("Dave Veleo"), Holly Hollywood, Regina Russell, Candace Washington, Jacy Andrews. R-rated VHS. Indigo (Playboy), 2001. SC.
Mona. Dir. Howard Ziehm. Prod. William Osco. 1970.
Mondo Rocco. Dir., writ., prod. Pat Rocco. 1970.
"Motel Magic." SC featurette. Dir. Valerie Landsburg. Prod. Tracy Paddock. Exec. prod. Elisa Rothstein. Perf. Sally Kirkland, Gabriella Hall. *Women: Stories of Passion.* Alta Loma (Playboy), 1997. TVMA. Showtime. 20 Mar. 2004 (3:30–4 A.M.).
Ms. 45. Dir. Abel Ferrara. 1981.
Mulholland Drive. Dir., writ. David Lynch. Prod. Mary Sweeney, Alan Sarde. Perf. Naomi Watts, Laura Elena Harring. R-rated DVD. Universal (StudioCanal), 2001.
My Tutor. Dir. George Bowers. Writ. Joe Roberts. Prod. Marilyn Tenser. Dir. phot. Mac

Ahlberg. Perf. Caren Kaye, Matt Lattanzi, Crispin Glover, Jewel Shepard, Kitten Natividad, Brioni Farrell, Katt Shea (uncredited). R-rated VHS. Crown (MCA), 1983.
Naked Obsession. Dir., writ. Dan Golden. Perf. William Katt, Maria Ford. 1990.
The Naked Venus. Dir. Edgar G. Ulmer. Prod. Gaston Hakim. Perf. Don Roberts, Patricia Conelle. Beaux Arts (Gaston Hakim), 1958. Unrated VHS. Something Weird, 2002.
The Naughty Stewardesses. Dir. Al Adamson. Prod. Samuel Sherman. 1973.
"New York Wildcats." SC featurette. Dir. Johnny Crash. Perf. Misty Mundae, Chelsea Mundae, Katie Jordon, John Fedele. 2002. Retro-Seduction (ei Cinema), 2005.
Night Call Nurses. Dir. Jonathan Kaplan. Prod. Julie Corman. Exec. prod. Roger Corman. 1972.
Night Eyes. Dir. Jag Mundhra. Writ. Andrew Stevens, Tom Citrano. Prod. Stevens, Ashok Amritraj. Perf. Stevens, Tanya Roberts, Larry Poindexter. Prism/Amritraj-Baldwin (Paramount), 1990.
Night Eyes 3. Dir., writ. Andrew Stevens. Prod. Ashok Amritraj. Exec. prod. Howard Baldwin. Perf. Stevens, Shannon Tweed, Tracy Tweed, Monique Parent. Unrated VHS. Sequel Productions (Prism), 1993. SC.
Night Rhythms. Dir. A. Gregory Hippolyte. Prod. Andrew Garroni. Exec. prod. Walter Gernert. Perf. Martin Hewitt, Delia Sheppard, Deborah Driggs, Julie Strain, Tracy Tweed, David Carradine. Unrated VHS. Axis (Imperial), 1992. SC.
The Notorious Cleopatra. Dir. Peter Perry ("A. P. Stootsberry"). Prod. Harry Novak. Global Pictures (Boxoffice International), 1970. Unrated DVD. Something Weird, 2002.
Novel Desires. Dir. Lawrence Unger. Writ. Dana Kelley. Ed. Kelley Cauthen. Prod. Richard Goldberg. Exec. prod. Marc Greenberg. Perf. Tyler Gains, Caroline Monteith, Lysa Hayland. CPV, 1991. TVMA. Showtime Too. 14 Jan. 2004. SC.
Olga's House of Shame. Dir. Joseph Mawra. Prod. George Weiss. 1964.
The Other Woman. Dir. Jag Mundhra. Writ. Georges des Esseintes. Prod. Alexander Gregory Hippolyte, Andrew Garroni. Exec. prod. Walter Gernert. Perf. Lee Anne Beaman, Craig Stepp. Unrated VHS. Axis (Imperial), 1992. SC.
Passion's Peak. Dir. John Quinn. Writ. Heather Carson, Edward Holzman. Prod. Kelly Andrea Rubin. Perf. Kelli McCarty, Bobby Johnston, Devinn Lane, Paul Logan, Monique Parent ("Scarlet Johansing"), Flower Edwards, Sebastien Guy. Unrated VHS. Indigo (Playboy), 2000. SC.
Peeping Tom. Dir. Michael Powell, 1960.
The People vs. Larry Flynt. Dir. Milos Forman. 1996.
Perfectly Legal. Dir. Cameron Davis (a.k.a. Lane Shefter). Prod. Jennifer Byrne. Exec. prod. Kelley Cauthen. Music Nicholas Rivera. Perf. Lauren Hays, Monique Parent ("Scarlet Johansing"), Tom Montreal, Edward Johnson, Rife Urquhart, Beverly Lynne. TVMA. Indigo (Playboy), 2002. Playboy TV. 1 Feb. 2004. SC.
Persona. Dir. Ingmar Bergman. 1966.
Personals 2: casualsex.com. Dir., prod. Kelley Cauthen. Writ. April White, Edward Gorsuch. Prod. Jennifer Byrne. Perf. Beverly Lynne, Christopher John Kapanke, Mia Zottoli ("Ava Lake"), Candace Washington, Tom Montreal, Eddie Jay. Indigo (Playboy), 2001. SC.
Picasso Trigger. Dir., writ. Andy Sidaris. Prod. Arlene Sidaris. Dir. phot. Howard Wexler. Perf. Steve Bond, Hope Marie Carlton, Dona Speir, Roberta Vasquez. Andy Sidaris Company, 1988. R-rated DVD. Malibu Bay, 2001.
A Place Called Truth. Dir. Rafael Eisenman. Writ., prod. Zalman King. Perf. Audie England, Jacqueline Lovell, Kira Reed, Anthony Addabbo. Zalman King (Playboy), 1998.

R-rated DVD. MGM Home Entertainment, 1999.
Play-Mate of the Apes. Dir., writ. John Bacchus. Exec. prod. Michael Raso ("Michael Beckerman"). Perf. Misty Mundae, Darian Caine, Debbie Rochon, Anoushka, John Bacchus, Shelby Taylor, Sharon Engert. Unrated DVD. Seduction (ei Cinema), 2002. SC.
Play Time. Dir., prod. Dale Trevillion. Writ. Mary Ellen Hanover. Prod. Nick Zuvic. Perf. Monique Parent, Jennifer Burton, Craig Stepp, David Elliott, Julie Strain, Tammy Parks. Cameo (Playboy), 1994. Unrated VHS. Triboro, 1995. SC.
Please Don't Eat My Mother. Dir., prod. Carl Monson. 1971.
Pleasures of a Woman. Dir. Nick Phillips (a.k.a. Steve Millard). 1972.
Pleasures of a Woman. Dir. Ted Crestview. Perf. Julian Wells, Darian Caine. Retro-Seduction (ei Cinema), 2002. SC.
Poison Ivy 2: Lily. Dir. Anne Goursaud. Writ. Chloe King. Prod. Paul Hertzberg, Catalaine Knell. Perf. Alyssa Milano. R-rated VHS. Turner (New Line), 1995. SC.
Porky's. Dir., writ., prod. Bob Clark. 1981.
Preppies. Dir., writ., prod. Chuck Vincent. Perf. Dennis Drake, Katt Shea, Linda Wiesmeier. R-rated VHS. Playboy/Platinum (Vestron Video), 1982.
Pretty as a Picture: The Art of David Lynch. Dir., prod. Toby Keeler. 1997.
Pretty Woman. Dir. Garry Marshall. 1990.
The Prince and the Nature Girl. Dir., writ., prod. Doris Wishman. 1965.
Private Duty Nurses. Dir., writ., prod. George Armitage. Exec. prod. Roger Corman. 1971.
Private Resort. Dir. George Bowers. 1985.
Private School. Dir. Noel Black. 1983.
The Profession. SC serial. Dir. Alexander Gregory Hippolyte ("Gregory Dark"). Perf. Kira Reed. Playboy, 1998.
Psycho. Dir. Alfred Hitchcock. 1960.
Red Shoe Diaries. Dir., writ., prod. Zalman King. Writ. Patricia Lousianna Knop. Prod. Rafael Eisenman, David Saunders. Perf. David Duchovny, Brigitte Bako, Billy Wirth, Anna Karin. Republic, 1990. First release: Showtime, 1992. Unrated DVD. Showtime, 2001.
The Red Shoes. Dir., writ., prod. Michael Powell, Emeric Pressburger. 1947.
Red Sonja. Dir. Richard Fleischer. 1985.
Reform School Girls. Dir. Tom DeSimone. 1986.
The Regina Pierce Affair. Dir. Madison Monroe. Writ. Louise Monclair. Prod. Pat Siciliano. Perf. Dan Hayden, C. C. Costigan, Holly Sampson, Amber Newman, Everett Rodd. Unrated director's cut. Surrender (Full Moon), 2000. SC.
Return to Two Moon Junction. Dir. Farhad Mann. 1983.
Romance. Dir., writ. Catherine Breillat. Prod. Jean-François Lepetit. Perf. Caroline Ducey. R-rated VHS. Flach (Trimark), 1999.
"Room 1503." SC featurette. Dir., writ. Cat X. Prod. Maricel Pagulayan. Exec. prod. Elisa Rothstein. Perf. Lisa Welti, Kendahl Thompson, Jack Lincoln ("Marklen Kennedy"). *Women: Stories of Passion.* Alta Loma (Playboy), 1997. TVMA. Showtime. 10 Mar. 2004 (1–1:30 A.M.).
Roommates. Dir., writ., prod. Chuck Vincent. 1981.
Roxanna. Dir. Nick Phillips (a.k.a. Steve Millard). 1970.
Roxanna. Dir. Ted Crestview. Prod. Michael Raso ("Michael Beck"). Perf. Misty Mundae, Darian Caine, Katie Jordon. Retro-Seduction (ei Cinema), 2002. SC.
"Runway." SC featurette. Dir. Rafael Eisenman. Writ. Melanie Finn, Zalman King. Exec. prod. King. Perf. Amber Smith, Daniel Blasco, Udo Kier. Showtime, 1993. *Red Shoe*

Diaries 7: Burning Up. Unrated VHS anthology. Republic, 1997.
"Safe Sex." SC featurette. Dir. Zalman King. Writ. Melanie Finn, Henry Cobbold. Exec. prod. King, Patricia Louisianna Knop. Perf. Steven Bauer, Joan Severance. Showtime, 1992. *Red Shoe Diaries 2: Double Dare.* Unrated VHS anthology. Republic, 1993.
Sapphire Girls. Dir. Joe Navilluso. Writ. Ted Newsom. Prod. Pat Siciliano. Perf. Mary Carey, Elizarah, Jodie Moore. Rosebud/Silhouette (Ambrosia/Blockbuster), 2003. SC.
Satan in High Heels. Dir. Jerald Intrator. 1962.
Savage Beach. Dir., writ. Andy Sidaris. Prod. Arlene Sidaris. Dir. phot. Howard Wexler. 1989.
Der Schlachter (a.k.a. *Le Boucher* or *The Butcher*). Dir. Claude Chabrol. 1970.
Score. Dir. Radley Metzger. Prod. Ava Leighton. 1972.
Screaming Dead. Dir., writ. Brett Piper. Prod. Michael Raso. Perf. Misty Mundae, Joseph Farrell, Heidi Kristoffer. R-rated DVD. Shock-O-Rama (ei Cinema), 2004.
"Screwed Up." SC featurette. Dir., prod. Gary Orona. Writ. A. G. Lawrence. Exec. prod. Alan Bursteen, Paul Hertzberg. Casting Anna Miller. Perf. Ava Vincent. *Hotel Erotica.* Cinetel/New City, 2003. TVMA. MoreMAX. 27 Jan. 2004 (10:35–11:05 P.M.).
Season Three Finale. TVMA episode of *7 Lives Xposed.* Dir., writ., prod. Tom Lazarus. Perf. Slide, Devinn Lane, Jools. Playboy, 2003. Playboy TV. 1 Feb. 2004 (9–10 A.M.).
Secret Games. Dir. Alexander Gregory Hippolyte. Writ. Georges des Esseintes. Prod. Andrew Garroni. Perf. Martin Hewitt, Michele Brin, Delia Sheppard, Monique Parent. Axis, 1991. Unrated VHS. Imperial, 1992. SC.
Secret Games 3. Dir. Gregory Hippolyte. Prod. Andrew Garroni. Exec. prod. Walter Gernert. Perf. Rochelle Swanson, May Karasun, Tammy Parks. Axis (Academy), 1994. SC.
The Secret Sex Lives of Romeo and Juliet. Dir. Peter Perry ("A. P. Stootsberry"). Prod. Harry Novak. Perf. Deirdre Nelson ("Dicora Carse"), Stuart Lancaster, William Rotsler ("Shannon Carse"). Global (Boxoffice International), 1969. Unrated DVD. Something Weird, 2002.
The Seduction of Inga. Dir., writ. Joe Sarno. Prod. Vernon Becker. Perf. Mari Liljedahl. Inskafilm, 1969. Cinemation, 1972. R-rated DVD. Retro-Seduction (ei Cinema), 2004.
The Seduction of Misty Mundae. Dir., writ., prod. Michael Raso. Writ. John Fedele. Perf. Misty Mundae, Julian Wells, Mario Duchi. Seduction (ei Cinema), 2005. SC.
Sensual Friends. Dir. Jay Madison. Writ. George Ayvas. Prod. Michael Feifer. Exec. prod. Marc Greenberg. Perf. Brandy Davis, Griffin Drew, Bobby Johnston, Kim Dawson. MRG, 2001. R-rated feature. Showtime. 6 Feb. 2004. SC.
Seven. Dir., writ., prod. Andy Sidaris. 1979.
Sex. Dir. Michael Ninn. Prod. Veronica Hart. 1994.
Sex Appeal. Dir., writ., prod. Chuck Vincent. Perf. Louie Bonanno, Candida Royalle, Veronica Hart. R-rated VHS. Platinum (Vestron), 1986.
"Sexposé." TVMA episode of *Night Calls.* Perf. Juli Ashton, Tiffany Granath. Playboy, 2003. Playboy TV. 31 Jan. 2004 (1:30–2 P.M.).
Sex, Secrets, and Betrayals. Dir. Dave Franks. Writ. Samm Croft. Prod. Debra Nichols. Exec. prod. Marc Greenberg. Casting Robert Lombard. Perf. Nikki Fritz, Daniel Anderson, Angela Davies, Jezebelle Bond. MRG, 2001. TVMA. Showtime. 10 Mar. 2004. SC.
Sex, Secrets, and Lies. Dir. Stan Allen. Writ. Elena Shuman. Prod. Debra Nichols. Exec. prod. Marc Greenberg. Perf. Randy Spears, Amber Newman, Edward Johnson, Julia Parton. R-rated VHS. MRG (Replay), 2002. SC.
Sexual Magic. Dir. Edward Holzman. Writ. Adele Bertei-Cecchi ("Eve Libertine"). Prod.

Kelly Andrea Rubin. Perf. Amber Newman, Jack Lincoln ("Jared Lincoln"), Jacy Andrews, Jezebelle Bond, Teanna Kai, Nikki Fairchild. Indigo (Playboy), 2001. SC.

Sexual Malice. Dir., writ. Jag Mundhra. Prod. Andrew Garroni. Exec. prod. Alexander Gregory Hippolyte, Walter Gernert. Casting Lori Cobe. Perf. Diana Barton, Doug Jeffery, Don Swayze, Samantha Phillips, Edward Albert, Kathy Shower. Axis (A-Pix), 1994. SC.

Sexual Predator (a.k.a. *Dangerous Desires* and *Last Cry*). Dir. Robert Angelo, Rob Spera. Writ. Ed Silverstein. Prod. Diane Cornell, Richard Goldberg. Exec. prod. Marc Greenberg. Perf. Angie Everhart, Richard Grieco, Gabriella Hall. Magic Hour/MRG, 2001. TVMA. Cinemax. 19 Jan. 2004. SC.

The Sexy Adventures of Van Helsing. Dir. phot. John Fedele. Writ. Bruce Hallenbeck, Helen Black. Perf. Darian Caine, Erika Smith, A. J. Khan, Andrea Davis. Prod. Michael Raso. Seduction (ei Cinema), 2004. SC.

Sexy American Idle. Dir. John Fedele. Writ. Fedele, Julian Wells. Exec. prod. Michael Raso, Jeff Faoro. Perf. Wells, Misty Mundae, C. J. DiMarsico, Anoushka, A. J. Khan, Darian Caine. Unrated DVD. Seduction (ei Cinema), 2004. SC.

Shock-O-Rama. Dir., writ. Brett Piper. Exec. prod. Michael Raso. Perf. Misty Mundae, Julian Wells, A. J. Khan. Shock-O-Rama (ei Cinema), 2006.

Showgirl Murders. Dave Payne ("Gene Hertel"). Writ. Christopher Wooden. Prod. Darin Spillman. Perf. Maria Ford, Matt Preston, Nikki Fritz, Doug Jeffery ("Jeffrey Douglas"). Unrated VHS. Califilm (Concorde–New Horizons), 1995. SC.

The Sign of the Cross. Dir. Cecil B. DeMille. 1932.

Sin in the Suburbs. Dir. Joe Sarno. 1962.

Sin Sisters. Dir. Tony Marsiglia. Prod. Michael Raso. Perf. Chelsea Mundae, Misty Mundae, Andrea Davis, Julian Wells. Director's cut DVD. Seduction (ei Cinema), 2003. SC.

Sinful. Dir., writ. Tony Marsiglia. Exec. prod. Michael Raso. Perf. Misty Mundae, Erika Smith. Seduction (ei Cinema), 2006.

Sinful Deeds. Dir. Dante Giove. Writ. Steve Martel. Prod. Debra Nichols. Exec. prod. Marc Greenberg. Casting Robert Lombard. Perf. Syren, Frank Harper, Brad Bartram, John Crown. MRG, 2001. TVMA. Showtime. 21 Jan. 2004. SC.

Sizzle. Dir. Chuck Vincent. 1980.

Slammer Girls. Dir., writ., prod. Chuck Vincent. 1987.

The Slaughter. Dir., writ. Michael, Roberta Findlay. 1970. (Unreleased basis for *Snuff.*)

Sliver. Dir. Phillip Noyce. Writ. Joe Eszterhas. 1993.

The Slumber Party Massacre. Dir., prod. Amy Jones. 1982.

Smooth Operator. Dir. Kelley Cauthen. Prod. Marc Laurence. Exec. prod. Marc Greenberg. Perf. Grace Nichols, Doug Jeffery, Jay Richardson, Tammy Parks. Magic Hour, 1995. SC.

Snuff. Dir., writ. Michael, Roberta Findlay. Prod. Allan Shackleton. 1976.

The Solitary Sin. Dir. Frederick Sullivan. 1918.

Some Nudity Required: The Naked Truth Behind Hollywood's B-Movies. Documentary. Dir., writ., prod. Odette Springer. Only Child, 1998. Unrated VHS. New Video, 1999.

Sorority Babes in the Slimeball Bowl-O-Rama. Dir., prod. David DeCoteau, 1988.

SpiderBabe. Dir. Johnny Crash. Prod. John Bacchus, Michael Raso. Perf. Misty Mundae, Julian Wells, Darian Caine. Unrated DVD. Seduction (ei Cinema), 2003. SC.

Spider-Man. Dir. Sam Raimi. 2002.

Stacey. Dir., writ., prod. Andy Sidaris. 1973.

Star Struck (a.k.a. *Deception*). Dir. Byron Werner. Writ. Stephen Johnston. Prod. Mark

Boot, Scarlett Pettyjohn, Emmanuel Itier. Perf. Nero Campbell, Amber Smith, Ursula Weiss. Unrated VHS. Santelmo/Red Violet (Avalanche), 2000. SC.
Star Wars. Dir., writ., prod. George Lucas. 1977.
Starlet! Dir. Richard Kanter. Writ., prod. David Friedman. Prod. William Allen Castleman. Perf. Deirdre Nelson, Stuart Lancaster, John Alderman, Kathi Cole, Sherri Mann. EVI, 1969. Unrated VHS. Something Weird, 2001.
Staying on Top. Dir., prod. John Quinn. Writ. Kristi Borgeous. Prod. Jennifer Byrne. Perf. Holly Sampson, Danny Pape, Mia Zottoli ("Ava Lake"), Angela Davies, Holly Hollywood. R-rated VHS. Indigo (Playboy), 2001. SC.
The Stewardesses. Dir., writ., prod. Alf Silliman, Jr. 1969.
Stigmata. Dir. Rupert Wainwright. Writ. Tom Lazarus. 1999.
The Story of Lady Chatterley (a.k.a. *The Loves of Lady Chatterley*). Dir. Lorenzo Onorati ("Frank De Niro"/"Pasqualino Fanetti"), 1989.
The Story of O. Dir. Just Jaeckin. 1975.
Straw Dogs. Dir., writ. Sam Peckinpah. 1971.
Strike a Pose. Dir., prod. Dean Hamilton. Writ. Riley Hays. Exec. prod. Marc Greenberg. Music Tane McClure. Perf. Robert Eastwick, Michele Brin ("Michele Lamothe"), Tamara Landry. Moving Forward (CPV), 1993. R-rated feature. Showtime. 9 Jan. 2004. SC.
Striporama. Dir., prod. Jerald Intrator. Dir. John Carroll. Writ. Alan Bodian. Perf. Georgia Sothern, Vicki Lynn, Lili St. Cyr, Betty Page ("Bettie Page"), Sally Rand. Venus Productions, 1953. Unrated VHS. Fine Arts, 1996.
Stripped to Kill. Dir. Katt Shea. Prod. Andy Ruben. 1987.
Stripped To Kill II. Dir. Katt Shea Ruben. Prod. Andy Ruben. Exec. prod. Roger Corman. Perf. Maria Ford. Concorde, 1988. R-rated DVD. Concorde–New Horizons, 2003.
Striptease. Dir., writ., prod. Andrew Bergman. 1996.
Student Affairs. Dir., writ., prod. Chuck Vincent. Perf. David Friedman. 1987.
The Student Nurses. Dir., prod. Stephanie Rothman. Exec. prod. Roger Corman. Perf. Brioni Farrell, Barbara Leigh. New World, 1970. R-rated DVD. Concorde–New Horizons, 2003.
The Student Teachers. Dir. Jonathan Kaplan. Prod. Julie Corman. 1973.
Suburban Pagans. Dir. William Rotsler ("Shannon Carse"). Exec. prod. Harry Novak. 1968.
Summer School Teachers. Dir., writ. Barbara Peters. Prod. Julie Corman. 1975.
Summer with Monika. Dir. Ingmar Bergman. 1953.
Superchick. Dir. Ed Forsyth. Writ. Cary Crutcher. Prod. John Burrows. Perf. Joyce Jillson, Candy Samples, Uschi Digart, John Carradine. Crown, 1973. R-rated DVD. Rhino, 2002.
Swedish Wildcats (a.k.a. *Every Afternoon*). Dir., writ. Joe Sarno. Prod., writ. Vernon Becker. Perf. Diana Dors, Cia Löwgren. Unicorn (Sherpix), 1972. R-rated DVD. Retro-Seduction (ei Cinema), 2005.
The Swinging Cheerleaders. Dir. Jack Hill. 1974.
Tales of Erotica (a.k.a. *Erotic Tales*). Anthology of four featurettes. Dir. Susan Seidelman ("The Dutch Master"), Ken Russell ("The Insatiable Mrs. Kirsch"), Melvin Van Peebles ("Vroom Vroom Vroom"), Bob Rafelson ("Wet"). Exec. prod. Regina Ziegler. Regina Ziegler Filmproduktion, 1994. R-rated VHS. Vidmark (Trimark), 1997.
Talk Sex. Dir. Dan Hyduk. Writ. Bill Dumas, Marc Leader. Prod. Kelly Andrea Rubin. Exec. prod. Edward Holzman. Perf. Kelli McCarty, Bobby Johnston, Tom Montreal, Renee Rea, Devinn Lane, Jezebelle Bond. R-rated VHS. Indigo (Playboy), 2001. SC.

Talking Walls. Dir., writ. Stephen Verona. Perf. Sybil Danning. 1987.
Teaserama. Dir., prod. Irving Klaw. Perf. Tempest Storm, Vicki Lynn. 1955.
Tell Me No Lies (a.k.a. *In the Midnight Hour*). Dir. Emmanuel Itier. Writ. Stephen Johnston, Erik Tomakin. Prod. Scarlett Pettyjohn. Exec. prod. Mark Boot. Perf. Amber Smith. R-rated VHS. Red Violet (Santelmo), 2000. SC.
Thelma and Louise. Dir., prod. Ridley Scott. 1991.
There's Something About Mary. Dir., writ., prod. Bobby Farrelly and Peter Farrelly. 1998.
Therese and Isabelle. Dir., prod. Radley Metzger. 1968.
This Nude World. Dir., prod. Michael Mindlin. 1932.
Through a Glass Darkly. Dir., writ. Ingmar Bergman. 1961.
Titanic. Dir., writ., prod. James Cameron. 1997.
Titanic 2000. Dir., prod. John Fedele. Writ., prod. Michael Raso. Perf. Tammy Parks, Tina Krause. Seduction (ei Cinema), 1999. SC.
Tomcat: Dangerous Desires (a.k.a. *Dangerous Desires*). Dir., writ. Paul Donovan. Perf. Richard Grieco, Maryam d'Abo. 1993.
Totally Exposed. Dir. Boots Rakely. Prod. Richard Goldberg. Exec. prod. Marc Goldberg. Perf. Kelli Konop, Tina Bockrath, Mark Jackson. CPV, 1991. SC.
The Touch of Her Flesh. Dir., writ., prod., perf. Michael Findlay ("Julian Marsh"). Prod., perf. Roberta Findlay ("Anna Riva"). Perf. Suzanne Marre, Peggy Steffans. Riva Marsh (American Film Distributing). 1967. Unrated DVD. Something Weird, 2003.
Tropical Heat. Dir., writ. Jag Mundhra. Writ. Michel Potts. Prod. Ashok Amritraj. Perf. Rick Rossovich, Maryam d'Abo, Lee Anne Beaman. Metro (Prism), 1993. SC.
Two Moon Junction. Dir., writ. Zalman King. Prod. Donald Borchers. Perf. Sherilyn Fenn, Richard Tyson, Martin Hewitt. Lorimar, 1988. R-rated DVD. Columbia TriStar, 2000.
Twogether. Dir., writ., prod. Andrew Chiaramonte. Perf. Nick Cassavetes. 1992.
Ultimate Taboo. Dir. Paul Thomas ("Toby Phillips"). Writ. Penny Antine. Prod. Steven Hirsch. Perf. Ginger Lynn Allen, Kim Dawson. R-rated VHS. Cinnamon (Ventura), 1995. SC.
The Unashamed. Dir. Allen Stuart. 1938.
Undercover (a.k.a. *Undercover Heat*). Dir. Gregory Hippolyte. Prod. Andrew Garroni. Exec. prod. Walter Gernert. Perf. Athena Massey. Axis (A-Pix), 1995. SC.
Unfaithful. Dir., prod. Adrian Lyne. 2002.
Vampire Seduction. Dir. John Bacchus. Seduction (ei Cinema), 1998.
Varietease. Dir., prod. Irving Klaw. Perf. Vicki Lynn, Betty Page ("Bettie Page"). 1954.
Visions of Passion. Dir. phot. Howard Wexler. Prod. Pat Siciliano. Perf. Mia Zottoli ("Ava Lake"), Regina Russell, Glenn Meadows, Everett Rodd. Rosebud (Silhouette), 2003. SC.
Vixen! Writ., dir., prod. Russ Meyer. 1968.
Voices of Desire. Dir. Chuck Vincent ("Mark Ubell"). 1970.
"Voodoo." SC featurette. Dir. Nandi Bowe. Writ. Robin Claire. Prod. Sonya Burres. Exec. prod. Elisa Rothstein. Perf. Daphnee Duplaix, Leroy Edwards. *Women: Stories of Passion.* Women Productions (Playboy), 1997. TVMA. Showtime. 16 Mar. 2004 (2–2:30 A.M.).
"Voodoun Blues." Featurette. Dir., writ., prod., perf. Misty Mundae. ei Cinema, 2004.
Voyeur Confessions. Dir. Tom Lazarus. Writ. L. L. Thomas (a.k.a. Tom Lazarus). Prod. Jennifer Byrne. Exec. prod. John Quinn. Music Matt Lazarus. Perf. Catalina Larranaga, Christopher Kapanke, Flower Edwards. R-rated VHS. Indigo (Playboy), 2001. SC.
W.A.R. (Women Against Rape). Dir., writ. Raphael Nussbaum. 1987.

Watch Me. Dir., writ. Lipo Ching. Prod. Sonya Burres ("Samantha Kash"). Perf. Jennifer Burton, Kehli O'Byrne (a.k.a. Kelly Burns). Casting Lori Cobe. Unrated VHS. Cameo/Playboy (Triboro), 1996. SC.

When Will I Be Loved. Dir. James Toback. 2004.

White Palace. Dir. Luis Mandoki. Perf. James Spader, Susan Sarandon. 1990.

White Slaves of Chinatown. Dir., writ. Joseph Mawra. Prod. George Weiss. 1964.

White Wife, Black Cock 2. Dir. Xavier. 2003.

Wicked Sins. Dir. Frank Carson. Writ. Barbara Fix. Prod. Debra Nichols. Exec. prod. Marc Greenberg. Casting Robert Lombard. Perf. Yvette Faulkner, Brad Bartram, Victoria Style, Justin Kyle, Samm Croft. MRG, 2001. TVMA. Showtime. 22 Mar. 2004. SC.

Wicked Temptations. Dir. Eric Gibson. Writ. Thomas K. Nash. Prod. Debra Nichols. Exec. prod. Marc Greenberg. Casting Robert Lombard. Perf. Monique Parent ("Scarlet Johansing"), Daniel Anderson, Keri Windsor, Chip Albert, Angelica Sin. MRG, 2001. TVMA. MoreMAX. 23 Jan. 2004. SC.

Wild Cactus. Dir., writ. Jag Mundhra. Prod. Alan Bursteen. Casting Lori Cobe. Perf. David Naughton, India Allen, Kathy Shower, Anna Karin. Unrated VHS. Imperial, 1993. SC.

Wild Orchid. Dir. Zalman King. Writ. Patricia Lousianna Knop, King. 1990.

Wild Orchid II: Two Shades of Blue. Dir., writ. Zalman King. Prod. Rafael Eisenman. 1992.

Wild Strawberries. Dir., writ. Ingmar Bergman. 1957.

Wild Things. Dir. John McNaughton. 1998.

Wild Things: Diamonds in the Rough. Dir. Jay Lowi. Writ. Andy Hurst, Ross Helford. Prod. Marc Bienstock. Exec. prod. Marc Greenberg, Richard Goldberg. Mainline, 2005.

Wildly Available. Dir., prod. Michael Nolin. 1996.

Wimps. Dir., writ., prod. Chuck Vincent. Perf. Louie Bonanno, Veronica Hart. 1986.

Witchbabe: The Erotic Witch Project III. Dir., writ. Terry West. Prod. Michael Raso ("Michael Beckerman"), John Bacchus. Perf. Laurie Wallace, Darian Caine, Misty Mundae, Debbie Rochon, Julian Wells, John Fedele. Unrated DVD. Seduction (ei Cinema), 2001. SC.

Without a Stitch. Dir. Annelise Meineche. 1968.

Women in Cages. Dir. Gerardo de Leon. Prod. Roger Corman. 1971.

Word of Mouth. Dir. Tom Lazarus. Writ. L. L. Thomaso (a.k.a. Tom Lazarus). Prod. April White. Exec. prod. Kelley Cauthen. Perf. Catalina Larranaga, Mark Pellegrino ("Robert Rand"), LoriDawn Messuri. Unrated VHS. Mystique (Playboy), 1999. SC.

"You Have the Right to Remain Silent." SC featurette. Dir. Zalman King. Writ. King, Rafael Eisenman, Henry Cobbold. Exec. prod. King, Patricia Louisianna Knop, David Saunders. Perf. Denise Crosby, Robert Knepper. Showtime, 1992. *Red Shoe Diaries 2: Double Dare.* Unrated VHS anthology. Republic, 1993.

Young and Seductive. Dir. Lucas Riley. Writ. April White, Edward Gorsuch. Prod. Debra Nichols. Exec. prod. Marc Greenberg. Casting Robert Lombard. Perf. Julian Wells, Robert Donovan, David Usher, Dru Berrymore, Felony. MRG, 2003. TVMA. Showtime. 4 Mar. 2004. SC.

Young Lady Chatterley. Dir., writ., prod. Alan Roberts. Perf. Harlee McBride. 1977.

Young Lady Chatterley II (a.k.a. *Private Property*). Dir., prod. Alan Roberts. Writ. Anthony Williams. Perf. Harlee McBride, Brett Clark, Sybil Danning, Steven Kean Matthews, Adam West. Park Lane (Playboy), 1985. Unrated VHS. Lion's Gate, 1988.

The Young Nurses. Dir. Clint Kimbrough. Writ. Howard Cohen. Prod. Julie Corman. 1973.

Young Nurses in Love. Dir., prod. Chuck Vincent. Perf. Annie Sprinkle, Veronica Hart. 1987.

Works Cited

Allen, Robert. *Horrible Prettiness: Burlesque and American Culture.* Chapel Hill: U of North Carolina P, 1991.
Allen, Robert, and Douglas Gomery. *Film History: Theory and Practice.* New York: Knopf, 1985.
Altman, Rick. *Film/Genre.* London: British Film Institute, 1999.
Andrews, David. "Convention and Ideology in the Contemporary Softcore Feature: The Sexual Architecture of *House of Love.*" *Journal of Popular Culture* 38.1 (Aug. 2004): 5–33.
———. "Just One of 'the Lesbian Vampire Guys': A Conversation with Seduction Cinema's Michael Raso." *Bridge* 13 (Dec. 2004/Jan. 2005): 31–37.
———. "One Filmmaker's 'Personal Journey' into the World of Soft-Focus: A Conversation with Playboy's Tom Lazarus." *Bridge* 12 (Oct./Nov. 2004): 26–32.
———. "An Oneiric Fugue: The Various Logics of *Mulholland Drive.*" *Journal of Film and Video* 56.1 (Spring 2004): 25–40.
Anonymous. Unsigned rev. of *Star Struck* (n.d.): 1–2. 23 Jun. 2004. <http://www.sreviews.com/starstruck.htm>.
Armstrong, Rod. "Zalman King: The Sultan of Soft-Core Speaks." Interv. Reel.com (2003): 1–6. 21 Jun. 2003. <http://www.reel.com/reel.asp?node=features/interviews/king>.
Atkins, Thomas, ed. *Sexuality in the Movies.* Bloomington: Indiana UP, 1975.
Backstein, Karen. "Soft Love: The Romantic Vision of Sex on the Showtime Network." *Television and New Media* 2.4 (Nov. 2001): 303–17.
Baldwin, Thomas, and D. Stevens McVoy. *Cable Communication.* Englewood Cliffs, N.J.: Prentice-Hall, 1983.
Barthes, Roland. "Striptease." 1955. In *A Roland Barthes Reader.* Ed. and intro. Susan Sontag. 1982. New York: Hill and Wang, 1998. 85–88.
Bauder, David. "TV Reacts to Flashy Halftime Routine." *Chicago Tribune* 6 Feb. 2004, sec. 1: 15.

Bazin, André. *What Is Cinema?* Vol. 1. Trans. Hugh Gray. Berkeley: University of California Press, 1967.
Beggan, James, and Scott Allison. "Tough Women in the Unlikeliest of Places: The Unexpected Toughness of the *Playboy* Playmate." *Journal of Popular Culture* 38.5 (Aug. 2005): 796–818.
Bellafante, Ginia. "Now, the Sex Files." *Time* 147.24 (10 Jun. 1996): 76.
Berger, John. *Ways of Seeing*. 1972. London and New York: British Broadcasting Corporation and Penguin, 1987.
Birken, Lawrence. *Consuming Desire: Sexual Science and the Emergence of a Culture of Abundance, 1871–1914*. Ithaca, N.Y.: Cornell UP, 1988.
Bordwell, David, Janet Staiger, and Kristin Thompson. *The Classical Hollywood Cinema: Film Style and Mode of Production to 1960*. New York: Columbia UP, 1985.
Bourdieu, Pierre. *Distinction: A Social Critique of the Judgement of Taste*. 1979. Trans. Richard Nice. Cambridge, Mass.: Harvard UP, 1984.
———. *Photography: A Middle-brow Art*. With Luc Boltanski, Robert Castel, Jean-Claude Chamboredon, and Dominique Schnapper. 1965. Trans. Shaun Whiteside. Stanford, Calif.: Stanford UP, 1990.
Bowen, Michael. "Doris Wishman Meets the Avant-Garde." In Mendik and Schneider 109–22.
———. DVD Commentary. *Abigail Leslie Is Back in Town*. Retro-Seduction (ei Cinema), 2005.
Brownlow, Kevin. *Behind the Mask of Innocence*. Berkeley: U of California P, 1990.
Brownmiller, Susan. *Against Our Will: Men, Women, and Rape*. New York: Simon and Schuster, 1975.
Buscombe, Edward. "Generic Overspill: *A Dirty Western*." In Gibson 27–30.
Butler, Judith. *Gender Trouble: Feminism and the Subversion of Identity*. 1990. New York: Routledge, 1999.
"Cable TV to Provide Free Channel-Blocking Gear." AP report. *Chicago Tribune* 24 Mar. 2004, sec. 1: 12.
Caro, Mark. "Two Naughty Movies Start 'Deep' Discussions." *Chicago Tribune* 24 Jan. 2005, sec. 5: 1, 4.
Carroll, Noël. *A Philosophy of Mass Art*. Oxford: Oxford UP, 1998.
Chamboredon, Jean-Claude. "Mechanical Art, Natural Art: Photographic Artists." In Bourdieu, *Photography* 129–49.
Chapman, Steve. "Freedom Evolves in Surprising Ways." *Chicago Tribune* 20 Nov. 2003, sec. 1: 31.
"Charles Band Biography." Full Moon Studios page (n.d.): 1. 7 Aug. 2004. <http://www.geocities.com/fullmoonfiend/page106.html>.
"Chris." "Main Policy." Policy Page. Cinebizarre, a.k.a. Atomic Cinema (2002): 1–7. 5 Sept. 2003. <http://www.cinebizarre.com/essay_eroticphil.htm>.
"Chris." Rev. of *Emmanuelle*. Softcore Reviews (n.d.): 1–2. 3 Mar 2003. <http://www.sreviews.com/emmanuelle.htm>.
Clover, Carol. *Men, Women, and Chain Saws: Gender in the Modern Horror Film*. Princeton, N.J.: Princeton UP, 1992.
Cohn, Jan. *Romance and the Erotics of Property: Mass-Market Fiction for Women*. Durham, N.C.: Duke UP, 1988.
Conroy, Marianne. "'No Sin in Lookin' Prosperous': Gender, Race, and the Class Formations of Middlebrow Taste in Douglas Sirk's *Imitation of Life*." In James and Berg 114–37.

Cook, Pam. "'Exploitation' Films and Feminism." *Screen* 17.2 (Summer 1976): 122–27.
Cook, John. "Will the FCC Go After Cable?" *Chicago Tribune* 8 Feb. 2004, sec. 7: 1, 13.
Coombes, Sam. "Sartre's Concept of Bad Faith in Relation to the Marxist Notion of False Consciousness: Inauthenticity and Ideology Re-Examined." Internet article. 30 Mar. 1998: 1–10. 3 Mar. 2004. <http://eserver.org/clogic/4-2/coombes.html>.
Corman, Roger, with Jim Jerome. *How I Made a Hundred Movies in Hollywood and Never Lost a Dime.* 1990. New York: Da Capo, 1998.
Cornell, Drucilla, ed. *Feminism and Pornography.* Oxford: Oxford UP, 2000.
Cox, Alex. "My Kind of Woman." *Guardian* 15 Dec. 2000: 1–3. 12 Feb. 2003. <http://film.guardian.co.uk/censorship/news/0,11729,660463,00.html>.
Crowther, Bruce. *Film Noir: Reflections in A Dark Mirror.* New York: Continuum, 1989.
Davis, Keith. *An American Century of Photography: From Dry-Plate to Digital.* New York: Abrams, 1999.
Davis, Scott. Rev. of *Lust for Dracula.* Horror Express (13 Dec. 2004): 1–3. 24 Dec. 2004. <http://www.horrorexpress.com/filmreview.php?id=549>.
DeGeorge, Gail. *The Making of a Blockbuster: How Wayne Huizenga Built a Sports and Entertainment Empire from Trash, Grit, and Videotape.* New York: John Wiley, 1996.
Douglas, Ann. *The Feminization of American Culture.* New York: Avon, 1977.
———. "Soft-Porn Culture." *New Republic* (30 Aug. 1980): 25–29.
Dyer, Richard. "Idol Thoughts: Orgasm and Self-Reflexivity in Gay Pornography." 1994. In Gibson 102–9.
———. *The Matter of Images: Essays on Representations.* 1993. New York: Routledge, 1995.
Eby, Douglas. "Elisa Rothstein." Interv. Wench.com (n.d.): 1–8. 2 Aug. 2004. <http://talentdevelop.com/Page105.html>.
Ehrenreich, Barbara. *The Hearts of Men: American Dreams and the Flight from Commitment.* New York: Anchor, 1983.
Elias, Justine. Rev. of *Delta of Venus. Village Voice* 41.2 (9 Jan. 1996): 62–64.
Epstein, Daniel Robert. "Zalman King: An Interview." Interv. Suicide Girls (n.d.): 1–4. 21 May 2004. <http://suicidegirls.com/words/Zalman+King/>.
Faludi, Susan. *Backlash: The Undeclared War against American Women.* New York: Crown, 1991.
Faoro, Jeffrey, and David Fine. "Legendary Erotica Director Joseph Sarno to Write, Helm New Seduction Cinema Feature." Seduction Cinema press release. 2003. 1–2.
"FAQ—Frequently Asked Questions." Unsigned policy page. Softcore Reviews (2001–2002): 1–3. 3 Nov. 2002 <http://www.sreviews.com/faq.htm>.
"FCC Seeks $755,000 Fine for Indecency." AP report. *Chicago Tribune* 28 Jan. 2004, sec. 1: 21.
Feasey, Rebecca. "'Sharon Stone, Screen Diva': Stardom, Femininity, and Cult Fandom." In Jancovich et al. 172–84.
Ferguson, Frances. *Pornography, the Theory: What Utilitarianism Did to Action.* Chicago: U of Chicago P, 2004.
Fine, David. "ei Cinema's Sexy Movie Spoofs to be Featured at Manhattan's Pioneer Theater." ei Cinema press release. 2003. 1–2.
Fishman, Pamela. "What Do Couples Talk About When They're Alone?" In *Women's Language and Style.* Ed. Douglas Butturff and Edward Epstein. Akron: U of Akron P, 1978. 11–22.
Ford, Luke. "Stuart Allen Profile." Interv. LukeFord.com (2 Jul. 2001): 1–2. 5 Jul. 2003. <http://www.lukeford.com/stars/male/stuart_allen.html>.

Foucault, Michel. *The History of Sexuality*. Vol. 1. Trans. Robert Hurley. 1976. New York: Pantheon, 1978.

Frazer, June, and Timothy Frazer. "*Policewoman*, Male Dominance, and the Cooperative Principle." In *The Text and Beyond*. Ed. Cynthia Goldin Bernstein. Tuscaloosa: U of Alabama P, 1994. 206–14.

Friedan, Betty. *The Feminine Mystique*. New York: Norton, 1963.

Friedman, David, with Don De Nevi. *A Youth in Babylon: Confessions of a Trash-Film King*. Buffalo, N.Y.: Prometheus, 1990.

Frug, Mary Joe. "The Politics of Postmodern Feminism: Lessons from the Anti-Pornography Campaign." In Cornell 254–63.

Gerli, Jake. "The Gay Sex Clerk: Chuck Vincent's Straight Pornography." In Linda Williams, *Porn* 198–220.

Gibson, Pamela Church, ed. *More Dirty Looks: Gender, Pornography and Power*. 1993. London: British Film Institute, 2004.

Goldman, Robert, Deborah Heath, and Sharon Smith. "Commodity Feminism." *Critical Studies in Mass Communication* 8 (1991): 333–51.

Gomery, Douglas. "Movies on Television." Online encyclopedia entry (n.d.): 1–3. 31 Jan. 2004. <http://www.museum.tv/archives/etv/C/htmlC/cablenetwork/cablenetwork.htm>.

"A Good Movie." IMDb user comment on *Poison Ivy II*. IMDb.com (27 May 2003): 1. 10 May 2004. <http://pro.imdb.com/title/tt0114151/usercomments>.

Gordon, Robert. "Victoria." Pictorial. *Penthouse* 34.10 (May 2003): 59–75.

Gorfinkel, Elena. "Radley Metzger's 'Elegant Arousal': Taste, Aesthetic Distinction and Sexploitation." In Mendik and Schneider 26–39.

Greenberg, Clement. "Avant-garde and Kitsch." 1939. In *Mass Culture: The Popular Arts in America*. Ed. Bernard Rosenberg and David Manning White. 1957. New York: Free-Macmillan, 1964. 98–107.

———. *The Collected Essays and Criticism: Arrogant Purpose, 1945–1949*. Vol. 2. Ed. John O'Brian. Chicago: U of Chicago P, 1986.

Griffin, Susan. *Pornography and Silence: Culture's Revenge against Nature*. New York: Harper and Row, 1981.

Gunning, Tom. "The Cinema of Attractions: Early Films, Its Spectator and the Avant-Garde." In *Early Cinema: Space, Frame, Narrative*. Ed. Thomas Elsaesser with Adam Barker. London: British Film Institute, 1990. 56–62.

Hallenbeck, Bruce. "Confessions of a Natural Beauty." Interv. *Misty Mundae: Girl Seduction, A Collection of Misty Mundae Featurettes, 1997–2002*. DVD booklet (#1029). Butler, N.J.: Seduction Cinema, 2003. 13–20.

———. "Joe Sarno's *Inga*." *Alternative Cinema* 20 (Spring 2003): 20–23.

———. "Lord of the Muse." *Alternative Cinema* 20 (Spring 2003): 38–43.

———. "Sixties Erotic Cinema." *Alternative Cinema* 20 (Spring 2003): 14–19.

Hardy, Simon. *The Reader, the Author, His Woman and Her Lover: Soft-Core Pornography and Heterosexual Men*. London: Cassell, 1998.

Hefner, Christie. "To Our Shareholders." *Playboy Enterprises 2000 Annual Report*. Inglewood, Calif.: Insync Media, 2001. 2–4. 4 Sep. 2004. <http://media.corporateir.net/media_files/ NYS/PLA/reports/PbyAR2000.pdf>.

Hefner, Hugh. "Hugh Hefner: Playboy Enterprises." *Fortune Small Business* 1 Sept. 2003: 1–2. 6 Sept. 2004. <http://www.fortune.com/fortune/smallbusiness/articles/0,15114,474264,00.html>.

Hollows, Joanne. *Feminism, Femininity, and Popular Culture.* Manchester: Manchester UP, 2000.

———. "The Masculinity of Cult." In Jancovich et al. 35–53.

"How We Rate Movies." Unsigned policy page. Softcore Reviews (2001–2002): 1–2. 19 Jul. 2004. <http:www.sreviews.com/ratings.htm>. (For the updated version of this page, see <http:www.sreviews.com/reviews/ratings.htm>.)

Hunt, Leon. *British Low Culture: From Safari Suits to Sexploitation.* London: Routledge, 1998.

Hunt, Nathan. "The Importance of Trivia: Ownership, Exclusion, and Authority in Science Fiction Fandom." In Jancovich et al. 185–201.

Hutcheon, Linda. *A Theory of Parody: The Teachings of Twentieth-Century Art Forms.* New York: Methuen, 1985.

Inness, Sherrie. *Tough Girls: Women Warriors and Wonder Women in Popular Culture.* Philadelphia: U of Pennsylvania P, 1999.

Jaehne, Karen. "Confessions of a Feminist Porn Programmer." *Film Quarterly* 37.1 (Fall 1983). 9–16.

James, David, and Rick Berg, eds. *The Hidden Foundation: Cinema and the Question of Class.* Minneapolis: U of Minnesota P, 1996.

James, Frank. "House Bill Increases Fine for Indecent Broadcasts." *Chicago Tribune* 12 Mar. 2004, sec. 1: 1, back p.

Jancovich, Mark. "Naked Ambitions: Pornography, Taste and the Problem of the Middlebrow." *Scope: An On-Line Journal of Film Studies* (Jun. 2001): 1–10. 2 Feb. 2004. <http://www.nottingham.ac.uk/film/journal/articles/naked-ambition.htm>.

———. "Placing Sex: Sexuality, Taste, and Middlebrow Culture in the Reception of *Playboy Magazine.*" *Intensities: The Journal of Cult Media* 2.1 (Autumn/Winter 2001): 1–10. 2 Feb. 2004. <http://www.cult-media.com/issue2/Ajanc.htm>.

Jancovich, Mark, Antonio Lázaro Reboll, Julian Stringer, and Andy Willis, eds. *Defining Cult Movies: The Cultural Politics of Oppositional Taste.* Manchester: Manchester UP, 2003.

———. "Introduction." In Jancovich et al. 1–13.

Jenkins, Henry. "Foreword: So You Want to Teach Pornography?" In Gibson 1–7.

Jenkins, Tricia. "'Potential Lesbians at Two O'Clock': The Heterosexualization of Lesbianism in the Recent Teen Film." *Journal of Popular Culture* 38.3 (Feb. 2005): 491–504.

Johnson, Eithne, and Eric Schaefer. "Soft Core/Hard Gore: *Snuff* as a Crisis in Meaning." *Journal of Film and Video* 45.2–3 (Summer-Fall 1993): 40–59.

Jones, Chris, and John Cook. "Radio Chief Says He's 'Ashamed.'" *Chicago Tribune* 27 Feb. 2004, sec. 1: 9.

Juffer, Jane. *At Home with Pornography: Women, Sex, and Everyday Life.* New York: NYU P, 1998.

———. "There's No Place Like Home: Further Developments on the Domestic Front." In Gibson 45–58.

Kendrick, Walter. *The Secret Museum: Pornography in Modern Culture.* 1987. Berkeley: U of California P, 1996.

Kennerson, Anthony. "A Conversation with Shauna O'Brien: Actress/Model/Web Diva." Interv. Softcore Reviews (2004): 1–6. 21 May 2004. <http://www.sreviews.com/shauna.htm>.

Kim, L. S. "'Sex and the Single Girl' in Postfeminism: The F Word on Television." *Television and New Media* 2.4 (Nov. 2001): 319–34.

Kipnis, Laura. *Bound and Gagged: Pornography and the Politics of Fantasy in America.* New York: Grove, 1996.
Kleinman, Geoffrey. "Zalman King: A DVD Talk Chat." Interv. DVD Talk: DVD & Movie Reviews (14 Mar. 2000): 1–7. 21 Jun. 2003. <http://www.dvdtalk.com/zalmantranscript.html>.
Koch, Gertrude. "The Body's Shadow Realm." 1989. In Gibson 149–64.
Landis, Bill, and Michelle Clifford. *Sleazoid Express: A Mind-Twisting Tour Through the Grindhouse Cinema of Times Square.* New York: Fireside, 2002.
Laqueur, Thomas. *Solitary Sex: A Cultural History of Masturbation.* New York: Zone, 2003.
Lazarus, Tom. "Q&A: A Conversation with Tom Lazarus, Writer/Producer/Director." Unsigned interv. Softcore Reviews (2003): 1–5. 22 Jun. 2003. <http://www.sreviews.com/tomlazarus.htm>.
———. "Re: it's Tom Lazarus." Personal e-mail to the author. 13 Dec. 2004. 1–3.
———. *Secrets of Film Writing.* New York: St. Martin's, 2001.
Lennig, Arthur. "A History of Censorship of the American Film." In Atkins 36–75.
Levine, Lawrence. *Highbrow/Lowbrow: The Emergence of Cultural Hierarchy in America.* 1988. Cambridge, Mass.: Harvard UP, 1990.
Lewis, Jon. *Hollywood v. Hard Core: How the Struggle Over Censorship Saved the Modern Film Industry.* New York: NYU P, 2000.
Loftus, David. *Watching Sex: How Men Really Respond to Pornography.* New York: Thunder's Mouth P, 2002.
Lombard, Robert. "A Journey Uphill." *Adult Industry News* (8 May 2003): 1–2. 23 Nov. 2003. <http://www.ainews.com/Archives/Story4899.phtml>.
———. "Re: One Other Quick Follow-Up." Personal e-mail to the author. 10 Feb. 2004. 1–7.
———. "Re: One Other Quick Follow-Up." Personal e-mail to the author. 30 June 2004. 1–9.
———. "Re: tiny addendum." Personal e-mail to the author. 14 Feb. 2005. 1–3.
———. "Robert Lombard: Casting & Talent Manager, Creative Image Entertainment." Unsigned interv. Softcore Reviews (2004): 1–6. 30 Jun. 2004. <http://www.sreviews.com/rlombard1.htm>.
———. "Robert Lombard: Industry Insider." Softcore Reviews forum posting (20 Jan. 2005): 1–2. 20 Jan. 2005. <http://sreviews.com/forum/viewtopic.php?p=5372>.
Lopez, Peter, and William George. "Men's Enjoyment of Explicit Erotica: Effects of Person-Specific Attitudes and Gender-Specific Norms." *Journal of Sex Research* 32.4 (1995): 275–88.
Losano, Wayne. "The Sex Genre: Traditional and Modern Variations on the Flesh Film." In Atkins 132–44.
Luckett, Moya. "Sexploitation as Feminine Territory: The Films of Doris Wishman." In Jancovich et al. 142–56.
Lury, Celia. *Consumer Culture.* New Brunswick: Rutgers UP, 1996.
Lynes, Russell. *The Tastemakers.* New York: Grosset and Dunlap, 1954.
Macdonald, Dwight. *Against the American Grain.* New York: Random House, 1962.
MacKinnon, Catharine. "The Roar on the Other Side of Silence." In Cornell 130–53.
Mair, George. *Inside HBO: The Billion Dollar War Between HBO, Hollywood, and the Home Video Revolution.* New York: Dodd, Mead, and Co., 1988.
"Manicottale, Luigi." "Doris Wishman Website": 1–7. 14 Sept. 2003. <http://www.doriswishman.com>.

Marcus, Steven. *The Other Victorians.* New York: Basic, 1964.
Marsiglia, Tony. "RE: Some Questions." Personal e-mail to the author. 19 Sep. 2004. 1–5.
Marsiglia, Tony, and Michael Raso. DVD commentary. *Lust for Dracula.* Unrated director's cut. Seduction (ei Cinema), 2004.
Martin, Nina. "*Red Shoe Diaries:* Sexual Fantasy and the Construction of the (Hetero)sexual Woman." *Journal of Film and Video* 46.2 (Summer 1994): 44–57.
Marx, Karl. *Capital.* Vol. 3. Chicago: Kerr, 1909. Trans. Ernest Untermann. Ed. Frederick Engels. Library of Economics and Liberty: 1. 12 Aug. 2005. <http://www.econlib.org/library/YPDBooks/Marx/mrxCpC47.html>.
May, Tons. "The Other Face of Love: Udo Kier's Career in the Erotic Genre." In Stevenson 140–58.
McNair, Brian. "'Not Some Kind of Kinky Porno Flick': The Return of Porno-Fear?" *Bridge* 11 (Aug./Sept. 2004): 16–19.
———. *Striptease Culture: Sex, Media and the Democratization of Desire.* London: Routledge, 2002.
McQueen, Jeff. "Inside *Basic Instinct.*" Interv. Paul Verhoeven. *Basic Instinct: The Original Director's Cut.* Dir. Verhoeven. Carolco, 1992. VHS. Live Home Video, 1993.
Mendik, Xavier, and Steven Jay Schneider, eds. *Underground U.S.A.: Filmmaking Beyond the Hollywood Canon.* London and New York: Wallflower, 2002.
Michelson, Peter. *Speaking the Unspeakable: A Poetics of Obscenity.* 1971. Albany: State U of New York P, 1993.
"Mick." Rev. of *House of Love.* Softcore Reviews (2002): 1–2. 25 Oct. 2002. <http://www.sreviews.com/wordofmouth.htm>. (For the updated version of this review, see <http://www.sreviews.com/reviews/wordofmouth.htm>.)
"Misty Mundae: From Skin to Scream." Documentary "extra" on *Screaming Dead* DVD. Written by David Fine. Produced by Michael Raso. Shock-O-Rama (ei Cinema), 2004.
Modleski, Tania. *Feminism Without Women: Culture and Criticism in a "Postfeminist" Age.* New York: Routledge, 1991.
———. *Loving with a Vengeance: Mass-Produced Fantasies for Women.* 1982. New York: Routledge, 1990.
Morris, Gary. "Notes Toward a Lexicon of Roger Corman's New World Pictures." *Bright Lights Film Journal* 27 (Jan. 2000): 1–3. 24 Feb. 2004. <http://www.brightlightsfilm.com/27/newworldpictures3.html>.
MRG. "Company Profile." Mainline Releasing/MRG Home Page (n.d.): 1–3. 5 Sept. 2004. <http://www.mainlinereleasing.com/>.
Mulvey, Laura. "Visual Pleasure and Narrative Cinema." 1975. In *Visual and Other Pleasures.* Bloomington: Indiana UP, 1989. 14–26.
Mumford, Laura Stempel. *Love and Ideology in the Afternoon: Soap Opera, Women, and Television Genre.* Bloomington: Indiana UP, 1995.
Naremore, James. *More Than Night: Film Noir in Its Contexts.* Berkeley: U of California P, 1998.
Neale, Stephen. "Art Cinema as Institution." *Screen* 22.1 (1981): 11–39.
———. *Genre.* London: British Film Institute, 1980.
———, ed. *Genre and Contemporary Hollywood.* London: British Film Institute, 2002.
Nochimson, Martha. *No End to Her: Soap Opera and the Female Subject.* Berkeley: U of California P, 1992.
"Not bad for softcore." IMDb user comment on *Friend of the Family.* IMDb.com (15 Mar. 2000): 1–3. 18 Jun. 2004. <http://pro.imdb.com/title/tt0113119/usercomments>.

Novak, Harry. DVD commentary. *The Secret Sex Lives of Romeo and Juliet.* 1969. Something Weird, 2002.
O'Toole, Laurence. *Pornocopia: Porn, Sex, Technology, and Desire.* London: Serpent's Tail, 1998.
Paglia, Camille. *Sex, Art, and American Culture.* New York: Vintage, 1992.
Petkovich, Anthony. "Gregory Hippolyte (aka Brown/Dark)." Interv. *Psychotronic Video* 26 (1997): 75–84.
Phoca, Sophia, and Rebecca Wright. *Introducing Postfeminism.* New York: Totem Books, 1999.
Playboy Enterprises 2000 Annual Report. Inglewood, Calif.: Insync Media, 2001. 4 Sep. 2004. <http://media.corporate-ir.net/media_files/NYS/PLA/reports/PbyAR2000.pdf>.
Powell, Michael. "Don't Expect the Government to Be a V-Chip." *New York Times* 3 Dec. 2004, sec. A: 29.
"Profile: Misty Mundae." Unsigned promotional bio. ei Cinema's "New Releases" catalogue (Feb.–Mar. 2004): 1–2.
"Programmers: Video Games Need Female Touch." AP report. *New York Times* 22 Jul. 2005: 1–2. 22 Jul. 2005 <http://www.nytimes.com/aponline/technology/AP-Game-Girls.html>.
Projansky, Sarah. *Watching Rape: Film and Television in Postfeminist Culture.* New York: NYU P, 2001.
Pust, Maren. "That's Why the Lady Is a Vamp: The Danish Origins of the Screen's First Dangerous Lady." In Stevenson 77–89.
Raso, Michael. "Re: PROJECTS." Personal e-mail to the author. 10 Dec. 2004. 1–2.
Ray, Fred Olen. *The New Poverty Row: Independent Filmmakers as Distributors.* Jefferson, N.C.: McFarland, 1991.
Rausch, Andrew. *Turning Points in Film History.* Foreword by Joe Bob Briggs. New York: Citadel, 2004.
Read, Jacinda. "The Cult of Masculinity: From Fan-Boys to Academic Bad-Boys." In Jancovich et al. 54–70.
Reich, Wilhelm. *The Discovery of the Orgone: The Function of the Orgasm.* Vol. 1. New York: Noonday, 1961.
———. *The Sexual Revolution: Toward a Self-Regulating Character Structure.* New York: Farrar, Straus and Giroux, 1945.
Richards, Allen. Rev. of *The Bizarre Case of the Electric Cord Strangler.* b-independent.com (2002): 1. 26 Sept. 2003. <http://www.b-independent.com/reviews/thebizarrecaseoftheelectriccordstrangler.htm>.
———. Rev. of *Hellcats in High Heels.* b-independent.com (2003): 1–2. 28 Sept. 2003. <http://www.b-independent.com/reviews/hellcatsinhighheels.htm>.
———. Rev. of *Witchbabe: The Erotic Witch Project III.* b-independent.com (2003): 1–2. 22 Jul. 2004. <http://www.b-independent.com/reviews/witchbabe.htm>.
Roberts, Alan. "Re: Fw: scholarly inquiry regarding past film work." Personal e-mail to the author. 11 May 2004. 1–3.
Rorty, Richard. *Contingency, Irony, and Solidarity.* Cambridge: Cambridge UP, 1989.
Rotsler, William. *Contemporary Erotic Cinema.* New York: Ballantine, 1973.
Rubin, Joan Shelley. *The Making of Middlebrow Culture.* Chapel Hill, N.C.: U of North Carolina P, 1992.
Russell, Diana. "Pornography and Rape: A Causal Model." In Cornell 48–94.

Sandler, Kevin. "Movie Ratings as Genre: The Incontestable R." In Neale, *Contemporary* 201–17.
Sartre, Jean-Paul. *Being and Nothingness*. 1943. Trans. and intro. Hazel E. Barnes. 1956. New York: Washington Square, 1984.
———. *Existentialism and Humanism*. Trans. P. Mairet. London: Methuen, 1966.
Schaefer, Eric. *"Bold! Daring! Shocking! True!": A History of Exploitation Films, 1919–1959*. Durham, N.C.: Duke UP, 1999.
———. "Burlesque Without Tassels: The Nudie-Cutie and Its Origin." Presentation. Society for Cinema and Media Studies Conference. Atlanta, 6 Mar. 2004.
———. "Gauging a Revolution: 16mm Film and the Rise of the Pornographic Feature." *Cinema Journal* 41.3 (2002): 3–26.
———. "RE: Thanks." Personal e-mail to the author. 20 Mar. 2004. 1.
———. "RE: Thanks." Personal e-mail to the author. 31 Mar. 2004. 1–2.
———. "The Triumph of Exploitation; or, From Exploitation Film to Exploitation Culture in Eight Easy Decades." *Bridge* 12 (Oct./Nov. 2004): 19–25.
Sconce, Jeffrey. "'Trashing the Academy': Taste, Excess, and an Emerging Politics of Cinematic Style." *Screen* 36.4 (Winter 1995): 371–93.
Seduction Cinema: Erotica 2005. Annual sales pamphlet for the American Film Market. Butler, NJ: ei Cinema, 2005.
Segal, Lynne. "Only the Literal: The Contradictions of Anti-Pornography Feminism." 1998. In Gibson 59–70.
Shields, Todd. "Activists Dominate Content Complaints." *Mediaweek* (6 Dec. 2004): 1–4. 12 Jan. 2005. <http:www.mediaweek.com/mediaweek/headlines/article_display.jsp?vnu_content_id=1000731656>.
Shiner, Larry. *The Invention of Art: A Cultural History*. Chicago: U of Chicago P, 2001.
Sibert, Jason. "On Zalman King, Softcore, and Film." Interv. Zalman King. Softcore Reviews (2004): 1–3. 30 Jul. 2004. <http://www.sreviews.com/zalmanking.htm>.
Sidaris, Andy, and Arlene Sidaris. *Bullets, Bombs, and Babes: The Films of Andy Sidaris*. Rockville Centre, N.Y.: Heavy Metal, 2003.
———. DVD commentary. *Hard Ticket to Hawaii*. Malibu Bay, 2001.
———. DVD commentary. *Picasso Trigger*. Malibu Bay, 2001.
Siemens xTronic ranges. Advertisement. *Chicago Tribune* 14 Dec. 2004, sec. 1: 17.
Simpson, Alan. Rev. of *Satan's School for Sluts*. SexGoreMutants (2003): 1–2. 3 Sept. 2003. <http://www.sexgoremutants.f9.co.uk/satangirls.html>.
Singer, Paul. "Justice Officials Targeting Porn." *Chicago Tribune* 23 Aug. 2003, sec. 1: 1, 16.
Smith, Lynn, and Richard Simon. "Cable TV Faces Indecency Crackdown." *Chicago Tribune* 12 Feb. 2004, sec. 1: 13.
Snitow, Ann Barr. "Mass Market Romance: Pornography for Women Is Different." 1979. In *The Powers of Desire: The Politics of Sexuality*. Eds. Snitow, Christine Stansell, and Sharon Thompson. New York: Monthly Review P, 1983. 245–63.
Soble, Alan. *Pornography: Marxism, Feminism, and the Future of Sexuality*. New Haven, Conn.: Yale UP, 1986.
———. *Pornography, Sex, and Feminism*. Amherst, N.Y.: Prometheus, 2002.
Sontag, Susan. *On Photography*. 1977. New York: Anchor, 1990.
———. "The Pornographic Imagination." 1967. In *Styles of Radical Will*. 1969. New York: Anchor, 1991. 35–73.
Springer, Odette, dir. *Some Nudity Required: The Naked Truth Behind Hollywood's B-Movies*. Documentary. 1998. VHS. New Video, 1999.

Squire, James, ed. *The Movie Business Book.* 1983. 3rd ed. New York: Fireside, 2004.
Staiger, Janet. *Interpreting Films: Studies in the Historical Reception of American Cinema.* Princeton, N.J.: Princeton UP, 1992.
Stallybrass, Peter, and Allon White. *The Politics and Poetics of Transgression.* London: Methuen, 1986.
Steinem, Gloria. "Erotica vs. Pornography: A Clear and Present Difference." In *Outrageous Acts and Everyday Rebellions.* New York: Holt, 1983. 247–60.
Stevenson, Jack, ed. *Fleshpot: Cinema's Sexual Myth Makers and Taboo Breakers.* 2000. Manchester: Critical Vision, 2002.
"Studio News—Spring 2005." Seduction Cinema online newsletter (26 May 2005): 1–2. 18 Aug. 2005. <http://www.seductioncinema.com/news_2005_spring.htm>.
Tawa, Renee. "Amateur Reviewers Gain Clout." *Chicago Tribune* 6 Apr. 2004, sec. 5: 1–2.
Testa, Bart. "Soft-Shaft Opportunism: Radley Metzger's Erotic Kitsch." *Spectator* 19.2 (Spring/Summer 1999): 41–55.
"Time to Enforce Internet Porn Law, Supreme Court Told." Tribune News Services. *Chicago Tribune* 3 Mar. 2004, sec. 1: 10.
Turan, Kenneth, and Stephen Zito. *Sinema: American Pornographic Films and the People Who Make Them.* New York: Praeger, 1974.
Twitchell, James. *Carnival Culture: The Trashing of Taste in America.* New York: Columbia UP, 1992.
"User Comments." 5 IMDb user revs. of *Sensual Friends.* IMDb.com (2001): 1–3. 19 Jul. 2004. <http://pro.imdb.com/title/tt0214106/usercomments>.
Vieira, Mark. *Sin in Soft Focus: Pre-Code Hollywood.* New York: Abrams, 1999.
Wachter, Carl. "Brief Encounter." Pictorial. *Penthouse* 34.10 (May 2003): 107–23.
Waller, Gregory. "Auto-Erotica: Some Notes on Comic Softcore Films for the Drive-In Circuit." *Journal of Popular Culture* 17.2 (Fall 1983): 135–41.
Waltz, Douglas. "Factory 2000, Seduction Cinema, and Misty Mundae: An Interview with Seduction Cinema Producer Michael Raso." 9 Sept. 2005: 1–2. Unpublished interview forthcoming at <http://www.penguincomics.net/>.
Ward, Tony. "Paulina." Pictorial. *Penthouse* 34.10 (May 2003): 87–95.
Waugh, Thomas. *Hard to Imagine: Gay Male Eroticism in Photography and Film from Their Beginnings to Stonewall.* New York: Columbia UP, 1996.
Wilinsky, Barbara. *Sure Seaters: The Emergence of Art House Cinema.* Minneapolis: U of Minnesota P, 2001.
Willemen, Paul. "For a Pornoscape." In Gibson 9–26.
Williams, Linda. *Hard Core: Power, Pleasure, and the "Frenzy of the Visible."* 1989. Berkeley: U of California P, 1999.
———. "Porn Studies: Proliferating Pornographies On/Scene: An Introduction." In Williams, *Porn* 1–23.
———, ed. *Porn Studies.* Durham, N.C.: Duke UP, 2004.
———. "Second Thoughts on *Hard Core:* American Obscenity Law and the Scapegoating of Deviance." In Gibson 165–75.
Williams, Linda Ruth. *The Erotic Thriller in Contemporary Cinema.* Edinburgh: Edinburgh UP, 2005.
———. "No Sex Please We're American." *Sight & Sound* (Jan. 2004): 1–6. Online edition. 16 Jan. 2004. <http://www.bfi.org.uk/sightandsound/2004_01/nosex.php>.
———. "The Oldest Swinger in Town." *Sight & Sound* 10.8 (Aug. 2000): 24–27.
Willis, Sharon. *High Contrast: Race and Gender in Contemporary Hollywood Film.*

Durham, N.C.: Duke UP, 1997.
Wilmington, Michael. "*Loved* Needs More Than Soft Porn to Satisfy." Rev. of *When Will I Be Loved. Chicago Tribune* 24 Sept. 2004, sec. 5: 1.
Woolf, Virginia. *The Death of the Moth and Other Essays.* 1942. New York: Harvest, 1974.
Wu, Harmony. "Trading in Horror, Cult, and Matricide: Peter Jackson's Phenomenal Bad Taste and New Zealand Fantasies of Inter/National Cinematic Success." In Jancovich et al. 84–108.
Zaitz, Leland. "A Conversation with Leland Zaitz: Writer, Former Director of Development for Indigo Entertainment." Interv. Softcore Reviews (2003): 1–7. 21 Jun. 2003. <http://www.sreviews.com/leland1.htm>.
Zizek, Slavoj. *The Art of the Ridiculous Sublime: On David Lynch's* Lost Highway. Seattle: Walter Chapin Simpson Center for the Humanities (U of Washington P), 2000.

Index

Italicized page numbers refer to illustrations.

7 Lives Xposed (serial), 218, 228–29, 283n30
9½ Weeks (Lyne), 110, 111, 116, 117, 119–21, 127, 146, 270n13, 271n28, 272n31
16mm films, 4, 79, 260n1, 262n10, 263n3, 275n33; and softcore thrillers, 133, 151–57, 209–10, 254, 275n27, 287n3; at Seduction Cinema, 231, 246, 250, 286n23, 286n28
35mm films, 4, 60, 147, 152, 210, 250, 260n1, 275n27

Abigail Lesley Is Back in Town (Sarno), 68, 265n31, 285n18
Academy Entertainment, 88, 143
Adamson, Al, 72
adultery: encouragement of female, 11, 91, 147–51, 166; restrictions on male, 11, 137, 147, 151, 155, 157; in erotic thrillers, 71, 132, 137, 147, 155–57; in suburban films, 70–72, 265n31
Adult Film Association of America (AFAA), 61
The Adult Version of Jekyll & Hyde (Mabe), 66
Adult Video News, xii
The Adventures of Lucky Pierre (Lewis), 264n12
aestheticism, 182, 216, 226, 247–48, 261n4, 285n22
Against Our Will (Brownmiller), 27, 63
The Agony of Love (Rotsler), 70, 148, 265n27

Ahlberg, Mac, 43, 56, 66–68, 92
AIDS, 135, 141
Alderman, John, 61–62, 104, 265n22
Allen, Robert, 51, 283n25
Alley Tramp (Lewis), 68, 71, 148
Allison, Scott, 214
All That Heaven Allows (Sirk), 269n12
Alta Loma, 281n7. *See also* Playboy Enterprises
Les Amants (Malle), 48, 260n6
Amazon, 187, 192, 197–99
American Independent Productions, 88, 194, 267n11
American Pie (Weitz), 95, 97
. . . And God Created Woman (Vadim), 36, 260n6, 264n14
Andrews, Michael, 106–8
Animal Instincts (Hippolyte), 147–48, 272n5, 274n21
Animal Instincts: The Seductress (Hippolyte), 143
antiporn ideology, 29, 70, 84, 87, 91, 94, 99, 262n11, 265n23; among cult fans, 196–97; among social conservatives, 29, 84, 87; impact on contemporary sexploitation, 4, 14, 30, 73, 78, 108–9, 200; within feminism, 13, 29–31, 84, 99, 164, 278n7
antisnuff campaign, 27, 84

A-Pix Entertainment, 143
Archer, Anne, 136, 141
art films: definition of, 260n6; and female desire, 14–15, 43, 46, 55, 66, 94; relation to sexploitation, 9, 14, 16, 35–36, 43, 46, 48, 66, 126, 164, 218, 244, 260n6, 268n4
arthouse: as classed and gendered site, 35–36, 112; and classical exhibition circuit, 3–4, 35–36, 81, 112, 244; as taste formation, 35, 83–84, 112, 165, 240, 249
artist-model motif, 48–49, 181–82
aspirational softcore, 72, 111, 161, 169, 182, 211, 219, 220, 275n2; definition of, 7; and exotic spectacle, 9; highbrow denunciations of, 7, 32, 34; literariness, 93–94; strategic blurring of art-porn distinction, 7, 205–6, 225–26, 216
At Home with Pornography (Juffer), 174
Audubon Films, 35
auteurism, 34–35, 41, 68, 130, 218–28, 232, 243–50, 257, 261n4, 2694, 269n7, 285n18, 285n20
"Auto Erotica" (King), 114, 175, 276n3
awakening-sexuality films, 57, 66–71, 98, 117, 149, 165–66, 243, 265n31; and tolerance of female desire, 15, 46, 56, 68–70, 112; male-identified variants of, 98
"Avant-garde and Kitsch" (Greenberg), 37
avant-gardism, 219, 244, 246, 249, 265n28
Axis Films, 5–6, 9, 14, 133, 135, 143, 145, 147, 152, 209–10, 215, 220, 254, 272n1, 274n20, 274n21, 274n25, 286n30

Backstein, Karen, 110, 160, 168–69, 173, 175–76, 179–81, 183, 276n13, 278n4
bad faith, xiii, 21, 22, 23, 32, 44, 184, 185, 187–89, 199, 203–4, 256
Bad Girls from Mars (Ray), 88, 99
Bako, Brigitte, 123, 270n16
Baldwin, Daniel, 152
Baldwin, Thomas, 82–83, 85, 86
Band, Charles, 230, 267n10
Bara, Theda, 141
Barbarian Queen (Olivera), 101–4 (*103*)
Barbarian Queen II (Finley), 101–4 (*103*), 268n18
Bardot, Brigitte, 36, 264n14
Bare Deception (Gibson), 153

Bare Witness (Cauthen), 152
Basic Instinct (Verhoeven), 1, 131–32, 133, 135–42 (*137*), 147, 272nn4–5, 273n6, 273n9
Basinger, Kim, 127, 270n13
Bazin, André, 41
Beach Babes 2 (DeCoteau), xii
Beaman, Lee Anne, 150
Beeftink, Herman, 6, 114
Beggan, James, 214
Behind Closed Doors (McLellan), 260n5
Behind the Green Door (Mitchell Brothers), 27
Behind the Mask of Innocence (Brownlow), 263n3
Bellafante, Ginia, 82, 110, 160, 168
Belle de Jour (Buñuel), 148–49
Berger, John, 107
Bergman, Ingmar, 36, 55, 67, 68, 244, 248, 285n17
Bertolucci, Bernardo, 269n4
The Best Sex Ever (serial), 160, 174, 176; episodes of, 181, 277n16
Beverly Hills Vamp (Ray), 88
Bikini Summer III (Blakey), 199
b-independent, 186, 194–96
Birken, Lawrence, 12, 15, 29, 66
Bite Me! (Piper), 231, 235, 241
"The Bitter and the Sweet" (Landsburg), 180, 277n19
Blake, Andrew, *21, 40,* 180, 263n24, 268n3
blank sex, 275n30
Blazing Stewardesses (Adamson), 285n19
Blockbuster Video, 1, 12, 87, 185, 210, 237, 253, 267n8
Blood Feast (Lewis), 265n19
Blue Movies (Koval, Fitzgerald), 88, 100
B-movies, 281n5; and classic *noir*, 273n13; conflation with exploitation, 3; Corman's overview of, 260n3
Body Chemistry (Peterson), 141–42, 155, 272n5, 273n7
Body Heat (Kasdan), 119, 134
Body of Evidence (Edel), 134
Body of Influence 2 (Smith), 274n20
"Bold! Daring! Shocking! True!" (Schaefer), 3
Bond, Steve, 108, 268n23
Bordwell, David, 3, 38, 235
Bourdieu, Pierre, 32–33, 36, 50, 189, 199,

Index

262n15
Bowen, Michael, 81, 285n20
Boxing Helena (Lynch), 269n7
Boxoffice International Pictures, 64–65, 70, 236, 284n7
Boyle, Barbara, 274n25
Boyle, Lisa, 142, 202, 215
Briggs, Joe Bob, 192, 194
Brin, Michele, 148
Brownlow, Kevin, 263n3
Brownmiller, Susan, 27, 63, 93, 212
"The Brunch Club" (Spera), 175
buddy films, 100, 214, 217
Buñuel, Luis, 149
burlesque, 105, 108, 200; comedy, 51, 55, 64–65, 104, 232, 233–36, 239, 244–46, 285n19; films, 14, 45–47, 49–53, 67, 78, 191, 235, 263n4, 264n6, 264nn8–10. See also classical exploitation; nudist films; Schaefer, Eric; sexploitation comedy
Buscombe, Edward, 284n5
Butler, Judith, 29, 108
Butterflies (Sarno) 67–70 (*67*), 97, 165, 265n29, 277n20

cable, 94, 208–9, 233; as alternative distribution mode, 169, 233; and female audiences, 15, 85–86, 112, 114, 167, 186, 198; and the Janet Jackson affair, 251, 253–56; premium cable, 1, 6, 15, 82–86, 100, 109, 112, 130, 160–61, 165, 168–69, 208, 237, 253–56, 267n8, 277n13, 278n1, 278n4, 281n8; and rape metaphors, 87; and the transition to contemporary sexploitation, 4, 80, 83–86, 208. See also Cinemax; HBO; Playboy Enterprises; Showtime
Cablevision, 83, 85
Caine, Darian, 231, 240, 286n28
Cameo Films, 6, 9, 142, 209, 273n16, 282n12. See also Playboy Enterprises
Camille 2000 (Metzger), 36
Campion, Jane, 270n15
Cannon Films, 68, 80, 84
career-woman film. See empowered babe, the; working-woman vehicles
Caress of the Vampire (Terranova), 233
Carlton, Hope Marie, 106, 108
Carmen, Baby (Metzger), 36

Carnal Crimes (Hippolyte), 4, 111, 140, 143, 145–47 (*145*), 151, 215, 273n17, 274n21
carnival: absence from corporate softcore, 9; in aspirational softcore, 9; in classical softcore, 65–66; in cult softcore, 9–10, 191, 232, 235–36, 239, 247, 284n7, 284n10; and *noir* and *noir*-romance hybrids, 119–21, 123
Carol, Linda, 146
Cattrall, Kim, 96
Cauthen, Kelley, 6, 152, 219
CBS, 252, 254
"Celeste" (Vance), 176, 177
Chamboredon, Jean-Claude, 188, 285n22
Chantal (Marsiglia), 235, 241, 246, 249, 285n13, 285n23
Chantal (Phillips), 246
Cheerleaders' Beach Party (Gotein), 74
Cherry Hill High (Gotein), 74
Child Online Protection Act, 253
children: absence from softcore, 19, 273n7. See also Young Person, the
Chiller Theater, 232, 233
ChromiumBlue.com (King), 128, 130, 269n8, 271n27, 271n30, 272n31
cinéma vérité, 218, 225, 283n25. See also mock documentaries; reality television
Cinemax, xi, 1, 7, 12, 82–84, 87, 90, 160, 254, 260n4, 276n9, 278n4, 286n3
Clark, Bob, 94
Clark, Brett, 92
Clarkson, Lana, 267n19
class and taste distinctions. See highbrow, the; lowbrow, the; middlebrow, the
classical exploitation, 34, 47–53, 60–61, 82, 232, 235; attitudes toward sexual desire, 15–16, 56, 278n6; distinctions from classical Hollywood, 3; Schaefer's definitions of, 3, 260n4, 264n7; transition to classical sexploitation, 3, 15, 49–53, 264n6. See also burlesque; nudist films; Schaefer, Eric; square-up, the
The Classical Hollywood Cinema (Bordwell et al.), 3
classical Hollywood, 3, 34, 47, 94, 113, 134, 169, 188, 197, 210–11, 218, 235–36, 240, 260n4, 276n3
classical sexploitation, 45–76; attitudes toward desire, 15–16, 46, 68; budgets, 60; competi-

tion with hardcore, 4, 5–6, 68–69, 79–80; competition with Hollywood, 4, 79–80, 133–34; decline of, 4, 78–82, 165; place in the cult nexus, 193–94, 231, 243–46; development, 3, 49–55, 58–60, 235–36, 264n6, 272n3; distinction from contemporary sexploitation, 3–6, 15–16, 45–46, 84–85, 133–34; emphasis on shock and transgression, 3, 12–13, 46, 56–59, 65–66, 73, 76, 194, 256; relative nonstandardization of, 45–46, 56, 75–76, 151, 249–50. See also classical exploitation; classical softcore; female subjectivity; Schaefer, Eric

classical softcore, 58–70, 231, 235–36, 277n20; development of, 3–4, 58–59, 265n19, 272n3; distinction from contemporary softcore, 3–6; distinction from classical sexploitation generally, 2, 5–6; formal impact of hardcore on, 62, 68–69, 79; and rape discourse, 62–66. See also classical sexploitation; contemporary softcore; rape motifs

Clinton, George, 114, 269n7

Close, Glenn, *134*, 136

Close Enough to Touch (Scabbert), 215–17, 225, 226

closure: devices, 167–68, 179; implications of, 68, 167–68, 179, 276n3; industrial utility, 168

Clover, Carol, 10–11, 63, 65, 72, 73, 101, 102, 122–23, 132, 162

Cohen, Howard, 101

Cohn, Jan, 115, 122, 269n10, 271n19, 271n20

Columbia, 4, 26, 30, 41, 80, 163, 262n12, 267n13

Columbia TriStar, viii, 118, 126, 152, 267n13

Comcast, xiv, 85

compensation, ideas of, 17–21, 59, 78, 102, 172–73, 182, 206

compilations, softcore, xii, 260n5

Concorde–New Horizons, 8, 103, 141, 230

The Concrete Jungle (DeSimone), 266n32

Conde, Manuel, 79

confessional forms, 161, 169, 228, 276n10

"Confessions of a Feminist Porn Programmer" (Jaehne), 85

Confessions of a Natural Beauty (Mundae), 241

Congress, United States, 251, 255

Conroy, Marianne, 33

Consumer Culture (Lury), 12

consumerism, 108, 130; of 16mm softcore thrillers, 154–57; and classical sexploitation, 12–13; and feminization, 12; and Playboy, 49, 90–91, 206, 212, 225; and tolerance of female desire, 15–16, 46, 47, 84, 113, 127–28, 132–33, 176, 192, 271n24. See *under* postfeminist

contemporary Hollywood, 4, 80, 83, 94, 100, 110, 134, 139, 169, 198, 200, 217, 218–19, 236, 243, 272n3, 273n10

contemporary sexploitation: deviations from classical sexploitation, 3–6, 15–16, 45–46, 84–85, 133–34; distinction with contemporary softcore, 2, 6 (*see also* just-shy-of-softcore sexploitation); promotion of, 84–85, 88, *103, 104, 105*, 185, 205; sequelling in, xii, 78, 266n1, 274n26; transition from classical sexploitation, 4–6, 45, 76, 77–78, 109, 165, 208

contemporary softcore: deflation in, 5–6, 16, 130, 152–53, 169, 174, 209–10, 224, 250, 253–54, 274n20, 274n25, 275nn27–28, 276n9, 277n18; development of, 4–6, 76, 77, 109–11, 130, 143–45, 165–66, 169, 253, 272n3; genre cues, xii, 1, 185; as a middle industry, 6, 16, 86, 184, 209, 273n16; middlebrow character, 5, 6–10; multiplicity of, xii, 1, 259n2, 260nn3–5, 260n2; negation and, 16–21, 184, 187–89, 196–99, 204, 205 (*see also* compensation, ideas of; structuring absence); paucity of scholarship on, xi, 259n1; relation to cult nexus, 8, 193–94, 202–4, 230–32; relation to hardcore, 5, 18, 86, 153, 200, 204, 208, 210, 236, 253, 267n14, 268n3, 275n29, 279n15, 280n18, 280n27, 282n17; roots in classical genres, 45–76; relative routinization of, 45, 78, 152; self-consciousness in, 16, 21, 44, 184–85, 187–90, 195–202, 204, 205, 232, 255–57; structuring inequities of, 11, 13, 18–21, 31, 112, 170–74, 180, 183, 189, 191; under-the-radar profile, xii, 1, 84–85, 185, 206, 237, 256, 278n1, 281n1. See *also* aspirational softcore; contemporary sexploitation; corporate softcore; cult softcore; softcore; softcore audiences

Index

Cook, Pam, 74, 165, 182, 263n1
Corman, Roger, 8, 73–74, 78–79, 80, 81, 83, 88, 99, 101–104, 141, 165, 194, 207, 230, 260n3, 264n13, 266n32, 267n10, 273n15
Corporate Fantasy (Randazzo), 214
corporate softcore, 9, 45, 72, 205–29, 230, 237, 240, 242, 275n2, 278n9, 281n1, 282n14; definitions, 7–8, 205; development and decline, 7, 209, 253–54, 282nn12–13; distinction from aspirational softcore, 7, 9, 205–6, 216–17; narrative-number format, 205–6, 216–17; promotion of, 88, 205, 212–13; routinization, 218–19, 249–50, 269n6; weightlessness, 91, 104, 157, 203, 205–7, 210–17, 220, 229, 256–57, 282n17, 283n24, 283n28
CPV (Cinema Products Video), 6, 86, 152, 154, 209, 217, 282n13
Crash, Johnny, 234, 246, 284n6
Creative Image, xiv, 153
Cresse, Bob, 63
Crosby, Mary, 141
Crown International, 73, 92
Crowther, Bruce, 210–11
cult audiences, 186, 192–97; misogyny and antifeminism, 193, 195; oppositionalism, 187, 193–97, 202–4; and paracinema, 8, 193, 197, 231; and softcore, 187–88, 193–97, 256, 284n4
cult softcore, 188, 230–50; and the cult nexus, 8–9, 186–87, 193–94, 230–31, 236, 243, 246–47; definition of, 8; distinctions with aspirational and corporate softcore, 8–10, 230, 240, 244, 247, 275n2, 284nn10–11, 286n29; links to classical sexploitation, 65, 235–36, 243–46, 250; and premium cable, 237, 267n11, 275n2; promotion of, 8, 231–32, 236, 240–50, 286n26; relative idiosyncrasy of, 8, 65, 230, 247, 249–50, 284n8. See also contemporary softcore, cult audiences
Curious Obsessions (Bacchus), 239, 244–45, 285n21
The Curse of Her Flesh (Findlay), 58, 60

D'Amato, Joe, 69
Damien's Seed (Holzman), 282n23
Dangerous Pleasures (Monroe), 1, 153, *154*, 275n30

Danning, Sybil, 91
Dark, Gregory. *See* Hippolyte, Alexander Gregory
Dash, Julie, 177
Davies, Angela, 176
Davis, Keith, 38, 39
Davis, Scott, 194, 196
Deadly Weapons (Wishman), 164
Dead On (Hemecker), 273n5
Deathstalker (Watson), 101
DeCoteau, David, 99
Deep Jaws (Dell), 79
Deep Throat (Damiano), 2, 26, 27, 42–43, 261n8
DeLaurentiis, Dino, 101
Dell, Perry, 79
Delta of Venus (King), 48, 110, 113, 114, 116, 123, 127–29, 178, 182, 261n6, 261n7, 269n10
DeMille, William, 37, 41
deregulation, 86, 267n7
The Devil in Miss Jones (Damiano), 27
The Dicktator (Dell), 79
Digart, Uschi, 74, 277n20
Disclosure (Levinson), 132, 141
disinterest, aesthetic, 16, 25, 36, 48, 196, 279n14
displaced abjection, 60–61, 269n4, 275n29; Schaefer's use of concept, 60
distribution: strategies to increase, 7, 12–13, 15, 35–36, 38, 42, 73, 77, 111–12, 128, 140, 152, 162, 164, 167, 172, 206, 237, 244, 282n17; constraints on, 12–13, 47, 81–82, 206, 237, 253–56, 274n25. *See also* feminization; postfeminist
Double Agent 73 (Wishman), 164
Douglas, Ann, 12, 23
Douglas, Michael, 132, 136–37, 141
Drago, Billy, 148
Dressed to Kill (De Palma), 134
Driggs, Deborah, 143
drive-ins, 3–4, 81–82, 112
Dr. Jekyll and Mistress Hyde (Marsiglia), 235, 239, 247–50
Duchovny, David, 121, 160
Dworkin, Andrea, 29, 93
Dyer, Richard, 17–18, 95, 96, 98, 107, 162, 178, 191–92, 265n26

early cinema, 47, 51, 232, 235–36
Ebert, Roger, 42
Ecstasy (Machaty), 35, 46
Edwards, Eric, 68
Ehrenreich, Barbara, 26, 211
ei Independent Cinema (ei Cinema), xiv, 67, 70, 190, 230–50, 283n2, 285nn14–16, 286n27, 286n30; After Hours, 236, 243, 246; Factory 2000, 241, 243; POPcinema, 283n1; Retro-Seduction Cinema, 69, 231, 243–46 (*245*), 266n4, 284n6, 285nn17–20; Seduction Cinema, 5, 7, 10, 14, 22, 87, 191, 194, 196, 210, 230–50, 267n11, 275n2, 277n20, 283n2, 284nn4–5, 284nn7–11; Shock-O-Rama, 231, 236–37, 249; Video Outlaw, 236, 246
Eisenman, Rafael, 268n2
"Elena" (Vance), 176, 177
Embrace the Darkness II (Kubilos), 214
Emmanuelle (Jaeckin), 4, 15, 26, 30, *41*, 42–44, 80, 89–91, 111, 149, 150, *163*, 165, 180–81, 262n12, 263n23, 263n25, 269n11
Emmanuelle 2 (Giacobetti), 180–81, 263n24
Emmanuelle in America (D'Amato), 69
empowered babe, the, 72–75 (*72*), 78–79, 100, 103, 106–7, 150, 214, 263n1, 266n32, 268n18. See also female empowerment; postfeminist; working-woman vehicles
England, Audie, 123
erotica, 25–27, 29–31, 115–16, 167, 196; literary, 114, 269n9; and the middlebrow, 26, 31; origin of the term, 25–26
The Erotic Adventures of Zorro (Freeman, Castleman), 60, 62–66, 237, 265n22, 265n26
erotic asphyxiation (or strangulation), 8, 155, 195, 243
Erotic Confessions (*EC*; serial), 159–60, 167, 176, 182; episodes of, 175, 176, 182
The Erotic Diary of Misty Mundae (Black), 239, 241
Erotic Obsessions (Monroe), *156*, 275n30
erotic thrillers, 16, 91, 100, 116, 119, 121–22, 130, 131–58, 214, 215, 225, 270n15, 287n3; hardcore thrillers, 157, 272n2; nontheatrical, 133, 140–58 (*144–45, 154, 156*), 259n1, 272n1, 272n3, 273n12, 274n26, 287n3; theatrical, 71, 109, 131–40 (*134, 137*), 153, 165, 259n1, 273n12. See also *noir;* softcore thrillers; Williams, Linda Ruth
The Erotic Thriller in Contemporary Cinema (Williams), 259n1, 272n1
The Erotic Witch Project (Bacchus), 233–34, 284n5
Escapade, 83, 85
Everhart, Angie, 152
EVI (Entertainment Ventures Incorporated), 60–66, 235–36, 284n7
Excelsior Pictures Corp. v. Regents of the University of the State of New York, 53
exhibitionism, 118, 123, 138, 155, 164, 235
The Exhibitionist Files (Lazarus), 218, 224, 226, 283n28
exotic: as spectacle, 9–10, 117–18, 162, 176, 270n14; and exoticization of social difference, 9, 92, 117, 119, 171, 176–79, 270n14, 277n19. See also carnival
Exposed (Williams), 283n28

Fabian, Ava, 159
face, emphasis on the female, 14, 46, 51, 66, 69, 84, 93–94, 96, 102, *126,* 265nn27–28, 283n27, 284n12. See also female subjectivity
Fallen Angels (Hippolyte), 135
Fancy Lady (Phillips), 277n20
fan groups, 278n2
fantasy: women's ability to distinguish reality from, 174–75; female, 112–13, 121, 124–30, 143, 159, 161, 170–71, 175, 178–79, 211, 213–14, 270n17, 272n30; male, 63, 65, 96–97, 224, 256; rape fantasy, 11, 63, 69, 175, 256
Farmer, Donald, 283n2
Faster, Pussycat! Kill! Kill! (Meyer), 23, 164
Fast Lane to Malibu (Cauthen), 189, 214
Fast Lane to Vegas (Quinn), 214
Fast Times at Ridgemont High (Heckerling), 74, 91, 94–95, 98
Fatal Attraction (Lyne), 1, 4, 122, 131–42 (*134*), 147, 165, 272nn4–5, 273n6
FCC (Federal Communications Commission), 85, 169, 251, 253–56
Feasey, Rebecca, 193, 203
Featherly, Susan, xii, 259n2
Fedele, John, 234

Index

Female Chauvinists (Jackson), 66
female authenticity rhetoric, 167, 169, 174, 179–80, 276n3
female empowerment, 14, 69–70, 76, 78, 97, 99–100, 108, 125, 147, 161–62, 167, 182, 228, 239–40, 261n9; in context of softcore postfeminism, 11, 182
female subjectivity, 14–15, 43, 46, 50–52, 54–58, 68–69, 117, 126–27 (*126*), 129–30, 170–71, 182, 214, 244
Femalien (Richards), 5, 9, 199, 202, 230, *231*
The Feminine Mystique (Friedan), 164
feminism, second-wave, 12, 27–31, 46, 72–74, 76, 102, 127, 135, 141, 162–65, 169–70, 239, 262n14, 278n7, 282n21. See also feminist criticism; postfeminist
feminist criticism: reception of softcore, 9, 10–12, 130, 160–61, 170–83, 275n1; and correctness, 161, 170, 173, 175–76, 178–79, 182. See also feminism, second-wave; postfeminist
feminization, 107, 256; as compensation, 19; and consumerism, 12, 132; as distribution strategy, 7, 15, 162, 167; in girl-girl scenes, 179–80, 277n20; and literariness, 93–94, 114, 271n25; in other cultural sectors, 12, 30, 262n13; at Playboy, 212–14; as diegetic transformation, 117–18, 121–23; as postfeminist stylization, 11, 30, 92, 109, 157, 256, 274n21; apropos the middlebrow, 7, 256; in the softcore serial, 160, 161, 175, 180, 183
The Feminization of American Culture (Douglas), 12
femme fatale, 75, 105–6, 119, 123, *134*, 136–43 (*137*), 146–47, 273n5, 273n14; the hidden femme fatale, 153–54, 275n31
Femme Fatale (De Palma), 134
Fenn, Sherilyn, 116, 269n7
Ferguson, Frances, 196
Film Quarterly, 85
Findlay, Michael, 55, 58–60
Findlay, Roberta, 55, 58–60, 79
Flesh for Olivia (Hellfire), 243
Forbidden (Kubilos), 202
Forbidden Highway (Cauthen), 214, 282n12
Forbidden Sins (Angelo), 153
Ford, Maria, 202, 273n5
Forsa, Marie, 68

Foucault, Michel, 43, 283n29
Frasier, David, 207
French Peep Show (Meyer), 49, 52
Frey, Douglas, 65
Friday, Nancy, 97, 159
Friedan, Betty, 164
Friedkin, William, 134
Friedman, David, 18, 49, 60–63, 79, 84, 207, 235, 264n12, 281n4
Friend of the Family (Holzman), 9, 202, 215–17
front-loaded spectacle, 133, 136, 141–42, 275n30
Full Moon Pictures, 7, 8, 152, 230–31, 250, 260n5, 267n10, 287n3

"Galatea's Wish" (Smith), 182
"The Games People Play" (Bunche), 176
Garroni, Andrew, 150, 274n18, 274n20, 274n25
"Gauging a Revolution" (Schaefer), 4
gender-bending, 105, 151, 272n31
genderlessness, 12–13, 29, 65–66, 108–9, 151, 157
Genre (Neale), 139
Gerli, Jake, 95–96
Gernert, Walter, 14, 143, 150, 274n18, 274n20, 274n25
Giacobetti, Francis, 263n24
Gibson, Eric, 275n30
girl next door, the, 214–15, 242
The Girl Next Door (Greenfield), 95
Girls Kissing Girls (Lee), 277n20
The Girl Who Shagged Me (Moose), 234, 237, 241
Gladiator Eroticvs (Bacchus), 194, 234, 237, 240
Goldberg, Richard, 275n31
Gorfinkel, Elena, 18, 34, 112, 277n20, 278n3
Goursaud, Anne, 48, 279n12
"Grading on a Curve" (Marchese), 181
Greenberg, Clement, 34, 37, 262n16
Greenberg, Marc, 6, 86, 152, 275n31, 281n1
Grieco, Richard, 152, 260n4
Griffin, Susan, 29
Griffith, D.W., 37, 39
grindhouse: as part of the classical circuit, 3–4, 35, 79, 81–82, 112; as classed and gendered site, 35, 84, 112, 244; tolerance of shock and transgression, 60, 84, 87

"Grip Till It Hurts" (Dash), 177
Gunning, Tom, 51, 235
Guy, Sebastien, 213

Hallenbeck, Bruce, 69, 249, 284n9, 286n29
Hall, Gabriella, 202
Hall, Landon, 176
The Happy Hooker (Sgarro), 80
The Happy Hooker Goes Hollywood (Roberts), 84
hardcore: classical, 4, 18, 61, 68–69, 189, 196, 225, 260n4; and compensation, 19–21; competition with classical sexploitation, 76, 79–80, 82; and displaced abjection, 60–62; edited, 95, 228, 267n14, 276n6; elevation *vis-à-vis* softcore, 23, 27–31; origin of the term, 26–27. *See also* contemporary softcore; hardcore-softcore distinction; hardcore thrillers; soft focus; Williams, Linda
Hardcore (Schrader), 135
Hard Core (Williams), 2, 13, 200, 260n4, 265n25
hardcore-softcore distinction, 22, 24–31; as gendered divide, 27–31, 37; relation to the erotica-porn distinction, 25–26, 29, 269n9
Hard Ticket to Hawaii (Sidaris), 23, 101, 105–9 (*105*), 266n1, 266n5, 268n22, 268n24
Hardy, Simon, 18, 117
Harring, Laura Elena, 249
Hart, Veronica, 97, 157
Hartley, Nina, 265n23
HBO (Home Box Office), 4, 82–86, 94, 160, 165, 168–69, 209–10, 254, 267n13, 276nn9–10, 278n4, 286n3
Hebdige, Dick, 12
Heckerling, Amy, 94
Hefner, Christie, 83, 212, 281n9, 282n18
Hefner, Hugh, 26, 42, 206–7, 212, 281n11
Hellcats in High Heels (Howard), 195–96
Hellfire, William ("Bill"), 195, 241
Herman, Pee Wee (Paul Reubens), 190
heterosexism, 2, 12–13, 30, 151, 256
Hewitt, Martin, 122, 143, 148
highbrow, the, 31–44, 262n15; rejection of the middlebrow, 6, 26, 31–37, 113, 269n5; rejection of by cable programmers, 86; rejection of soft focus, 38–39, 41–44,

283n26. *See also* lowbrow, the; middlebrow, the
Hill, Jack, 265n32
Hinton, Darby, 107
Hippolyte, Alexander Gregory (a.k.a. Gregory Dark), 9, 25, 111, 135, 140, 142, 145–50, 180, 202, 211, 220, 226, 261n5, 263n23, 274n19, 286n30
Hollows, Joanne, 162–63, 183, 193, 195, 261n8
Hollywood Chainsaw Hookers (Ray), 88, 99, 267n12
Hollywood Hot Tubs (Vincent), 95, 99, 266n1, 268n17
Hollywood Sex Fantasy (Cauthen), 214, 217
Hollywood Sins (Holzman), 213–14
Hollywood Video, 185, 237, 253
Holmes, John, 28
Holzman, Edward, 215, 219, 282n23
home video, 87–88, 274n25; and cult softcore, 230, 237, 275n2; as diversity of tastes, 87; and the transition to contemporary sexploitation, 4, 80, 267n10
"Homework" (Riley), 181
hommes fatals, 107, 112, 119, 121, 123, 148–49
horror films, 8, 16, 72, 194, 214, 230–33, 236, 240, 249, 250, 284n12, 285n12, 286n30
Hotel Erotica (serial), 160, 174, 176; episode of, 276n4
Hot Line (serial), 160, 176; episode of, 175
House of Love (Lazarus), 73, 202, 218, 221–22, *223*, 226, 227, 283n29
housewife, the, 70–72, 133, 148, 150
Hunt, Leon, 32, 37, 63, 71
Hunt, Nathan, 193, 195
Hustler, 281n10
Hutton, Hal, 214

I am Curious (Yellow) (Sjöman), 66
I, a Woman (Ahlberg), 43, 56, 66, 265n27
I Like to Play Games (Lobato), 9, 142, 202, 214, 273n16, 282n12
"Illicit Affairs" (Nicholas), 181, 277n21
Illicit Dreams (Stevens), 147, 151
Ilsa, 57, 65
IMDb (Internet Movie Database), 187, 197–99, 272n4, 273n17, 279n11, 279n16, 285n15
The Immoral Mr. Teas (Meyer), 3, 15–16, 49,

52–54, 55, 56, 95, 207, 235, 264n13, 281n3
Imperial Entertainment, 143
impressionism, 37, 38
I'm Watching You (Brown), 214
In Dangerous Company (Preuss), 273n14
indecency, xii, 18, 80, 172, 240, 264n11; and the FCC, 251, 253–57
The Indelicate Balance (Sarno), 285nn17–18
Independent-International, 73, 81, 266n4
Indigo Entertainment, 7, 206, 209–10, 223, 228, 250, 274n27, 282n24. See also Playboy Enterprises
Inga (Sarno), 15, 67–70 (*70*), 111, 243–44, 248
Inness, Sherrie, 106
Inskafilm, 68
Internet, the, 139, 186, 193, 194, 196–99, 232, 274n24, 279n16
In the Cut (Campion), 270n15
In the Realm of the Senses (Oshima), 155
Intimate Sessions (serial), 160, 176; episodes of, 176, 177
Intrator, Jerald, 49, 67
Invasion of the Bee Girls (Sanders), 75, 165
I Spit on Your Grave (Zarchi), 101

Jade (Friedkin), 134
Jaeckin, Just, 4, 7, 9, 15, 26, 34, 38, 41–44, 90, 111, 114, 149, 163, 221, 226, 263n24, 269n11, 283n26
Jaehne, Karen, 5, 15, 84, 85–86, 87, 152, 165, 173, 189, 262n12
"Jake's Story" (Karbelnikoff), 269n6, 271n23, 277n16
James, David, 17
Jancovich, Mark, xiii, 31–33, 42, 187, 193, 196, 199, 262n14, 263n21, 284n8
Janet Jackson affair, 102, 251–55 (*252*)
Jenkins, Henry, 30, 193
Jeremy, Ron, 98
Jillson, Joyce, 75
Joe Bob Report, 186, 194
Johnson, Caroline Key, 176
Johnson, Ed Lee, 177
Johnson, Eithne, 27, 54, 84, 265n20, 278n3
Johnson, Paul, 156
Johnston, Bobby, 215
Jordan, Marsha, 28, 71
Journal of Popular Culture, 214
Juffer, Jane, 31, 86, 87, 169, 173–74, 180, 183, 185, 212, 262n14, 267n8, 269n9, 276n8, 276n13, 278n1, 281n11, 282n23
Justice Department, United States, 253
just-shy-of-softcore sexploitation, 7, 94, 115–16, 129, 138, 141–42, 145–46, 158, 273n7, 278n1; as distribution strategy, 111, 113

Kapanke, Christopher John, 225, 278n5
"Kat Tails" (Pagulayan), 179–80, 276n4
Kaufman, Lloyd, 194
Kaye, Caren, 92
Kendrick, Walter, 25–26, 29, 273n7, 278n7, 284n10
Killer Looks (Thomas), 147
King, Chloe, 268n1
King, Zalman, 5, 7, 9, 15, 22, 34, 42–44, 48, 77–78, 92, 94, 109–31, 141, 146, 158, 160, 165–70, 178, 180, 202, 206, 211, 214, 220, 226, 263n23, 268nn1–4, 269nn5–8, 269nn11–12, 270nn13–18, 271nn19–30, 272n31, 274n19, 274n21, 283n26; Zalmanesque, the, 113–16, 219–20. See also *Red Shoe Diaries* (King); *Red Shoe Diaries* (serial)
kinkies, 3, 46, 54–55, 57–59, 73, 74, 101, 103, 272n3
Kinky Kong (Bacchus), 234
Kipnis, Laura, 31, 263n21, 278n7
The Kiss of Her Flesh (Findlay), 58
Klaw, Irving, 57–58
Knop, Patricia Louisianna, 268n1
Koch, Gertrud, 189
Kristel, Sylvia, *41, 43, 163*
Kubilos, Robert, 219
Kubrick, Stanley, 36, 286n23

Lake Consequence (Eisenman), 9, 109, 116, 117–18, 120–22, 124, 268n2, 274n19
Lancaster, Stuart, 61
Laqueur, Thomas, 66, 97, 190–91, 278n7
Larranaga, Catalina, 202, 221, 222, 224
Lattanzi, Matt, 92
Lawrence, D. H., 90
Lazarus, Tom, xiv, 22, 113, 180, 190, 202, 207, 218–29, 247, 281n2, 282n14, 283nn25–26, 283nn28–30
Lee, Sheryl, 269n7, 271n23
Lefkowitz, Gillian, 268n1

Leigh, Barbara, 74
Leighton, Ava, 268n1
Lewis, Jon, xiv, 4, 26, 48, 60, 79, 80, 90, 236, 262n12, 266n2, 267n8, 272n3, 273n10
Liljedahl, Marie, 68, 243
Lincoln, Jack, 225
"Locked Up" (Bunche), 175
Loftus, David, 132, 280n19, 280n24
Lombard, Robert, xiv, 5, 6, 152, 153, 154, 156, 172, 203, 209, 240, 254, 267n8, 275n28, 280n21, 280n27, 282n14, 286n30, 286n3
Lord of the G-Strings (West), 231, 234, 237–38 (*238*), 239, 246, 284n9
Lorna (Meyer), 54–56 (*55*), 57, 63, 68, 71, 164, 264n15
Losano, Wayne, 189
Lost Highway (Lynch), 248, 261n4, 286n24
Love Camp 7 (Frost), 63
Love Games (Monroe), 156–57, 275n30
Lovell, Jacqueline, 130
The Lover (Annaud), 94
Love Street (serial), 86, 160, 167, 181–82; episodes of, 181–82
Love Toy (Wishman), 58–59, 265n19
lowbrow, the, 112, 120–21, 228–29, 233–36, 239, 263, 284n10; counterintuitive relation to high culture, 31, 32, 34, 246–49; relation to masculinity, 270n15. *See also* highbrow, the; masculinization; middlebrow, the
low-budget softcore paradigm, 152, 209, 273n16, 274n27, 282n15
low hero, the, 9, 112–13, 116–28, 178, 269n12, 270n13, 271nn21–22; subjectification of, 121, 127
Luckett, Moya, 71–72
"The Lucky Bar" (Bertei-Cecchi), 177
Lury, Celia, 12, 13, 177, 203
Lust for Dracula (Marsiglia), 235, 247, 249, 286n23, 286nn27–28
Lust for Laura (Sarno), 235, 243, 285n18
Lustful Addiction (Mundae), 241, 243
The L Word (serial), 169, 180, 255
Lyne, Adrian, 110, 134, 135–36, 141, 147
Lynne, Beverly, 278n5
Lynn, Vicki, 51, 108
Lynch, David, 114, 196, 232, 248–49, 261n4, 269n7, 286nn24–25

Macdonald, Dwight, 33–34
Macherey, Pierre, 217
MacKinnon, Catharine, 29, 278n7
Magic Hour Pictures. *See under* Mainline Releasing
Magnum Entertainment, 143, 145
Mainline Releasing, 152, 154, 156, 274n26, 275n31; Magic Hour Pictures, 152–53, 274n26, 275n31; MRG (Mainline Releasing Group), 5–7, 86, 133, 152–57, 172, 203, 205, 209, 210, 214, 217, 236, 250, 254, 267n6, 267n8, 274n26, 275nn27–28, 275nn30–31, 275n2, 276n9, 281n1, 282nn13–14, 283n28, 286n3, 287n3. *See also* softcore thrillers
Mair, George, 80, 82–84, 168, 208
Maitland, Lorna, 56, 207
The Making of Middlebrow Culture (Rubin), 33
male disempowerment, 78, 95–100, 191, 240. *See also* sexploitation comedy; teen sex comedy
Malibu Bay Films, 104, 105, 266n5
Malibu Express (Sidaris), 101, 104–7, 268n21, 268n22, 268n24
Malle, Louis, 48, 260n6
Mantis in Lace (Rotsler), 58–59 (*59*), 75, 265n19, 272n3
Marcus, Steven, 25–26, 36, 261n6, 278n7
Married People, Single Sex (Sedan), 220
Marsha, the Erotic Housewife (Davis), 71
Marsiglia, Tony, xiv, 196, 219, 226, 235, 246–50, 285nn22–23, 286nn24–28
Martin, Nina, 114, 117, 129–30, 170–75, 178–80, 183, 272n32, 277n15
masculinization, of burlesque, 52; of the cult nexus, 8–10, 78, 193; of empowered babes, 75; of the grindhouse, 87; of hard, pure forms, 24, 34, 38–39, 44, 261n4; of Hollywood paradigms, 77; of the lowbrow, 9, 120; of Playboy softcore, 211–14; and rape discourse, 64; in roughies and kinkies, 57; at Seduction Cinema, 239, 244; of sex-action films, 100–109; and sexploitation comedy, 94–100, 265n26, 272n3; in erotic thrillers, 142, 270n15; of the softcore serial's visual biases, 180–81; of the Zalman King heroine, 117–18, 124–25
masochism, female, 63–65, 78, 142, 264n14;

Index

male, 16, 100, 112, 138, 161, 174, 199
masturbation, 189–92, 234; and burlesque films, 51–52, 191; and devaluation of softcore, 16, 188, 195–96, 279n14; female, 11, 15, 19, 69–70, 97–98, 126, 155, 190–92, 228, 278n5, 278n10, 280n24; and feminism, 97–98, 165, 190–92; male, 19, 97–99, 189–92, 203, 223, 228, 278n8; and narrative-number format, 97, 195–96; restrictions on male, 11, 190–92, 278nn7–9; and technology, 190, 192. *See also* raincoat brigade
Mawra, Joseph, 57–58
May, Tons, 263n22
McBride, Harlee, 90
McCarty, Kelli, 226, 278n2, 282n22
McClure, Tane, 153
McNair, Brian, 135, 138
McVoy, D. Stevens, 82–86
Media Home Entertainment, 267n10
Medium Cool (Wexler), 283n25
Meese Commission, 29, 262n11
Mellencamp, Patricia, 139
Men, Women, and Chain Saws (Clover), 116
Metzger, Radley, 7, 9, 15, 34–38, 42, 46, 55–56, 67, 68, 79, 111–12, 114, 149, 157, 165, 180, 226, 265n30, 268n1, 269nn4–5, 277n20, 283n26
Meyer, Russ, 3, 14, 35, 49, 52–56, 73, 95, 104, 164–65, 207, 235, 269n4
M&G's (moans and groans), 96–97, 267n15, 268n22
Michelson, Peter, 212
midbudget softcore paradigm, 133, 146–51, 157, 209, 253, 259n1, 272n1, 273n16, 274nn20–21, 274n25, 282n15
middlebrow, the, 6, 31–37, 83, 112, 114, 189, 228, 236, 246, 257, 262n16, 271n25; difficulties for interpreters, xiii, 32–33, 262n15; origin of the concept, 33–34. *See also* highbrow, the; lowbrow, the
middlebrow heroine, the, 9, 14, 93, 112, 114–24, 161, 178, 214, 269n12, 270n13, 270n16, 271nn21–23
middle feminism. *See under* postfeminism
Miller v. California, 4, 79, 253
Mills, C. Wright, 33
"Mind's Eye" (Fishel), 170, 175
Ministry of Film, 176

Mirror Images (Hippolyte), 143
misandry: as byproduct of softcore's postfeminist identity, 11, 174, 181, 270n15; as result of mainstream distribution, 16; in classical sexploitation, 71–72, 74–75; in softcore serials, 161–62, 167–68, 174, 178–82, 199, 277n21; in softcore thrillers, 148–49, 199, 270n15; as reflected by sexual double standards, 11, 16, 148, 151, 162, 256
misogyny: in art films, 149, 182, 249–50; as result of nonmainstream distribution, 10, 54; in cult films, 195, 249–50; in *noir* and the erotic thriller, 132, 140–42, 153–54, 158, 273n14; at Playboy, 212, 228–29; in roughies and kinkies, 55–59; in softcore serials, 182; in sword-and-sorcery films, 102–3, 268n18
Mistress Frankenstein (Bacchus), 234, 240, 249–50
"Misty Mundae: From Skin to Scream" (Seduction), 240–41
mock documentary, 218, 220, 224–25, 228. *See also cinéma vérité;* reality television
"Model Situation" (Bunche), 182
The Model Solution (Holzman), 213–14 (*213*)
modernism, 33–34, 39, 194, 227
Modleski, Tania, 10, 30, 32, 217, 261n1
Mona (Ziehm), 4, 60
Mondo Rocco (Rocco), 191
Monroe, Madison, 275n30
Monson, Carl, 264n13
Morality in Media, 84–85
Morgan, Robin, 262n11
"Motel Magic" (Landsburg), 177
Movie Channel, The, 7, 82, 160, 278n4
MPAA (Motion Picture Association of America), 18, 60, 80, 169
MRG (Mainline Releasing Group). *See under* Mainline Releasing
MTV (Music Television), 228, 252, 254, 255, 269n8
Mudhoney (Meyer), 164
Mulholland Drive (Lynch), 240, 248–49, 285n23
multiculturalism and diversity, 162, 176–79, 203–4, 277n18, 283n30
Mulvey, Laura, 107, 118
Mumford, Laura Stempel, 276n3
Mundae, Misty, 194, 195, 231, 240–44, 248,

250, 283n2, 284nn12–13, 285n15, 286n23, 286nn28–29
Mundhra, Jag, 144, 146, 147, 150, 260n3, 270n15, 274n25
Mystique Films, 206, 209, 222. *See also* Playboy Enterprises
My Tutor (Bowers), 92, 181

Naked Obsession (Golden), 155, 260n2, 270n15
The Naked Venus (Ulmer), 47–48, 181
Naremore, James, 9, 87, 119, 134, 136, 139, 143, 147, 166, 194, 260n3, 273n13, 274n20
narrative: and gender bias, 14, 16, 56, 71–72, 78, 94–100, 140–41, 146–54, 161–62, 171–75, 179–83, 212–14, 244, 264n14, 270n15; development, 18, 54–56, 66–70, 101–4, 112–13, 115–30, 133, 136–39, 147–50, 154–57, 167–68, 179, 215–17, 233–37, 255–56, 266n32, 269n10, 283n29, 284n9; Hollywood, 34; integration with number, 49, 56, 115–16, 139, 197–98, 200, 206, 224–25, 234–36, 249, 265n19, 279n12, 282n24, 283n24, 284n9; reception of softcore, 21, 187–88, 196–202, 279nn12, 279nn15–16, 280n19
narrative-number format. *See under* corporate softcore. *See also* masturbation; softcore; softcore audiences
National Cable and Telecommunications Association, 255
The Naughty Stewardesses (Adamson), 62, *72,* 73, 81, 266n4, 285n19
Neale, Stephen, 139
network television, 80
New City Releasing, 5, 7, 176, 205, 209, 214, 215, 217, 254, 275n2, 286n3
New Hollywood, 4, 135
New World Pictures, 73–75, 80, 103, 265n32
"New York Wildcats" (Crash), 235, 284n6, 285n18
Night Call Nurses (Kaplan), 73
Night Calls (serial), 228
Nightcap (serial), 160, 174, 181; episodes of, 181, 277n21
Night Eyes (Mundhra), 144–46 (*144*), 153, 274n21
Night Rhythms (Hippolyte), 142–43, 274n21
Nin, Anaïs, 110, 178, 269n11

Ninn, Michael, 268n3
Nochimson, Martha, 276n3
noir: classic, 9, 67, 116, 119, 135, 140, 210–11, 218, 273n13; *noir* hero, 138, 142–43, 146, 154, 273n14; *noir*-romance hybrids, 22, 77–78, 109, 111–12, 119, 130, 140, 145, 146, 158, 165–66, 270n12, 270n15, 274n19; *noir* stylization, 140, 142–44, 146, 149, 151, 152, 158, *166,* 175, 261n4, 269n7, 270n15; sexploitation *noir,* 139, 142, 273n15; softcore *noir,* 139, 142. *See also* erotic thrillers; softcore thrillers; Williams, Linda Ruth
The Notorious Cleopatra (Perry), 63–65, 265n25
Novak, Harry, 4, 60, 64, 235, 265n24
Novel Desires (Unger), 86
Noyce, Phillip, 134
nudie cuties, 3, 14, 49–50, 52–54, 56, 78, 94–95, 214, 235, 240
nudist films, 3, 47–50, 53, 263n4
number: distinction from spectacle, 2, 56, 115–16, 224–25. *See also* just-shy-of-softcore sexploitation

objectification: female, 14, 16, 47, 54, 75, 106, 126–27, 171–74, 180–83, 286n28; male, 14, 105–8, 117–18, 126, 171–74, 178, 268n23; *to-be-looked-at-ness,* 107, 118; inequities in, 13–14, 16, 112, 161–62, 171–74, 180–83. *See also under* subjectification
O'Brien, Shauna, 215, 275n29, 278n1
Olga's House of Shame (Mawra), 57
orgasm, female, 96–97
Oshima, Nagisa, 155
The Other Woman (Mundhra), 146, 150–51, 270n15, 274n21
Otis, Carré, 121, 270n14
O'Toole, Laurence, xiii, 29, 137, 139, 180, 191, 262n9, 263n24, 265n23, 278n4, 278n7

Page, Betty (a.k.a., Bettie Page), 50–52, 57, 264n18
Paramount, 146
Paramount Decrees, 80, 266n3
Parent, Monique, 6, 147, 149, 202; as Scarlet Johansing, 215
Parents Television Council, 251, 267n9
parody, 233–35, 240, 245–46, 248–49, 268n24

Index

Passion Cove (serial), 160, 281n7
Passion's Peak (Quinn), 214
paternalism, 43, 65–66, 79, 84, 87, 108–9, 174, 181, 267n9, 26n24
pathologization of sexual desire, 68, 148, 265n28
pay-per-view distribution, xii, 82, 190, 208–9, 236, 253–54, 275n28, 286n3
Peckinpah, Samuel, 63
Peeping Tom (Powell), 227
Penthouse, 38, 42, 208, 242, 263n21, 275n29, 281n10
Perfectly Legal (Davis), 214, 228
Persona (Bergman), 248, 286n25
Personals 2 (Cauthen), 214, 278n5
Pescia, Lisa, 141
Peterson, Kristine, 141
Phillips, Nick (Steve Millard), 243–44, 246, 265n28, 277n20, 285n16
Picasso Trigger (Sidaris), 101, 106–8, 266n1, 266n5, 268n23
pictorialism, 37–39, 41, 149, 262n18
Piper, Brett, 235, 247, 250, 284n12
A Place Called Truth (Eisenman), 130, 271n21, 272n31
Platinum Pictures, 95
Playboy Enterprises, xiv, 6, 22, 83–84, 90–91, 130, 142, 152, 173–74, 205–29, 234, 247, 250, 261n7, 275n2, 276n13, 281n2, 281n4, 281n11, 282n15, 282n17, 282n19, 282n21, 282n24, 283n28; Playboy Entertainment, 206, 208, 222, 267n8, 274n27, 281n7, 281n12, 282n14, 282n20, 282n22; *Playboy* magazine, 26, 38, 42, 49, 106, 187–88, 199, 206–9, 242–43, 263n21, 264n13, 281nn3–5, 281n8, 281n10, 282nn20–22, 284n10; Playboy TV (formerly called the Playboy Channel), xii, 83, 90, 94, 95, 190, 207, 208, 209, 218, 220, 227–28, 276n6, 277n13, 281n6, 281n9, 282n15, 282n17
Playboy philosophy, the, 49, 206, 211–12; and the Playboy lifestyle, 212–14; and the Playboy male, 212, *213*, 214. See also consumerism
Play-Mate of the Apes (Bacchus), 194, 199, 234, 237, 239, 284n5
Playmates, *Playboy*, 105–6, 207–8, 214, 281nn4–5
Play Time (Trevillion), 9, 202, 273n16, 278n9, 282n12
Please Don't Eat My Mother (Monson), 264n13
Pleasures of a Woman (Phillips), 244
The Pleasure Zone (serial), 160
Poison Ivy 2 (Goursaud), 48, 279n12
Porky's (Clark), 4, 74, 91, 94, 95, 96
porno-chic, 2, 24, 25, 26–27, 30, 61, 69, 84, 91
porno-fear, 135, 139
pornography: devaluation of, xiii, 25, 186, 216–17; distinction from erotica (*see under* hardcore-softcore distinction); evasion of the concept, 7, 111, 113, 115–16, 129, 180, 185–86, 197, 199, 216, 225, 236, 256, 262n12, 269n9; origin of the term, 25
postfeminist, 10–14, 30–31, 78–79, 86, 114, 126, 162–70, 246, 277nn14–15; anxiety, 11, 87, 100–101, 104, 108–9, 150; apolitical aspect, 11, 128, 161, 163, 271n29; backlash, 11, 135, 143, 164–65, 178, 274n22; consumerism, 12, 76, 105–6, 109, 125, 127–28, 132, 139, 152, 157, 164, 192, 206, 212, 221, 228; definitions of, 10–12, 162–64, 261n8; and middle feminism, 46, 66, 72–75, 91, 103–5, 165; postfeminism as a constraint on genderlessness, 133, 139, 151, 157, 249–50, 272n31; propriety, 93, 170, 172, 175, 180–83, 214, 256; stylization, 11, 30, 92, 109, 169, 256, 274n21. See also consumerism; female empowerment; feminism, second-wave; feminization; misandry; soft focus
postmodernism, 34
Potter, Bridget, 84
Powell, Michael, 251, 255–56
pre-Code Hollywood, 36, 39–40, 42, 48
Preppies (Vincent), 95–99, 282n15
Prism Entertainment, 5, 144, 146, 152, 209, 273n13
Production Code, the, 3, 36, 40, 47, 60, 80, 94–95, 169, 262n19
productivist values, 12, 15, 50, 91, 129, 138, 211, 279n14
The Profession (serial), 220
Projansky, Sarah, 11, 12, 63, 102, 163–64, 177, 183, 261n8, 277n14
Psychotronic Video, 186

Quarry, Peter, 237
Queer as Folk (serial), 69

Quigley, Linnea, 240
Quigley, Martin, 263n20
Quinn, John, 219

race, 19, 117, 162, 171, 176–79, 203, 228, 256, 264n14, 270n14
raincoat man (or raincoat brigade), the, 36, 53, 189–92, 196, 202, 278n3. *See also* masturbation
rape motifs: and attitudes toward rape fantasy, 11, 63–64, 93, 174–75; in classical sexploitation, 46, 55–56, 59, 61–65, 102, 265n22; in contemporary sexploitation, 79, 93, 268n24, 286n28; in hardcore, 265n23; nonconsensual scenes, 63, 65, 93; rape tease, 101–2; semiconsensual scenes, 56, 63–65, 91–93, 265n25, 280n25; rape-revenge films, 63, 101–4, 268n18; transition from male-identified to female-identified, 63–65
Raso, Michael, xiv, 190, 194, 231–43, 246, 249, 284n4, 285n18, 286n27, 286n30
rating systems: and Blockbuster Video, 1, 267n8; and cable, 169, 254–55, 276n8; and the MPAA, 79–80, 169, 266n2
Ray, Fred Olen (a.k.a. Nicholas Medina), 4, 81, 88, 99, 267nn11–12
Rea, Renee, 214
Read, Jacinda, 10, 162, 183, 193, 195
Reagan, Ronald, 29, 80, 86, 109, 135, 267n7
realism, 31, 34, 39, 41, 51, 69, 113, 168–69, 179–80, 201, 206–7, 210–11, 218–28, 234, 237, 247, 250, 261n10, 265n30, 281n10, 282n20, 283n25
reality television, 207, 218, 220, 228–29, 276n10
Real Sex (serial), 276n10
Red Shoe Diaries (*RSD;* King), 7, 9, 110, 112, 116, 117, 120, 121, 12–25, 129–30, 165, 167, 270n17, 270n18, 271n25
Red Shoe Diaries (*RSD;* serial), 5, 7, 30, 94, 110–14, 116, 121, 125, 129, 130, 160–61, 163, *166*, 167–78, 182, 220, 268n2, 269n7, 271n25, 271n28, 272n31, 274n19, 274n22, 276n9; episodes of, 114–15, 174–75, 269n6, 271n21, 271nn23–24, 276n3, 276n5, 277nn16–17
"*Red Shoe Diaries:* Sexual Fantasy and the Construction of the (Hetero)sexual Woman" (Martin), 129–30, 170
Reed, Kira, 130
Reems, Harry, 68
Reich, Wilhelm, 27
Retro-Seduction Cinema. *See under* ei Independent Cinema
Return to Two Moon Junction (Mann), 123, 271n22
Rexroth, Mary, 28, 30
Richards, Allen, 194–97, 239
Ritz Brothers, the, 235, 285n19
Rivera, Nicholas, 114
Roberts, Alan, xiv, 78, 83, 89–94, 114, 146, 207, 208, 263n23, 282n15
Roberts, Tanya, 146, 176
Rocco, Pat, 28
Rochon, Debbie, 240
romance fiction, xi, 23, 63, 93, 102, 112, 114–18, 122–23, 127, 159, 190, 261n1, 269n10, 269n12, 271nn19–20, 278n5
"Room 1503" (Cat X), 179–80, 276n4
Rosebud Entertainment, 209
Roth (*Roth v. United States*), 26, 27
Rothman, Stephanie, 74
Rothstein, Elisa, 9–10, 97, 159, 173–74, 178, 180, 261n7
Rotsler, William, 4, 26, 45, 58, 60–61, 64, 70, 265n24, 272n3
roughies, 3, 14, 18, 46, 54–59, 73, 78–79, 101, 103, 272n3
Rourke, Mickey, 117, 270n13
Roxanna (Crestview), 239
Roxanna (Phillips), 243, 248, 265n28
Royalle, Candida, 21, 98, 180, 268n16
Rubin, Joan Shelley, 33
"Runway" (Eisenman), 174, 271n21, 277n16
Russell, Diana, 14, 29–31, 99, 276n12
Russell, Ken, 90
Ryan, Tracy, 202, 221, 259n2

Saalman, Raelyn, 175
sadism, 8, 57–58, 63, 65, 73, 104, 124–27, 138, 149, 266n32, 271n28
"Safe Sex" (King), 269n6
same-sex spectacle, 11, 13, 180, 242, 277n20; boy-boy, 157, 265n30; girl-girl, 2, 8, 43, 52, 149, 150, 161, 179–80, 203, 232–33,

Index

237–40, 242, 244, 248–50, 263n1, 277n20, 285n14. *See also* sexual identity
Sapphire Films, 209
Sarno, Joseph, 7, 34, 38, 46, 56, 67–71, 79, 97, 111, 114, 149, 165, 180, 243–47, 265n28, 268n1, 269n4, 277n20, 284n6, 285nn17–18
Sartre, Jean-Paul, 185–86, 188–89
Satan in High Heels (Intrator), 67
satiation factor, 5, 151
Savage Beach (Sidaris), 101
Schaefer, Eric, xiv, 2, 3, 4, 9, 15–16, 18, 27, 36, 47–52, 54, 55, 59, 60–61, 65, 72, 81, 84, 117, 207, 232, 235, 240, 260n3, 260n4, 260n6, 262n10, 263nn3–4, 264nn6–9, 264n16, 265n20, 266n3, 275n33, 278n3, 278n6. See also *"Bold! Daring! Shocking! True!"*; burlesque; classical exploitation; nudist films; "Gauging a Revolution"
Schnuit, Jason, 215
Schrader, Paul, 135
Sconce, Jeffrey, 8, 188, 192, 195, 230–31
Score (Metzger), 157, 265n30
Screaming Dead (Piper), 231, 235, 247, 249, 284n12
scream queens, 240, 250
Screen, 8, 192
Screen Actors Guild (SAG), 6, 151–52, 209
"Screwed Up" (Orona), 276n4
Secret Games (Hippolyte), 71, 147, 148–50, 215, 274n21
Secret Games 3 (Hippolyte), 149
The Secret Museum (Kendrick), 25
The Secret Sex Lives of Romeo and Juliet (Perry), 4, 64, 237, 265n24
Secrets of Film Writing (Lazarus), 218
Sedan, Mike, 202, 220
The Seduction of Inga (Sarno), 68
The Seduction of Misty Mundae (Raso), 10, 241, 243, 285n18
Seduction Cinema. *See under* ei Independent Cinema
self-reflexivity, 61, 98–99, 114–15, 119, 226–27, 237–38, 244–45, 265n21, 268n17, 269n11
Severance, Joan, 121
sex-action films, 73, 75, 78, 100–109
Sex and the City (serial), 169
Sex Appeal (Vincent), 95, 97–99, 267n16, 268n17
SexGoreMutants, 194, 202

sexploitation comedy, 74, 83, 88, 90–100, 181, 191, 214, 230, 268n22, 272n3. *See also* burlesque; teen sex comedy; male disempowerment
"Sexposé" (Playboy), 228
Sex, Secrets, and Betrayals (Franks), 1, 275n32
Sex, Secrets, and Lies (Allen), 1, 275n32
sexual identity: bisexuality, 57, 108–9, 138, 149, 157, 248, 272n31, 285n14; heterosexuality, 96–97, 106, 112, 129, 169, 272n31, 277n20; homosexuality, 65–66, 96, 98, 106–7, 169, 176–77, 179–80, 191, 277n20, 283n30. *See also* genderlessness; heterosexism; same-sex spectacle
Sexual Magic (Holzman), 214
Sexual Malice (Mundhra), 146
Sexual Predator (Angelo, Spera; a.k.a. *Dangerous Desires*), 1, 152–53, 260n4
sexual revolution, 24, 26–27, 30, 38, 76, 212, 257
The Sexy Adventures of Van Helsing (Fedele), 234, 283nn2–3
Sexy American Idle (Fedele), 234–35
Shackleton, Allen, 265n20
Shea, Katt, 96–97, 265n19
Sheppard, Delia, 143, 148
Sherman, Sam, 81, 266n4, 285n19
Shock-O-Rama. *See under* ei Independent Cinema
Shock-O-Rama (Piper), 231
shot-on-video productions, 37, 151–52, 231, 244–46, 250, 254, 260n5, 260n1, 283n2, 285n21, 286n3
Showgirls (Verhoeven), 139
Showtime, xi, 4, 7, 82–83, 85–86, 90, 94, 110, 112, 130, 160, 165, 166, 168–69, 174, 180, 209–10, 254–55, 261n7, 270n17, 276n7, 276n9, 278n4
Shumate, Nathan, 194
Siciliano, Pat, 260n5, 281n1, 282n12
Sidaris, Andy, 75, 78–79, 101, 104–9, 118, 194, 207, 266n1, 266n5, 268n20, 268n22, 268n24, 281n4
Sidaris, Arlene, 105, 108, 268n20, 268n23
Silhouette romance, 115, 122, 269n10
Simpson, Alan, 194, 196
Sinema (Turan, Zito), 18, 27–29
Sinful (Marsiglia), 235, 241, 249, 286n23
Sinful Deeds (Giove), 155

Singer, Marc, 141
Sin in Soft Focus (Vieira), 39
Sin Sisters (Marsiglia), 235
Sirk, Douglas, 269n12
slasher, the, 100, 132, 140
The Slaughter (Findlay, Findlay), 59, 265n20. See also *Snuff*
Sliver (Noyce), 134, 139, 227
The Slumber Party Massacre (Jones), 100
Smith, Amber, 174
smooth jazz, 114, 269n8, 270n17
Snitow, Ann Barr, 25
Snuff (Findlay, Findlay), 84, 265n20. See also *The Slaughter*
soap opera, xi, 147, 167, 211, 215, 261n1, 276n3, 282n22
Soble, Alan, 99, 190, 262n11
softcore: definition of, 2, 267n14; as exemplified by *Emmanuelle*, 42–43; as a gendered concept, 27–31, 37; narrative-number format in, 2, 47, 58, 110–11, 115–16, 133, 139, 157, 167, 184, 195–200, 221, 224–25, 230, 233–35, 256, 273n9, 279n12, 279n15, 282n24, 284n5; origin of the term, 26–27; as a pejorative, xiii, 23–24, 27, 31, 37, 184–86, 198–99, 204, 261n3, 279n12, 279n15
softcore audiences, 54, 112, 171–72, 184–204, 275n1, 279nn10–16, 280n19, 280nn22–23, 284n4; and emphasis on detail, 279n11; and links to objectification practices, 112, 119, 284n4; and links to the observer figure, 54, 191; make-up of, 198, 203, 279n16; and the narrative-number format, 21, 184, 187, 195–200, 206, 233, 235–36, 279n12, 279n15; and negation or interpretive amputation, 20–21, 187–88, 196–202, 275n1, 279n15 (*see also* compensation); self-consciousness of, 21, 185–89, 195–202, 204, 280n18; and evaluation, 21, 196–202, 279nn12–13, 279n15, 280n17. *See also* masturbation
softcore featurettes, 4–5, 167–68, 179, 276nn5–6. *See also* softcore serials
Softcore Reviews, xii, xiv, 172, 187–88, 192, 199–204, 269n5, 274n24, 280nn17–18, 280nn20–23, 280nn25–27
softcore serials, 4–5, 22, 130, 158, 159–183, 230, 275nn1–2; narrative biases of, 174–75, 177, 179–82; non-adversarial aspect, 161–62, 176–83. *See also* softcore featurettes
softcore thrillers, 4, 22, 71, 77–78, 109, 111, 131–33, 136, 139, 140, 142–58, 166, 211, 220, 230, 259n1, 270n12, 272n1, 272n3, 273n7, 274nn20–21, 275n30. *See also* erotic thrillers; *noir*; Williams, Linda Ruth
soft focus: as aspirational style, 7, 37–43, 62, 68, 206, 211, 239, 276n5; and beauty, 37, 39–40, 43, 90, 221–22, 263n25; in classical softcore, 62, 68; as compensation, 17–19; in cult softcore, 239; devaluation of, 23–24, 38, 44, 113, 218–19; and distribution, 38, 42; and *Emmanuelle*, 41–44 (*41*), 263n21, 263n24; feminization of, 38–39, 43–44, 147, 211, 257; in hardcore, 20–21; in Lazarus's work, 219–25, 283n26; overview of, 37–44, 262n17; at *Playboy* and *Penthouse*, 38, 42, 281n10; as postfeminist style, 11, 43, 109, 147; in softcore thrillers, 147, 149. *See also* aspirational softcore; feminization; postfeminist
"Soft Porn Culture" (Douglas), 23
"Soft-Shaft Opportunism" (Testa), 36–37
Solitary Sex (Laqueur), 97
Some Nudity Required (Springer), 273n15
Something Weird Video, 193, 196, 243, 265n24
Sontag, Susan, 39
The Sopranos (serial), 169
Sorority Babes in the Slimeball Bowl-O-Rama (DeCoteau), 99
Spader, James, 175, 270n17
Speir, Dona, 106, 268n24
SpiderBabe (Crash), 234, 237, 241, *242*, 285n14
Springer, Odette, 273n15, 284n4
square-up, the, 49, 50, 264n7
Stacey (Sidaris), 75, 105
stag films, 17, 47, 61–62, 263n2
Staiger, Janet, 3
Stallybrass, Peter, 60, 120, 124, 239, 270n15
Star 80 (Fosse), 135, 207
Starlet! (Kanter), 10, 19, 26, 61–63, 265n21
Star Struck (Werner), 1, 19, 184
star systems, 147, 207–8, 232, 240–43, 250, 278n2, 281n4, 282n14, 284n11, 285n12, 285n15

Index

Staubach, Roger, 84, 87
Staying on Top (Quinn), 214
St. Cyr, Lili, 52
Steadman, Ken, 142
Steffans-Sarno, Peggy, 268n1
Steinem, Gloria, 29–30, 212
Stevens, Andrew, 146
Stevens, Brinke, 240
Stevenson, Jack, 4, 81, 206, 263nn2–3, 266n3, 281n3
The Stewardesses (Silliman), 66, 73–74
Stieglitz, Alfred, 39
Stigmata (Wainwright), 218
Stone, Sharon, 136, *137*, 281n5
Storm, Tempest, 50, 52
The Story of Lady Chatterley (Onorati), 90
The Story of O (Jaeckin), 269
straight photography, 39
Strain, Julie, 104, 202
Straw Dogs (Peckinpah), 63
Strike a Pose (Hamilton), 154
Striporama (Intrator), 49, 50, 51–52
Stripped to Kill (Shea), 265n19
striptease, 2, 17, 52, 235
Striptease (Bergman), 139
structuring absence, 17, 192, 256. *See also* compensation
Struss, Karl, 221, 263n20, 263n24
Struss Pictorial Lens, 262n18
Student Affairs (Vincent), 95, 268n17
The Student Nurses (Rothman), 73–74, 103, 165
subjectification, 43, 121, 123, 126–27; through objectification, 14, 16, 54, 75, 76, 78, 95, 164, 240, 256, 274n18. *See also* objectification
suburban film, the, 15, 46, 66, 70–72, 148, 265n31
Suburban Pagans (Rotsler), 70
Summer with Monika (Bergman), 68
Super Bowl halftime show (2004), 102, 251, *252*, 254–55
Superchick (Forsyth), 73, 74–75, 82, 100
Surrender Cinema, 5, 7, 8–9, 87, 194, 210, 230, 231, 250, 260n5, 284n11. *See also* Band, Charles; Full Moon Pictures
Swanson, Rochelle, 149
Swedish Wildcats (Sarno), 240, 246, 284n6, 285n18

The Swinging Cheerleaders (Hill), 73
sword-and-sorcery movies, 101–4
Syren, 153, 155, 280n27

Talk Sex (Hyduk), 214, 225
Teaserama (Klaw), 49, 51–52
teen sex comedy, 74, 78, 91–92, 94–99, 109, 110, 126, 133, 214, 267n13
Testa, Bart, 36–37, 66–67
A Theory of Parody (Hutcheon), 244–45
Therese and Isabelle (Metzger), 15, 36, 66, 67, 111
This Is Sexy?, 187, 274n24
This Nude World (Mindlin), 47–48, 264n5
Thomas, Michael, 234
Thomas, Paul (a.k.a. Toby Phillips), 147, 207
Thompson, Kristin, 3, 39, 262n18
Titanic 2000 (Fedele), 233–34
Torchlight (Full Moon), 8, 87
Torchlight (New City), 275n28, 287n3
The Touch of her Flesh (Findlay), 58
Tough Girls (Inness), 106
"'Trashing' the Academy" (Sconce), 192–93
Troma, 10, 284n7, 284n11
Turan, Kenneth, 3, 18, 27–29, 36, 45, 54, 55, 71, 73–74, 189, 269nn4–5, 281n3
tutor motif, 92, 161, 180–81
Tweed, Shannon, 147, 153, 201, 202, 208, 278n2
Twin Peaks (serial), 269n7
Twitchell, James, 34
Two Moon Junction (King), 9, 110, 113, 116, 117–29 (*118, 126*), 270n18, 271nn24–25
Tyson, Richard, 116

ultra-low-budget paradigms, 88, 100, 151–57, 231, 250, 275n27, 283n2, 284n5, 286n28
Unfaithful (Lyne), 122, 134, 136, 147, 273n8
Universal, 95, 101, 218, 219

Vadim, Roger, 36, 55
Vampire Seduction (Bacchus), 234, 283n3
Vance, Marilyn, 176
Varietease (Klaw), 49, 51
Variety, xii, 266n2
Ventura Marketing, 234
Verhoeven, Paul, 134, 135, 139
vertical integration, 80, 212
Vestron Video, 90, 135

Viacom, 83, 254–55, 267n8
victim heroes, 100, 102, 268n24
video sexploitation, 87–88, 100. *See also* home video
Vieira, Mark, 39–40, 48, 262n18, 263n20
Vincent, Ava, 153
Vincent, Chuck, 83, 95–100, 191, 207–8, 266n1, 267n16, 282n15
violence, 54–59, 62–66, 79, 87, 100–109, 132, 134–36, 139, 141, 148, 151, 153, 155, 157, 250, 268n24, 272n3, 273n10, 274n24
Vivid, 157, 210, 218–19
Vixen! (Meyer), 164
Voices of Desire (Vincent), 95
"Voodoo" (Bowe), 177, 178, 277n19
"Voodoun Blues" (Mundae), 241
Voyeur Confessions (Lazarus), 218, 224–27, 283n28
voyeurism, 16, 53–54, 117–18, 125–27, 224–26, 229; and the observer figure, 53–54, 191, 264n13
Vraney, Mike, 193

Waller, Gregory, 73, 74, 82
Watching Rape (Projansky), 163
Watching Sex (Loftus), 280n19
Weiss, George, 57–58, 264n17
Wells, Julian, 155, 231, 243, 248–50, 286n28
West, Adam, 92
West, Terry, 196, 246–47, 284n9
Wexler, Haskell, 283n25
Whirry, Shannon, 147, 148, 202
White, Allon, 60, 120, 124, 239, 270n15
White Palace (Mandoki), 175, 270n17
White Slaves of Chinatown (Mawra), 57
Wicked Sins (Carson), 1, 153, *156*
Wicked Temptations (Gibson), 1, *156*, 275n30
Widdemer, Margaret, 33
Wiesmeier, Linda, 97
Wild Orchid (King), 110, 116, 117, 121–22, 270nn13–14
Wild Orchid II (King), 114, 116
Wild Strawberries (Bergman), 68
Wild Things: Diamonds in the Rough (Lowi), 274n26, 275n31
Williams, Linda, 2, 13, 17–19, 21, 23, 29–31, 47, 52, 96, 153, 190, 200, 225, 260n4, 262n11, 263n2, 264n10, 265n23, 265n25, 278n3, 283n29. *See also* hardcore; *Hard Core*
Williams, Linda Ruth, xiv, 5, 14, 16, 23, 27–28, 30–31, 43, 54, 111–12, 135, 137, 139, 143, 144, 146, 172, 174, 188, 190–92, 193, 211, 220, 225, 253, 259n1, 260n3, 260n2, 261n9, 261n3, 261n5, 265n19, 270n12, 270n15, 272n4, 273n6, 273nn10–12, 273n17, 274n18, 274n20, 274n25, 275n31, 275n1, 277n20, 278n10, 281n5, 286n30. *See also* erotic thrillers; *The Erotic Thriller in Contemporary Cinema*; softcore thrillers
Wimps (Vincent), 95, 268n17
Wirth, Billy, 117
Wishman, Doris, 58, 164, 239, 285n20
Witchbabe (West), 197, 234, 246
woman's film, the, 116, 150, 269n12, 279n16
Women Against Pornography (WAP), 27, 84–85
women-in-prison film, 75, 100, 165, 265n32
Women: Stories of Passion (*WSP;* serial): 10, 97, 130, 159–61, 167–69, 173–80, 182, 261n7, 276n9, 277n19, 281n7; episodes of, 170, 175, 177–80, 276n4, 277n19
working-woman vehicles, 66, 72–75, 99,114, 150, 165, 167, 178, 274n22. *See also* empowered babe, the
Woolf, Virginia, 33–34
Word of Mouth (Lazarus), 201–2, 218, 220–27 (*222*)
Wu, Harmony, 236
Wynorski, Jim, 284n4

"You Have the Right to Remain Silent" (King), 271n24, 277n16
Young and Seductive (Riley), 156, 250
Young Lady Chatterley (Roberts), 84, 89–91 (*89*), 282n15
Young Lady Chatterley II (Roberts), 78, 84, 89–94, 181, 208
Young Nurses in Love (Vincent), 99
Young Person, the, 136, 273n7
Zaitz, Leland, 210, 217, 282n24

Zane, Billy, 117
Zarchi, Meir, 101
Zito, Stephen, 3, 18, 27–29, 36, 45, 54, 55, 71, 73–74, 189, 269nn4–5, 281n